MW00784183

ARCHITECTURE, CULTURE, AND SPIRITUALITY

*In gratitude for all who have contributed to the collective efforts of the
Forum for Architecture, Culture, and Spirituality*

Architecture, Culture, and Spirituality

Edited by

THOMAS BARRIE
North Carolina State University, USA

JULIO BERMUDEZ
The Catholic University of America, USA

PHILLIP JAMES TABB
Texas A&M University, USA

Routledge
Taylor & Francis Group

LONDON AND NEW YORK

First published 2015 by Ashgate Publishing

2 Park Square, Milton Park, Abingdon, Oxon OX14 4RN
711 Third Avenue, New York, NY 10017, USA

Routledge is an imprint of the Taylor & Francis Group, an informa business

First issued in paperback 2017

British Library Cataloguing in Publication Data
A catalogue record for this book is available from the British Library.

Library of Congress Cataloging-in-Publication Data
Architecture, culture, and spirituality / [edited] by Thomas Barrie, Julio Bermudez and Phillip James Tabb.
     pages cm
 Includes bibliographical references and index.
  ISBN 978-1-4724-4171-3 (hardback) -- ISBN 978-1-4724-4172-0 (ebook) -- ISBN 978-1-4724-4173-7 (epub) 1. Spirituality in architecture. 2. Architecture and society. I. Barrie, Thomas, editor. II. Bermúdez, Julio Cesar, editor. III. Tabb, Phillip, editor.
  NA2540.A6125 2015
  720.1'08--dc23
                                                                          2015011906

ISBN 978-1-4724-4171-3 (hbk)
ISBN 978-1-138-29684-8 (pbk)

Contents

PART IV: SACRED LANDSCAPES

PART V: SPIRITUALITY AND THE DESIGNED ENVIRONMENT

List of Figures

List of Tables

Notes on Contributors

Nader Ardalan is President of Ardalan Associates, LLC, and a practicing architect with a long and distinguished international career in the fields of environmentally sustainable and culturally relevant design with a particular focus on Islamic countries. He holds a Bachelor of Architecture from Carnegie-Mellon University and a Masters in Architecture from the Graduate School of Design, Harvard University. Academically, as of 2011 he is the Senior Research Associate and Senior Editor of the *Persian Gulf Encyclopedia for Sustainable Urbanism* at the Harvard Graduate School of Design. Prior to that he was Director of the Persian Gulf Research Project at the Harvard Center for Middle East Studies, and with anthropologist Dr. Steven Caton co-authored *The New Arab Urbanism in the Persian Gulf.* He is the co-author of *The Sense of Unity, the Sufi Tradition in Persian Architecture* (Chicago University Press), author of *Blessed Jerusalem* (Harvard University), and a number of other publications. He has been a Visiting Professor at Harvard, Yale, MIT and Tehran University. He was a founding member of the Steering Committee of the prestigious Aga Khan Award for Architecture, and is a member of the Executive Committee of the Forum for Architecture, Culture, and Spirituality.

Thomas Barrie, AIA is a Professor of Architecture at North Carolina State University where he was School Director from 2002–07. His research focuses on alternative histories of architecture and, in particular, the interrelationship of a culture's architecture, its cultural/religious beliefs and its socio-political, doctrinal and ritual agendas. His research has brought him to sacred sites around the world, and he has published numerous articles and lectured extensively on his subject area. He is the author of *The Sacred In-Between: The Mediating Roles of Architecture* (Routledge, 2010), and *Spiritual Path, Sacred Place: Myth Ritual and Meaning in Architecture* (Shambhala, 1996). Barrie has received numerous teaching and design awards, and has taught at a number of schools of architecture, nationally and internationally. He co-founded the Forum for Architecture, Culture, and Spirituality in 2007.

Michael Benedikt is the Director of the Center for American Architecture and Design (CAAD) at the University of Texas at Austin, where he holds the Hal Box Chair in Urbanism and teaches design studio and architectural theory. He is a graduate of the University of the Witwatersrand in South Africa and of Yale University. Although he has run a small, mainly residential, architectural practice, he is best known for his teaching and writing. His books include *For an Architecture of Reality* (1987), *Deconstructing the Kimbell* (1991), *Cyberspace: First Steps* (1991), *Value* (1997), *Value 2* (1998), *Shelter: The 2000 Raoul Wallenberg Lecture* (2001), *God Is the Good We Do: Theology of Theopraxy* (2007), and *God, Creativity, and Evolution: The Argument from Design(ers)* (2008). He is Executive Editor of the book series *CENTER: Architecture and Design in America*, with recent volumes such as *On Landscape Urbanism* (2007), *Latitudes: Architecture in the Americas* (2012), and *Space + Psyche*. He has lectured widely on design theory, the esthetic of ethics, phenomenology, economic philosophy, and the future of architecture, all of which, in his own mind, are "one thing." In 2004, he was named a Distinguished Professor by the Association of Collegiate Schools of Architecture.

Julio Bermudez, Ph.D. is an Associate Professor at the Catholic University of America School of Architecture and Planning where he directs the Sacred Space and Cultural Studies graduate concentration. He holds a Masters of Architecture and a Ph.D. in Education, both from the University of Minnesota. His expertise covers architectural phenomenology and the relationship between architecture, culture and spirituality. Bermudez has widely lectured, led symposia, and published in these areas. His current research includes an fMRI study of architecturally induced contemplative states and a large survey on profound experiences of place. His book *Transcending Architecture* was published by CUA Press in 2015. He co-founded the Forum for Architecture, Culture, and Spirituality in 2007. Bermudez has received many recognitions including the 1998

AIA Education Honors Award, the 2004–05 ACSA Creative Achievement Award, the 2005 Premio Trayectoria Creativa Arturo Montagu (by SIGraDI, Latin America), and the 2010 Sasada Award (by CAADRIA, Asia).

Prem Chandavarkar is the managing partner of CnT Architects: an architectural practice based in Bangalore, India. CnT has produced award-winning and published work throughout a history that stretches back across generations to being Bangalore's first architectural firm. Prem is a former Executive Director of Srishti School of Art Design & Technology in Bangalore. He is an academic advisor and guest faculty at Indian and international architecture colleges. Besides his design practice at CnT, he writes and lectures on architecture, urbanism, art, cultural studies, and education.

Hyejung Chang, Ph.D. is currently an Assistant Professor in the Department of Landscape Architecture at Clemson University and teaches undergraduate and graduate design studios as well as seminar courses such as Master's Thesis Project, Dr. Chang's scholarly interests lie in design theory and practice that promote shared values for healthy communities and human wellbeing. Her research centers on aesthetics, environmental ethics and the culture and value of urban landscapes and place-making, and sacred landscapes—all in relation to environmental sustainability. Key Issues in Landscape Architecture, Research Methods, and Introduction to Landscape Architecture.

Dr. Michael J. Crosbie, Ph.D. is the editor of *Faith & Form* magazine, the Interfaith Journal on Religion, Art, and Architecture, and writes and lectures extensively on its topics. He is Associate Dean of the College of Engineering, Technology, and Architecture, Chair of the Department of Architecture, and Professor of Architecture at the University of Hartford. He is a member of the College of Fellows of the American Institute of Architects, and a recipient of the Edward S. Frey Memorial Award in recognition of his contributions made to religion, art, and architecture bestowed by the Interfaith Forum on Religion, Art, and Architecture, and the AIA. He is also an active member of the Forum for Architecture, Culture, and Spirituality.

Anat Geva, Ph.D., is an architect (registered in Israel, Associate of AIA), and a Professor of Architecture at Texas A&M University. She teaches architectural design studios, and seminars on sacred architecture, history of building technology, and introduction to historic preservation. She is a Faculty Fellow of the University's Center of Heritage Conservation and the Religious Studies Program. She has served as President of the South East Chapter Society of Architectural Historians, and serves on the Executive Committee of the Forum for Architecture, Culture, and Spirituality. Dr. Geva's book *Frank Lloyd Wright's Sacred Architecture: Faith, Form, and Building Technology* was published by Routledge in 2012. She is a co-editor of the journal *Preservation Education and Research*, and has published and presented articles in the areas of sacred architecture, historic preservation, and the history of building technology. She is a recipient of several awards and research grants including the prestigious James Marston Fitch National Award for innovative research in historic preservation. She co-founded the Forum for Architecture, Culture, and Spirituality.

Rumiko Handa, Ph.D. is a Professor of Architecture at the University of Nebraska-Lincoln. She holds a B.Arch. from the University of Tokyo and a M.Arch., M.S.Arch., and Ph.D. from the University of Pennsylvania. She has received the American Institute of Architecture Students' 2002 National Educator Honor Award, and grants from the Graham Foundation for Advanced Studies in the Fine Arts, the Huntington Library, and the University of Michigan's Center for Japanese Studies. She has organized and chaired conference sessions for the Association of the Collegiate Schools of Architecture, the Society of Architectural Historians, the International Association for the Studies of Traditional Environments, and the Forum for Architecture, Culture, and Spirituality. She is the author of *Allure of the Incomplete, Imperfect, and Impermanent: Designing and Appreciating Architecture as Nature* (Routledge, 2015), and co-editor of *Conjuring the Real: The Role of Architecture in Eighteenth-and Nineteenth-Century Fiction* (University of Nebraska Press, 2011). Her articles have appeared in *The Encyclopedia of Twentieth-Century Architecture*; *Architectura: Elements of Architectural Style*; *Transportable Environments: Theory, Context, Design and Technology*; and the journals of the Society of Architectural Historians, the Bibliographical Society of America, the Design Research Society, and Nexus: Architecture and Mathematics.

Lindsay Jones, Ph.D. is a Professor in the Department of Comparative Studies and Director of the Center for the Study of Religion at The Ohio State University. As a historian of religions (Ph.D., University of Chicago), he is interested in both the cross-cultural comparison of religious phenomena, and in the theories, methods and history of the academic study of religion. His early training in design issues led to continuing interests in sacred architecture and the arrangement of space in all contexts, with special concerns for the peoples, cultures and religions of Mesoamerica. He is author of *Twin City Tales: A Hermeneutical Reassessment of Tula and Chichén Itzá* (University Press of Colorado, 1995) and a 2-volume study entitled *The Hermeneutics of Sacred Architecture: Experience, Interpretation, Comparison* (Harvard University Press, 2000). Additionally, he is editor-in-chief of a revised second edition of Mircea Eliade's 16-volume *Encyclopedia of Religion* (Macmillan Reference USA, 2005).

Rebecca Krinke is Professor of Landscape Architecture at the University of Minnesota. She holds degrees in art and design and has a multidisciplinary practice that includes sculpture, installations, public art, site works, and social practice. In broad terms, all of her work deals with issues related to place and emotion. Krinke disseminates her work through permanent and temporary public works and gallery shows. She is co-convener of the international artist-academic network: *Mapping Spectral Traces* and a member of the UK-based group *PLaCE*, an artist-academic collective for place-based practice and research. Krinke is a frequent guest lecturer and critic; nationally and internationally. She was co-editor of *Contemporary Landscapes of Contemplation* (Routledge, 2005). She is a current member of the Executive Committee of the Forum for Architecture, Culture and Spirituality.

A.T. Mann graduated from the Cornell University College of Architecture, and worked for prominent architects in New York City and Rome. He lived in Europe for 28 years and has written 14 books on a variety of subjects, most recently *Sacred Architecture*, *Sacred Landscapes* and *The Sacred Language of Trees*. He lectures and teaches all over the world, and is working on documentary films about the presence of the sacred in the world, and the connection between neuroscience and spirituality. He lives in Hudson, NY.

Phillip James Tabb, Ph.D. is Professor of Architecture at Texas A&M University where he is the holder of the Liz and Nelson Mitchell Professor of Residential Design. He served as Head of the Department from 2001–05, and was Director of the School of Architecture and Construction Management at Washington State University from 1998–2001. He completed a Ph.D. dissertation on "The Solar Village Archetype: A Study of English Village Form Applicable to Energy Integrated Planning Principles for Satellite Settlements in Temperate Climates" in 1990. Among his publications are *The Greening of Architecture* (Ashgate, 2014), and *Solar Energy Planning* published (McGraw-Hill, 1984). Tabb is the master plan architect for Serenbe Community—a sacred and sustainable community near Atlanta, Georgia. He received his Bachelor of Science in Architecture from the University of Cincinnati, Master of Architecture from the University of Colorado, and Ph.D. from the Architectural Association in London. Dr. Tabb is a practicing urban designer and licensed architect, and holds a NCARB Certificate. He is a current member of the Executive Committee of the Forum for Architecture, Culture and Spirituality.

Randall Teal is a writer, teacher, painter and designer. His pedagogical and research interests are in design fundamentals and architectural theory with a significant influence from Continental thought. His writing focuses primarily on understanding and promoting situated dialogue between creative processes and the built environment. He is an Associate Professor and Chair of the Architecture Program at the University of Idaho. He holds a B.S. Psychology and a MIARC, Interior Architecture, University of Oregon.

Paul Tesar, Ph.D. studied architecture at the T.U. Wien (Dipl.Ing. 1968). He was awarded a Fulbright Grant to study at the University of Washington Seattle (M.Arch. 1971). Before joining the faculty at North Carolina State University in 1975, he held teaching appointments at the T.U. Wien and Rensselaer Polytechnic Institute. His scholarship centers on aesthetics, theory, and vernacular Architecture. He has numerous publications to his credit and has lectured, taught, and served as a studio critic in architecture schools in the U.S. and abroad. His dissertation (Ph.D., T.U. Wien, 1992) examines the social phenomenology of Alfred Schütz for its applicability to architectural theory. Tesar was named Alumni Distinguished Professor at NC State in 1992, and received the UNC Board of Governors Award for Excellence in Teaching in 2005. He served as Head of the Department of Architecture in 1990–91 and as Director of the School of Architecture in 2007–08.

Dennis Alan Winters is a landscape architect with degrees in landscape architecture (M.L.A., Cornell University) and architecture (B.Arch., University of Florida), and urban design studies (Teknillinen Korkeakoulu, Finland), and professional work in environmental analysis and regional land use planning. He designs, builds and writes about gardens for meditation and sacred landscape through his Toronto studio, *Tales of the Earth.* He is the author of *Searching for the Heart of Sacred Space* (The Sumeru Press, 2014), a book on deep relationships among landscape, Buddhism and personal awakening that focuses on sites in Kyoto and Western Tibet.

Foreword

Alberto Pérez-Gómez

Most basically, spirituality concerns the air, *spiritus*, and thus evokes the *invisible* dimension that is always present in everyday experience, epitomized by our living breath. Spirituality therefore is not primarily something mystical (meaning secret), or arcane, but encompasses the availabilities and vulnerabilities that are part of perception in its most mundane sense, like the back of the apple that makes the visible apple present in all of its evocative sensuousness; our ever-present susceptibilities to destructive emotions and our personal mortality; the corridor behind the door in the room where I now sit, and the topographical, ecological and geographical conditions of the building I inhabit that are very much part of the present atmospheric meaning that gives me *place* to dwell. All of this is made possible by the fact that *subject*, *object* and *action of perception* are *invariably co-emergent*. It is ultimately impossible to identify an autonomous existence of any of the three terms that make up the phenomenon of human embodied consciousness or *mind*, present in a range between deep dreamless sleep and intellectual awareness, and subtended by an invisible unity that may appear "empty" for its ephemeral existence in a mortal world, yet "full" of purpose like our primary biological life.

In our present age the disregard of *spiritus*, in this broad yet fundamental sense, one vastly more encompassing than the chemical contamination of the atmosphere, makes our life less healthy, even difficult to bear. Everything (including the "self"), becomes objectified and reduced to matter, while places become coordinates in a GPS map, reinforcing societies' consumerist and nihilistic tendencies.

While the so-called Fine Arts can often be distorted to appear merely decorative, be kept in museums or stored in basements; architecture, to be truly named so, concerns itself with psychosomatic health, with the spiritual (literally "atmospheric"), dimensions of life. In order to address life as lived, a life always and already possessed of sensorimotor skills afforded by cultures, architecture must create transformative atmospheres to properly accommodate habits and to bring about productive (poetic and ethical) change, a power that emulates the classical gods' in the physical realm, already present in the meanings and uses of the Greek word *atmós*.

In Ancient Greek, *atmós* doubled as both vapor and steam, and was sometimes associated with breath; it could be poisonous or beneficial, like the divine haze emanating from the ground in Delphi that inspired the Oracle. By tracing the roots of the term back to Sanskrit we find *Atman*, which means "inner self" (or mind—in a non-dualistic sense), or the "first principle" or true self of the individual before identification with phenomena. In Hinduism, in order to be liberated, the individual must realize that one's true self (*Atman*), is identical with the transcendent self. According to Plutarch, the *atmós* of moving water or foggy air can bear fleeting images—like the imagination of the inner self (or soul);[1] it can carry words like the human breath. From the Latin *spiritus* (breath), we inherit the words "spirit" and "spiritual." In architecture, pre-reflective transformative atmospheres can indeed create places for reflective poetic images, completing its cognitive and communicative function; affective and intellectual. *This is in essence, its spiritual function.*

After Nietzsche's questioning of monotheism in *The Gay Science* (1882–87), any discussion about spirituality in modern culture possesses little legitimacy if bound by discredited dogmas and fanatical ideologies. Mallarmé sharply realized that he must kill the God (of monotheisms), to get in touch with the underlying divine ground; this defined his poetic task: "Having discovered Nothingness, I have found the Beautiful."[2] As recipients of this cultural condition, we may productively consider that the old sharp divisions between the sacred (literally: that which is "set apart"), and the profane, famously set out by Mircea Eliade and easily extrapolated into our architectural heritage, are no longer valid, and thus the spiritual might be expected to appear in the realm of everyday life, with architecture as one of its important mediations.

George Lakoff and Mark Johnson remind us that a major function of the embodied mind is empathic.[3] Our capacity for imaginative, mimetic projection is a vital cognitive faculty, the origin of our social selves. Contrary to Sartre, who postulated the ultimate alienation of the seemingly unknowable "Other," Maurice

Merleau-Ponty's phenomenology demonstrates that we only know ourselves through such projection: we know ourselves *through* the other, in embodied communication, situated through architecture and urban space. Experientially, this primary knowing is a form of "transcendence." Lakoff and Johnson add that imaginative empathic projection is a major part of what has been called spiritual experience, as cultivated in meditative practices. Philosopher and cognitive scientist Alva Noë has recently argued that the environment is actually part of our consciousness; our consciousness doesn't simply end at our skull.[4] The environment is potentially never an "other" or a collection of things, a *res extensa* at odds with our "thinking" or "spiritual substance" (as René Descartes wrongly imagined and contemporary cultures—and many religions—usually take for granted); but rather is indeed part of our being. Through empathic projection we understand that we are part of the environment.

In some religious traditions, however, a connection with the natural world is regarded as an encounter with the divine present in all things. This is known in theology as panentheism, simultaneously affirming both the transcendence and the immanence of God, where God does not exist as a separate being "out there." God is more than everything, yet everything is in God. God is "right here" even if it is also more than "right here."[5] This condition may describe the possibility of an authentic spirituality for modernity in the wake of dualism. For this reason Hölderlin goes beyond and behind the gods to arrive at the pure divine or "immediate": *enargeîs*.[6] The sacred is the awesome itself; the alignment of *cháos* and *nómos* is precisely what Heidegger admired in Hölderlin's poetry. For the poet, chaos is the sacred, reminding us of the relationship between *cháos* and *chóra*—cultural space—that Plato draws in *Timaeus*. Chaos is the gap where light appears and which itself flaunts all location in measurable time and space."[7]

Granting the possibility of a panentheistic spirituality for non-dualistic embodied consciousness in the contemporary world, it is easy to recognize that appropriate environments are crucial to this aim. If as recent cognitive science now affirms, perception is something "we actively do" (unlike digestion), and a self-conscious life appears as a result of our bodily sensorimotor articulation in the world, then the environment is the "equipment" of consciousness (in the sense of Heidegger), and architecture is an event. Architecture must be resonant, or "empathic," for us to attain a spiritual wholeness. Postindustrial environments are seldom receptive to empathy, but they could be, as is amply demonstrated in literature and cinema, and they must be part of everyday life: no longer "set apart" like old ritual spaces. Architecture is not an encounter with an unusual, uncanny or even supernatural dimension that is deployed somewhere beyond everyday life experience, rather, if it is magical, it discloses a dimension, *Stimmung*—an attunement of Being, that is always operative beneath conventional consciousness, in that carnal realm of exchange with our animal bodies, our true embodied minds. Thus, great architecture and moving urban spaces do not simply sweep you away, they gather you up into the body of the present moment so thoroughly that explanations can fall away; revealing the ordinary in all its plain and simple outrageousness and allowing it to shine.[8]

The challenge that this book faces is beautifully summarized by Octavio Paz who writes: "On the one hand, I believe that poetry and religion spring from the same source and it is not possible to dissociate the poem from its pretension to change man without the risk of turning the poem into an inoffensive form of literature. On the other hand, I believe the Promethean thrust of modern poetry consists in its belligerence toward religion, the source of its deliberate will to create a new 'sacred,' in contradistinction to the one that churches offer us today."[9]

Endnotes

1   http://www.perseus.tufts.edu/hopper/text?doc=Perseus:text:2008.01.0392:section=47&highlight=a%29tmoi%3Ds
     (accessed July 6, 2014). With gratitude to Dr. Lisa Landrum for this reference.
2   Calasso, Roberto (2001). *Literature and the Gods.* New York, NY: Vintage, p. 112.
3   Lakoff, George and Mark Johnson (1999). *Philosophy in the Flesh. The Embodied Mind and its Challenge to Western Thought.* New York, NY: Basic Books, pp. 565–6.
4   Noë, Alva (2009). *Out of Our Heads: Why You Are Not Your Brain, and Other Lessons from the Biology of Consciousness.* New York, NY: Hill and Wang.
5   Ibid., p. 567. Citing E. Borg.

6   Calasso (2001). *Literature and the Gods*, p. 31f.
7   Ibid.
8   I am paraphrasing a description of "magic" in Abram, David (2011). *Becoming Animal.* New York, NY: Vintage, p. 224.
9   Cited by Hejduk, Renata and Jim Williamson (2011). Introduction, in R. Hejduk and J. Williamson (eds), *The Religious Imagination in Modern and Contemporary Architecture*. New York, NY: Routledge, p. 4.

Chapter 1
Introduction

Thomas Barrie, Julio Bermudez, and Phillip James Tabb

In a world whose complexity is both exhilarating and bewildering, its paradoxes are perhaps the most accessible. This may not be a phenomenon unique to our time but it is arguably one that defines it. Parts of the world enjoy unprecedented prosperity, longevity, political continuity, and energy and food security, while others have very little—and there is everything in between. Communication technologies have connected humans in ways that have rendered traditional notions of space and time obsolete, while ideological misunderstandings and national, cultural, and religious divisions have persisted. Globalized economies have resulted in egalitarian opportunities for economic advancement while also supporting political and economic hegemonies. Technologies formally reserved for a few are now available globally, but resource depletion and ecological consequences threaten the advances they set out to achieve. The rise in worldwide living standards, all of which are dependent on increased consumption of material and technological resources, are also attributable to global climate change and vast environmental destruction, perhaps the most significant imperatives of our time and ones that are most attributable to human activity and the built environment. Complicating matters further is that these transformations and challenges are happening at a speed and scale never before encountered and that our success at resolving these enormous challenges remains fundamentally elusive. For certain, there is a need for more reflective, effective, and insightful approaches to creating and sustaining habitation.

This book, its authors and its chapters, are firmly positioned within this contemporary milieu. The authors recognize that the design professions and built environment can be similarly characterized according to the paradoxes outlined above, yet they often propose that complementary viewpoints, supplemental philosophies, and new means are required to arrive at promising perspectives and appropriate solutions. The focus of the work is the intersection of the built environment, culture, and spiritual traditions, and as such presumes that they retain a certain degree of potency and veracity to address the complexities of our era. Religious and spiritual beliefs, explorations, and practices are brought into focused consideration through the lens of the built environment. The authors do not shy away from the paradoxes inherent in such strategy, and, in fact, many base their arguments on the incongruities that one often finds in contemporary religion and by extension the artifacts built to serve them. However, not all essays are concerned with architecture designed to serve traditional religions, some are more interested in consciousness, culture, landscapes, and the more secular everyday, individual, and indigenous expressions of spirituality in the built environment.

However within all of these contexts some inevitable questions arise. Why study religion and spirituality? Why focus on sacred architecture and sacred places, in a world that many say has rendered them, for the most part, obsolete? How can metaphysical beliefs and practices survive the devastating blows of contemporary empirical science and post-structuralist critique? Isn't religion at best irrelevant, at worst tribal and territorial? Aren't the numbers of religious adherents and practitioners dwindling, and haven't most state religions died, putting in jeopardy the whole viewpoint and strategy advanced in this book? The answers to these questions are yes—and no.

If religion could be rendered obsolete by science or philosophy, it would have happened long ago.[1] If positivism, empiricism and rationalism had proven to be superior approaches there would not be a need for reconsiderations. And, even though the death of religion has been long predicted as the result of a progressive diminishment inverse to scientific, economic, and technological advancement,[2] it has not come to pass. Rather, it is ever transforming, some say even thriving albeit in different ways.[3] Certainly, there is no shortage of religious adherents, believers, and practitioners—from orthodox sects to spiritual seekers, and a good majority of the population today continues to use religious or spiritual beliefs and practices as their compass to assess and guide their lives. For example, a recent survey revealed that a significant percentage of the world's population identify themselves as religious.[4] In the United States, polls have consistently shown that spiritual matters are a concern to a large majority of people,[5] and the success of broadcast programs covering faith issues only affirms this finding.[6] Lastly, even though religion may have emerged from, at least in part, cultural and territorial claims, at its best it transcends both and may actually integrate, harmonize, and heal such differences.

That said, there is no denying the reluctance of many people to include religion and spirituality in the public arena. A general ignorance (and consequent bias), of the spiritual beliefs of others, the violent expressions of recalcitrant religious fundamentalisms, and the influence of religious groups on governments and economic systems, breed people's fear, mistrust, and even revulsion towards organized faiths. Consequently, religion appears rather powerful or at least concerning enough to avoid, suppress, or sugar coat with a politically correct but unwise tolerance—all poor if not dangerous responses.[7] All of which seems to suggest that we are simultaneously dwelling in two seemingly irreconcilable realities: one where we "successfully" conduct our lives dislocated from religious contexts, and the other where spiritual values and practices provide us with meaning. The limited engagement of religions or other spiritual practices with contemporary culture restricts their potential to address today's pressing problems, which at their root demand an acknowledgment of the ultimate meaning, wholeness, or transpersonal nature of reality and all beings. Concurrently, without some openness to the contemporary milieu, religion remains stuck in regressive perspectives and practices that truncate its ability to address the challenges of the 21st century. Resolving this quandary demands a reconciliation of this dichotomy.

The resilience of spirituality around the world and the number of people that see their lives, situation, or reality in relation to some 'other' transcendent (one assumes) realm, suggests, at least, the potential for a broadened point of view. As a result, at least theoretically, such spiritual mindsets may be harnessed to effect positive changes in the world. For example, the contemporary interest in health and wellbeing is partially the reason for growing research in active spirituality in disciplines as diverse as nursing,[8] health and wellbeing,[9] higher education,[10] psychiatry, and psychology,[11] and brain-mind sciences.[12] The results have been so positive[13] that many scientific teams, medical centers, and prestigious institutions are actively engaged in research of this type, often with the support of federal and private grants,[14] and the results routinely reported in popular media.[15] Additionally, an increasing number of people have adopted a range of spiritual practices to address a variety of challenges, resulting in the recent growth of new or "alternative" religious interests and movements. Studies show that by providing a transcendental framework, spirituality imbues life with meaning, hope, authenticity, and a sense of belonging, equanimity and compassion. Given this, one might conclude that many consider a proactive reengagement with spirituality to be a means to engage our contemporary paradoxes.

This growing appreciation of spirituality is occurring at a time of recognition that culture is a fundamental force not only shaping quality of life, social change, and welfare, but also economic development, productivity, and environmental responses.[16] Interesting enough, this expanding consideration of culture is not coming from fields traditionally associated with it, such as anthropology, sociology, philosophy, and theology, but from architects, landscape urbanists, and city planners, and is grounded in the fact that humanity is increasingly an urban phenomenon. Support for the importance of culture in the life of cities has been growing, both at the theoretical and empirical levels, advanced in recent years by work done by UN Habitat and a number of non-profit organizations.[17] Furthermore, and despite the disagreements, confusing overlappings, and lack of data sources for gauging the function of culture in human settlements, there is accord that the built environment plays a central role in preserving, sustaining, and advancing cultural identity, authenticity, and wellbeing. The coincidental growth in interest, research, and work in both spirituality and culture at this time is not fortuitous, because both are fundamental and interrelated components that address how we aesthetically, ethically, physically, and socially respond to reality—and both are most synthetically expressed in the built environment.

Unsurprisingly, some of the chapters in this book discuss the built environment as a cultural artifact and, more specifically, study sacred places or religious architecture as building types that are so significantly embedded in culture that we can access those cultures in particular and potent ways. Consequently, in a world still defined by territorial, cultural, and religious conflicts, the material evidence of architecture and the built environment may provide certain insights into these contemporary conditions, and perhaps offer more transformative solutions through revealing common grounds that were formerly inaccessible. It may also be a means to challenge our contemporary prejudices and presumptions. One predominant contemporary belief Julio Bermudez sets out to dismantle is that of the irreconcilability of science and religion. Bermudez takes that one step further to illustrate how empirical science can be used to recover and illuminate aspects of the human condition and our inhabitation of the world.

Figure 1.1   Considering the relationship between architecture, culture, and spirituality demands
                addressing its unavoidable phenomenological dimension and the first-person experiences
                that evoke the transcendent. Machu Picchu, Peru
Source: Photograph courtesy of Julio Bermudez, 2005.

Overall, the authors recognize that they operate within design professions that, even though they engage in the design and scholarship of religious or spiritually motivated buildings, urban contexts, landscapes, interiors and furnishings, seem truncated in their ability to incorporate the motivating factors underneath these endeavors into their discourse. This, of course, is not surprising given the dominance of so-called "professionalism" in the design professions that privilege the technical, productive, material, and intellectual over the experiential, receptive, immaterial, and emotional—a tendency complicit with the dominant values of contemporary culture.[18] Opposition can also be explained by the risks, misunderstandings, and difficulties associated with engaging the sensitive matters of spirituality and religion, as many scholars have discussed elsewhere.[19] This explains why, despite beginning to identify the relationship between global climate change and the built environment, and the necessity of more sustainable building, the design professions are largely unable to integrate into their considerations religious or spiritual perspectives that may simultaneously address issues unidentified in more technological or material approaches. According to Michael Crosbie this reluctance is almost a taboo, what he terms the "S word," in contemporary architectural discourse, which relegates aspects of human moral, ethical, and spiritual aspirations and capacities to the backwater of theoretical and professional research and practice.[20] You will not find chapters in this volume that instruct how to design a more spiritually-oriented building or landscape, but you will find many that provide perspectives regarding the spiritual and ethical responsibilities, and the benefits of spiritual orientations.

The Forum for Architecture, Culture, and Spirituality (ACS) emerged from the cultural, religious, and professional conditions outlined above. Its founders identified many of the issues that the authors in this book, attendees of ACS symposia, and members of the organization, considered preeminent. The ACS forum was created in 2007 with the expressed intention of addressing what our discipline was avoiding:

Figure 1.2   Scholarship on architecture, culture, and spirituality has traditionally included the empirical
                study of sacred buildings with the purpose of learning what "measurable" attributes make
                them successful at facilitating visitors' access to what architect Louis Kahn named the
                "immeasurable." Oculus, the Pantheon, Rome
Source: Photograph courtesy of Julio Bermudez, 2004.

the interrelationship of culture, spirituality, and the built environment. Its members believed then, and continue to profess now, that the discipline should engage in insightful study, reflective making, critical assessment, and open dissemination regarding the transcendent in the built environment. By "transcendent" they mean considerations associated not only with the sacred or metaphysical, but ones that also facilitate human health and wellbeing, caring for the environment and other beings, and nurturing interpersonal connections and community. They also understand that, by its very nature, ACS has to engage an international audience and operate under a process that is inclusive, integrative, interdisciplinary, diverse, ecumenical, multicultural, and rigorous, and on the leading edge of scholarship and practice, while also remaining humble, and open to new approaches and conclusions.

   This book constitutes an acknowledgment and celebration of this vision, made possible through the efforts of many people. More concretely, it summarizes the scholarly findings and output of ACS members during its first five years of existence. Its content is a crafted elaboration of papers selected from four annual symposia conducted from 2009 to 2012. These symposia, which followed a strict peer-review process, were conducted at places of spiritual significance and natural beauty including Mt. Angel Abbey in St. Benedict, Oregon (2009);

Figure 1.3   Scholarship on architecture, culture, and spirituality also includes the ethical, compassionate, and empathic ways in which the built environment can help us traverse our hardest existential challenges, such as sickness and death. Maggie's Cancer Caring Centre, 2013, Tuen Mun, Hong Kong

Source: Photograph courtesy of RLPhongkong, September 30, 2013, Wikipedia Creative Commons Attribution-Share Alike 3.0 Unported license.

St. John's University in Collegeville, Minnesota (2010); Serenbe Community in Chattahoochee Hills, Georgia (2011); and Chichén Itzá in the Yucatan Peninsula, Mexico (2012).

Key to understanding the scholarly focus of ACS is an exploration of the three terms architecture, culture, and spirituality. *Architecture* stands for a variety of disciplines and scales of application including art, architecture, building technology, landscape and interior architectures, urban design, and planning. *Culture* refers to the important roles that communal traditions, beliefs, rituals, languages, economics, politics, religion, technologies, arts, heritage, and nature play in shaping and being shaped by the built environment. Lastly, *spirituality* may be the most challenging to delineate but, as discussed, is of central concern to ACS's vision and mission. William James's definition of spirituality as "the attempt to be in harmony with an unseen order of things"[21] is perhaps the most succinct, but Keith Critchlow's "the power of levity in the physical, emotional, intellectual, inspirational and ontological realms, always dedicated to raising experience to a more inclusive and comprehensive unity and integrity," gives us a more nuanced interpretation.[22] Spirituality addresses the human need for understanding our place in the world, connections to others and the self, and experience of the transcendent.[23]

Sacred architecture is, of course, a problematic term, and the book provides a range of interpretations of its definitions. Sacred sites and buildings have a lengthy lineage in the history of architecture and in many ways define these histories. Less clear are the specific roles that architecture has served in conceptualizing and materializing the sacred and accommodating their associative rituals. Our contemporary position provides an objective distance that both supports and hinders our ability to truly understand the significance and meaning of sacred places. As many of the authors argue, we most effectively engage sacred architecture through applying contemporary thinking and theory to the subject. It is important to add that not all intersections between architecture, culture, and spirituality result in sacred spaces. Some of the book authors are acutely aware of this and focus less on formally-motivated expressions and more on ethical or meaningful manifestations that support socio-physical needs, recognize human dignity, and/or protect the earth and its sentient life.

Arguably, the *meaning* of the built environment is potentially the most challenging and problematic topic of the book. For some, formal and spatial characteristics are sufficient to postulate the meaning and significance of examples. For others, it is the capacity of ritual to both create and animate architecture that confers meaning to buildings. There are positions that emphasize more what architecture is asked to do rather than what it actually does, and others that see no dependable means to establish a modicum of understanding of the meaning of place. Overall, the range of approaches of the essays firmly ground them in today's condition of fluidity, multivalency, and criticality.

The book's primary argument is, that even though the mentioned cultural and civilizational conditions have transgressed, degraded, or superseded shared belief systems and symbolic languages, the built environment can again retain its experience, significance, and meaning with veracity and potency. Put differently, despite the ephemerality of contemporary media and consumerism and the placelessness attendant to globalization, the solidity and stability of architecture can provide a stable framework to facilitate transcendent experiences and meaning. This is at least the message that recognized experts in architecture, urbanism, landscape architecture, and other disciplines deliver in this book. Additionally, the book's contributors advance a number of timely and pertinent questions including: What is missing in the contemporary discourse regarding the built environment? Are there perspectives from the past that are still relevant? What are new ways to approach and understand what occurs at the intersection between architecture, culture, and spirituality? And, in what ways can the practice, design, and stewardship of buildings assist in meeting today's challenges? Throughout the authors examine ways that professionals and scholars can respond to the contemporary milieu: to reflectively and strategically recover forgotten, repressed or suppressed perspectives; and to revive and apply new philosophical, scientific, and theoretical thinking to envision an improved and more hopeful future.

Despite their different fields, topics, methodologies, attitudes, and hypotheses, the authors agree on the need to rediscover, redefine, or reclaim the sacred in everyday experience, scholarly analysis, and design, and that the sacred remains relevant because it is where architecture, culture, and spirituality most readily and obviously converge. As Thomas Barrie argues in *The Sacred In-Between: The Mediating Roles of Architecture,*[24] sacred spaces are mediating vehicles through which we gain connection to, propitiate experiences of, and find and express meaning associated with, the transcendent. Scholars have described these meaningful places as "possessing wholeness" (Alexander), "sublime" (Burke), "beautiful" (Schopenhauer), "numinous" (Otto), "immeasurable" (Kahn), and "ineffable" (Le Corbusier). Given their remarkable nature, it is not surprising that the book authors align, to a certain degree, in the aspiration to reconsider, reposition, and advance understandings of the built environment through how architecture symbolizes, houses, and facilitates spiritual connections.

The authors in this collection share the position, often posited by their predecessors, that architecture can be productively understood as a cultural artifact that has the capacity to both express and reveal the cultural motivations that produced them. They depart from them, however, in providing interpretations from contemporary perspectives. In the book the dialectic between architecture and spirituality is less of a historical account or detached ethnographic observation and more of a vibrant and ever-present condition. Consequently the chapters range from applications of contemporary theories, to considerations of natural and built environments, to the science of transcendent experiences, to reflections on how to design places that uplift the human spirit. The direct experience of place and the body's role in structuring meaning finds prominence in some chapters. For some authors the experiential and ontological positions of phenomenology provide a means to objectify the subjective. History and historicism also appear in chapters as dependable departure points for contextualizing specific eras or examples. Other authors share distrust in the solidity of historical positions, viewing them as more fluid and porous, and the interpretive methodologies of hermeneutics find particular potency in this context. Lastly, professional practice is often positioned as both a professional and spiritual practice that recognizes the capacity of the built environment to help uplift, elucidate, and connect. All share the aspiration to establish some modicum of dependability regarding the cultural and spiritual significance of architecture.

The book is organized according to topical themes and constellations of divergent perspectives, which include: *Being in the World*; *Sacred, Secular, and the Contemporary Condition*; *Symbolic Engagements*; *Sacred Landscapes*; and *Spirituality and the Built Environment*.

The *Being in the World* theme focuses on the embodied experiences engendered by the built environment, and the capacity of sacred places to contribute to expanding and uplifting the human spirit. **Michael Benedikt** introduces the subject through a discussion of Martin Buber's thesis regarding the interpersonal condition of human discourse to position the understanding of the sacred as fundamentally relational. He argues that the divine is essentially present in all relationships, and that understanding this, as well as our individual and cultural prejudices that often truncate this understanding, is essential to the analysis and conceptualization of sacred places. **Randall Teal** approaches the subject through the lens of Martin Heidegger's essay *Building, Dwelling, Thinking*. He applies Heidegger's concept of the fourfold to address everyday encounters with the sacred dimension. Teal argues that mature understandings of the built environment transcend the limitations of notions regarding the spiritual, and that divinity is best understood not as intrinsically sacred but as a setting with the capacity to provide transcendent experiences. **Julio Bermudez** insists on the primacy of "lived experience" as a means to understand the depth of architecture. Paradoxically (yet borrowing from Merleau-Ponty's idea of a "naturalized phenomenology"), his approach applies Western scientific survey methods to reach its conclusions. Thousands of respondents to his empirical survey instrument corroborate his argument regarding the reciprocity between places designed to elicit corporal, emotional, and spiritual responses, and their direct experience. Bermudez concludes that the application of statistical science to analyze subjective experience is a potent means to conceptualize the creation of ontologically potent architecture.

In contrast to the preceding theme, the *Sacred, Secular, and the Contemporary Condition* section more directly addresses societal and professional cultural issues. **Michael Crosbie** identifies the reluctance of most designers to use the term "spirituality" to describe their work. The discomfort elicited by the "S Word" and what it suggests, is a symptom of truncated approaches to design. For Crosbie, the antidote is an expanded discourse that accurately uses this term and applies its meanings to architecture and the built environment. **Hyejung Chang** sets out to recover the terms "spirit of place" and "placemaking." To do so she applies selected theories of John Dewey and Abraham Maslow to argue that the design of places that more accurately matches these terms emerges from consummatory relations that incorporate a full range of ethical, social, and environmental issues. **Paul Tesar** suggests that effectively formulating alternatives to the dominant design culture depends on recovering traditional spiritual perspectives. The contemporary focus on the novel, inventive, and unfamiliar (what he terms "neophilia"), needs to be balanced by the familiar and the habitual. For Tesar, it is the quotidian rituals of everyday life and their settings that promise a certain kind of resolution.

The *Symbolic Engagements* theme addresses the capacity of the built environment to embody and express symbolic content. **Thomas Barrie** uses the special case of the domicile to explore the enduring human need to structure through built form their understandings of the world and their place within it. Barrie incorporates a broad range of sources to this end—from traditional sacred settings that employed domestic symbols, to literature that presents aspects of domesticity. All contribute to his argument that the desire to make a "home in the world" is a role that the built environment has often been asked to play, and has had a particular, symbolic capacity to provide. **Anat Geva** focuses on the symbolic power of mountains, stones, and light to embody spiritual qualities in the built environment. To this end, two chapels designed by Mario Botta are analyzed in depth: the Chapel of St. Mary of the Angels in Monte Tamaro, and the San Giovanni Battista Church, in Mogno, both in Switzerland. Even though each respond to their mountainous settings differently, both illustrate the interplay of symbolism these settings evoke. **Lindsay Jones** also focuses on symbolism, but from the perspective of the multiple and often conflicting "stories" certain sites evoke. The case study of Chichén Itzá illustrates what he terms the "autonomy and superabundance of architecture." For Jones the symbolic capacity of architecture is never in doubt, it is its ability to produce a plethora of interpretations, often over long periods of time, that is a means to more thoroughly understand them.

Figure 1.4   Participating in carefully choreographed rituals has long been a fundamental element of the
                experience and significance of sacred spaces. Walking the labyrinth at Chartres Cathedral,
                Chartres, France

Source: Photograph courtesy of Daderot, April 10, 2005, GNU Free Documentation License, Version 1.2; and Wikipedia
Creative Commons Attribution-Share Alike 3.0 Unported license.

The *Sacred Landscapes* theme examines the elements and organizations of spiritually responsive and
expressive environments, and the ways in which they are enlivened by ritual and participatory experience.
Rebecca Krinke articulates how the constructs of mapping and writing in installation works can serve to
uncover and express our emotional and spiritual lives. In three built examples she presents how these specific
means illustrate the value of new approaches to the design of built environments. **Dennis Alan Winters**
addresses the potential for spiritual transactions in the experience of natural environments. To do so he applies
Buddhist philosophical systems to explain the diversity of engagements engendered by the experience of the
beautiful in nature, and how they may be used in the design of sacred landscapes. **A.T. Mann** describes sacred
architecture and natural places as thresholds to the divine with potential to trigger spiritual experiences. He
argues that the impetus to create sacred environments is rooted in the human quest for transcendent modalities
often accessed through immersion in the natural environment. In this context, both sacred buildings and
landscapes perform related roles of connecting us with what otherwise would be inaccessible, inculcating a
reverence for "this marvelous and mysterious planet."

The final theme, *Spirituality and the Built Environment,* presents additional distinctive reflections on
the interrelationship of architecture, culture, and spirituality, with particular attention to design and built
works. **Phillip James Tabb** outlines the theoretical background for sacred-secular communities, employing
archetypal patterns in the design of the built environment extrapolated from the works of Christopher

Alexander, Charles Moore, Edward Casey, Belden Lane, and Michael Brill. As the architect of the Serenbe Community in Georgia, Tabb is well situated to describe how the application of what he terms "placemaking patterns," including geometry and ritualized spaces, can result in places that facilitate community, a spirit of place, and an intimate relationship with the land. **Rumiko Handa** addresses the endurance of ruins to express particular attributes of human existence. She asserts that the qualities they embody, incompleteness, imperfection and impermanence, are ones that are not currently valued and are in need of rehabilitation. These, for Handa, provide a counter-project to the often slick and sanitized depictions of contemporary architecture, which, when properly understood, can result in a richer experience of places and objects that engage us in ways that may explicate aspects of our ontological position in the world. **Prem Chandavakar** uses the term "aura" to describe materially transcendent places. For Chandavakar, even though it cannot be rationally described, the "aura" of a place is a primary element of the numinous. The means to access this phenomenon is through "wonder," and he sets out to explain it in a manner that both incorporates and advances predominant intellectual preoccupations. In the last chapter, **Nader Ardalan** discusses the lineage of mysticism (e.g., Sufism, Gnosis, Cabala, Yoga, Zen, and other esoteric traditions), to illustrate its enduring relevancy to contemporary design. He states that, even though these sacred orientations have been suppressed in contemporary discourse, they have remained intrinsic to creative endeavors. To illustrate, he explains how the Abstract Movement of the early 20th century was fundamentally mystical in its philosophy and goals, and that it, along with the mystical traditions it was aligned with, can serve as a timely approach to contemporary design. For all, these expanded positions provide a path to a certain kind of "mastery" regarding the understanding and design of spiritually propitious places.

In short, the authors of the chapters that follow present a panoply of perspectives about the conjunction of architecture, culture, and spirituality. Some reach definitive conclusions, others pose more questions; all seek for and examine the roles architecture has been asked to play in structuring our understanding of the world and our place in it. Collectively the authors present reasoned, proactive, and hopeful perspectives. But, even though they share the view that the contemporary built environment and our approaches to its design are deficient and that its improvement depends on new approaches, they argue that how one does so has multiple and nuanced aspects, principles, and strategies. The book may not have an explicit social and environmental agenda, but throughout the authors profess that spiritual grounding constitutes an auspicious and often successful way to respond to the imperatives of our time. They see a more reverential, humanist, and transcendent orientation as holding the key to more collective objectives and responsible actions. In other words, it is by shifting our priorities to this spiritual grounding that we might create built environments that more thoroughly live up to our needs and aspirations. Ultimately, however, the readers are challenged to reach their own conclusions.

Endnotes

1. Mature cultures throughout history have actually furthered science and rational thought while also remaining centered on religion.
2. Berger, Peter L. (1967). *The Sacred Canopy: Elements of a Sociological Theory of Religion*. New York, NY: Anchor. Habermas, Jürgen (2008). *A "Post-secular" Society—What Does that Mean?*, paper presented at the Istanbul Seminars organized by Reset Dialogues on Civilizations in Istanbul, June 2–6, http://www.resetdoc.org/story/00000000926 (accessed December 16, 2014). Weber, Max (1971). *The Protestant Ethic and the Spirit of Capitalism*. London, UK: Unwin.
3. Cox, Harvey (2010). *The Future of Faith*. New York, NY: Harper-One. Taylor, Charles (2007). *A Secular Society*. Cambridge, MA: Harvard University Press.
4. A 2012 WIN-Gallup International poll on religiosity and atheism concluded that 59% of the world's population is religious, 23% are not religious (but do not call themselves "atheist," suggesting an openness to non-organized spiritual belief or practice) and only 13% report to be atheist. Refer to http://www.wingia.com/web/files/news/14/file/14.pdf (accessed December 16, 2014).
5. Adler, Jerry (2005). In Search of the Spiritual, in *Newsweek: Spirituality in America* (August, 29–September 2005 issue). MSNBC. ARDA (American Religion Data Archive), URL: http://www.thearda.com/quickstats/. Associated Press

(2006). Survey: Americans more religious than believed, *MSNBC.com*, http://www.msnbc.msn.com/id/14782908/. Pew Research Center's Forum on Religion & Public Life (2008). Religious Landscape Survey. (June 23), Washington, D.C., http://religions.pewforum.org/reports. Pew Research Center's Forum on Religion & Public Life (2012). "Nones" on the Rise: One-in-Five Adults Have No Religious Affiliation (October 9) Washington, D.C., Polling Reports.com (various dates and data). See in particular Gallup Poll December 11–13, 2009, Gallup Poll. May 10–13, 2007, and CBS News Poll. April 6–9, 2006, http://www.pollingreport.com/religion2.htm. Tanner, Lindsey (2005). Survey: Most U.S. docs are influenced by God. *The Salt Lake Tribune*, A-10 (June 23) (all accessed December 16, 2014).

6   For example, public television and radio in the United States has been successful at securing and growing an audience over the past decade and more. Perhaps the most successful is Krista Tipett's National Public Radio (NPR) program *On Being* that reached more than 600,000 weekly listeners on nearly 300 public radio stations in the U.S. and was available globally online in mid-2013, with its podcasts downloaded over nine million times in the preceding year. See http:// americanpublicmedia.publicradio.org/press/archive/pr_130709.html (accessed December 16, 2014). Other programs such as *Interfaith Voices*, also in NPR, has been also quite popular and in continuous broadcasting since 2002. In Public TV, *Religion & Ethics Newsweekly* has been aired since 1997 and recognized with over 115 industry awards.

7   Prothero, Stephen (2010). *God is Not One, The Eight Rival Religions That Run the World—And Why Their Differences Matter*. New York, NY: Harper Collins. Rorty, Richard (1994). Religion as Conversation-stopper. *Common Knowledge* 3(1), pp. 1–6.

8   Dyson, Jane, Cobb, Mark and Dawn Forman (1997). The Meaning of Spirituality: A Literature Review. *Journal of Advanced Nursing* 26, pp. 1183–8. Hussey, Trevor (2009). Nursing and Spirituality. *Nursing Philosophy* 10(2), pp. 71–80. Tanyi, Ruth (2002). Toward Clarification of the Meaning of Spirituality. *Journal of Advanced Nursing* 39(5), pp. 500–509.

9   See research publications from Dr. Richard Davidson's Laboratory for Affective Neuroscience at the University of Wisconsin-Madison at http://psyphz.psych.wisc.edu/ (accessed December 16, 2014). Additionally, refer to Koenig, Harold D. (2008). *Medicine, Religion and Health. Where Science and Spirituality Meet*. West Conshohocken, PA: Templeton Foundation Press. Lee, Bruce and Andrew Newberg (2005). Religion and Health: A Review and Critical Analysis. *Zygon* 40(2), pp. 443–68.

10   Chickering, Arthur, Dalton, Jon and Liesa Stamm (2005). *Encouraging Authenticity and Spirituality in Higher Education*. San Francisco, CA: Jossey-Bass. Jones, Laura (2005). What Does Spirituality in Education Mean? *Journal of College and Character* VI(7) article. Tisdell, Elizabeth (2003). *Exploring Spirituality and Culture in Adult and Higher Education*. San Francisco, CA: Jossey-Bass.

11   Grof, Stanislav (2000). *Psychology of the Future: Lessons from Modern Consciousness Research*. New York, NY: SUNY Press. Hayes, Steven (2002). Acceptance, Mindfulness and Science. *Clinical Psychology Science and Practice* 9(1), pp. 101–6. Slife, Brent, Hope, Carolen and R. Scott Nebeker (1999). Examining the Relationship Between Religious Spirituality and Psychological Science. *Journal of Humanistic Psychology* 39(2), pp. 51–85.

12   Austin, James (1998). *Zen and the Brain*. Cambridge, MA: MIT Press. Dalai Lama, Benson, Herbert, Thurman, Robert, Gardner, Howard and Daniel Coleman (1991). *MindScience: An East-West Dialogue*. The Harvard Mind Science Symposium. Wisdom Publications. Mind and Life XIII: Investigating the Mind (2005). *The Science and Clinical Applications of Meditation*. Washington, D.C. (November 8–10) http://www.investigatingthemind.org/ (accessed December 16, 2014). Newberg, Andrew and Mark Robert Waldman (2010). *How God Changes Your Brain*. New York, NY: Ballantine Books. Newberg, Andrew, D'Aquili, Eugene and Vince Rause (2001). *Why God Won't Go Away, Brain Science and the Biology of Belief*. New York, NY: Ballantine Books. Pinker, Steven (1997). *How the Mind Works*. New York, NY: W.W. Norton & Company.

13   For example, growing empirical evidence in the fields of psychology, psychiatry, and neuroscience demonstrate that the contemplative practices of several religions (e.g., Zen and Tibetan Buddhism, Catholic centering prayer, etc.) significantly improve cognitive and affective performances, enhance immunological response, foster brain growth and plasticity, provide a better sense of wellbeing, reduce stress, depression, loneliness, and anxiety, increase motivation, and raise pain thresholds. So impressive have the scientific findings been that hundreds of centers around the world now offer mindfulness-based therapies for a variety of disorders.

14   For example, the Center for Mindfulness in Medicine, Health Care, and Society at the University of Massachusetts Medical School (http://www.umassmed.edu/cfm/), the University of Wisconsin 'Body-Mind Center' (http://aging.wisc. edu/research/mindbody.php), and 'Lab for Affective Neuroscience' (http://psyphz.psych.wisc.edu/), the Jefferson-

Myrna Brind Center of Integrative Medicine in Philadelphia (http://jeffline.jefferson.edu/JMBCIM/research/) and the Neuroscience Institute in La Joya (California) (http://www.nsi.edu/) (all accessed December 16, 2014).

15   For instance: *National Geographic* (March 2005), *Newsweek* (August 29, 2005), *Scientific American MIND* (since 2004), *Time* (January 27, 2007 and August 4, 2003), *Wired* (December 2002), etc. Consider also the amount of radio, (cable, public and open), television, and internet content that has been dedicated to the subject.

16   For example, see UNESCO (1996). *Towards a World Report on Culture and Development. Constructing Cultural Statistics and Indicators*, http://unesdoc.unesco.org/images/0012/001241/124173eo.pdf. McKinley, Terry (1997). *Cultural Indicators of Development*, Geneva, Switzerland: UNRISD & UNESCO. UNESCO (2003). *Convention for the Safeguarding of the Intangible Cultural Heritage*, http://www.unesco.org/culture/ich/en/convention. Gordon, John C. and Helen Beilby-Orren (2007). *International Measurement of the Economic and Social Importance of Culture*. Paris, France: Organization for Economic Co-operation and Development, http://www.oecd.org/std/na/projectontheinternationalmeasurementofculture.htm (all accessed December 16, 2014).

17   Agenda 21 for Culture (2004). http://www.agenda21culture.net/index.php/documents/agenda-21-for-culture. Badham, Marnie (2010). *The Menace of Measurement. A Discussion about Arts Indicators*. Saskatchewan Arts Alliances/University of Melbourne, https://www.academia.edu/1366194/. IFACCA (2005). *D'Art Report Number 18: Statistical Indicators for Arts Policy*, http://media.ifacca.org/files/statisticalindicatorsforartspolicy.pdf. Meyer, Todd (2014). Exploring Cultural Urbanism. *Planning* 80(4) (April) pp. 15–19. The Urban Institute (2006). *Cultural Vitality: Interpretation and Indicators*, http://www.urban.org/publications/311392.html. United Nations Human Settlements Program, 2012, *State of the World's Cities Report 2012/2013: Prosperity of Cities*, http://sustainabledevelopment.un.org/content/documents/745habitat.pdf. Hawkes, Jon (2001). *The Fourth Pillar of Sustainability*. Melbourne: Common Ground Publishing (all accessed December 16, 2014).

18   The Forum for Architecture, Culture, and Spirituality's 2007 founding whitepaper articulated this situation. See http://www.acsforum.org/ACS_founding_whitepaper_2007.pdf (accessed December 16, 2014). Arguments and evidences explaining the biases of the architectural discipline against the qualitative, experiential, and axiological may be found in several books. For example, Pérez-Gómez, Alberto (1985). *Architecture and the Crisis of Modern Science.* Cambridge, MA: MIT Press; Harries, Karsten (1997). *The Ethical Function of Architecture.* Cambridge, MA: MIT Press; Harries, Karsten, (2007). The Ethical Significance of Environmental Beauty, in Gregory Caicco (ed.), *Architecture, Ethics, and the Personhood of Place.* Lebanon, NH: University Press of New England. Additionally, we are always reminded of Luis Barragán's 1980 Laureate Acceptance Speech, Pritzker Architecture Prize, http://www.pritzkerprize.com/1980/ceremony_speech1 (accessed December 16, 2014). Related to this is Pérez-Gómez's argument that the taboo against addressing this area of inquiry is endemic to all institutions that must confront something at their core that is mystical, numinous, immeasurable. See his book (2006). *Built upon Love: Architectural Longing after Ethics and Aesthetics.* Cambridge, MA: The MIT Press, p. 84.

19   Karla Britton discusses the bias against the sacred and spiritual in contemporary architecture in her book (2010). *Constructing the Ineffable: Contemporary Sacred Architecture.* New Haven, CT: Yale School of Architecture. See also Hejduk, Renata and Jim Williamson (2011). Introduction: The Apocryphal Project of Modern and Contemporary Architecture, in Renata Hejduk and Jim Williamson (eds), *The Religious Imagination in Modern and Contemporary Architecture: A Reader.* New York, NY: Routledge. Michael Benekikt offers more evidence of this bias in the introduction to his book (2008). *God, Creativity and Evolution. The Argument from Design(ers).* Austin, TX: Center for American Architecture and Design. Bermudez provides further arguments in (2009). The Extraordinary in Architecture. Studying and Acknowledging the Reality of the Spiritual. *2A—Architecture and Art Magazine*, Autumn Quarter(12), pp. 46–9.

20   Refer to Michael Crosbie's chapter in this book.

21   James, William (2004), *The Varieties of Religious Experiences: A Study in Human Nature.* New York, NY: Barnes and Noble Classics.

22   Critchlow, Keith (1980). What is Sacred in Architecture? *Lindisfarne Letter* 10, Stockbridge, MA, pp. 4–6.

23   Dyson, Jane, Cobb, Mark and Dawn Forman (1997). The Meaning of Spirituality: A Literature Review. *Journal of Advanced Nursing*, 26, pp. 1183–8.

24   Barrie, Thomas (2010). *The Sacred In-Between: The Mediating Roles of Architecture.* New York, NY: Routledge.

PART I
Being in the World

Chapter 2
On Architecture, Divinity, and the Interhuman

Michael Benedikt

When architects talk about sacred space, it might be about the holy sites they've visited, or the sanctuaries they've designed, or the experiences they've had of secular buildings that seem, somehow, to slow time, capture eternity, or partake of nature's intricacy, vastness, perfection, and majesty.

Other religious sensibilities than these are reflected in different architectural preferences. The simplicity and silence sought by monastics of all traditions, for example, is reflected in the architecture of wood-floored cabins, quiet quadrangles, and remote locations. The liveliness of sacred space sought by religious people of more social temperament is reflected in radiant, elaborately decorated temples, perfumed with flowers and bodies, alive with ceremony and music, or, for more reserved believers, simple communal houses, as austere as they are clean, set in a field of grass. Whatever kind of space one considers sacred, however, *the primary relationship being cultivated is that between the individual and the divine, or God.* Architects and clerics—sacred space makers both, one by physical, one by rhetorical means—aim to facilitate this relationship.

Moreover, when humans *do* experience God (or the divine, or their Buddha-nature), they do so individually, one by one, one on One. People might pray and sing together in a lofty hall, or meditate together in a darkened room, or stand in awe on a mountaintop with others, but the relationship *between* people at these times is muted. Even as one sits (or stands) shoulder-to-shoulder, the enlightenment experience is an internal one, a private one, whose only outward manifestation might be a smile or a tear.

This echoes the modern view that *all* experience is private. After all, "experiencing" happens in brains; and brains, like bodies, are privately owned and operated. *The world* might be public, out there, as nature is; but it is experienced "in here," locally, individually, and uniquely. And experience is what counts. Thus: to each person *a* world of experience—a world of his or her own, you yours and me mine. In the West, we live in cultures strongly inclined to defend and celebrate the very multiplicity of those worlds, those "subjectivities."

I have just sketched a version of *solipsism*, the philosophy that claims that "the self can know nothing but its own modifications, and that the self is the only existent thing." In *Appearance and Reality* (1897), F.H. Bradley put it this way: "I cannot transcend experience, and experience is *my* experience. From this it follows that nothing beyond myself exists; for what experience is, is the self's states."[1]

How do buildings fit in to the solipsistic if pluralistic picture? Buildings are certainly part of the world "out there." They are paradigmatically real and often public. But they too are privately experienced, if by many at once. More to the point of this essay, however, is that, on the solipsistic view, if a building successfully presents itself *to me* as cosmic, eternal, and unfathomable, if it seems to me to be intricate, vast, perfect, and majestic like the sun on a mountain or the stars in the sky—if it even points to such things and marks itself off from "profane" space—then it *is* all these things, and I am offered a minute or two in ([the] mind of) divinity.

Should *you* have a similar experience, well, all the better.

Eastern religions give us an alternative to solipsism: to wit, that the inner and the outer, the private and the public, the self and the other are One, that the separation between experiencer and world, created and creation, you and me, is illusory. In Buddhism (deriving many of its categories from Hinduism), Brahman (the Absolute) is without borders, embracing all being and non-being. Brahman gives rise to Atman (Self or spirit) and thus to individuality and the need for language. But by virtue of its priority and continuity and eternity, Brahman gives reason for human beings to act with compassion for all things: for all things are of its substance, including ourselves.

Recognizing, intuiting, and ultimately identifying oneself with Brahman is one way to challenge solipsism, for it follows that we are all in This together, or better, we are all each other already. On the other hand, we might see this doctrine as solipsistic in the extreme: I am Brahman and so are you, and so we are both equally, at the center of existence as a whole. For his 2003 film *Wheel of Time*, Werner Herzog interviewed

His Holiness the Dalai Lama. H.H.D.L.: "Ultimately, we ourselves, one individual, *that* is the center of the universe. So for me, this place is the center of the universe, because the concept—the conception—of the whole universe comes from *here*, so therefore, I am the center of the universe. So, similarly, in your case, *you* are the center of the whole universe!" [Laughs]. W.H.: "Thank you. That makes me feel very good. I shouldn't tell my wife."[2]

We will return to the theological theme. But for now, I would like to make an observation that is more sociological than mystical, to wit, that architects tend to focus on how people relate to their physical environment, whereas ordinary people are preoccupied with how people relate to each other.[3]

For evidence that architects, at least professionally, are more interested in space and things than they are in people we might take the summary treatment human figures have received in architectural illustrations going back hundreds of years. Students of architecture are typically not taught how to draw people *doing things* in their buildings, not even in outline. Rather, in schools as in practice, ready-made clip-art people are brought into drawings like so many extras, walking, standing, at best clumping like tourists, each one happy in him or herself and generally admiring their surroundings. Their purpose is to "give scale," to murmur behind the lead actor that is the building. Buildings are only in the last place seen as *arrangers of people*—of people, moreover, who are primarily concerned not with architecture but with the intentions, actions, and opinions of the *people* around them.

Or take the vagueness and generic-ness of most programs: lots of talk about the "areas" needed (as in "reception area," "dining area," "service area") and little talk about what could or should go on in these places in any detail, i.e., with any richness of *social* experience. Perhaps that's why so many architect-designed buildings look so generic, and why rooms in them do too (if there are rooms at all rather than areas). Very few architects are capable of envisioning in any detail what "activities" (the word betrays) a building's "users" (there's another one) will undertake, nor what experiences users will have *of each other*. They are much better at envisioning what users will experience of their *buildings*. Hence how common CAD-generated "fly-throughs" are … of empty buildings.

Now let us turn the discussion back to matters theological.

Differences of relationship among people are revealed in how they dispose themselves *spatially*, in "formations." One can identify three everyday patterns: there are quasi-random, standing-about formations; there are more organized face-to-back column and shoulder-to-shoulder row formations; and there are face-to-face, "dialogical" ones, often expanded to create inward-facing circles and arcs. I point out these three formations only because, in a religious context, a different the vision of divinity is conjured by each. The first, "standing-about" one, favors architecture or places acting as demonstrations of cosmic harmony and scale, where one simply stands in awe, looking around. The second, queuing and shoulder-to-shoulder formations favor architecture or places serving as gateways or thresholds to worlds above and beyond this one.[4] This all-but theatrical pattern can be found in most organized religions.

Face-to-face, dialogical formations suggest that divinity enters the world in, as, and because of the quality of the relationships *between* people, and more specifically in, as, and because of their *regard for one another*. This line of thinking leads to proposition that divinity *is nothing other than* human action of a certain kind, namely, ethically creative (or creatively ethical) action with and towards others; and this is radically educated not by private experiences of the cosmos (or, by extension, of "cosmic" buildings), or by experiences of communal solidarity addressing a Beyond or superior being, but by witnessing, deepening, and multiplying the occasions of positive, dialogical, interhuman regard. On this view, God is not "in" people. Nor are people "in" God; but God is *between* them, in—and perhaps, as—a sort of transactional electricity. Think about a jazz ensemble with God as the music.

We will now look into this "interhuman" view, and then return to its implications for architectural design.

The philosopher most closely associated with the interhuman view is Martin Buber. Polish by birth but Austrian by culture, a student of Ludwig Feuerbach, Buber lived from 1878 to 1965. The book that accounts for Buber's considerable influence on Jewish and Christian socio-religious thought in the 1960s and 1970s was the essay he published in 1923 called *Ich und Du*, translated in 1937 as *I and Thou*.

I and Thou begins with a distinction that will seem familiar to readers of the previous few pages. Human experiencing occurs not in a vacuum, but through one of two possible *relationships* to other entities in the world. These he named I-You, and I-It.

To man the world is twofold in accordance with his twofold attitude.

The attitude of man is twofold, in accordance with the twofold nature of the primary words which he speaks.

The primary words are not isolated words, but combined words.

The one primary word is the combination *I-You.*

The other primary word is the combination *I-It,* wherein, without a change in the primary word, one of the words *He* and *She* can replace *It.*

Hence the *I* of man is also twofold.

For the *I* of the primary word *I-You* is a different *I* from that of the primary word *I-It.* [5]

Every phenomenon—physical, chemical, biological, social—derives from relationships, and according to Buber, in the human world it is no different; except that I-You and I-It are foundational to all the others. There can be no "I" without a "You" or "It" to relate to; no "You" or "It" without an "I" to make it so. I-you and I-It are the two "primary words" uttered by consciousness.

I-It relationships are ones in which one person relates to another, or to an animal, or to an inanimate object, as a means to an end. As "-Its," others are objectified, assessed: they are well formed or not, useful or not, suitable or not, edible or not, intelligent or dull, amenable or problematic. I-It relationships are not *ipso facto* bad; they can be good or bad. Indeed, they are essential to the functioning of any society that would provide safety, goods, and livelihoods for its citizens. We all agree to become "Its" for certain others—employees and employers, partners, coworkers, servers, even spouses—and we treat many others as "Its" ourselves. There is no blame to be apportioned here, except that I-It relations tend to dominate I-You ones, which are just as essential, but more fragile.

In I-It relationships, people expect things from each other and respond to one another by virtue of their roles and positions in society, as in a game—a game that everyone plays, ideally, by the rules, even as the rules are under construction in some higher-yet game. In I-It relationships there is no interest in what the other is really thinking, except that knowing what they're really thinking allows one to "work with them" all the more effectively. As "-Its," others are there to give you pleasure, and you they. Others are there to give you information, and you they. I-It relationships also allow us to take esthetic pleasure in each other's poses and appearances without thinking of them as addressed to us specifically, and thus having to respond.

In I-You relationships one cannot see the other objectively. To look into the eyes of another is to look through the night of their pupils into a sort of infinity. It is to address others fearfully or lovingly, but in any case, fragilely. It is to say: you matter to me and I think I matter to you. It is to say: I acknowledge an immensity in you equal to the immensity that I feel in myself; I recognize your freedom as I recognize my own, your fears as I do my own, your ambitions as I do my own.

In I-You relationships, computation of debt and advantage are at a minimum. Accounting, if there is any, is long term, loose, even irrational.

Contrary to philosophers who argue, following Kant, that detachment is necessary to esthetic enjoyment, esthetic enjoyment does not vanish in I-You relationships, it just occurs differently, more able to get past superficial ugliness, more able to ride swells of emotion. Think of Rembrandt's self-portraits, or Van Gogh's. Who are they looking at?

I-You relationships cannot be experienced from the side, as it were. They involve the whole of our beings and they block out the world, if only for a moment. Rare? Not at all. "Hello" and "goodbye" are I-You words that briefly perform that magic. And so we might say hello to a cat as he or she turns towards us (or should I say *if* …?). We might also say hello *sotto vocé* to a praying mantis, a sapling, or a building, meaning: I recognize the you-ness of you and that in some way *you experience me* in your subjectivity, such as it can maximally be. We regard each other. We are in dialogue.

In I-It, people deal with each other.

In I-You, they meet.

There's a temptation to equate Buber's "I-You" with love. No doubt this was what enthused Buber's Christian admirers, followers of the Gospel according to John. But I-You relationships are not necessarily agapic; they are just direct and non-depersonalizing.[6] Can I-You be anthropomorphizing? Yes. But while entering an I-You relationship with an inanimate object is objectively silly, doing so is not at all uncommon[7] among artists and designers, who might say: "Unless I thought that non-sentient things, like this sculpture I am making or building I am designing, had the right to exist in its own way (i.e., had integrity), unless I thought it could answer to my presence or yours as you and I answer to its with the fullness of our beings and memories ... I could not design it well. And nor, in the end, would it have the qualities that allow ordinary people to 'relate to it' at all."

Buber was not the first to discuss the difference between instrumental I-It relationships and interpersonal I-You ones. One can find the idea in Kant, Hegel, and Feuerbach, as well as Sartre and Levinas. But Buber was who made the most of the distinction, poeticized it, drove home how deeply existential the difference was, and showed what social, political, spiritual, and theological consequences flowed from it.[8]

Let us go directly to the last consequence, the theological, since we are trying to limn how architecture participates in divinity. Here are three questions: (1) Are human beings best in an I-It relationship to divinity, or an I-You one? (2) Does it matter which? And then, assuming the answer to (2) is yes: (3) does it matter to architects and architecture which?

Some prefatory remarks before looking at how Buber answers the first two questions. To hear what Buber has to say about divinity, there must be at least *one* sense in which God credibly exists for the reader. (Which is to say, if you are an atheist then what Buber [and I] have to say is nonsense, or at least, non-science.) If you are a *deist*, then God for you exists as Creator of the Universe—a long-gone creator it sometimes seems, but certainly one who left us free. For others, divinity is Being itself, in totality, or the Ground of Being, or Brahman, or Tao, wise beyond our understanding of these words. Here is Buber's first point: when God is conceived of in *any* of these ways, then the proper relationship between humans and God is an I-It one. An "-It God" is not a God one listens for, listens to, argues with, begs, thanks, or confides in. It is a God one watches dazzled by "his" (or its) power and beauty. It is a God one learns about and "obeys" or is simply, ineluctably part of, in as much as the laws of nature apply everywhere and always to everyone. It is Spinoza's God and Einstein's.

Now, most liberal, college-educated believers are happier with this rendition of divinity than they are with God as some unpredictable (yet influenceable) all-powerful and eternal patriarch, who can speak to prophets or have a human son. But Buber could no more subscribe to deism and its "-It God" than he could to traditional monotheism. Buber was modernly Jewish and sympathetic to all religions that strove to bring out the best in human beings ethically. In the earlier part of his career, Buber was a well-known interpreter of Jewish (Hasidic) mystical literature, like the Zohar, which is laced through with ecstatic descriptions of a God-beyond-description. But by 1923 Buber had become convinced that everyday *life* and *relationships* were more important than *theology* and *description* for leading "the life of the spirit" and enjoying the capabilities that came with it. Direct I-You relationships were intrinsically more ethical than rational or mystical I-It relationships, be they to people individually, people in togetherness, or to God. Certainly, I-You was the relationship that prophets had to God. He saw the same pattern in the lives of the great Hasidic rabbis: a relationship to God—as to people—that was eye-to-eye and utterly sincere, seemingly naïve but not at all so in fact. Go along with Buber in this, even in trial, and the whole theological question transforms. It becomes not "Who or what is God in and of 'Him-' or It-self that I should believe in 'Him' (or 'It')?" but "How is God to human beings, and how are we to "Him" and each other, when mutual I-You-ness is the defining relationship?"

In maintaining an I-You *relationship to* divinity rather than an I-It *belief in* it, there are (at least) two options.

Option One: God could appear to us in a vision, as an entity or voice in dialogue with us, as He legendarily did to Moses and to the prophets before and after him. Here, we (or the prophets anyway) speak to God and God replies, or He calls out to us first and we reply.[9] Of course, to say today that "I did x because God told me to" is to court ridicule in many quarters. And yet many people claim to have felt addressed "out of the blue" by an entity or argument or situation that results in ethically creative action beyond that which would derive from utilitarian or even judicial considerations. To know that feeling—the feeling of being addressed and then of wanting to respond (to no one actually there) with "You mean *me*? *Now*?" and then "But I ..."—is to appreciate the power of thinking of divinity as that which, or "He" who, having somehow gotten our number, calls us to do right, right here, right now, and probably at some risk.

A deist, indeed an atheist, would patiently explain that in this case—with this "option" as I am calling it—we are simply listening to *conscience*, which is a mental process in our brains, the product of long socialization, and not anything *cosmic*.[10] But Buber would want us to note that the voice in which (or with which) conscience addresses us is not simply our own (or our parents' or priest's) or a psychotic, delusional voice, but a rapidly dawning cognitive clarity that *this* action now *is* right and good, even if at our personal expense. More than a shedding of present guilt, more than an avoidance of future shame, this energy, this coalescence of intentionality, this sense of going backward in time and forward in time simultaneously, is *ethical creativity* at work, *inaugurated by a variety of heeding*. God thought of this way, i.e., as ethical creativity emergent from life taken personally, from life lived I-You-ly on this planet, is "cosmic" enough.

Option Two: The option I am about to describe is the one slightly favored by Buber himself, perhaps because it is less prone to objectification, perhaps because it is less malleable to unethical purposes, or perhaps because it keeps "God" a distinct singularity consistent with ancient monotheism. It deploys a new metaphor of radiance. Buber located God behind the eyes, as it were, of every other who is addressed as You. God is the You of all You's, the point towards which all forms of direct address between people converges, or equivalently, the point *from* which all You-ness originates, radiates. To say, "Oh, you mean God is *love*" over-simplifies. God, for Buber, is what makes addressing other creatures in the second person—as "you"—both possible and necessary, for some animals possible and necessary in glimmering, for humans, possible and necessary in full. God has had quasi-human form in the religious imagination, then, not out of naïve anthropomorphism in an I-It mode of belief, but because *people* have faces and voices, and because *people*, living a life of I-You relation to each other and to all sentient creatures, are the site of goodness's repeated emergence into an otherwise indifferent and mechanical world. God may be Love, but love, properly understood, is always *between* different beings ("between" was a word Buber liked to capitalize) and forever being tested. It is not a melding of them into one.

By way of recap: In the first Option, God is who, from the swirl of an evolving situation, entrains your intuition with a whisper that grows into a voice that wants you—you!—to intervene on behalf of all life here and now. ("If not now, then when?" asked Rabbi Hillel. "And if not me, then who?") In the second Option, God is who looks at you—you!—through the eyes of an actual other who needs you. Both involve the opening of an I-You channel, as it were, between oneself and divinity; and both are preferable, in Buber's view, to the deist-scientist's I-It God, which is a conviction chasing a chimera: the conviction that all things have a beginning or reason chasing the chimera of complete understanding and control. The deist-scientist's vision of God obliges us to exercise, eat right, and perfect ourselves for the chase. The scientific mystic, for his part, contemplates the "grandeur" and laughs: The universe is neither large nor small, he knows; it is neither old nor young, neither beautiful nor ugly nor good nor bad. It just *is*. It does not care for us, and it is we who, pathetically or heroically in our own judgment, insist on finding it "large" and "old" and "beautiful" and "good."

This sounds utterly modern and cool-headed if you are going to believe at all. But we are post-post-Enlightenment now, and can more easily imagine the universe not as a mechanical thing, like a clock, but as a complex, evolving system with new, emergent, complexity-dependent phenomena and entities, including ourselves and what we think and do.[11] The process that engenders truth-seeking and esthetic and moral agency on earth might itself—"himself"—be younger yet, a tender new flower of Being with a wavering, still-forming ontological status. This view is not Buber's exactly, but more Hegel's.[12] Entirely with Buber, however, we might go on to think this: that whether we garb divinity in personhood, knowing full well that this is projection, or whether we prefer to leave God's ontological status uncertain, a perpetual blooming/becoming of the good on this planet and probably many others, it is in the second person—in saying *you*—that divinity moves the air.[13]

Does it matter whether God is related to I-It-ly or I-You-ly? Let us consider this question answered in the affirmative, and turn to whether it matters to architecture specifically. After all, not all buildings aspire to making sacred space either I-It-ly or I-You-ly (whatever that might mean). Supermarkets do not aim to put us in mind of God at all, much less to bring divinity into being, and most architects are relieved: society has charged them with designing safe, practical, and handsome buildings for everyday life. It has not charged them with being prophets, or clerics, or mystical seers.

And yet historically influential architects have not shied away from religiosity of some sort, from providing narratives that locate their work metaphysically and ethically in some larger context. From Vitruvius to Palladio to Wren to Sullivan to Wright to Kahn, the profession has had its prophets.[14] Even journeyman architects can recall their youthful dedication to timeless beauty or selfless service on the basis of architectural "prophecy." Are all-but-religiously-held metaphysical and ethical ideals necessary, then, for practicing architecture at its highest levels? Most would say no. But for those who think they are (and that includes this author), four framing possibilities remain, each resulting from the choices made between two pairs of alternatives.

First alternative: only high-culture venues or explicitly religious building-types offer appropriate venues for sacred space (e.g. churches, libraries, art museums, memorials) *or all* building-types could be venues for spiritually ambitious architecture and contain sacred space (e.g., retail stores, hotels, factories, schools, houses …). Second alternative: achieving architectural perfection of light, material, space, proportion, construction, in cooperation with nature is how divinity is revealed, *or* having people relate to each another more compassionately, generously, truthfully, creatively, and so on, is how divinity is revealed. It's this second pair that we have been addressing. Here is a table, labeling the four framing permutations **A**, **B**, **C**, and **D**:

Table 2.1   Four framing permutations

	High-culture venues	All venues
Divinity through architecture	**A**	**B**
Divinity through people	**C**	**D**

Frame A represents the view among architects that sacred space arises when buildings of high moral and esthetic purpose (like churches and art museums) are perfectly designed, constructed, and cared for, where "perfect design" entails, among other things, geometric and geomantic sophistication, orientation to the sky, and/or cosmic references and attunements.

Frame B represents the view that perfect design, construction, and care should grace *every* building type, making sacredness a matter not of altars and star-alignments, but of sensitivity-of-layout, cleanliness, generosity, integrity, sophistication, and craftsmanship everywhere.

Frame C does not look to architecture to open gates to divine realms at all, but to the power and beauty of people engaged in orchestrated religious, artistic, or civic rituals. In its secular manifestation, **C** would have us see divinity in the genius of great statesmen, scientists, and artists, and to be knowledgeable about their times. **C** would have us behave solemnly at ceremonies, inaugurations and concerts, and attend them well attired.

Frame D holds that divinity happens (or God reveals itself/Himself) every time and in every place that people are doing something good and decent or meeting I-You-ly. It happens in shacks and chateaus, formally or casually, whenever kindness, courage, and ethical creativity meet a human (or sentient animal's) need. It happens whenever a person reaches, and by example teaches, excellence in some small or large undertaking.

Some readers might find themselves identifying with one of these permutations more than the others … and then suddenly wondering why they should have to choose among them. "God is not limited in any way," they might think. "God is always 'all of the above' when the options are good, and so, too, should *we* try to be, *imitatio dei*."

Indeed, why choose?

I say architects should focus on **C** and **D** because of their relative neglect. Architects in search of spiritual seriousness have difficulty seeing how enhancing human (or inter-species) relationships can be the *point* of their work *and* inform architectural form. They are *architects*, after all. They want form itself, architecture alone, to sing God or nature's praises in the **A** or **B** frame. Their implicit theology rests on Design or perhaps Process,[15] not on the ethics of interpersonal encounter.

Frames **C** and **D**, and what we have learned from Buber, show the way to a new sort of humanism in architecture, perhaps even a religious humanism. Religious or not, this humanism would be shaped by renewed and careful attention to human character and human social behavior in space. It would also look again at the Architecture of Humanism, so named by Geoffrey Scott in 1914. It would be nourished most deeply, however, by compassion and introspection under the sign of I-You. This architecture too would be spiritual.

How to go about it? At this point, and in this short chapter, one can only offer pointers.[16]

Visit an architecture school during review week, and instead of looking at the work on the walls, listen to the conversation. Listen in particular to the language of appraisal: the compliments, the misgivings, even the descriptions. Through the jargon of the day (oh, the jargon), you will be struck by how many of the compliments and critiques offered are more appropriate to people than to buildings. While *ad hominem* criticism of a student is rare ("George, you were lazy!"), you might very well hear "your *building* does not work hard enough" to "negotiate the landscape" or "organize services" or "articulate the program." You will hear buildings complimented for their *integrity* and *honesty*, dissed for their *incoherence* or *pretension*. Cognates of "strong" and "weak" having little to do with engineering soundness will abound, as will cognates of "sensitive" and "insensitive," "elegant" and "clumsy," "ingenious" and "obvious," "rigorous" or "sloppy," "mature" or "undeveloped." These are all epithets that properly apply to people, not things.

We should not be surprised. We relate to many designed objects as though they had personalities and attitudes. Buber's notion that near-to-I-You relationships can be established with inanimate objects is borne out daily in the teaching of design. The animism of ancient religious practitioners lives among designers, together with belief in the magical efficacy of gestures.[17] Now add that sometimes students' characters *are* being assessed by the "conversation" about their work—slyly, and often along social class lines[18]—and one sees how deeply anthropomorphic the processes of architectural design and appreciation are, for all the functional, constructional, and "systems talk" being put forward.

Or take the phenomenon of *posture*. Buildings communicate by how they make us feel, and part of how they make us feel is through empathy—body-empathy—which uses our "mirror neurons."[19] Buildings, like people, have *bodies* set on the ground in a pose or posture: they sit or stand, heavily or lightly; they can hang from a cliff, they can hover over water; they squat, swivel, soar, lean, leap; they can seem defeated or yearning. And because of our mirror neurons, they make us feel that way too, merely by looking at them. Facing towards us or facing away, they can seem proud or ashamed of themselves, informative (here's my door! look at how I'm built) or inscrutable (mirror glass and a faraway stare). As soloists or in company, buildings communicate through dance one might say, albeit frozen dance: posture.[20] And one cannot see any of this if a building is merely an –It.

Bringing social relationships to the topic of design is troubling for many architects. It represents an invasion by ethics (or politics) of esthetics (or design). Humans are deeply and ineluctably social, they would admit, but the creation and appreciation of beauty must come out of consciousness itself, i.e., consciousness quieted of commentary and cleared of involvement.[21] As Paul Valery put it: "Seeing is forgetting the name of the thing one sees."[22] In this view, beauty is respite, art is respite, and spirituality is respite from social intercourse and obligations, making no building's altruism an excuse for its ugliness. The debate is ongoing, however, as to whether this respite is desirable or even possible. Elaine Scarry, in *On Beauty and Being Just*, makes the case that ethical fairness and esthetic fairness are related.[23] Our sense of justice and our sense of beauty, she argues, share a central concept, fairness, which in turn reflects the world's *symmetries* at biological, physical, and mathematical levels.

These two meanings of "fairness" might be verbal coincidence, not to be made too much of. After all, there are other meanings of fairness that do not work at all. But Scarry also discusses the experience most people have had of *having been wrong in one's judgment about what is beautiful* and then correcting oneself. The experience is telling not only because it indicates that there is *some* objectivity to beauty—that there is something *there* one can be wrong *about*—but because correcting an earlier judgment is more than an abstract, balancing-out, or symmetry-seeking exercise. For example, as a young person, you might have hated Italian opera or Renaissance painting. In later life, and/or after some education, you might develop a love of both and feel embarrassed by your earlier ignorance. What is this "mechanism" but a way of injecting a touch of guilt—which is a social, ethical emotion—into the viewer's otherwise-distant relationship to inanimate esthetic objects? What one eventually finds beautiful (or innocent) one owes an apology to, I-You, for past ignorance or condemnation, and this multiplies the emotion with which one regards it now. One has not just changed one's mind or "grown." One has redeemed oneself from error; one has *converted* from one whole frame of reference to another. I do not think it far-fetched to claim that great beauty cannot be experienced without this conversion experience admixed.[24]

In sum, if a building's virtues often sound like human ones, it's because of our empathetic engagement with inanimate objects, and especially of artifacts, which are known to be made for us, and presented to us, by other human beings. This is not a bad thing if you think that relationships among sentient beings, not inanimate objects, are the site of divinity's possible appearance.

It's easy to see how greater attention to I-You relationships could help an architecture firm thrive: more genuine and personal client and employee relations would likely result in better buildings and more work. But it's not easy, Scarrie's idea of fairness notwithstanding, to indicate exactly how sensitivity to human relationships—and especially I-You ones—might inform the spatial and material choices architects must make as designers.

For this, one ought to be able to cite research in journals like *Environment & Behavior*. But, as Thomas Fisher points out, almost 45 years of scientific investigation into how buildings influence human behavior has had little or no effect on architects in practice, and one has to wonder why.[25] Is it because of the "two-cultures" divide between the sciences and the arts famously lamented by C.P. Snow? Or the similar divide between researchers and practitioners frequently lamented by engineers as Fisher suggests. Or is it because the direct effect of a building's spaces and materials on most people's psyches is, in fact, so subtle as to be negligible? And might *that* be because non-architects are intrinsically much more interested in other people than they are in buildings, as we have noted?

It may well be that the effect of buildings on people has less to do with "the masterly, correct and magnificent play of masses brought together in light," as Le Corbusier proclaimed, and more to do with the choreographies buildings impose upon the comings and goings, appearances and disappearances, elevations, facings, dispositions, groupings, processions, and closeness of people with respect to one another.[26] In this view, space does not derive from the meshwork of light ricocheting between surfaces, but from the diaphanous *fabric of glances* between people. Currently, we have no *theory* of that, no system of representation.

Louis Kahn called the plan "a society of rooms." Few of us stop to contemplate the profundity of this apothegm. Kahn is not simply directing us to think about the people in rooms, but is personifying rooms themselves. If the room is a person, then a plan (consisting of rooms) is also a statement either of the actuality or of the idealization of human relationships. More generally, Kahn is asking, what approach to spatial arrangement—other than maximizing convenience to us—might emerge from thinking about the environment anthropomorphically and animistically, as did Le Corbusier? What if things were aware of their surroundings? Might they be conscious of each other's characters, intentions, and attitudes? Are spaces—rooms, streets, squares—not bodies of air, and thus also bodies of sound- and light-borne information? And if they are *bodies*, might they have some of the properties of bodies-proper, yours and mine: posture, facing, elevation, entrance and exit, their own structure, inclinations, curiosities, desires, and affiliations?

Concerning rooms: do the rooms of a building know where the other rooms are? And if not, why not? Do they care? Are they in conversation with each other or oblivious? Do they know which way they face, or what's being done in them? Are they happy when lived in and sad ("empty-feeling") when abandoned? Are they trying, always, to move, drift, lift? Are they trying to get away, or huddle, or dance? Can they see the outdoors? And if so, is *their* seeing ("The living room looks out at the ocean") just ours in potential? These are just some of the questions one could ask once we opened the gates between our natural social intelligence and our cultivated design and form intelligence.

Could the categories "I-It" and "I-You" apply to relationships between buildings and rooms, as between furniture, objects, trees, etc., *apart* from us as well as relative to us?[27] And if so, why would anyone create architecture that does not include *rooms* at all, which is where some current trends in architectural design are taking us?

Again, we simply do not have the language yet to talk about these things psychologically or politically, much less the science to back it up.

Which brings us to the science that, in theory, could. A major task for academicians of architecture could be writing a digest of the findings accumulated by *Environment & Behavior* and the *Environmental Design Research Association*, edited and formatted as a ready reference for architects. Because the majority of these studies are premised on one person at a time facing a physical environment, also needed is a digest from studies further afield, e.g. coming out of *social* psychology, that offer insight into what Edward T. Hall long ago called "proxemics," i.e., how human beings move, group, isolate themselves from, and orient themselves towards each other in space depending on the *relationship* between them and *tasks* before them (a) uninfluenced by architecture (i.e., in the open field) and then (b) influenced by architecture. Online efforts at summary of, and access to, environment behavior studies under the rubric of Evidence Based Design, like InformeDesign, are to be praised even if they do not reach the depths really required.[28]

Also needed is a resource that confirms what one would expect about the environment's effects on "socialization" but goes much further.[29] Amenity provision is a simple business, physically if not politically. But one has to wonder what would happen were this simple business to evolve into the complexity of art: places and spaces not just pleasing to the eye in a general way, but cleverly wrought to multiply and enhance people's I-You experience of each other.

And finally, and importantly for designers, needed are ways to represent humans and human social life in buildings, and to do that artistically, practically, technically, poetically, using new kinds of drawings, movie-based video techniques, and narratives of observation. Teachers of design have a special responsibility here.

We seem to have drifted off topic: what does any of this have to do with *divinity*?

Everything—if you think divinity manifests itself in how human beings set themselves in relation to other beings, rather than in how stones are set against the sky.

Endnotes

1 Bradley, F.H. (1930). *Appearance and Reality*. Oxford, UK: Clarendon Press (reprint of 1897 edition), p. 218.

2 https://youtu.be/rkzoMJtk8Qk, 0:15-0:32 (accessed June 29, 2015).

3 Indeed, it seems that non-architects are roughly 150 times more interested in other people than they are in buildings or light or natural objects. This strangely empirical claim is based on my unpublished Masters of Environmental Design (M.E.D.) Thesis at Yale University (The Information Field: A Theoretical and Empirical Approach to the Distribution and Transfer of Information in the Physical Environment, 1975). In an experiment performed under supervision of Dr. Michael Kubovy of the Psychology Department, I examined the temporal order-of-recall and completeness-of-recall of the elements of two, complex, urban scenes. The result pertaining to relative interest comes from the completeness-of-recall measure: people remembered far, far more about the people in the scene (who occupied a tiny fraction of it spatially) than anything else. In the temporal-order-of-free-recall measure, however overall setting (geometry and weather etc.), summarily described, came first. The "solid angle" measure was computed from the relative area of the image (as a percentage of the whole) devoted to people, buildings, planting, signs, etc. The area of an image on the retina is a direct linear function of the solid (i.e., 3-D) angle subtended at the eye by an object of given size and distance in the world, see http://en.wikipedia.org/wiki/Solid_angle (accessed June 29, 2015).

4 For an eloquent modern account of this view, see Barrie, Thomas (2010). *The Sacred In-Between: The Mediating Roles of Architecture*. Abingdon, UK: Routledge. Martin Heidegger had done much to revive the rather Nordic and ancient trinary image of man-on-earth, gods-in-heaven, and temple between-earth-and-sky. This image had a strong influence on architectural theory through Christian Norberg-Schulz's 1971 book *Existence, Space, and Architecture* (London, UK: Studio Vista). Also influential on architects in this vein was *Sacred and Profane* by Mircea Eliade (New York, NY: Harcourt Brace Jovanovich, 1987 [1959]) in describing how spaces are traditionally demarcated as one or the other.

5 Buber, Martin (2000 [1958]). *I and Thou*. New York, NY: Scribner. The reader may be wondering: what happened to "Thou"? As Walter Kaufman, the book's second translator, noted, the English title of Buber's book should have been *I and You* which is closer to *Ich und Du*. It would seem that the book's first translator, Ronald Gregor Smith, wanted the book's religious ambition to be signaled.

6 Buber addresses this in many places, but see especially, (1965). *Between Man and Man*. New York, NY: Macmillan, pp. 20–21, where he contrasts dialogic *I-You-ness* with love.

7   It may even be necessary. Certainly it has a long history as Stuart Guthrie in (1993). *Faces in the Clouds: A New Theory of Religion.* New York, NY: Oxford University Press, shows. One might also remember Theodor Lipps' theory of *einfuhling*, or empathy, as essential to art creation and appreciation.

8   This essay is too brief to discuss Buber's intellectual relationship to Martin Heidegger (they were contemporaries) except to say this: Buber thought Heidegger's terms *Dasein* ("being here humanly") and *mitsein* ("being-with") inadequate to describing human relationships. Even admitting and encouraging *fürsorge* ("solicitude"), as Heidegger did, Heidegger's worldview rotated still around the self—around the Cartesian *cogito* or "I-I" relationship—which left divinity in "heaven," indifferent, unimaginably superior, and identified with *Sein* (Being) rather than in/as *Dasein*. See Gordon, Haim (2001). *The Heidegger Buber Controversy: The Status of the I-Thou.* Connecticut: Praeger/ Greenwood Press.

9   Exodus 33:11 is especially striking: "And the Lord spoke to Moses face to face, as a man speaks to his friend." The theme is expanded in Abraham Joshua Heschel's (1995). *God in Search of Man.* New York, NY; Aronson and Heschel (1969). *The Prophets.* New York, NY: Harper Colophon. Heschel knew Buber and they agreed in what Hasidic tradition taught (both were raised in it): to wit, that, for all His glory and ineffability, *God needs human beings in order (fully) to be God*, just as human beings need God in order (fully) to be human. In the context of deism as well as orthodox Judaic, Christian, and Islamic theism, Heschel's and Buber's views, though different, are radical in that they both challenge belief in God's perfection, omnipotence, and self-sufficiency. In liberal Christian theology, this line of thinking goes by the name "the open view of God."

10   For an eloquent recent account of the evolution of morality, see Boehm, Christopher (2012). *Moral Origins: The Evolution of Virtue, Altruism, and Shame.* New York, NY: Basic Books.

11   Buber had studied C. Lloyd Morgan's *Emergent Evolution* (Williams and Norgate, 1923), which was an early expression of a basically Hegelian view, and would himself alternate between the idea of God as the eternal all-knowing Source somehow incomplete without us, and God as a being "himself" emergent from the complexities of human social consciousness. The influences of Alfred North Whitehead's process theology (Part V of *Process and Reality*, 1928), and of Henri Bergson's 1911 *Creative Evolution* are evident. In Buber's lifetime too, the cosmic theology of Pierre Teilhard de Chardin became popular (e.g., *The Phenomenon of Man*, 1959).

12   And this author's. For an explorations of this view, see Benedikt, Michael (2007). *God Is the Good We Do: Theology of Theopraxy.* New York, NY: Bottino Books and (2011). Another Word on 'God in the 21st Century.' *Tikkun* 26(2), p. 14. The first, especially, traces the origins of the idea.

13   Compare Exodus 33:18–23. Interesting also is that "you" in most languages is a non-gender-specific pronoun. Ditto "I" and "me;" a property shared with the collective pronouns "we," "they," "us," and "them." See Anna Siewierska, "Gender Distinctions in Independent Personal Pronouns," *The World Atlas of Language Structures Online* at http:// wals.info/chapter/44 (accessed June 29, 2015).

14   See Benedikt, Michael (2010). *God, Creativity, and Evolution: The Argument from Design(ers).* Austin, TX: Center for American Architecture and Design; and (2011). Shiva, Luria, Kahn, in R. Hejduk and J. Williamson (eds), *Religious Imagination in Modern and Contemporary Architecture.* Abingdon, UK: Routledge.

15   See *God, Creativity, and Evolution: The Argument from Designers*, op. cit.

16   A more extended treatment will appear in *Relationism: Architecture beyond Experience* (in preparation).

17   Guthrie, Stuart (1993). op. cit., argues that even modern religious thought is built on the ancient human habits of animism and personification.

18   See Benedikt, Michael (2000). Class Notes. *Harvard Design Magazine*, 11 (Summer).

19   See Gallese, Vittorio (2001). The Shared Manifold Hypothesis: From Mirror Neurons to Empathy. *Journal of Consciousness Studies* 8(5–7), pp. 33–50, available at http://didattica.uniroma2.it/assets/uploads/corsi/33846/ Gallese_2001.pdf (accessed June 29, 2015). On Theodor Lipps' prefiguring of mirror neurons with in his theory of Einfuhlung ("feeling into") in the 1890s, see Montag, C., Gallinat, J. and A. Heinz (2008). Theodor Lipps and the Concept of Empathy: 1851–1914. Lipps was to have great (and I think salutary) influence on the theory of modern art and architecture. For an example of the latter, see Scott, Geoffrey (Sir) (1914). *The Architecture of Humanism.* London: Constable, still in print.

20   For a short essay devoted to this, see Benedikt, Michael Posture (August 2012). *The Issue: Collective,* http://mbenedikt. com/posture_rev4.pdf (accessed June 29, 2015).

21   As I wrote in (1992). *For an Architecture of Reality.* New York, NY: Lumen Books, the "direct, esthetic experience of the real" requires that four characteristics coexist in the object contemplated: presence, significance, materiality,

and emptiness. Of the four, significance causes the most trouble, since seeing or creating significance *at the same time* as emptiness is difficult. Seeing "emptiness," which is a Buddhist notion, is not the same as regarding beauty with "disinterestedness," as Kant explained it. See also my essay (2011). Love and Beauty. *2A Magazine: Art and Architecture* 17, guest edited by Nader Adalan and Phillip Tabb, http://mbenedikt.com/love_and_beauty_1s.pdf (accessed June 29, 2015).

22 Used by Lawrence Wechsler in his book (largely) about the artist Robert Irwin, (1982). *Seeing is Forgetting the Name of the Thing One Sees.* Oakland, CA: University of California Press.

23 Scarry, Elaine (1999). *On Beauty and being Just.* Princeton, NJ: Princeton University Press.

24 Art critic Peter Schjeldahl is eloquent on this score. See his essay (1998). "Notes on Beauty" in Bill Beckly (ed.), *Uncontrollable Beauty.* New York, NY: Allworth Press, pp. 53–5.

25 Fisher, Thomas (2004/2005). Architects Behaving Badly: Ignoring Environmental Behavior Research. *Harvard Design Magazine* Fall/Winter, pp. 1–3.

26 Le Corbusier (1923). *Vers une architecture* [Towards a New Architecture]. It's instructive to try replacing "masses" with "people" in Le Corbusier's definition of architecture. But Corbusier goes on: "Our eyes are made to see forms in light; light and shade reveal these forms; cubes, cones, spheres, cylinders or pyramids are the great primary forms which light reveals to advantage; the image of these is distinct and tangible within us without ambiguity. It is for this reason that these are *beautiful forms, the most beautiful forms.* Everybody is agreed to that, the child, the savage and the metaphysician."

27 It goes without saying that animals participate in this. There is also a case for plants literally registering and reacting to their environment through temperature, air-borne chemicals (smell), touch, and spectral-directional "vision." See Chamowitz, Daniel (2012). *What a Plant Knows: A Field Guide to the Senses.* New York, NY: Scientific American/ Farrar, Straus and Giroux.

28 Informe Design seems to have stopped being added to in 2009. See http://www.informedesign.umn.edu (accessed June 29, 2015).

29 See for example, Semenza, Jan C. and Tanya L. March (2009). An Urban, Community-Based Intervention to Advance Social Interactions. *Environment & Behavior* 41(1) (January), pp. 22–42, where we learn that public amenities like benches, safe places to walk, kiosks, and greenery encourage positive social interaction among people who would otherwise live isolated and afraid of each other.

Chapter 3
Encountering Significance:
Architecture, Place, and Heidegger's Gods

Randall Teal

… an inkling that is not for him to decide … godhood enowns itself solely out of be-ing.[1]

Martin Heidegger

The goddess reveals her true identity by the mode of her epiphanies and her interventions … she herself is properly the decision.[2]

Walter Otto (on Athena)

Prologue

When my daughter was 1½ years old we took her to "Santa Park," a theme park at the Arctic Circle in Finland. Although well crafted, it was still a theme park; meaning that there were plenty of attractions, lots of "souvenirs," a hefty entrance fee, and a healthy dose of adult cynicism (me). However, an interesting thing occurred when we entered the central cave to a lively "elf" review, my daughter started spontaneously (and vigorously) dancing. In this turn of events, affected by her joy, my cynicism dissolved. Although this event only lasted for a few minutes, I will always remember how my hardness was replaced with connection to my daughter and, ironically, to this place. In this experience, the "decision" to be cynical was mine, but only partially so. This, I think, says something interesting about the reciprocal relationship between individual and place.

I cite this particular example as a lead-in to a discussion of significance and place because it occurred in what some might consider an environment of the lowest architectural achievement and the highest consumerist contrivance.[3] However, I think this is exactly the kind of conflicted territory that designers must take the most notice of: first, because it is a challenging illustration of how place can foster significance; and second, because the encounter with significance in such a place questions the often singular authority of design and what counts as good design.[4] As such, I believe this example offers a fine sense of what German philosopher Martin Heidegger meant when he said, "secular spaces are always the privation of often very remote sacred spaces."[5] I like this idea because it suggests that imperfect is not the same as depthless; and it points to the way that the smallest of things can help "sacredness" become less remote.[6]

However, as I proceed, I intentionally make limited use of terms like sacred and spiritual. I do this not because I am against those experiences typically considered eternal and harmonious; but to check certain connotations of purity, harmony, and beauty that are unnecessarily limiting when pursuing design within the often messy and contradictory nature of the world in which we live. Thus, in this chapter, I inquire into an understanding of affective encounters that exceed simple novelty or entertainment through Heidegger's thinking on the "divinities;" particularly, how this idea opens the potentialities for encountering phenomena of significance.

Significant Events

Throughout his life, Heidegger was concerned with the relationship between significance and place.[7] In fact, in a late seminar he described how his work evolved from thinking "the meaning of being" to "the truth of being" to "the topology of being."[8] Much of his interest in topology stems from the Greek *topos*, which indicated that "place belongs to the thing itself."[9] Here, Heidegger is suggesting that place is not first an empty space that is later filled with things; rather, he finds the presencing of place is often experienced as what Edward Casey calls "exemplary cases of things-as-locations."[10]

Figure 3.1   Copenhagen
Source: Photograph courtesy of Randall Teal.

However, Heidegger wanted equally to highlight place as an energetic temporal state. For example, in a late essay he says cryptically, "out of the ringing mirror-play the thinging of the thing takes place."[11] His text focuses on place, not as a kind of object, but as an event—taking-place. And in this passage he emphasizes this active quality of place through dynamic terms like "ringing," "thinging," and "mirror-play." In this passage, Heidegger is making reference to his well-known "Das Geivert," or "the fourfold," namely mortals, earth, sky and divinities. Following his active and relation-based conceptualization, the fourfold should be considered, more generally, as an attempt to account for the contingent manner in which meaning is encountered in the world.[12] And within the fourfold, place becomes a process activated through human involvement with both the material and ephemeral, the divinities being a primary exponent of the latter.

Heidegger, a source of inspiration for many of the more static and romantic visions of place, might seem a strange person to turn to for a more dynamic and plural description of the significance of place;[13] yet, there is much more in Heidegger's thought than pure and harmonious pastoralism. To be fair, cursory readings of Heidegger beg these kinds of conclusions, exactly because of the examples he draws upon: farmhouses, cathedrals, temples, peasants' shoes, hammers, and wine jugs. However, it is important to realize that what is intended and is most instructive in these examples is how these things are used to illustrate complex relationships in time. In fact, Heidegger is explicit on his purpose for using such examples, "primitive phenomena are often less concealed and less complicated (and) can be positively helpful in bringing out the ontological structure of phenomena in a genuine way."[14] Here, it is up to readers to go beyond the literal, static, qualities of his examples, using them instead as catalysts for new ways of thinking and navigating specific contemporary contexts and issues.

Considering the divinities in this way begins by *not* thinking of them in strictly spiritual or religious terms.[15] Importantly, Damon Young says, "Heidegger's notion of divinity cannot be understood outside its context of poetic phenomenological hermeneutics."[16] In other words, one should not connect this concept to the typical images and tropes of God but must attempt to understand how the term is being used to describe, evoke, and think about specific phenomena of existence. Jeff Malpas suggests the poetic intent of Heidegger's divinities is partly determined by "Greek thought and experience," and directs readers to Walter Otto's *Homeric Gods,* published in German in 1929 for further illumination of this connection.[17] The following description of the Greek gods in Otto provides a fair analogue to what Heidegger has in mind with the divinities:

> There has never been a religion in which the miraculous, in the literal sense of transcending the natural order, has played so slight a role as in the ancient Greek. The reader of Homer must find it remarkable that despite frequent reference to the gods and their power the narrative contains virtually no miracles ... In their world the divine is not superimposed as a sovereign power over natural events; it is revealed in the forms of the natural, as their very essence and being ... the natural has become one with the spiritual and eternal, without surrendering a whit of its abundance, warmth, and immediacy in the amalgam ... the ancient Greek religion comprehended the things of this world with the most powerful sense of reality possible, and nevertheless—nay, for that very reason—recognized in them the marvelous delineations of the divine.[18]

In a similar vein Heidegger says, "the holy is the essence of nature."[19] Yet, at the same time, he also wants to emphasize that nature is not something "higher." So elsewhere he questions, "does nature therefore resemble a god or goddess? If this were so then 'nature,' which is, after all, present in everything, even the gods, would be measured by the 'divine,' and would not be 'nature' any longer."[20] In other words, Heidegger thinks it a disservice to the richness of nature to ascribe its 'holy' moments to something that transcends it. Thus, the gods cannot be thought of as merely natural or simply material. In fact Heidegger says, "the default of God and the divinities is absence. But absence is not nothing; rather it is precisely the presence ... of the hidden fullness and wealth of what has been and what ... is presencing."[21] Here, Heidegger's divinities might be regarded as virtual (in a Deleuzean sense); which is to say, immanent *by way of* their absence.[22] In any case, they are not "beyond" as Heidegger states clearly, "eternal gods are no gods."[23] Perhaps John Caputo puts the gods' peculiar way of being best when he says (referring to Heidegger's divinities), "'God' is not the clearing itself ... 'God' makes an appearance within this clearing."[24] In short, the gods are *both* material and immaterial; and their relation to place must be considered seamless, non-hierarchical, and interdependent.[25]

Humans too are bound up in this interdependency. As such, significance is not something that is ours to ascribe to things; but rather it is a relationship one enters into. Heidegger states, "as the Dasein gives itself over immediately and passionately to the world itself, its own self is reflected to it from things."[26] Similarly, according to Otto, for the Greeks "the notion of divine essence and power proceeds not from the desiring subject (as in the case of Eros), but from the beloved object."[27] For Heidegger this power underlies all encounters. He states: "to undergo an experience with something—be it a thing, a person, or a god—means that this something befalls us, strikes us, comes over us, overwhelms and transforms us."[28] Thus, understanding means *to be affected*, and to act upon the insight that arises from being overwhelmed and transformed. And, by acknowledging one's own particular possibilities for response and taking up a certain trajectory through action one "owns" a given situation.[29]

However, when one thinks of responding to the call of things it is important to note that this does not indicate mere determinism; rather, the action of the gods depends upon (and favors) the individual who is receptive and takes action. Here Otto points to the god's appreciation for Odysseus' cleverness. Otto states,

> But if we look more closely at the occasions when these divine interventions take place, we find that they always come at the critical moment when human powers suddenly converge, as if charged by electric contact, on some insight, some resolution, some deed ... something must nevertheless proceed out of man to enable the god to enter and attach himself to him ... man has to start out if he is to encounter the god.[30]

Heidegger too emphasizes a receptive/action-taking disposition saying, "work, deed, poetizing, thinking, gifting, building, shelter-conceal the truth of being in things."[31] In other words, becoming involved galvanizes the potentials of things. And truth opens up when, like the Greeks, one experiences "gods and men in their ... reciprocal relation."[32] Or in architectural terms, Farshid Moussavi says, "subjectivity ... is a reciprocal interaction between built forms and people ... meanings are not produced by architects, but by individuals. Architects produce affects."[33] This comment highlights the uncertainty of design and the way this uncertainty plays out via the on-going reciprocations between people and things. Heidegger's term *stimmung* can be seen to describe this process of reciprocation. Although, initially translated by Macquarrie and Robinson as "mood," *stimmung* is most interesting because it means both mood and attunement. The importance of this point, as William Blattner notes, is that the notion of mood "is too narrow, since 'attunement' ('*stimmung*') is meant to cover all of Dasein's affective states (emotions, passions, and even ... important aspects of character traits and sensibilities).[34] And importantly, the attunement of *stimmung* also connects this idea to Heidegger's thinking on the Greek gods, who he refers to as the "attuning ones."[35]

In German, *stimmung* refers to the tuning of an instrument; thus Heidegger is evoking the interplay between instrument (thing) and musician (*Dasein*) and how the quality of the instrument's sound depends upon both the sound itself and the responsive (and skilled) disposition of one who is tuning. In this image, Heidegger has provided an analog to the process by which one comes into understanding: one must be affected by (hearing) the mood of a given situation, and move to align their actions with the "frequency" of the mood, or alter the frequency through other actions. In this way, mood does not tell one what to do, it reveals a range of shifting possibilities for one to respond to. Blattner put it this way: "something that might show up as aggravating when you're angry shows up as comical when you're feeling silly."[36] Such plurality is at the heart of both the architectural encounter and life itself. As such, the potentialities for significance are vast. Perhaps this is why Heidegger says, "chaos is the holy itself."[37]

Figure 3.2   Libraries
Source: Photograph courtesy of Randall Teal.

Significant Pluralities

In seeking *gods* instead of God, Heidegger opens the prospect that it is only through significance *as multiplicity* that we get anything that can be considered significant—there is no single "significance." In this way, for Heidegger the holy points to questions of significance that are best answered by asking "which one," rather than "what is it."[38] Such multiplicity interests Heidegger, in part, because it points to "truth" as being situational and thus unstable; and thus requires a way of conceiving understanding in which different types of truths can be encountered. This kind of undecidablity is reminiscent of both the specific of truths each different Greek god delivered, as well as, the shifting favors of the individual gods. For example of Hermes, Otto says:

> Hermes protects highwaymen and thieves, and even though he conducts pious wayfarers safely past them, it
> is the thieves who seem particularly close to his nature and heart. This signifies a huge expansion of the divine
> sphere of operation. Its compass is no longer delimited by human wishes but rather by the totality of existence.[39]

A similar kind of specificity and contingency of truth can be seen in the way "things" gather the fourfold. As David Weinberger explains, "the jug can be what it is (i.e., a jug) because it gathers the fourfold in way that a sieve or a stool does not."[40] Further, it is not just that there are different things that can gather the fourfold differently, it is also that one jug might gather differently than another jug; and as Blattner explained of *stimmung*—the same jug in different occasions with different people might find different resonances—be differently significant. Critically, none of these truths are limited by having an absolute end like the "correct" or "good."

Here, exclusionary categories become less important than effective descriptions and understandings of what something does, how it works, and its implications. In other words, like the different appearances of the Greek gods, for Heidegger, a thing's "truth" (the way it gathers the fourfold) is not absolute or categorical; as such, it must be discerned in terms of its workings, its relationships, and how humans and other things fit into these workings and relationships. The importance of understanding this gathering can be seen in Heidegger's emphasis of the etymological link between the holy (*Heilige*) and being "whole" (*heil*).[41] This link highlights the appropriateness of both knowing what counts as a "part" of a given whole, and how the introduction of a "part" might result in the creation of a new whole. In this way, Heidegger's divinities ask not a yes or no question—not *the* good—but *a* "good" that can only be understood in relative terms.[42]

In architecture, the problem with the search for more absolute notions of good—the "right way" to do architecture—was called out recently in a conversation between Peter Eisenman and Mark Wigley. In this conversation they discussed how they understood such a limiting definition of architectural worth being posited and promoted by what they referred to as "architectural phenomenology."[43] Wigley stated plainly, that architectural phenomenology is hypocritical. And he believes this to be true, because architectural phenomenology:

> Travels in the guise of wisdom but is relentlessly cynical in its approaches and motivations because it
> excludes so many of the very experiences it would claim to value … phenomenologists have a limited set of
> architectural objects they are willing to describe the experience of. Certain kinds of objects are good, certain
> kinds of objects are bad.[44]

The conclusion they draw is that any tendency towards closed-mindedness or a kind of consensus about architectural appropriateness is problematic. Of course in moving to condemn the phenomenologists, Eisenman and Wigley are treading the same water. In their case, through elevating questionability, uncertainty, and non-presence to a higher plane, they seek to delegitimize everything that is its opposite. But, certainly, to elevate either the "phenomenological" or the "conceptual" as superior is unproductive. In fact, it is the avoidance of such petty opposition that moved Heidegger, in part, to eschew the "higher" in terms of source, cause, or God. And a similar concern led Finnish architect and theorist Riema Pietilä to comment, "no single future: I believe for the progress of architecture, a plurality of goals and means is vital."[45]

However, to promote plurality does not simply mean to promote the adoption of an uncritical "everything is good" attitude.[46] Instead, it means finding more open dispositions to the world and more expansive definitions of what is to be considered architecturally significant. For David Salomon, this definition is found in the notion of "taste." Following Hume, Salomon says taste is: "neither universal nor infinitely fragmented. It is plural, yet specific with regard to history and medium."[47] And importantly, taste means "having a specific sensibility or preference for one thing does not mean negating other equally valid ones."[48] The notion of taste aligns with the divinities, because in both the demand is placed on the human participant to discern the gestalt of the thing or situation so as to be able to take appropriate action. This attitude shifts away from questions of good or bad, significant or insignificant, to inquiring into the means for creating legibility of different types of significance.

Salomon cites Susan Sontag's discussion of Camp and how an appreciation of Camp demands the cultivation of the "taste" for it. In other words, the Camp aesthetic has particular values and codes that one can learn to "read"—become attuned to—and ultimately develop understandings of what makes good Camp or bad Camp. And importantly, inquiring into Camp *as Camp*—not as beauty—is to understand it to be a material practice that communicates a particular significance. In short, appreciation of Camp depends upon becoming literate in the sensibilities of Camp.[49]

Others in architecture also have interests in this notion of being able to read a plurality of significances. For instance, Jeffery Kipnis has called this ability "discrimination," Stan Allen "legibility," and Sarah Whiting has used both "legibility" and "judgment" as terms to describe engaging architecture in this way.[50] In developing such abilities, Whiting sees a re-visioning of "reference meaning, process meaning, (and) phenomenological meaning."[51] I take this to mean a re-visiting, re-evaluation, and expansion of the ways that have been used to valuate architecture—the employment of disciplinary knowledge as a means of evaluating different kinds of architectural moves and architectural wholes.

In addition to knowledge of the disciplinary tropes and techniques that enable discrimination one must also be able to "read" the temporal conditions *made possible* by the particular material and substantial constructs of places. This refers back to what Moussavi said above: designers do not *create* significance explicitly through their built works–they can only create affects.[52] Elizabeth Grosz provides a good explanation of affect as it is employed by Gilles Deleuze and Felix Guattari:

> The work of art, whether pictorial, tactile, or sonorous, is a block of intensities, a compound of sensations and affects, of intensities that have gone beyond a subject to become entities themselves. But these sensations and affects do not in themselves make up art (on the contrary, art is composed of materials, sounds, colors, textures, melodies and not affects or sensations). They are the products of art, what art makes, what enables art to stand on its own, independent of its creator and of the circumstances of its creation.[53]

It is important to grapple with this slipperiness of concept because as Brian Massumi has suggested:

> Affect is central to understanding our information and image-based late capitalist culture in which so-called master narratives are perceived to have foundered … (yet) there is no cultural-theoretical vocabulary specific to affect. Our entire vocabulary has derived from theories of signification that are still wedded to structure even across irreconcilable differences.[54]

Put differently, affect theory becomes critical the moment one moves to engage any of the a-signifying effects of architecture and the a-subjective processes of design. However, the "standing on its own" of affect does not mean designers have no creative agency; rather it simply assigns "things" their deserved agency. And importantly, like plurality not being an "anything goes" proposition, a focus on affect is not a vision of atomized individual experience without collective significance. Here, it is useful to refer to Heidegger's discussion in *Being and Time* about the "publicness" of certain phenomena, suggesting that although there is always variation, it would be a completely a-typical condition where everyone was literally compartmentalized in their own understanding.[55] For example, the mood of many libraries affects a sense of quiet from most people yet they achieve this end by different means. So although, the way people feel about the specific instantiations and arrangements is always subject to variation and cultural expectations, the perception of qualities such as shiny, heavy, dark, quiet has some degree of predictability. However, because particular qualities and affective arrangements do not guarantee the "arrival of the divinities," so to speak, designers must be attentive to the multiple processes and events that can occur in response to, or facilitated by, architecture.

Here, design might be said to be, as Rem Koolhaas does, an art of "staging uncertainty."[56] For example, Preston Scott Cohen and Stan Allen have discussed the capacity for staging multifarious functions in the Columbia University Library stairs as what is particularly remarkable about this architectural intervention in this particular location.[57] In short, significance is not the designed object *as such*, rather significance is sheltered in the *domain* of the designed object; it resonates through the temporal phenomena that are supported or freed by the specific qualities and affordances of architecture. And, learning to evaluate such ephemeral phenomena—just like architectural language itself—cannot be solely an intellectual enterprise. Alberto Perez-Gomez has stated, design cannot be reduced to a "syntax of style … controlled by reason."[58] Rather, it depends on practice, tacit knowledge, and having a capacity for being affected; that is, to discern (and foster) the fleeting intimations of significance; or as Kipnis claims, "*performance* in architecture is … as much if not more a question of elusive qualities than of measurable effects.[59]

Elusive Measures

Heidegger calls the process of discerning (and fostering) significance "measure taking." However, he does not mean typical definitions of "measure," such as ascertaining the quantitative dimensions of some physical interval. For Heidegger, "measure taking gauges *the between*."[60] That is, it reveals being itself, which he calls "the longest bridge of the 'between.'"[61] Here, taking measure means *to become* the specific conditions of a given situation.

In directing us to this "between," Heidegger is working to correct one of the primary restrictions to "seeing" the gods at all: the deep-seated history of metaphysical thinking itself. He states that the gods will only be able to "announce themselves" when the "metaphysically grounded history 'goes under.'"[62] He says that this encounter is blocked by "calculation," "explanation," and "divinization;"[63] that is, the human tendency to impose *its own* measures upon situations that need no external justification or explanation. And for Heidegger, escaping those "highest" forms of knowledge—the representational, the instrumental, the calculative—requires standing *in* the "clearing," rather than standing *above* it.

Figure 3.3   Between
Source: Photograph courtesy of Randall Teal.

In addition to being an argument against pure objectivity, this point means that knowing *how* (everydayness) must be infused by an affective capacity for knowing *what matters* (significance). In other words, there is a direct connection between the way we feel about certain situations and what we do; and this connection creates a link between events of significance and human know-how.[64] Without this connection, human actions lose their basis of meaning. For example, it is one thing to know *how* to speak, it is another to know *when* to speak and *what* manner of speaking is appropriate in a given instance. A similar ability is necessary in architecture, particularly if one acknowledges that design, as Salomon says, is not simply a way of solving problems that have multiple answers (instrumental reason), instead it is "the creation of objects and events via aesthetic means."[65] In other words, the language of architecture requires both thinking *and feeling*; or perhaps *thinking-feeling*.

The need to account for the intelligence of feeling, and to enable and attend to temporal and transient phenomena—something metaphysical thinking cannot do—leads Heidegger to the "measure taking" of poetry. He is interested in poetry, in part, because it does not explain; it does not try to convince, or as he says, "the poet who preaches is a poor poet."[66] Instead, the poetic indicates one's capacity for the non-representational, the non-categorical, and the non-instrumental. In this way, Heidegger presents poetry as *poiesis*, to be linked with a kind of Pre-Socratic thinking.[67] Which means, it is a more open and holistic thinking than mere intellect, because it is underpinned by feeling. The openness of this thinking helps dematerialize the hardness of thought that occurs when thought reigns over things. This shift occurs as one becomes attuned to the "visible inclusions of the alien in the sight of the familiar."[68] Which is to say, when one becomes more attentive to small convergences and disjunctions—to recognize what is special within what is routine. Leibniz called the results of this kind of attention "minute perceptions."[69] And, for Heidegger, such perceptions deliver a kind of precision of understanding about the possibilities of a given situation or, in terms of the divinities, "in this strangeness (the god) proclaims his unfaltering nearness."[70] In short, such discernment amounts to learning to "read" significance. However as thinking-feeling, reading poetry as poetry, design as design, or architecture as architecture means knowing that the locus of their potency is found in their affect. Or as Ben Van Berkel says of architecture, "quality of meaning can only be experienced if it is like in music, if it is felt.[71]

In this way, significance can be experienced but it cannot be known—it must be held in one's attention *in its evanescence*—which is why Heidegger claims, "the god who remains unknown must by showing himself as the one he is, appear as the one who remains unknown. God's manifestness—not only he himself—is mysterious."[72] In short, much of what we count as being significant cannot be pointed to directly. In fact, to make significance explicit and unequivocal is often to eliminate significance altogether. Thus, when one talks about "seeing" in this context it cannot refer to the acuity of vision, rather it must refer to the immersiveness of embodied realization—including its temporal dimensions—what Heidegger calls "spanning."

The being of this "span" is the natural disposition of human beings. Or in Heidegger's words: "man is man at all only in such spanning … he can block this spanning, trim it, and disfigure it, but he can never evade it."[73] Which is to say, the temporal nature of existence means that human beings—by default—inhabit a place of plentitude "spanning" across a past and a future and bridging relations with shifting orders of things. The uncertainties associated with being this span leads to the attempts to "trim" or "disfigure" it; and these occur through non-participation and attempts to fix uncertainty through calculation—standing above the clearing, as it were. Such behavior excludes the divinities; it excludes understandings of significance. Conversely, to participate in life *as uncertainty* brings "heaven and earth, to one another."[74] And, in this way one measures the difference between those things under human power and those things that must be bestowed from outside one's self. It is to know being itself. This is why Heidegger calls spanning "the measure against which man measures himself."[75]

Attending to this temporal stretch allows the divinities to be their fullest. That is, a real measure of significance can only really be found if durational qualities are included. For example, a lack of durational significance is why it is problematic to judge architectural worth solely at the moment of finished construction. Not only do such practices neglect performance and durability as factors of architectural worth, but they also neglect the degree to which the enduring presence of the building facilitates (or not) well-being for its users over time. By incorporating durational significance one understands that gods do not simply appear, and that gods are both effect and affect. Which is to say, it is only through the wholeness of life, like in Aristotle's *eudaimonia*, that one can determine such things as happiness, goodness, and holiness.

Figure 3.4   Zchair
Source: Photograph courtesy of Randall Teal.

Epilogue

Here, I return to Santa Park: maybe the real key to the significance of this experience was the loss of my hardness. Which leads to one of the more interesting statements Heidegger makes about the divinities. He says, "as long as this arrival of kindness endures, so long does man succeed in measuring himself not unhappily against the godhead."[76] That is, kindness initiates the sacred encounter. Thus, at Santa Park the architectural qualities played a role in the happening of this experience, but the architecture itself was not in the foreground. Instead, the place created atmospheric conditions that some might call fun, some might call banal, some might call contrived, some might call whimsical; but, it became differently significant for me—perhaps holy—through the fleeting event it facilitated.

Now, this is not to say that particular places cannot, through their material power, affect humans in profound ways. However, what my experience at Santa Park does suggest is that perhaps there is less of a line between the sacred and the profane (or at least the prosaic) than is often allowed; and, perhaps the line is only there because we, as thinking subjects, have made it. In other words, perhaps one can be equally, but differently, spiritually affected by going to Santa Park as to Central Park; or taking in a sunrise in one's own kitchen as sitting in the colored light of Chartres Cathedral.

Regardless of this bigger question, Santa Park highlights the fact that prosaic architectural environments often hold hidden opportunities for profundity; and these are freed only when one allows them to happen. Or Heidegger says, "the god shows himself 'everyday' and 'far about' by reconciling himself to his concealment, for the sake of looking callers."[77] So, unlike being jolted into awareness by the new, the novel, or the innovative, "knowing" this kind of significance depends upon developing a practice of being affected by what is strange in the everyday. In other words, tuning one's perception to afford more precise contact with the world. And when this occurs one allows things to be things and not just one of "the countless objects everywhere of equal value."[78]

Architecturally speaking, I think the emphasis Heidegger places on the role of the human in attunement is both interesting and useful, because such an outlook suggests that there are opportunities to encourage encounters with the special significances of the holy in any project. However, it is important to remember that building for Heidegger means: "all the works made by man's hands *and through his arrangements* (my emphasis)."[79] Thus, one of the most important "buildings" designers make is the arrangement of intimacy for the actors and elements in a given environment—through particular languages of architecture. This is a language that arises when, through design, one continuously and rigorously questions how certain orders of objects create certain effects, how architectural conditions can catalyze events, and how things "thing" to arrange human contact. Here, Heidegger's divinities point to an advantageous condition of plurality whereby significances of form and space become entwined with the significances of event; and when we ourselves are prepared to become part of this entanglement kindness endures and the world becomes a measure of our humanity.

Endnotes

1   Heidegger, Martin (2006). *Mindfulness*, translated by Parvis Emad and Thomas Kalary. New York, NY: Continuum, p. 211.

2 Otto, Walter Friedrich (1954). *The Homeric Gods: The Spiritual Significance of Greek Religion*, translated by Moses Hadas. New York, NY: Pantheon, pp. 44, 48.

3 A heated debate occurred on the ACS list-server in February–March 2014 regarding a similar topic and a "Sacred Disney" controversy ensued. Many of the critics were staunchly opposed to the idea that there might be any co-existence of sacredness and consumerism.

4 Others have gone further to call out the exclusionary aspects of design expertise as actually being detrimental to the formation of place. See for example: Awan, Nishat, Schneider, Tatjana and Jeremy Till (2011). *Spatial Agency: Other Ways of Doing Architecture.* Abingdon, UK: Routledge. Or, Schneekloth, Lynda H. and Robert G. Shibley (2000). Implacing Architecture into the Practice of Placemaking. *Journal of Architectural Education* 35(3).

5 Heidegger, Martin (1973). Art and Space. *Man and World* 6(1) (February), p. 5, pp. 1–8

6 Earlier in his career Heidegger tended to be more pessimistic about the arrival of the divinities. For example in 1938–39 he said: "Since long ago man is without attunement, that is without that which at times enjoins his ownmost to the relentlessness of preserving an openness wherein be-ing enowns itself. Thus far lack of attunement is replaced by enticement of emotions and lived-experiences which merely 'dehumanize' man into the fortuitousness of what he happens to pursue and obtain through calculation." ("attunement" is a reference to the gods). *Mindfulness*, p. 210.

7 Jeff Malpas sees place as the primary question of his philosophy. See Malpas, Jeff (2006). *Heidegger's Topology: Being, Place, World.* Cambridge, MA: MIT Press.

8 Heidegger, Martin (2003). *Four Seminars*, translated by Andrew Mitchell and François Raffoul, Studies in Continental Thought. Bloomington, IN: Indiana University Press, p. 41.

9 (1959). *An Introduction to Metaphysics*, translated by Ralph Manheim. New Haven, CT and London: Yale University Press, p. 66.

10 Casey, Edward (1987). *Remembering: A Phenomenological Study.* Bloomington, IN: Indiana University Press.

11 Heidegger, Martin (1971). The Thing, in *Poetry, Language, Thought.* New York, NY: Harper & Row, p. 178.

12 *Das Geviert* or fourfold is made of seemingly simple elements—mortals, earth, and sky, divinities—and like Heidegger's other primitive examples, it is a concept that demands an eye for the relationships of temporality, absence and affection. For example, the "mortals" are actual flesh and blood humans, but the word mortal, "those who can experience death as death," also evokes virtual qualities such as human finitude and questions about one's ability to allow ends to be ends. Or in another example, "earth," geology and geological time, flora and fauna and thus biological time (evolution and growth) are all evoked simultaneously. To go on: nothing of the earth can exist without the light of the sun, the nourishment of the rain, and atmospheric mix of gases that allow for life and movement of the earth itself which is witnessed as night and day and the seasons of the year. Conversely, the sky needs the material of the earth, without which it would be nothing but the vacuum of deep space. The sky also suggests the light of intelligibility. As counter point to humans the divinities are temporal in two ways. First, somewhat paradoxically, they exist in time by being immortal. Second, their presence is always fleeting. That is, although they are not subject to death, their presence can only be experienced in its transience. In this way, the fourfold is a complex existential structure that points not simply to particular things critical to existence, but critical *relations* of things in time.

13 See for example, Norberg-Schulz, Christian (1980). *Genius Loci: Towards a Phenomenology of Architecture.* New York, NY: Rizzoli. Or, Sharr, Adam (2007). Heidegger for Architects, in Adam Sharr (ed.), *Thinkers for Architects*. New York, NY and London, UK: Routledge. Or, Kenneth Frampton's comment that "… place is … in itself concrete and static." Frampton, Kenneth (1996). On Reading Heidegger, in Kate Nesbitt (ed.), *Theorizing a New Agenda for Architecture: An Anthology of Architectural Theory, 1965–1995*. New York, NY: Princeton Architectural Press, p. 444.

14 Heidegger, Martin (1962). *Being and Time*, translated by John Macquarrie and Edward Robinson, 7th edn. San Francisco, CA: Harper and Row, pp. 76; ibid.

15 He says there is a "common tendency to think (improperly) of the gods in religious terms." Malpas, *Heidegger's Topology: Being, Place, World*, p. 274.

16 Young, Damon (2005). Being Grateful for Being: Being, Reverence and Finitude. *Sophia* 44(2), p. 39.

17 Malpas, *Heidegger's Topology: Being, Place, World*, p. 274.

18 Otto, *The Homeric Gods: The Spiritual Significance of Greek Religion*, pp. 6, 7, 10.

19 Heidegger, Martin (2000). *Elucidations of Hölderlin's Poetry.* Amherst, NY: Humanity Books, p. 82.

20 Ibid., p. 76.

21 Heidegger, The Thing, p. 182.

22 For example Deleuze states, "The virtual is opposed not to the real but to the actual. The virtual is fully real in so far as it is virtual. Exactly what Proust said of states of resonance must be said of the virtual." Deleuze, Gilles (1995). *Difference and Repitition*, translated by Paul Patton. New York, NY: Columbia University Press, p. 208.

23 Heidegger, *Mindfulness*, p. 223.

24 Caputo, John (1982). *Heidegger and Aquinas: Being, Place, World.* New York, NY: Fordham University Press, p. 282.

25 Part of Heidegger's interest in this complex interdependence of divine and natural comes from limits he sees in the so-called ontotheological view of being (God as the cause and source). Heidegger, understands this view to be an inattentive simplification, rooted in a fallacy of linear causality; the notions of causality or source, for Heidegger, can only be a fraction of the full state of being. And he draws upon *physis*—the Greek natural-temporal notion of nature/being—to imbue his thinking with dynamic becoming.

26 Heidegger, Martin (1982). *The Basic Problems of Phenomenology.* Bloomington, IN: Indiana University Press, p. 104.

27 Otto, *The Homeric Gods: The Spiritual Significance of Greek Religion*, p. 101.

28 Heidegger, Martin (1971). The Nature of Language, in *On the Way to Language.* New York, NY: Harper One, p. 57.

29 In early Heidegger this understanding arose as a three-part "equiprimordial" structure of temporality. Here, Heidegger's *befindlicheit* (affectedness) corresponds to the past, *verstehen* (understanding) the future and *verfallen* (falling) to the present (roughly speaking). I point to this structure here only because, much of this thinking underpins the Heidegger's thinking of the fourfold. Specifically, for Heidegger this structure describes how one is always becoming futural; that is, one is always moving into relationships with things and moving into these relationships uncover (and are conditioned by) the significance of the past.

30 Otto, *The Homeric Gods: The Spiritual Significance of Greek Religion*, pp. 6, 195. Walter also says "The gods belong on the side of life. In order to encounter them the living must move, go forward, be active. Then the gods encompass the living with their strength and majesty and in sudden revelation even show their heavenly countenance." Ibid., pp. 265–6.

31 Heidegger, *Mindfulness*, p. 213.

32 Heidegger, Martin (1992). *Parmenides*, translated by Andre Schuwer and Richard Rojcewicz. Bloomington, IN: Indiana University Press, p. 110.

33 Moussavi, Farshid (2009). The Return of Nature: Organicism Contra Ornament. Symposia on Architecture 1 at Harvard GSD, http://harvard.vo.llnwd.net/o18/gsd/09162009_ReturnOfNature.mp4 (accessed June 29, 2015).

34 Blattner, William (2011). Some Terminology in Being and Time, http://www9.georgetown.edu/faculty/blattnew/heid/terms.htm (accessed April 28, 2014).

35 Heidegger, *Parmenides*, p. 111.

36 Blattner, Some Terminology in Being and Time.

37 Heidegger, *Elucidations of Hölderlin's Poetry*, p. 85.

38 Or as Deleuze says, "which one?" (qui) means this: "what are the forces which take hold of a given thing, what is the will that possesses it?" Deleuze Gilles (2006). *Nietzsche and Philosophy*, translated by Hugh Tomlinson. New York, NY: Columbia University Press, p. 77.

39 Otto, *The Homeric Gods: The Spiritual Significance of Greek Religion*, p. 121.

40 Weinberger, David (1984). Earth, World, and Fourfold. *Tulane Studies in Philosophy* 32, p. 105.

41 Heidegger, *Elucidations of Hölderlin's Poetry*, p. 85.

42 The good would constitute a ground, and the basic temporality of existence means there is no ground; or, it must be a ground that grounds itself. Heidegger calls this *ab-grund.* See Heidegger, Martin (2000). *Contributions to Philosophy (from Enowning)*, translated by Parvis Emad and Kenneth Maly. Bloomington, IN: Indiana University Press.

43 Jeffrey Kipnis refers to something similar via the term "new authenticity," see Kipnis, Jeffrey (2007). Lecture at UIC. University of Illinios-Chicago, http://www.youtube.com/watch?v=iNkOQoOZAss (accessed March 12, 2014).

44 Eisenman, Peter and Mark Wigley (2012). Wobble: The Cat Has Nine Lives. Lecture at Columbia GSAPP, https://www.youtube.com/watch?v=Gu4-ErX6hDA (accessed March 12, 2014).

45 Norri, Marja-Riitta et al. (eds) (1985). *Pietilä: Intermediate Zones in Modern Architecture.* Helsinki: Museum of Finnish Architecture, p. 95.

46 Similar view of the value of plurality, have been argued in other fields as well. For example, Paul Feyerabend claims, "Proliferation of theories is beneficial for science, while uniformity impairs its critical power." Feyerabend, Paul (1988). *Against Method.* London, UK: Verso. See also: Mouffe, Chantal (2000). For an Agonistic Model of Democracy, in *The Democratic Paradox.* London, UK: Verso; and Guattari, Felix (2000). *The Three Ecologies*, translated by Ian Pindar and Paul Sutton. London, UK: Continuum.

47   Salomon, David (2011). Taste is Critical. *The Cornell Journal of Architecture* 8, p. 5.

48   Ibid.

49   Ibid.

50   Kipnis, Jeffrey (2013). Discrimination. Lecture at Harvard GSD, https://www.youtube.com/watch?v=vur3TRzFztQ (accessed April 28, 2014). Whiting, Sarah, New Directions in Architecture Education. ANCB, http://www.ancb.de/sixcms/detail.php?id=9708635#.U225vF7nAZY (accessed April 28, 2014). Or, Legibility. Columbia GSADD, http://www.youtube.com/watch?v=fHVQ9SNUpAY (accessed April 28, 2014); Allen, Stan, Projective Landscape. https://www.youtube.com/watch?v=pYPJQRHwJH8 (accessed April 28, 2014).

51   Whiting, Legibility.

52   In this statement Moussavi is no doubt referring to Deleuze and Guattari's assertion in that artists create "blocs of sensation" called "percepts and affects." Deleuze, Gilles and Felix Guattari (1994). *What is Philosophy?*, translated by Janis Tomlinson and Graham Burchell. New York, NY: Columbia University Press, p. 164.

53   Grosz, Elizabeth (2008). *Chaos, Territory, Art: Deleuze and the Framing of the Earth.* New York, NY: Columbia University Press, p. 59.

54   Massumi, Brian (2002). *Parables for the Virtual: Movement, Affect, Sensation.* Durham, NC: Duke University Press, p. 27.

55   For example, in regards to the publicness of time see, Heidegger, *Being and Time*, p. 391.

56   Koolhaas, Rem (1995). Whatever Happened to Urbanism? *Design Quarterly* 164, p. 29.

57   Cohen, Preston Scott and Stan Allen (2011). Discussions in Architecture: Stan Allen with Preston Scott Cohen. Lecture at Harvard GSD. http://www.youtube.com/watch?v=2IFVnJT55ZQ (accessed April 28, 2014).

58   Perez-Gomez, Alberto (1982). Architecture as Drawing. *Journal of Architectural Education* 36(2), p. 5.

59   Kipnis, Jeffrey (2013). A Question of Qualities, in *A Question of Qualities: Essays in Architecture.* Cambridge, MA: MIT Press, p. 2.

60   Heidegger, … Poetically Man Dwells …, p. 219.

61   Heidegger, *Mindfulness*, p. 224.

62   Ibid., p. 222.

63   Ibid., p. 211.

64   This connection underpins much of the basis of *Being and Time*, where Heidegger is interested in the way the networks of equipment that humans use and are implicated by are largely engaged pre-reflectively. For example, the famous "hammer" is used to illustrate both how the hammer itself is first and foremost significant as something used to perform certain actions in world, namely hammering. Here, understanding of what a hammer is, is enacted through using the hammer. Further, when in use, the significance of the hammer, immediately activates a whole collection of other "ready-to-hand" beings (i.e., nails, 2x4s, measuring devices, saws, building plans, etc.). These too are engaged pre-reflectively. In short, one's know-how of, say, carpentry connects one to those things significant within the world of carpentry.

65   Salomon, Taste is Critical, p. 7.

66   Heidegger, Martin (1983). Hebel, Friend of the House. *Contemporary German Philosophy* 3, p. 96.

67   Ferrari Di Pippo, Alexander (2000). The Concept of Poiesis in Heidegger's an Introduction to Metaphysics. *Thinking Fundamentals: WM Junior Visiting Fellows Conferences* 9.

68   Heidegger, … Poetically Man Dwells …, p. 223.

69   Leibniz says, "But it is impossible that the soul can know clearly its whole nature, and perceive how this innumerable number of small perceptions, piled up or rather concentrated together, shapes itself there: to that end it must need know completely the whole universe which is embraced by them, that is, it must be a God." Leibniz, G.W. (1985). *Theodicy: Essays on the Goodness of God, the Freedom of Man, and the Origin of Evil*, translated by E.M. Huggard. La Salle, Ill: Open Court, p. 403.

70   Heidegger, … Poetically Man Dwells …, p. 224.

71   Van Berkel, Ben (2012). What Happened to Architectural Objectivity?, Lecture at Columbia GSAPP, https://www.youtube.com/watch?v=UTPshW9zogk (accessed April 28, 2014).

72   Heidegger, … Poetically Man Dwells …, p. 220.

73   Ibid., p. 218.

74   Ibid., p. 219.

75   Ibid., pp. 220–21.

76   Ibid., p. 227.

77 Heidegger, *Elucidations of Hölderlin's Poetry*, p. 194.
78 Heidegger, The Thing, p. 180.
79 Heidegger, ... Poetically Man Dwells ..., p. 214.

Chapter 4
Phenomenology of the Architectural Extraordinary and Merleau-Ponty's Philosophy

Julio Bermudez

The Rapture: Stricken by Architecture[1]

We arrived at the Salk and just walked out into the courtyard without going into the reception office first. Within the first 5 minutes of being in the courtyard and seeing the horizon, I remember having a tremendous rush of joy. I remember coming to a (sudden) realization that I was now involved with something that was connected to something powerful and bigger than I ever imagined possible. I remember a physical feeling in my chest: like my "heart in my throat," which I do not remember feeling before (but have felt since). I also recall wanting to jerk into motion – I wanted to run; swing my arms; do anything other than just stand in place. It was like I suddenly knew something that I didn't know before. I also recall thinking about the fact I could not make a direct correspondence between what I was feeling and the architecture, per se. It's that strangeness that in retrospect points me to the feeling that … I was in touch with something really awesome and bigger than the structure itself. Joy and optimism.

The Salk Institute, La Jolla, California, 1971

I felt this building more deeply than I have ever felt any piece of architecture. As soon as I entered the baths, I felt that I had been reduced to nothing but senses and emotions. I touched the expertly crafted stone to my fingers and toes. I dipped my body into each individual pool, marveling at the sensations each change in temperature caused. I breathed in the sweltering black heat of the sauna. I smelled the mineral water and swished its metallic coolness in my mouth. I watched the green mountains from the outdoor pool. I was overcome. Such overwhelming simplicity in design and material was closer to divinity than I had felt in any other man-made design. As I surrounded myself with the purity of living rock, water, mountain, and light, I couldn't help but crying for the beauty and deep spirituality of it all. I felt the spirit of the place. I cried and cried at the realization of the deeper meaning of it all. Zumthor had captured the immaterial and the immortal. I had no idea that someone could do this in architecture.

Therme Vals Bath, Switzerland, 2007

I walked into the monastery through a small wooden entrance door and entered the dimly lit, small cavernous chambers. Walls were covered with icons blackened over time from the candle smoke. I entered the main chamber, looked up at the dome where the white angel wings shone in almost fluorescent glow. The whole room felt like a womb, dark and comforting, deeply touching, deeply spiritual, filling my heart with feelings that can't quite be put into words. I stood there and wept. And then the feeling was gone, but to this day I can still bring it back as if it had just happened a moment ago.

Saint Roman Monastery, Serbia, 2007

Let us say that you have had one of the most profound experiences in your life. Let's further say that such an event was provoked by architecture. You were visiting a building when its presence unexpectedly overwhelmed you to the point of tears. For a few moments, something happened that you can't really explain but know was "extraordinary." You have been shaken to your core and, after giving yourself some time to 'digest' it (10 days, 10 weeks, 10 years), you are ready to seek some understanding. What was that? Was it beauty? How did it happen and what does it mean?

Figure 4.1   Main courtyard of the Salk Institute by Louis Kahn. La Jolla, California
Source: Photograph courtesy of Shawn Benjamin.

The Quest: Seeking Understanding

Faced with this situation, the most logical thing to do is to compare your experience with that of other individuals who have undergone a similar event. This would go a long way to avoid errors attributable to self-delusion, sickness, momentary madness, or some external mirage, not to mention helping you to grasp the meaning, nature, and details of your rapture. And what better place to find such testimonies than in architecture—the discipline most interested in understanding the effects of building in people? But, as incomprehensibly as this may be, you will discover a profession with a dismal understanding of profound phenomenologies of architecture. For starters, the vast majority of studies on aesthetic experiences have traditionally focused on formal appearances and therefore interested in buildings as objects. The scholars that have investigated the phenomenological nature of architecture have focused on topics only indirectly relevant to profound aesthetic experiences (e.g., environmental perception, place making, existential space, meaning, ethics, etc.).[2] Seeking public testimonies about extraordinary experiences of architecture from recognized sources is bound to reach a dead end as well. Except for the always cited but by now overused reference to Le Corbusier's epiphany at the Acropolis in 1911,[3] the published record is problematically thin not only for its small sample size but also for its content: the few available testimonies suffer from either (a) analytical detachment that fails to address the embodied and psychological nature of the experience; or (b) inspiring words that offer no details of the actual experience.[4] Scholars have directed some of the blame for such poor record to an architectural discipline biased against anything even moderately spiritual or religious, something that the architectural extraordinary inevitable points at.[5] Regardless of the reason, you will find very little help from the architectural profession in your search for answers about your remarkable experience.

Undeterred you turn to philosophy, a field interested in beauty since antiquity. Yet, despite the great wisdom embedded in this discipline, you will soon realize that the available conversation tends to be highly abstract, removed, and relative to the philosopher and philosophy you look at. Certainly, and oversimplifying a bit, Premodern and Modern philosophies will offer you very different views of aesthetic experiences. For example, a Premodern position will normally present beauty as a disinterested, non-rational and emotionally arousing experience that is immediately accessible through sense-perception, and with the ability to deliver profound insights and pleasures—and possibly the transcendent (e.g., Kant, Schopenhauer, Stolnitz, etc.). It will point at a positive or negative sublime (Burke) or numinous (Otto) phenomenology that is beyond practical and pure reason (Kant) and ultimately locked within the confine of one's experience. In this sense, Premodern aesthetics will certainly affirm that what you experienced is possibly true and real but, in the end you will be left wanting, as little detail or discussion on architecture will be offered by any of these philosophers.[6] Unfortunately, whatever clarity or assurance you may have gained from reading Premodern philosophers will be lost when you consider Modern and Postmodern thinkers (e.g., Wittgenstein, Danto, Foucault, etc.). Even with their otherwise vast differences, both viewpoints will tell you that "aesthetic appreciation" depends on mental abilities and not sensual and emotional faculties because, in the end, there is a fundamental difference between the content and the appearance of something and that it is the content that truly matters—its meaning retrievable only through intellectual effort based on knowledge, reason, culture, and/or interpretation. Generally speaking, Modern/Postmodern philosophy's lack of interest in extraordinary aesthetic experiences, in tandem with its strong semiotic, critical and detached approach, will put you back where you started. Just before giving up with latter-day philosophical thinking, you will surely hear that phenomenology may perhaps offer you some help. But this would be true only to some extent since, with the notable exception of Hans-Georg Gadamer,[7] phenomenology has avoided extraordinary aesthetics and concentrated instead in uncovering structures and processes underlying our ordinary consciousness of things, art and places.[8] Furthermore, this work suffers from a level of generality that reveals very little about the phenomenological texture and detail so central to even ordinary aesthetic experiences.[6] In paradoxical contrast, French philosopher Maurice Merleau-Ponty who was never really interested in beauty (although he dealt with the arts) offers plenty of details applicable to aesthetic experiences in two of his master works (*The Structure of Behavior* and *Phenomenology of Perception*) and his last published paper while alive (*Eye and Mind*).[9] His success in addressing this area comes from realizing the primary role that perception plays in consciousness. This position guarded him (at least initially) from falling prisoner to the intellectual and linguist biases of 20th-century philosophy. Still, despite Merleau-Ponty's insights, the transference of these observations into a phenomenology of aesthetics is far from done. Therefore, and while potentially useful in your quest, there is little you can take from Merleau-Ponty at this point.

Considerations of how philosophy may illuminate your extraordinary experience of architecture cannot finish without acknowledging philosophy's poor record in engaging architectural matters. Few philosophers have really studied architecture,[10] and even fewer interrogated its relationship to beauty and experience in any depth. Certainly neither the sporadic references to architecture by Gadamer nor the interrogation of buildings by Gaston Bachelard,[11] Martin Heidegger[12] and Roger Scruton[13] directly illuminate the matter that preoccupies you here. In short, it is hard to avoid being unimpressed with what philosophy provides toward understanding extraordinary encounters with architecture. At best, that is if you avoid getting confused and lost in the process, you will gain some vague understanding at the price of trapping your exceptional experience inside a rigid intellectual jail that gives little meaning or information beyond generalities.

Lastly, you may seek understanding from available research on "altered," "non-ordinary," and "peak" states of consciousness in fields as diverse as the psychology of religion, medicine, neuroscience and positive psychology. Here you will find some parallels between your moment of truth and Mihaly Csikszentmihaly's "flow experience"—when one is so engaged in a situation that awareness and action merge and give rise to peak performances and an exalted sense of wellbeing and presence.[14] Reading William James' 100-year-old psychological discussion of "unio mystica"—the instant when believer and God become "aligned" and a blissful religious experience ensues—will give you confidence that incredible events are indeed possible.[15] You will certainly notice the convergences among meditative, aesthetic, spiritual and even psychedelic states that are being found in neuroscience and clinical studies,[16] only to realize how many scientific disagreements on definitions, taxonomies and results remain, fueled by the little data available, methodological challenges, and the distorting bias of contemporary aesthetics.[17] Finally, you may find affirming narrative and data in edgy (if not controversial) reporting such as Elizabeth Lloyd Mayer's "extraordinary knowing."[18] However, even after all this mind-expanding inquiry, you will be left with few specific responses to your extraordinary experience because, for all their goods, none of these studies has considered architecturally-induced non-ordinary states of consciousness.

Frustrated yet determined you decide to take the matter into your own hands and solicit public testimonies of the architectural extraordinary. It cannot be true that you are the only person that has ever enjoyed an exceptional experience of architecture, can it? However, even if you managed to gather some responses, your gained insights will be dismissed by the rationalist, skeptic, empiricist, and/or expert. They will claim that such testimonies represent a few instances that cannot be objectively verified, and therefore considered as genuine examples of a real phenomenon. The only recourse left at your disposal at this point would be to request the help of science. In this case, it would mean to gather a very large number of testimonies that permit you to tackle the situation collectively and validate your study via statistical and interpretive analyses.

In other words, phenomenology would be the way forward in your quest, ***BUT*** (and this is a big but) you would need to expand its traditional methods of small-scale self-observation and comparative hermeneutics to include very large numbers of experiential accounts and enlist the help of science. This would mean to engage in a *naturalization* of phenomenology, an idea advanced by Merleau-Ponty, and a topic of current debate.[19] Your project would surely find resistance from two fronts. The traditional phenomenologist will reject your using empirical methods to approach something so qualitative as the experience of beauty, not to mention what he/she will see as an implicit project of subordinating phenomenology to science! On the other hand, the hardcore scientist will reject any epistemology not grounded on positivist principles that disqualify anything that cannot be quantitatively measured or empirically observed and repeated. But, forcing a choice between phenomenology and science or the subordination of one to the other are false options.[20]

The Action: Asking for Testimonies (The Surveys)

Based on the ongoing conversation, it is not surprising to learn that, until eight years ago, almost nobody had ever applied the idea of "naturalizing" phenomenology to the study of the architectural extraordinary.[21] And while we can endlessly debate whether a systematic methodology to gather and analyze a massive number of testimonies can ever deliver useful insights, it is far preferable to do it than to continue to ignore the architectural extraordinary or employ the same old approach and expect different results. It was for this reason, that I decided to carry out two parallel and independent online surveys (one in English and the other in Spanish) over the course of one full year (April 2007–April 2008). The polls gathered information about people's most profound, lasting, and/or intense experiences of architecture. The surveys defined Extraordinary Architectural Experiences (or EAEs) as:

> an encounter with a building or place that **fundamentally alters one's normal state of being**. By "fundamental alteration" it is meant a powerful and lasting shift in one's physical, perceptual, emotional, intellectual, and/or spiritual appreciation of architecture. In contrast, an ordinary experience of architecture, however interesting or engaging, does not cause a significant impact in one's life.

The surveys produced the largest number of personal testimonies of EAEs ever collected: 2,892 (1,890 in English and 982 in Spanish). Following, I will limit myself to briefly present survey results germane to the concerns of this article. I do not have room in this chapter to argue or explain the survey guiding criteria, design, scope, methodology, responding population, statistical analysis, etc. Those interested in knowing more may refer to an array of publications covering these issues in detail.[22] Two quick clarifications before going into the findings. First, participants in the surveys represent skewed versions of their general populations: they predominately (a) have college education (90%) and (b) report architecture as their field of study (59%). Although skewed representations may be problematic for certain studies, it serves the purposes of this investigation quite well. Having a well-educated population whose majority understands architecture is particularly relevant in our case because we are dealing with issues that are very hard to detect, measure, and describe. Second, while there were disparities in the responses of English and Spanish populations, the data that we will be considering are for the most part immune to such differences. This in itself has important implications as we shall see.

The Result: The Phenomenology of the Architectural Extraordinary[i]

Are These Phenomenologies Significant?

Given that the tacit assumption of this paper is that extraordinary architectural experiences are real and significant, we must first check if such events do exist and if they are truly remarkable. The surveys clearly answer in the affirmative to both questions in unmistakable ways.

The first is through popular response. The strong wording behind the definition of EAE was not a deterrent to people's participation. Hence, we must assume that barring massive misunderstandings, at least 2,872 individuals affirmed the actuality of these events. Regarding their relevancy, nothing insignificant gets so many responses from educated people in our time, particularly when we are talking of a time consuming, unsupervised survey that offers no rewards (except a raw record of the results) and deals with something most would consider esoteric. The second is through the reported level of impact, accounted as memory recall and transformative power. Nature reserves lasting memory only to those events that are significant in our lives. When asked about the vividness of recall of their EAE, the majority of respondents agreed that it was "strongly vivid" (64%) with "moderately vivid" a clear second at 34%. "Vague" memory was chosen by only 3% of the people. Regarding transformative impact, participants decidedly reported that the EAE had permanently changed their understanding and appreciation of architecture (81%). This is truly significant because we are talking of changing something supposedly well known to the majority of the participants.

The importance of EAEs is made even more apparent when, despite their reported rarity (61% of the respondents indicated to have had less than five EAEs in their entire lives) *and* short duration (49% timed them at less than 30 minutes), participants still rated EAEs to be as or more memorable and vivid than other "very strong life experiences" (87%).[23]

What Is Their Character and How Are They Felt?

When asked to describe the main qualities of their architectural rapture, participants defined them as fundamentally "emotional" (72%), "sensual/perceptual/physical" (64%), "timeless" (46%), and "pleasurable" (40%). The top two qualifiers affirm that EAEs are first and foremost perceptive engagements: inward perceptions (gauged by feelings—*sentiency*) *and* outward perceptions (done by the senses—*sensibility*), both tied to the body. Indeed, their overlapping percentage suggests that EAEs involve a simultaneous perception of both sides of the subject-object interface. Describing EAEs as "timeless" implies that such perception has been slowed down to a standstill and momentarily freed from its eternal fleeting destiny. In this condition, the brightness and fullness of the present instant are seized and, as Gadamer would say, time is "fulfilled."[24] And if "timelessness" could be associated with disembodiment or mental detachment, the "emotional" and "sensual/ perceptual/physical" qualifications as well as the fourth character descriptor "pleasurable" (an adjective with strong visceral connotations) dispel any confusion.

---

i   *Note:* unless indicated, all the percentages represent the compounded results of both surveys.

Figure 4.2   The south face of the Parthenon in late afternoon. This building was one of the most cited
               places to elicit Extraordinary Architectural Experiences by respondents of both English and
               Spanish surveys

Source: Photograph courtesy of Thermos, December 5, 2005, Wikimedia Creative Commons Attribution-Share Alike 2.5
Generic license.

Survey participants added that they arrived at a "surprising" (77%) and "introspective/silent" (87%) state "suddenly" (56%). *They further* characterized the event as being "spontaneous" (82%) and at a "higher level of awareness than normal" (89%). They universally agreed that the event was lived "intensely," "profoundly," and "vividly" (all over 80%).[25] Consistent with such descriptions, 53% reported "strong body reactions" (goose bumps, heart pounding, shivers, throat throbbing, immobilization) and "weeping" (21%).[26] In depth statistical analyses of the correlations among all these variables confirmed that embodiment and emotion play a central and unavoidable role in the phenomenology of the architectural extraordinary.[27]

The lack of any major reference to "analytical/intellectual" functions to characterize EAEs is noticeable. This absence is not due to a lack of survey choices but it reflects respondents' view that thought has a secondary role in the architectural extraordinary. In fact, participants placed mental ruminations in the fifth rank, tied with "personal/private" at 35%. Of course, this does not make the intellect irrelevant: it only recognizes its modest importance when encountering the extraordinary in architecture. This is particularly evident when considering the responses "strong body reactions" and "weeping." We find out our body and emotional reactions only as they happen (i.e., suddenly, surprisingly, spontaneously). In fact, there is a natural interdependency between feelings and body: emotions trigger and are triggered by strong body reactions. Since it is hard if not impossible to voluntarily fabricate such corporal and emotional responses in the context of an experience of architecture, we would have to conclude that they must precede our consciousness of them. Only after becoming aware of such responses do we begin to deal with them. In other words, thinking appears to operate as a derivative of coming to terms to what is happening.[28] This explains how weeping can take place even when our society clearly disapproves the public display of strong emotions.[29] The fact that 1 in 5 individuals still cried indicates that EAEs may be bypassing cultural and intellectual (conscious and unconscious) mechanisms of censorship.

Outcomes, Distancing, and Communicability of EAEs

When survey participants were asked to assess what they got out of the experience, they reported "insight" (55%), "beauty" (51%), "*joy*" (43% in the English Survey) or "satisfaction" (44% in the Spanish poll), and "peace" (38%).[30] While these survey results align the architectural extraordinary with a Premodern view of beauty as delivering fulfillment and wellbeing, they also bring attention to their mental or cognitive effects. This is relevant for at least two reasons. First, because the data shows that, although outwardly driven, EAEs 'move' or impact us inwardly.[31] Since the architectural discipline pays little attention to the psychological, the results of the surveys instruct us to consider conditions that make subjective states more propitious to the aesthetic engagement of buildings. Second, when we consider all the survey results (i.e., the character of the experience, its qualities, its significance, etc.) it becomes evident that the mind undergoing an EAE is not one burdened by analytical or interpretive operations. Instead, it is one that is effortlessly and immediately gaining insight via the body, sensations, emotions, and intuitions. In other words, the data points to Premodern or Classical aesthetics as more in line with what is actually occurring during EAEs. Given the stronghold of contemporary (i.e., Modern/Postmodern) aesthetics on architecture and the arts, this survey result urges us to reconsider the theories, methodologies and pedagogies currently deployed in the architectural discipline.

Another important survey discovery was that substantial travel distance is a determining factor in arriving at the architectural extraordinary: the average distance reported for the 10 buildings most cited to induce EAEs was 3,428 miles (5,517 km) in the English poll and 3,912 miles (6,295 km) in the Spanish survey. Reasons underlying this phenomenon are not hard to find. Since negotiating such distances is not trivial in terms of the physical, temporal, and economic efforts placed on the traveler, a "pilgrimage" type of effect is likely to facilitate a state of awe and openness to the experience. As (if not more) important is the cultural distance implied: a thousands-of-miles journey implies that subjects most likely had their EAEs in another country with a different society, culture, and language (if not ethnicity and religion as well). Once immersed in an alien environment, many of our assimilating structures of cognitive operation are rendered ineffective. As a result, direct perception, emotion, and intuition become the drivers of consciousness, at least initially—de-facto causing a phenomenological reduction, a concept and discussion that we shall cover at the end of this essay.[32]

Figure 4.3   Overlooking the city of Cuenca, Spain. It took thousands of miles away from home for
              this person to encounter the architectural extraordinary. Drawing, silence, concentration,
              and solitude within a foreign context generated the necessary "distancing" to conjure up
              the ineffable. It is in moments like this that beauty transforms our lives
Source: Photograph courtesy of Jeffrey Tuft and Aaron Day.

When we also consider that, according to the surveys respondents, these exceptional experiences did not serve
any purpose except their own occurrence nor dispense goods suitable for concrete gain, we again find out that
Premodern philosophical tenets of "disinterestedness" and "distancing" match the phenomenology of EAEs
much better than those of the Modern/Postmodern model.[33] Again, this highlights the need to re-evaluate the
premises directly or indirectly shaping the contemporary practice, teaching and research of architecture.

    Finally, looking at what survey participants said about using language to communicate their EAEs, we
find clear support for the "ineffability" claim so often made regarding extraordinary aesthetic states of any
kind and, in particular, architecture. We are talking of the indescribable, inexpressible, or incommunicable
nature of profound experiences of architecture, what Le Corbusier called "ineffable space."[34] Rudolf Otto
presented a similar condition: when people encounter the "Holy Other" through beauty, their experience

(that he called "numinous") resists and transcends human communication and/or language.[35] In our case, the remarkable situation is that the majority of survey participants agreed with the fundamental incommunicability of the architectural extraordinary but this understanding didn't stop them from trying to share it with others anyway.[36] Skepticism surely arises from these responses. If EAEs cannot be communicated, then, how much can we trust the surveys' results? And how do we reconcile the paradox of people realizing their inability to convey the experience while still trying to? An answer to both questions starts by explaining the latter contradiction pointing at the basic human need to (a) share important life events with others (our social nature), (b) rationalize such powerful events to ourselves or others (a necessity that drives the narrative of this chapter), and in the process (c) validate such ungraspable events to ourselves and others. The second counterpoint to the paradox is that while the extraordinary or sublime cannot be fully expressed, something may be said and transmitted. And, while these pointers are not the "thing" or "event" itself, they certainly describe some of its qualities. As we gather multiple such descriptions a more holistic picture arises that, again, while not completely depicting the event, provides us with a better, multidimensional, and more nuanced sense and understanding of its nature. I believe the findings and arguments presented in this chapter support this claim.

Implications

To further illuminate our understanding of EAEs. I will now consider how the presented surveys findings intersect two important areas in Merleau-Ponty's philosophy: the primacy of perception and pre-reflective consciousness. I will differentiate between *early* Merleau-Ponty[37] and *late* Merleau-Ponty[38] because of the different positions he championed at different times of his career. I will conclude this section by considering Husserl's phenomenological reduction in the light of the data with the hope to further clarify our understanding of the architectural extraordinary and, perhaps advance phenomenology at large.

The Primacy of Perception

In agreement with *early* Merleau-Ponty, the survey results unambiguously affirm the primacy of perception in EAEs. These events were found to be "products" of a strongly embodied consciousness deeply embedded in emotion, the body, and the world. And while not necessarily applying to all human experiences, these findings back the "dominance" of perception in our consciousness of the physical-sensible world at large.[39] Also consistent with *early* Merleau-Ponty, the surveys assign a secondary role to language and the intellect during EAEs. Since reflection about the object of perception is *not* the object of perception, verbal language and thinking can never fully "hold" or communicate architectural experiences. This explains in part why there are so few accounts of EAEs available and their poor quality—something survey respondents recognized when affirming the ineffability of their experience. It also shows why the architectural extraordinary cannot be limited, studied or explained as/by thinking and related cerebral activities alone. In fact, as art historian and critic James Elkins argues, the intellect may need to be kept at bay (phenomenologically reduced) if the architectural extraordinary is to unfold uninhibited.[40] The fundamentally physical, emotional, and subjective quality of EAEs not only explains the primacy of perception while they last but also their remarkable mnemonic longevity, power, and fascination.

Pre-Reflective or Tacit Cogito

As *early* Merleau-Ponty realized, recognizing the primacy of perception in consciousness naturally leads one to accept the existence of some type of "pre-reflective or tacit cogito." By this he meant an immediate and essential consciousness operating *before* language and thought. The *late* Merleau-Ponty, however, reversed this view indicating that a "tacit cogito" was a nostalgic impossibility since words are the ultimate ruler of consciousness.[41] The "linguistic turn" of *late* Merleau-Ponty, though consistent with his 1950s and 1960s zeitgeist, presents a challenge to the results of the surveys. In this regard, it is important to consider the remarkable harmony between Spanish and English speakers in the survey responses. Despite the great distance in space, culture, *and language*, both groups "happened" to closely agree in the vast majority of responses, something difficult to explain without resorting to some "deeper" or more fundamental level of cogito than language.

What seems to be happening is that anytime we reflect about an ongoing perception, thinking (analysis, commentary, association, evaluation, etc.) overwhelms the experience. The mental chat takes over, something we all have experienced. Such intellectual derivative will appear to the introspective mind as if thinking and language were framing consciousness. But this is only partially true. The introspective challenge is to phenomenologically access the ground from which consciousness arises and determine if the primacy comes from perception (*early* Merleau-Ponty) or from language (*late* Merleau-Ponty).[42] The recognition of the ultimate incommunicability of the architectural extraordinary via language unmistakably supports *early* Merleau-Ponty.

Of course, it would show little humbleness, if not stupidity, to argue against thought and language as *the* framers of consciousness. After all, we would have to wrestle not only with *late* Merleau-Ponty but also Martin Heidegger and many other positions ranging from Analytic Philosophy to Post-Structuralism. Instead, let us contemplate the hypothesis that both *early* and *late* Merleau-Ponty might be right. Under ordinary circumstances pre-reflective consciousness is subsumed to language and thought, but in extraordinary situations (e.g., EAEs), "tacit cogito" dominates. This is not trying to politically resolve the disagreement between *early* and *late* Merleau-Ponty. Rather, it may be what is actually happening. Let us consider this in architecture. Normally, architectural perceptions operate in concert with the semiotic engagements. However, in extraordinary conditions, as the surveys demonstrate, perception dominates. This strongly hints at the existence of at least two types of architectural phenomenologies at play: ordinary and extraordinary. While some may question such a move, we should remember that very much like we cannot speak of one unique paradigm to describe all phenomena in Physics (Quantum, Newtonian and Relativistic models are necessary to work at different spacetime scales), we should not expect that one type of phenomenology will address the inexhaustible realm of human consciousness.[43]

The Phenomenological Reduction

Our discussion on "tacit cogito" opens the opportunity to visit the "phenomenological reduction," a central consideration in phenomenology. The idea of "reduction" was first advanced by Edmund Husserl[44] as a method for "bracketing" anything unrelated to the ongoing experience in order to immediately access the unspoiled contents of consciousness alone, or unconditioned reality. Although Merleau-Ponty never accepted Husserl's arguments that the reduction could deliver an actual grasp of the essence of things, he was ready to adhere to a "weaker" version of it. Contemporary phenomenology scholar Bernard Flynn clarifies Merleau-Ponty's position:[45]

> The reduction, as Merleau-Ponty conceives it, disrupts our absorption in the world, thereby destroying its "ordinary character." The Russian formalists claimed that the function of poetic language is to "defamiliarize" language. It is in this sense that Merleau-Ponty wishes to retain a version of Husserl's notion of "reduction."

Notice the particular emphasis given to the disruption of the 'ordinary' and 'familiar' in order to access a level of perceptual discernment—a situation that may be referred, in contrasting difference, as "extraordinary" and "unfamiliar." The spatial and cultural distancing that survey participants report should be seen in this light. Hence I propose that *the architectural extraordinary effects a de-facto "phenomenological reduction"* because it allows consciousness to enter into a radically more open and less conditioned perceptive state.[46] *Late* Merleau-Ponty seems to endorse this view. In his article "Eye and Mind," he writes how a painter is able to bypass the "literal" or "ordinary" perception of the world (e.g., objects) and see the fundamentals behind the scene (e.g., light and shadow). His implication is clear: the artist's aesthetic sensibility is executing a phenomenological reduction. And while the architectural extraordinary is different,[47] the essential idea of a "reduction" through aesthetics is the same.

Figure 4.4   Interior of the Chartres Cathedral
Source: Photograph courtesy of Jörg Bittner Unna, September 20, 2014, Wikimedia Creative Commons Attribution-Share Alike 3.0 Unported license.

Now, since all "phenomenological reduction" aims at gaining insight into the nature of "consciousness-as-is," we must consider the type of results afforded by the 'architectural reduction' (i.e., the EAE). Having just finished defending the existence of a "tacit cogito" during extraordinary experiences, I will advance the hypothesis that the fundamental outcome gained through an "aesthetic (or architectural) reduction" *is* the "tacit cogito" itself. The reductive act would be the suspension of inhibiting intellectual activities including some biases, expectations and the likes. And while it is true that the attitude, decision, and even preparation for the "reduction" may depend on words (as *late* Merleau-Ponty argued in order to refute the "tacit cogito"), the actual reduction, while happening, is fundamentally non-verbal and not intellectually-driven.[48] It may include words or thinking, but they are of peripheral importance and cause no disturbance, as the surveys participants report.[49] Arriving at and maintaining such "mental silence" is an event of rare natural occurrence and especially hard to fabricate at will. Surveys respondents attested to this fact: shifting consciousness from ordinary to extraordinary perception demanded nothing short of a surprising, sudden, spontaneous, intense, vivid, and profound architectural shock—something that rarely takes place in one's life and doesn't last too long.

More specifically, survey participants said that the architectural extraordinary was essentially an *emotional, sensual/physical/perceptual, timeless* and *pleasurable* experience that delivered *insight, beauty, joy/satisfaction,* and *peace.* Notice that except for "insight," all the other qualifications of (what we might now term) the "architectural reduction" portray an experience of high "contentment" with itself, that is, an experience joyous, satisfied, and at peace with what is being experienced. In other words, it is an experience in full alignment with the situation as given. There is no friction or resistance. Nothing is missing, nothing can be added. Everything is perfect as it is: the building, the place, the time, the weather, the people, the self. As John Dewey puts it when summarizing the phenomenology of beauty, the experience *becomes* the experience—a description in agreement with Martin Heidegger who says that in such circumstances the experience "*appears*" (as experience in consciousness).[50] For this reason, it is not surprising to discover that the discernments people report having from their EAEs are not about formal aesthetics or other objective aspects of the world or architecture, although, they surely matter and many survey respondents refer to them. Rather, as the testimonies quoted at the beginning of this essay exemplify, the insights are about something more profound that architecture helps to present: being. The realization and appreciation of the *experience as experience* cause an intense, deep and spontaneous recognition of being. In this sense, while *late* Merleau-Ponty's "chiasmic ontology" is right arguing that Being is forever hiding and cannot be fully retrieved, some glimpses are possible and reported under extraordinary conditions. Indeed, "tacit cogito" is nothing other than a sighting of Being. Contemporary phenomenologist philosopher Jean-Luc Marion's own version of the reduction help us see what the architectural extraordinary brings forth from a different and clarifying perspective. According to Marion,[51] a "reduction" gives us access to the "given" as given and as gift. In the context of this essay, I would say that the architectural extraordinary presents the underlying "givenness" of a world-embodied consciousness that is revealed in its total perfection as given (insight), and appreciated as a completely fulfilling gift (beauty, joy/satisfaction, peace). Now whether the revelation of such givenness stops at the roots of an existential being-in-the-world (Heidegger) or continues into the transcendent (Being) due to its saturation/excess (Marion), is a subject that needs a whole another discussion. Interesting enough, Finnish architect Juhani Pallasmaa comes to the very same conclusion. At its best, he tells us, architecture turns us not toward the building or the world but rather toward ourselves, thus making *being* opaque to realization. In so doing, and Pallasmaa goes one step further (which finds support in the surveys' results), the architectural extraordinary inevitably leads us into silence and the transcendental realm, the domain of the sacred.[52]

The irony of the reduction is that whatever beautiful or insightful glimpse of Being we may gain, it is ultimately incommunicable and ungraspable. For the moment we shift emphasis from perceiving "*it*" to speaking or thinking "*about it*," we lose the "tacit cogito" and with it our direct glance. In other words, making the experience *rhetorically* meaningful or understandable to ourselves or others demands the loss of our extraordinary experience.[53] We trade the "reduction" for a "report-of-the-reduction," the tacit for the explained, being for knowing.[54] This is why American writer, filmmaker and social critic Susan Sontag so eloquently spoke against interpretation and over-intellectualization in the arts[55]—which of course is nothing really new: the sages said it millennia ago:

The Tao that can be told is not the eternal Tao.[56]

Figure 4.5   The Pavilion Barcelona in Spain is another building cited by many survey participants to occasion the architecturally extraordinary

Source: Photograph courtesy of Jacob Gines.

Conclusion

What started with a very frustrating lack of help to elucidate the architectural extraordinary has been turned around with inspiration from Merleau-Ponty's life-long vision of a mutually beneficial dialogue between science and phenomenology. The survey results have enriched science by illuminating its operations with phenomenological intention and interpretation, whereas phenomenology has been able to more completely define EAEs.

In effect, on one hand the polls' findings validated Merleau-Ponty's position regarding the central role the body and perception play in all phenomenology. Similarly, the surveys directed us toward a more nuanced understanding of Hussserl's phenomenological reduction and call for different models to address ordinary and extraordinary aesthetic phenomenologies. In this sense, this research effort shares commonalities with Experimental Philosophy ("X-Phi"), a relatively new and developing reflective practice focused in the empirical examination of philosophical topics that have resisted scrutiny on the basis of analytical reasoning, phenomenological inaccessibility, and/or mistrust of science.[57]

On the other hand, we learned that EAEs are de-facto phenomenological reductions occasioned by an architectural presence that brings perception to the foreground of experience instead of relying on semiotically-driven automatic cognition. The outcome is a phenomenology of sudden and surprising arousal, intense/profound/vivid impressions, high state of awareness, silent/introspective manners, and remarkable levels of recall. The highly sensorial, emotional, and embodied experience is not only pleasurable, relaxed, and spontaneous but, sometimes, provides access to the transcendent. Furthermore, the survey data convincingly indicated that EAEs are (a) not essentially tied to intellectual operations (i.e., criticism, analysis, etc.), and (b) prompted by spatial, cultural, and other types of "distancing"—results that in conjunction with the other findings fundamentally undermine the claims of Modern and/or Postmodern aesthetics. In other words, the present investigation demonstrates the strong currency of Premodern aesthetics when addressing the architectural extraordinary. As a consequence, our inquiry encourages a reconsideration of many assumptions shaping architecture and its allied disciplines today.

It should be also noted that although survey results affirmed that EAEs are facilitated by extraordinary buildings, ordinary settings still accounted for a large number of cited places. The fact that quotidian architecture does induce the extraordinary brings attention not only to those places but, more poignantly, to the personal or subjective side of the encounter (i.e., attitude, stress, effort, expectation, health, emotional state, etc.). In this sense, an important outcome of this study is the recognition that the architectural extraordinary is more likely if we approached architecture with states of embodiment, distancing, and emotionality similar to those found under EAEs. The obvious corollary is that our architectural training too often blinds us from realizing that subjective conditions are as important as objective circumstances (e.g., the place "itself") when dealing with aesthetics. We should never forget their interdependence. In this spirit, a fruitful next step for the present investigation would be to correlate subjective responses (survey results) and the objective or factual dimension of buildings with the goal of developing indicators and methods that facilitate a better design of the built environment.

But the most important contribution of this work may be the application of science to understand the reality, rarity and relevancy of the architectural extraordinary. In so doing, this effort begins to dispel the doubts, silence, and ignorance that has surrounded the topic for far too long and allows for an open recognition and engagement of this area in architectural scholarship, education, and practice.

Acknowledgment

I want to thank the thousands of individuals worldwide who gave their time to participate in the surveys. Each one of these selfless acts not only helps advance the state-of-the-art of our knowledge of architectural phenomenology but, more importantly, they are living proof of the true and staying power and relevancy of architecture in our lives.

Endnotes

1   The three stories in this section are portions of the 1,093 narratives shared by the participants of two large surveys about extraordinary architectural experiences. For more information on the surveys, read sections 3 and 4 of this chapter. For other examples of stories entered by survey participants, refer to publications in endnote 22.

2   See for example: Hiss, Tony (2006). *The Experience of Place.* New York, NY: Knopf; Gomez, Alberto Perez (2006). *Built upon Love.* Cambridge, MA: MIT Press; Norberg-Schulz, Christian (1985). *The Concept of Dwelling.* New York, NY: Rizzoli International Publication and (1971). *Space, Existence and Architecture.* New York, NY: Praegger Publishers; Rasmussen, Steen (1962). *Experiencing Architecture.* Cambridge, MA: MIT Press; Seamon, David (1993). *Dwelling, Seeing, and Designing.* Albany, NY: State University of New York Press; Tuan, Yi-Fu (1977). *Space and Place, the Perspective of Experience.* Minneapolis, MN: University of Minnesota Press.

3   Le Corbusier (1987). *Journey to the East,* edited and translated by Ivan Zaknic in collaboration with Nicole Pertuiset. Cambridge, MA: MIT Press. In particular, refer to the chapter entitled "The Parthenon." I recently conducted a thorough study of this event focusing precisely on its extraordinary aesthetic nature. See Bermudez, Julio (2015). Le Corbusier at the Parthenon, in Julio Bermudez (ed.), *Transcending Architecture. Contemporary Views on Sacred Space.* Washington, D.C.: The CUA Press.

4   For instance, see Bruno Taut at Katsura in Kyoto [Taut, Bruno (1937). *Houses and People of Japan.* Tokyo: The Sanseido Co.]; Frank Gehry at the Chartres Cathedral [(2002). Frank O. Gehry, in Yoshio Futagawa (ed.), *Studio Talk: Interview with 15 Architects.* Tokyo: A.D.A. EDITA, pp. 6–57]; Philip Johnson also at Chartres Cathedral [(1973). Philip Johnson, in John W. Cook and Heinrich Klotz (eds), *Conversations with Architects.* New York, NY: Praeger Publishers Inc., pp. 11–51]; Bernard Tschumi while visiting the city of Chicago [(2002). Bernard Tschumi, in *Studio Talk: Interview with 15 Architects,* pp. 512–41]; Antoine Predock at the Alhambra [Predock, Antoine (2002). Antoine Predock on the Alhambra, in Susan Gray (ed.), *Architects on Architects.* New York, NY: McGraw-Hill, pp. 146–53]; Tadao Ando at Ronchamp [Ando, Tadao (2002). Tadao Ando on Le Corbusier, in *Architects on Architects,* ibid., pp. 11–17]; Steven Holl at the Pantheon [Holl, Steven (1994). Archetypal Experiences of Architecture, *A+U: Questions of Perception,* pp. 121–35]; Juhani Pallasmaa at Karnak [Pallasmaa, Juhani (2011). The Aura of the Sacred, in Renata Hejduk and Jim Williamson (eds), *The Religious Imagination in Modern and Contemporary Architecture: A Reader.* New York, NY: Routledge, see especially p. 237]; Alberto Campo Baeza at the Pantheon [Campo Baeza, Alberto (2012). *Principia Architectonica.* Madrid: Mairea Libros, 85–92]; Peter Zumthor at an urban scene in Europe [Zumthor, Peter (2005). The Magic of the Real, in *World Architecture* 1(175), pp. 18–20.

5   Refer to Crosbie, Michael. The Sacred Becomes Profane, a chapter in this book, but also in the following: Benedikt, Michael (2008). *God, Creativity and Evolution. The Argument from Design(ers).* Austin, TX: The Center for American Architecture and Design; Bermudez, Julio (2009). The Extraordinary in Architecture. *2A–Architecture and Art Magazine* 12, pp. 46–9; Bermudez, Julio (2015). Le Corbusier at the Parthenon; Britton, Karla (2010). *Constructing the Ineffable.* New Haven, CT: Yale University Press; and Hejduk, Renata and Jim Williamson (2011). Introduction: The Apocryphal Project of Modern and Contemporary Architecture, in Renata Hejduk and Jim Williamson (eds), *The Religious Imagination in Modern and Contemporary Architecture. A Reader.* New York, NY: Routledge, pp. 1–9.

6   For instance, there is very little information regarding concrete aspects of extraordinary aesthetic experiences such as how they actually unfold, what they feel like, why and when they happen, how long they usually last, what psychological and corporal signatures they have or the type of insights gained through them. There is also not much on how architecture provokes such events or what is unique about this particular phenomenology vis-à-vis other aesthetic experiences.

7   Gadamer, Hans-Georg (1986). *The Relevance of the Beautiful and Other Essays,* translated by Nicholas Walker. New York, NY: Cambridge University Press.

8   This avoidance could be seen in response to the often harsh scientific, structuralist and post-structuralist critiques of phenomenology.

9   Merleau-Ponty, Maurice (1964). Eye and Mind, in James Edie (ed.), *The Primacy of Perception.* Evanston, IL: Northwestern University Press; (1963). *The Structure of Behavior,* translated by Alden Fisher. Boston, MA: Beacon Press; and (1962). *Phenomenology of Perception,* translated by Colin Smith. New York, NY: Routledge.

10 Graham, Gordon (2003). "Architecture" in Jerrold Levinson (ed.), *The Oxford Handbook of Aesthetics.* New York, NY: Oxford University Press, pp. 555–71 (Chapter 31).

11 Bachelard, Gaston (1964). *The Poetics of Space.* Boston, MA: Beacon Press.

12 Heidegger, Martin (1971). *Poetry, Language, Thought.* New York, NY: Harper & Row Publishers.

13 Scruton, Roger (1979). *The Aesthetics of Architecture.* Princeton, NJ: Princeton University Press.

14 Csikszentmihalyi, Mihaly (1990). *Flow: The Psychology of Optimal Experience.* New York, NY: Harper & Row.

15 James, William (2004). *Varieties of Religious Experiences.* New York, NY: Touchstone.

16 Much research has been done in the past two decades in areas related to our concerns such as "Neurophenomenology," "Neuroaesthetics," and "Neurotheology." Among them, the reader may consider: Eugene d'Aquili, Eugene G. and Andrew B. Newberg (2000). The Neuropsychology of Aesthetic, Spiritual, and Mystical States. *Zygon* (2000) 35(1), pp. 39–51; Keltner, Dacher and Jonathan Haidt (2003). "Approaching Awe, a Moral, Spiritual, and Aesthetic Emotion." *Cognition and Emotion* (2003) 17(2), pp. 297–314; Carhart-Harris, Robin L., Erritzoe, David, Williams, Tim, Stone, James M., Reed, Laurence J., Colasanti, Alessandro, Tyacke, Robin J., Leech, Robert, Malizia, Andrea L., Murphy, Kevin, Hobden, Peter, Evans, John, Feilding, Amanda, Wise, Richard G. and David J. Nutt (2012). "Neural Correlates of the Psychedelic State as Determined by fMRI Studies with Psilocybin." *PNAS* (February 7), 2012, 109(6), pp. 2138–43; and Dietrich, Arne (2003). "Functional Neuroanatomy of Altered States of Consciousness: The Transient Hypofrontality Hypothesis." *Consciousness and Cognition* (2003) 12, pp. 231–56.

17 Danto, Arthur, Harowitz, Gregg, Huhn, Tom and Saul Ostrow (1998). *Wake of Art: Criticism, Philosophy, and the Ends of Taste.* Abingdon, UK: Routledge; Elkins, James (2001). *Pictures and Tears.* New York, NY: Routledge. Nehamas, Alexander (2007). *Only a Promise of Happiness.* Princeton, NJ: Princeton University Press.

18 Lloyd Mayer, Elizabeth (2008). *Extraordinary Knowing: Science, Skepticism, and the Inexplicable Powers of the Human Mind.* New York, NY: Bantam Books.

19 Petitot, Jean, Varela, Francisco, Pachoud, Bernard and Jean-Michel Roy (1999). *Naturalizing Phenomenology: Issues in Contemporary Phenomenology and Cognitive Science.* Stanford, CA: Stanford University Press. The explosion in neuroscience research in cognition, contemplation, and more over the past 10–15 years owes much to investigating the correlations between first-person (i.e., phenomenological) experience and third-person (i.e., objective or empirical) observations—nothing other than a naturalization of phenomenology. See also Varela, Francisco (1996). Neurophenomenology: A Methodological Remedy for the Hard Problem. *Journal of Consciousness Studies* 3(4), pp. 330–49; and Damasio, Antonio (2012). *Self Comes to Mind: Constructing the Conscious Brain.* New York, NY: Vintage Books.

20 I discuss this situation at some length in my article: Bermudez, Julio (2014). Considering the Relationship Between Phenomenology and Science. *Environmental & Architectural Phenomenology Newsletter* 25(3), 51–4.

21 There are two exceptions that I know of. First is the work of *James Elkins* in the visual arts who, while not carrying out a systematic survey, did try to address this matter at a general level. See James Elkins, *Pictures and Tears.* The other is the *Landscape Journal* devoting a large portion of its Fall 1993 issue to essays by recognized practitioners describing the most influential landscape experiences in their lives. In this latter case, the article limited itself to only publish the text without any further analysis or comments. Refer to *Landscape Journal* (1993). (eds). Most Influential Landscapes. *Landscape Journal* 12(2), pp. 169–89.

22 Bermudez, Julio and Brandon Ro (2014). Measuring Architectural Phenomenology through Qualitative Analysis: Studying Written Narratives of Extraordinary Architectural Experiences, in J. Carney and K. Cheramie (eds), *Proceedings of EDRA 45.* New Orleans, LA: EDRA, pp. 386–7; Bermudez, Julio and Brandon Ro (2013). Memory, Social Interaction and Communicability in Extraordinary Experiences of Architecture, in C. Jarrett, K-H. Kim and N. Senske (eds), *Proceedings of the 2013 Architectural Research Centers Consortium.* Charlotte, NC: University of North Carolina, pp. 677–84; Bermudez, Julio and Brandon Ro (2013). The Effect of Gender, Age, and Education in Extraordinary Aesthetic Experiences, in J. Wells and E. Pavlides (eds), *Proceedings of EDRA 44.* Providence, RI: EDRA, pp. 279–80; Bermudez, Julio and Brandon Ro (2012). Extraordinary Architectural Experiences: Comparative Study of Three Paradigmatic Cases of Sacred Space (The Pantheon, The Chartres Cathedral and the Chapel of Ronchamp), in J.-P. Thibaud and D. Siret (eds), *Proceedings of the 2nd International Congress on Ambiances.* Montreal, Canada: Canadian Center for Architecture, pp. 689–94; Bermudez, Julio (2011). Profound Experiences of Architecture. The Role of 'Distancing' in the Ineffable. *2A –Architecture and Art Magazine* 17, pp. 20–25; Bermudez, Julio (2011). Empirical Aesthetics: The Body and Emotion in Extraordinary Architectural Experiences, in P. Plowright and B. Gamper (eds), *Proceedings of the 2011 Architectural Research Centers Consortium.* Detroit, MI: Lawrence Tech University, pp. 369–80; Bermudez, Julio (2011). Outcomes of the Architectural Extraordinary: An Empirical Study, in J. Bermudez and P. Tabb (eds), *Collected Abstracts of the Third Architecture, Culture & Spirituality Symposium (Electronic Publication).* Serenbe, GA: The ACS Forum, http://www.acsforum.org/symposium2011/papers/bermudez.pdf (accessed November 9, 2014); Bermudez, Julio (2009). Amazing Grace. New Research into "Extraordinary Architectural Experiences" Reveals the Central Role of Sacred Places.

Faith & Form 42(2), pp. 8–13; Bermudez, Julio (2008). Mapping the Phenomenological Territory of Profound Architectural Atmospheres. Results of a Large Survey, in *Electronic Proceedings of the International Symposium "Creating an Atmosphere."* Grenoble, France: Ecole Nationale Supériure d'Architecture, http://www.cresson.archi.fr/PUBLI/pubCOLLOQUE/AMB8–1Bermudez.pdf (accessed November 9, 2014).

23 The fact that these extraordinary experiences have a lasting consequences in the lives of people *and* professionals has been argued by Hiss, Tony (1990). *The Experience of Place*; Ivy, Robert (2006). The Essence of Education. *Architectural Record* 7(17); Jones, Lindsay (2000). *The Hermeneutics of Sacred Architecture*. Cambridge, MA: Harvard University Press; Perez-Gomez, Alberto (2006). *Built Upon Love*; and the Landscape Journal, "Most Influential Landscapes."

24 Gadamer, *The Relevance of the Beautiful and Other Essays*.

25 Notice that "intensity" and "vividness" are nouns usually employed to describe emotional and bodily states rather than intellectual experiences. And while we can get into deep intellectual states, these words tend to describe experiential conditions other than thought.

26 The different responses in the English and Spanish speaking populations perhaps suggest a higher cultural tolerance for the external display of emotions (weeping) in Spanish speakers which may explain their diminished need for "sublimation" into *"strong body reactions."*

27 Bermudez, Empirical Aesthetics: The Body and Emotion in Extraordinary Architectural Experiences.

28 This interpretation is consistent with the growing body of research in neuroscience indicating the existence of a measurable delay between neural activation and conscious experience. This is often referred to as the "neural processing time factor." See Libet, Benjamin (2006). Reflections on the Interaction of the Mind and Brain. *Prog Neurobiol*, February–April, 78(3–5), pp. 322–6 (ePub 2006 May 3). Libet, Benjamin (1999). How Does Conscious Experience Arise? The Neural Time Factor. *Brain Research Bulletin* 50(5–6), pp. 339–40. This phenomenon also finds and gives support to the mounting evidence in psychology and neuroscience that cognition is fundamentally embodied.

29 Elkins, *Pictures and Tears*. In this spirit, see Reiner, Andrew (2015). The Tracks of my Tears. *The Washington Post Magazine* (Sunday January 25), pp. 18–21.

30 These results are more nuanced than I am able to discuss here. Those interested in more detail, please refer to Bermudez, Profound Experiences of Architecture. The Role of 'Distancing' in the Ineffable; and "Outcomes of the Architectural Extraordinary."

31 The importance of the internal or psychological dimension of EAEs must be highlighted. However such turn inward is not about mind-wandering, self-narrative, or intellectual rumination. Rather, the experience is one of moving beyond architecture into an experience of consciousness. See Bermudez, The Extraordinary in Architecture; and Pallasmaa, The Aura of the Sacred.

32 The phenomenological reduction was proposed by Edmund Husserl in (1931). *Ideas: General Introduction to Pure Phenomenology*. London, UK: G. Allen & Unwin Ltd.

33 Danto, Arthur (2003). *The Abuse of Beauty*. Chicago, IL: Carus Publishing Company; Nehamas, Alexander (2011). *Only a Promise of Happiness*; Roger Scruton, *Beauty. A Very Short Introduction*. New York, NY: Oxford University Press.

34 Le Corbusier (1948). *New World of Space*. New York, NY: Reynal & Hitchcock.

35 Otto, Rudolf (1970). *The Idea of the Holy*. New York, NY: Oxford University Press.

36 I don't have the space to discuss the nature and rationale of this phenomenon but readers may refer to refer to Bermudez and Ro, Memory, Social Interaction and Communicability in Extraordinary Experiences of Architecture, for such conversation.

37 *Early* Maurice Mereau-Ponty's position is articulate in his books *Phenomenology of Perception*; and *The Structure of Behavior*.

38 *Late* Maurice Merleau-Ponty is best presented in his books (1969). *The Primacy of Perception*; and *The Visible and the Invisible*, translated by Claude Lefort. Chicago, IL: Northwestern University Press.

39 The application of these surveys results pertaining to architecture to encounters with the physical-sensible world is based on the fact that buildings basically operate like nature by setting a spatial-material environment that interacts with us at an unconscious level most of the time. During the peer-review of this book, one of the readers commented on the obvious primacy of perception in architecture and therefore hinted to the redundancy of such survey finding (didn't we already know that architecture comes through the senses?!). Although the power of perception to lead the experience of architecture may seem obvious, the actual cognitive engagement is much more subtle and complex. In reality, there is a strong a-priori interpretive dimension to human cognition that fundamentally "bends" or shapes what and how we engage architecture (and the world). In most familiar situations, we don't even notice architecture to

start with and if we do, we deploy existing pre-defined systems of apprehension. We see and pay attention to what we have been taught to see. In this sense, there is no "perception" as Maurice Merleau-Ponty and most phenomenologists understand it. Even when we make an effort to openly engage a scene or building, we usually force expectations, analysis, memories, or other biases to the perceptual act which, again, more or less deforms the encounter, sometimes to a very large extent—for example, to the point of making us emotionally insensitive to it as James Elkins argues in his book *Pictures and Tears*. However, and this is the finding of the surveys, under extraordinary circumstances, our existing cognitive, cultural, and professional lenses are sufficiently bypassed as to allow a perceptual opening that produces the breakthrough: the "tacit cogito." This non-reflective or "pre-reflective" act of perception, since it inhibits our ordinary cognitive frameworks, is appropriately termed a "phenomenological reduction."

40   Elkins, *Pictures and Tears*.
41   Reynolds, Jack (2005). Maurice Merleau-Ponty. *The Internet Encyclopedia of Philosophy*, http://www.iep.utm.edu/merleau/ (accessed November 9, 2014).
42   What is notable about *late* Merleau-Ponty's "linguistics turn" is that he himself advocated for the constant critical monitoring of all thinking because, he contended, sooner or later thought naturally becomes blind to idealization and itself—he called this type of alert intellectual screening "hyper-dialectics" or "hyper-reflection." Yet, despite so much warning, *late* Merleau-Ponty seems to succumb to the seduction of words!
43   Bermudez, Julio (2010). Non-Ordinary Architectural Phenomenologies: Non Dualist Experiences and Husserl's Reduction. *Environmental & Architectural Phenomenology (EAP)* 21(2), pp. 11–15.
44   Husserl, *Ideas: General Introduction to Pure Phenomenology*.
45   Flynn, Bernard (2008). Maurice Merleau-Ponty, in Edward N. Zalta (ed.), *The Stanford Encyclopedia of Philosophy*. (Fall edition), http://plato.stanford.edu/archives/fall2008/entries/merleau-ponty/ (accessed November 9, 2014).
46   Bermudez, Non-Ordinary Architectural Phenomenologies: Non Dualist Experiences and Husserl's Reduction.
47   There are two differences. First, Merleau-Ponty is talking of a way of artistic operation that while uncommon to the lay person, is definitely ordinary to the painter and, since he gives no further details, cannot be assumed to be causing extraordinary phenomenological state in the artist. Second, the painter is intentionally conducting the reduction whereas EAEs are for the most part involuntary reductions in the sense that people are drawn into them without being asked. As we saw in the survey result, individuals find themselves undergoing an EAE surprisingly, suddenly, and spontaneously.
48   These characteristics (i.e., non-thinking, non-reflective, non-analytical, and non-self-centered phenomenologies) draw parallels to what is termed "peak" or "flow" experience in Positive Psychology. See Csikszentmihalyi, *Flow: The Psychology of Optimal Experience*.
49   For example, recent neuroscience research has showed growing hypofrontality (i.e., downregulation of the Prefrontal Cortex) the deeper the architectural experience of contemplative buildings. See Bermudez, Julio et al. two-part lecture "fMRI Study of Architecturally-Induced Contemplative States" at the Academy of Neuroscience For Architecture 2012 and 2014 Conferences at the Salk Institute in San Diego, CA. Available online at http://youtu.be/PalHtOrY9E4 and http://youtu.be/ipcuDiI1jYA (accessed November 9, 2014). I should add that the five contemplative buildings used in this scientific study were chosen from the top 10 most cited places in the EAE English survey.
50   Dewey, John (1934). *Art as Experience*. New York: Wideview/Perigee Book; Heidegger, *Poetry, Language, Thought*.
51   Marion, Jean-Luc (1998). *Reduction and Givenness: Investigation of Husserl, Heidegger and Phenomenology*. Evanston, IL: Northwestern University Press.
52   Pallasmaa, Juhani (2015). Light, Silence and Spirituality in Architecture and Art, in Julio Bermudez (ed.), *Transcending Architecture. Contemporary Views on Sacred Space*. Washington, D.C.: CUA Press.
53   I use the word *rhetoric* because in most cases the verbal discourse is used to persuade ourselves or others of the value, truth, and/or beauty of what was perceived.
54   Language is one of several frameworks that collapses any insight into discursive understanding, thus making ordinary what was extraordinary. Others are culture and level of personal development (cognitive, emotional, ethical, etc.). See Wilber, Ken (2000). *Integral Psychology*. Boston, MA: Shambala.
55   Sontag, Susan (1966). *Against Interpretation and Other Essays*. New York, NY: Dell.
56   First verse of Chapter 1 of the *Tao Te Ching* by Lao Tsu. Translated by Gia-Fu Feng and Jane English (1989). New York, NY: Vintage Books.
57   Knobe, Joshua and Shaun Nichols (eds) (2008). *Experimental Philosophy*. New York, NY: Oxford University Press.

PART II
Sacred, Secular, and the Contemporary Condition

Chapter 5
The Sacred becomes Profane

Michael J. Crosbie

This chapter starts with questions: Why do many architects seem uncomfortable with using the word "sacred" in discussing such spaces? Do young architects and architecture students share this reticence, or are they willing (maybe even eager) to use such words? What makes a thing sacred, how do we define it? Can we create a sacred architecture, or can we only create an architecture of the sacred? What is the role of the architect in the creation of such spaces? Is there room for a spiritual dimension in architecture that is not for religious purposes? How might we approach such an idea?

The motivation to consider such questions here grew out of a series of personal encounters over the past few years that brought them into focus. The trigger event was at a gathering in New York early in 2012 at Cornell University's New York City Center for a celebration and discussion of two important, recently published books: *The Religious Imagination in Modern and Contemporary Architecture* edited by Renata Hejduk and Jim Williamson, and *Constructing the Ineffable: Contemporary Sacred Architecture* edited by Karla Britton. The structure of the evening was a discussion by a panel that included AIA Gold Medalist Steven Holl (designer of the Chapel of St. Ignatius at Seattle University); Mark Taylor, a theologian-philosopher; architect Anne Rieselbach of the New York Architectural League; and Britton and Williamson. The discussion was prefaced by remarks by me to provide a context for discussion (or not, as it turned out).

My comments focused on the prevalent cultural quandary regarding religion, belief, spirituality, concepts of the sacred, and the design of sacred space. Today sacred art and architecture are battlefields. Where a century ago the debate for such noted church architects as Ralph Adams Cram or Bertram Goodhue might have turned on the most appropriate stylistic response for a church, the question today is ... do we need a building at all to be religious? People of all ages are turning away from organized religion, but they are not choosing to be atheists. Rather, they are looking for a more genuine, personal experience of the spiritual in their lives. They are suspicious of the institutional power of all religions, and the corruption they see as bound to come with such worldly influence.

Recent surveys bear out this shift. In 2008 the Trinity College "American Religious Identification Survey" found that 15% of the adults surveyed said that they are not affiliated with any organized religion, are agnostic or atheist, or described their religious affiliation as "None." This was the second largest group in the survey—larger than any single denomination or sect of believers, except for Roman Catholics. The same study found further declines in mainline religions, but increases in the Buddhist and Muslim faiths.[1] A study in 2012 by the Pew Research Center's Religion and Public Life Project found that "Nones" accounted for 20% of the U.S. population.[2] Obviously, the landscape of faith is changing. How are designers of sacred space to respond? How do we educate future architects, who are among the very people who are changing their attitudes about religion the fastest?

Instead of engaging this change in the spiritual beliefs of people, the assembled panel at the Cornell Center that night quickly veered away from a discussion of personal beliefs and the role of a sense of the sacred in architecture, particularly as a human experience. Instead, the discussion of "the sacred" was kept at a safe distance. The panelists were more comfortable intellectualizing about the role of architecture itself as a "sacred" object that should be worshipped and revered. They spoke about architecture that is "immeasurable," "ineffable," "oceanic," "possessing absence," a "void," or a "vanishing point." Most of the panelists were uncomfortable with the very word "sacred," freighted as it is with the requirement of human belief and spiritual passion —something quite outside the control of the architect. One panelist declared that this discussion was a more profound assessment of transcendent architecture for the very fact that it did not engage in the "purely instrumental, functional aspects" of sacred space.[3]

Figure 5.1   Interior of the Chapel of St. Ignatius, Seattle University, designed by Steven Holl
Source: Photograph courtesy of JessyeAnne/flickr, https://creativecommons.org/licenses/by-sa/2.0/.

The panelists were much more comfortable speculating on a "secular" sacred architecture as an intellectual construct, not a spiritual experience—abstract and safe, one that does not demand human engagement to sanctify it. Only Anne Rieselbach dared to use the "S" word to question whether architects can indeed create a space that calls forth the sacred—one shaped by liturgical needs that serves a religious belief system. She even ventured the possibility that a space itself cannot be sacred, that it is only through its setting as a place of gathering for worship, contemplation, prayer, meditation, or fellowship that architecture can become sacred. One could argue that it is the very instrumental nature of architecture—its functional aspect—that helps to call forth the sacred.

The palpable discomfort of many architects and academicians in using such "S" words as "sacred" and "spiritual" could be a symptom of their own disbelief or uncertainty. But it is more likely that such self-censorship is the product of two conditions: the secular context that most architects are educated and practice within; and a belief on the part of professionals in the creative power of the architect to create potent sacred space through design alone.

The first condition of self-censorship is a product of a larger cultural context of Modernism and education that has kept certain discussions "off the table," so to speak. It is the atmosphere of the academy and its unstated yet well-understood rules of engagement that Michael Benedikt captures so well when he points out: "Believers are hard to find in the halls of academe. Faith has no place in the class or committee room unless it is viewed anthropologically or with the proper critical distance: *their* faith, not mine." Benedikt goes on to offer a warning: "To reflect in conversation upon God or the cosmos, or to say out loud that one is searching for transcendent meaning in the act (or result) of *design*, would be to betray a serious absence of 'cool.'"[4] Benedikt's gage of the un-cool factor is just the tip of the iceberg of suppression of discussion of spiritual belief in architecture school, particularly as it relates to the creation of sacred space and the experience of such spaces. Modernism ushered in a censorship of such dialogue that has only recently began to lift—membership in organized religion maybe down, but more people (students, faculty, architects, and the people they design for) have expressed a thirst for meaning and the spiritual dimension in everyday life.

Most practicing architects today have been educated in professional architecture programs that concentrate on quantifiable knowledge about the way buildings are designed and constructed, how they perform, and how people interact with the built environment. The programs of architecture education, which are governed by regulatory agencies such the National Architectural Accrediting Board (NAAB) and the National Council of Architectural Registration Boards (NCARB), focus on such areas as statics and strength of materials; methods of assembly; environmental control systems; cultural factors and human behavior in the built environment; architectural history and the study of design precedents; building economics; construction documents and specifications; codes and standards; professional practice conventions; visual, written, and oral communication; and professional collaboration. This body of "quantifiable" knowledge is expected to be the foundation upon which architects base their designs, as explored in the design studio, which is the centerpiece of the architectural enterprise. There is little, if any, room to consider design factors that are not easily quantified. The nature of the "sacred," of course, sits squarely in the realm of the non-quantifiable. Sacred space might be considered as part of architectural history and its precedents, and an expression of a cultural belief, but in schools of architecture and at professional gatherings it is generally off limits as a topic of discussion as anything other than from an anthropological/cultural standpoint as an expression of material culture.

One corner of the architectural curriculum that has allowed the discussion of "the sacred" is architectural theory. The realm of architectural theory allows architects and architectural students to probe the secular belief systems of designers in an effort to understand the motivations behind architectural design. Theories go in and out of fashion, and any architect worth studying usually has developed a design theory that reveals the intellectual underpinnings of one's approach to design. However, the architectural theory of an architect rarely, if ever, ventures into the "sacred" because it is understood as an expression of organized religion or spirituality. Instead, what may be considered "sacred" in the architecture discipline has to do with beliefs, rituals, figures, and practices of what could be provocatively termed the "religion of architecture." For example, the architectural canon recognizes a certain sainthood in the creation of architecture, such as Le Corbusier, Frank Lloyd Wright, and Louis Kahn (who are revered by many architects who were educated between the 1950s and 1970s), and currently practicing architects whose work takes on certain spiritual overtones (one thinks of Peter Zumthor, Rafael Moneo, Santiago Calatrava, Tadao Ando, and Steven Holl). Many of these architects have designed sacred spaces and describe their work in spiritual dimensions, yet the discussion of spirituality tends to stay safely in the realm of the "religion of architecture," not a spirituality that exists outside of architecture.

Wright is perhaps the best example of an architect who saw his architecture as sacred, and was not shy about speaking about it in that way. In her book on Wright's design of religious buildings, Anat Geva notes that, "Wright considered all of his architecture as sacred."[5] For Wright, it was an expression of a living spirit that builds, and that the act of building was a sacred act, creating a sacred place. Nature, first and foremost, was for Wright a way to express the sanctity of God's creation; essentially, the experience of nature was a way to experience God, and this is why he included nature in many of his buildings, religious or not, and described their design as "organic."[6]

The second condition of self-censorship mentioned above is the investment on the part of professionals in the creative power of the architect to produce potent spaces through design alone. In the discussion at the event at the Cornell Center mentioned earlier, the focus was on those architectural qualities of the "ineffable" and the "immeasurable." The important distinction is that the sacred, for many of these panelists, is the architectural object itself.

Le Corbusier famously used the term "ineffable space" to describe the highest experiential quality that architecture may provoke—something that he equated with the phenomenon of faith and therefore at the level of the sacred. In an interview about his work at La Tourette monastery in Eveux, France, Le Corbusier said that this quality of "ineffable space" is attained when a work of architecture "… reaches a maximum of intensity, when it has the best proportions and has been made with the best quality of execution, when it has reached perfection …."[7] When this happens, the work starts to "radiate," and give the space a quality that "does not depend on dimensions but on the quality of its perfection. It belongs to the domain of the ineffable, of that which cannot be said."[8] Le Corbusier went one step further to strengthen the importance of architecture in creating what for him could be described as a sense of the sacred when he wrote, in a different context, "I am not conscious of the miracle of faith, but I often live that of ineffable space, the consummation of plastic emotion."[9] Le Corbusier suggests that the sense of the sacred (the "ineffable") is provided or created by the architecture itself, a product of its material design, proportions, harmony, and craft, attained, one might add, through the architect's creative capacity to call it into being. In other words, the creative power of the architect sanctifies the space, makes it sacred. Many have observed that certain architects tend to have a "God complex," but it is probably more accurate to describe such architects as priests in the "religion of architecture." Through the architecture, the architects function as shamans, high priests that impart through creativity, vision, and determination an aura of holiness to their buildings. In reading Le Corbusier it is hard not to think that architects are capable of a kind of secular trans-substantiation, turning mere concrete, steel, and glass into sacred objects that "radiate" and can exert their power to make places sacred.

The terms of architecture's sacredness are most often described as physical qualities that impart a sense of the sacred. Le Corbusier talks about proportion, harmony, plasticity, boundless space, aesthetics, and the fourth dimension as the instruments of "ineffable space."[10] For Wright, it is the presence of nature, captured and framed by the building, which provides architecture with a sense of holiness. Tadao Ando recalls Wright in his use of nature and especially light in his architecture, sacred and otherwise. Ando's reliance on these qualities causes at least one observer, Kenneth Frampton, to question the mixed messages of what is sacred and why it is sacred, with the more explicit belief systems of those he designs for, in projects such as the Church of the Light and the Water Temple. Frampton queries: "… in most cases the secular character of his spirituality poses the question: how should we relate his all but animistic conception of nature to the institutions that continue to house orthodox traditional religious practices within contemporary Japanese society?"[11]

Frampton's observation brings up the issue of a shared sense of the sacred: does the architect need to share it with the people whom the architecture will serve, and how does the architect respond when the shared sense of the sacred is not shared?

Figure 5.2   Interior of the Cathedral of Our Lady of the Angels, Los Angeles, designed by Rafael Moneo
Source: Photograph courtesy of Clinton Steeds/flickr, https://creativecommons.org/licenses/by-sa/2.0/.

Rafael Moneo addressed this very dilemma openly and with humility in his design of the Cathedral of Our Lady of the Angels in Los Angeles. In beginning the project, Moneo found himself questioning how to proceed with a building of such religious and cultural significance in an age when the sense of the sacred has become more a personal belief than one dictated by an institution. "The architect, facing the challenge of building a church or a temple, cannot rely on a vision of the sacred shared by those who will use the building," Moneo explains, "but instead must risk offering his or her version of sacred space."[12] The architect thus must use the only means available to him or her as the creative agent: the shaping of space, the manipulation of light and sound, the expression of materials, textures, colors, and religious symbols.

Yet Moneo sensed that the architect's reliance on marshaling the materials of architecture in an effort to create something sacred might fall short. He confesses that he did not feel "... capable of projecting a transcendent space able to incite a sensory experience in the individual ... nor did I expect to build a perfect machine like those ... from the cathedral builders of the Middle Ages. The alternative was to design the cathedral conscious of those spaces which could be understood as metaphors of religious experience."[13] Moneo here expresses his awareness of the limitations of architecture to "create" the sacred, and of his own personal crisis of confidence to be able to design a space that becomes sacred through the sheer power of the architecture. What he can offer honestly as a designer is the creation of a setting, a space that suggests or recalls the images of sacred spaces throughout history, as metaphors that might allow or invite the believer to enter into a state, personally and in the shared presence of others, through which the sacred can be experienced—not defined, or contained, or quantified. The elusive nature of the sacred, like a firefly in a jar on a summer's night, can never be captured and held.

Moneo's crisis of confidence in the design of such a sacred space seems a sincere reflection on the limitations of architecture to create sacredness merely through the instruments of light, materials, and sound—the architect's tools of trade. It is an awareness echoed by the architect Fariborz Sahba, in his design of the Lotus Temple in New Delhi, India. Sahba used the image of the lotus flower for the temple design to express the unity of religions espoused by the Bahá'i faith. He explains that the process of designing and building the temple made him realize that the architecture itself could not make the temple sacred. Establishing a direct connection with people's souls and spirits constitutes a sacred space and a sacred monument. Sahba states, "I do not think it is the geometry, material beauty, or grandeur of the Taj Mahal that has made it so special to people ... rather it is the building's story, mystery, and aura which have made it a sacred edifice. There is a fifth dimension in the space beyond length, width, height, and movement; it is a dimension of inherent relation in the essence of things, the realities of things. ... This relation is so delicate, so special. And this is what makes it sacred."[14]

What Sahba and Moneo describe is that architecture can provide a setting for the sacred to transpire, but it cannot create the sacred through an arrangement of architectural elements. Such an idea might be anathema to architects who see their role as conjurers, in which the building itself is the sacrament. This belief system can only take place within the "religion of architecture" which is instilled in architecture school and tended by the high priests of the profession. Architecture can and often does—through the skillful manipulation of light, sound, materials, texture, color, water, flame, and shadow—become transcendent. Human experience of such spaces can take us out of our quotidian existence and transport us to another state of being. But does the architecture actually make a place sacred, does it sanctify it? Is the sacredness of a space *dependent upon* the mystical combination of elements that the architect has mastered? I, and others, might argue that it does not.

This does not mean that architecture does not have an important role in creating a place where we can experience the holy. Indeed, the entire history of the greatest works of architecture is mostly about the creation of sacred space. The important distinction is whether the architecture itself is sacred (or actually makes a place sacred) or that architecture is an instrument that calls forth the sacred. These are two different conditions. In the first it is the very matter of the architecture—its presence—that is sacred. In the second, the architecture creates a space, a mood, a physical setting that helps people to experience the sacred, deeply inside or outside themselves. Theologian Sigurd Bergmann observes that architecture can function beyond as simply a place for transcendence; it can be the agent of belief itself, "... not only a 'locus theologicus,' but as an autonomous agent of theology itself."[15] It is like the difference between a musical instrument and music. The horn is not music. But the horn (through its careful design and construction) allows human breath to fill it, and music is made.

Figure 5.3   Lotus Temple, New Delhi, designed by Fariborz Sahba
Source: Photograph courtesy of Jools Asher from England, 21 October 2003, Wikimedia Creative Commons Attribution 2.0 Generic license.

Architecture can serve as a vessel to convey a sense of the sacred, but is not sacred in and of itself. Religion scholar Diana Eck notes that architecture functions as a frame to experience—on a personal level—the sacred, not to create the sacred itself. Architecture is often the lens through which we are able to orient ourselves to the presence of the sacred, the "numinous" (to use Rudolf Otto's word for it). "It is through the windows," explains Eck, "that we are able to see in ways our unfettered gaze cannot comprehend. Architects do not, in that sense, construct the sacred. How could anyone do that? But they do enable us to see it, and in that sense architecture is a revelatory art. It is training the eye to see, training the soul to deep seeing."[16]

In this light, we might better understand, for several different reasons, the resistance on the part of architects and academicians to use the "S" word, whether "sacred" or "spiritual," in discussing their work. On one level it is taboo and a serious threat to one's quotient of "coolness" (as Benedikt warns us) to parley in the language of religion, especially if such a discussion might identify one as a believer. Second, most architects have been trained to talk about design using words that are acceptable in the profession; "light," "space," the "immeasurable," the "void," and "ineffable" are all in the preferred vocabulary. It also keeps the focus on the work of architecture itself, which architects are most confident and enjoy talking about, and over which they ultimately have some measure of control (giving form, choosing materials, selecting colors, etc.).

At another level, architects could find it uncomfortable or simply useless to discuss a realm that they have little control of actually bringing about through their actions as designers. The position taken by one of the participants in the Cornell event was that a discussion of "purely instrumental, functional aspects" of sacred space was less critical to the creation of transcendent architecture. Such an assessment appears based on an assumption that architecture as a setting for ritual is secondary to its provision of a religious experience, but many would argue the opposite. Paul Goldberger's summary comments on the "Constructing the Ineffable" conference at Yale University in October 2007 takes architects to task for thinking it is the architecture, not the community of believers, that delivers transcendence:

... even when these experiences, the aesthetic and the sacred, co-exist, we as architects tend to assume that the power of the experience comes wholly or largely from the architecture. I think this is architectural hubris. While great architecture surely can and often does enhance religious experience, it is not particularly likely to create it. The qualities that most architecturally aware people respond to, the qualities that we might feel confer sanctity, are not always the ones that make space sacred for the people for whom it was, at least ostensibly, created. It is transcendent for them because of what they bring to it at least as much as because of what the architecture has done with it.[17]

Virtually all religions locate the creation of the sacred in the actions of people drawn to celebrate and share belief. Karsten Harries describes the sacred as the function of people gathered to remember: "Architecture is properly sacred, I want to suggest, only as a site of sacred memory."[18] Harries believes that such sacred memory helps to define identity, is communal, and expresses a concern for the future, what we might also describe as an afterlife. Harries' description suggests that sacred architecture needs to fulfill a certain function, provide a space for human action to transpire, through which sacredness might be achieved. If this is the case, we can see the careful attention to how the built environment accommodates ritual, or the function of a place of prayer, meditation, or solace, as the highest calling in architecture's service to the sacred.

Where the "S" Word is (Almost) OK

While architects and architectural academics might be loath to utter the "S" word, it is by no means a universal prohibition. With the climate toward religion and spirituality changing, its evolution is happening fastest in the academy itself, and the reasons for this are multiple. One is demographic. Over the past several years, socially we have experienced a shift away from organized religion and a focus more on personal spirituality. As discussed, this is reflected in several studies, such as the "American Religious Identification Survey" cited earlier, which Trinity College in Hartford, Connecticut has conducted since 1990. Its last survey (2008) found that 15% of the adults were not affiliated with an organized religion, agnostic or atheist, or described their religious affiliation as "None." The greatest growth was from 1990 to 2001, when the percentage of "Nones" jumped from 8.2% to 14.1%.[19] Also mentioned earlier, the Pew Center for Research 2012 study saw "Nones" climb to 20% of population. Demographically, "Nones" account for 32% of people aged 18–29, the largest share of any of the five age brackets in the study, and of course the group that numbers college students. It is important to note that "Nones" are not necessarily atheists or agnostics. The Pew Center notes: 68% of "Nones" say they believe in God, 58% say they often feel a deep connection with nature and the earth, 37% describe themselves as "spiritual" but not "religious," while 21% say they pray every day.[20]

Young people are challenging what is and isn't acceptable to talk about on college campuses, and appear to have an intellectual thirst for topics regarding the spiritual. Karla Britton, Lecturer at the Yale School of Architecture, describes today's campus atmosphere as one where questions of faith and belief are continuously assessed through the lens of the needs of a young and new culture. The American literary theorist and public intellectual Stanley Fish, notes Britton, asserts that religion, "including issues of faith, belief, and spirituality—has succeeded theory and issues of race, gender, and class as the center of intellectual energy in the academy."[21] Other evidence is found in the growth of religious studies courses at several institutions. Harvard theologian Harvey Cox recalls that when he began teaching at Harvard in 1965, courses in religious studies were unheard of. When he retired in 2009, he described an atmosphere radically different: "We can't add enough courses to respond to all the interest," and also noted a surge in worship among students of all different faiths, "... a vast variety of ways of worshipping, and being spiritual, religious." Cox described the students as intellectually curious, with many on a "personal quest."[22]

Some institutions of higher learning have included the growing student interest in religion and spirituality as part of their educational mission. In the late 1990s secular Wellesley College started its "Beyond Tolerance" program, which not only recognizes and celebrates the diversity of religious traditions that the student body represents (including those who considered themselves "spiritual" outside of any tradition), it has an educational component as well. According to Victor Kazanjian, former dean of religious and spiritual life at

Wellesley, the focus is on "… interreligious understanding and dialogue intended to equip students with the intellectual and practical skills necessary to be citizens of a religiously diverse world."[23]

While architecture programs at secular institutions are at this time far from being settings for discussions about the creation of sacred space, schools that are faith-based are more likely to entertain such dialogue. But even at religiously affiliated institutions, the topic can be sensitive. For instance, in the early years of this century, The Catholic University of America School of Architecture and Planning created a concentration of sacred architecture at the graduate level. According to CUA architecture Dean Randall Ott, the title of the concentration was carefully nuanced as "Cultural Studies/Sacred Space" at the insistence of several faculty members who felt uncomfortable giving too much prominence to the word "sacred" in an architecture program, even at Catholic University, as it might be assumed that the sacred space under consideration was only Roman Catholic. Even worse, outsiders might detect it as evidence of religious zealotry in the architecture program. The term "cultural studies" served to defuse the power of the word "sacred," clothing it in the vestments of anthropology as a way of making it safe for academics to talk about, if they ventured to talk about it at all.[24]

When Professor Julio Bermudez arrived at CUA in 2010 to head up the graduate concentration, he insisted that the name be changed to "Sacred Space/Cultural Studies."[25] Bermudez welcomes such dialogue; several years earlier he co-founded the Forum for Architecture, Culture, and Spirituality for the expressed purpose of creating a "space" where religion and spirituality could be addressed by academics and others in the field of architecture and design without apology (see this book's Introduction). Even with more pushback from some faculty members, Bermudez prevailed. Yet the program appears, at least on the CUA Website, to have a schizoid personality. On some web pages it is still referred to as the "Cultural Studies/Sacred Space" concentration, while on others it is "Sacred Space/Cultural Studies." In one instance, both titles are used on the same page.[26]

Architect Duncan Stroik, whose practice has concentrated on the design of religious buildings (mostly Roman Catholic), describes a similar situation at the University of Notre Dame School of Architecture. Stroik, who has taught at Notre Dame since 1990, offers a seminar on religious architecture for architecture students and those outside the discipline, and has headed thesis studios at the school. He notes that some faculty (mostly those in their late 50s and 60s) are reserved about discussing the element of the "sacred" with their colleagues or with students, while younger faculty appear more open to dialogue. According to Stroik, architecture students seem comfortable with in-class discussions regarding spirituality and architecture, some actively seeking it. He estimates that about 10% of the undergraduate architecture students chose to study at this Roman Catholic institution because they are interested in architecture's spiritual dimensions and about a quarter of the graduate students came to Notre Dame because they want to design religious buildings. He describes the students' orientation in this realm as "catholic," with a small "c"—their interest in sacred architecture are comprehensive, cutting across religious traditions globally, extending into spirituality.[27]

Stroik says that some students at Notre Dame are unabashed about the role of "beauty" in architecture, sacred or not. Considering the dimension of beauty has long been taboo in most architecture schools, and is a carry-over from the influence of Modernism that continues to influence the majority of programs. "Functionalism" was the Modernist equivalent of "beauty"; if a design were functional it would be beautiful (although the "B" word was not used). Stroik says that students at Notre Dame, with its Vitruvian approach to architecture, instead see beauty as the third leg of Sir Henry Wotton's translation of the Roman architect's dictum that architecture should have "firmness, commodity, and delight." For Stroik's students, good architecture equates with beauty, and a sacred building should be the most beautiful of all.[28]

Pursuing a faith-based architectural education that is overt in its alignment with religious beliefs and ethics is an option at schools such as Judson University in Elgin, Illinois, which describes itself as "Evangelical Christian" and was founded by the American Baptist Church. The architecture program began in 1997, became NAAB accredited in 2004, and offers undergraduate and professional-degree graduate programs. At 150 students, the architecture department is the biggest on a campus of about 1,200 students, and according to the department website, represents "… the Church at work in higher education and aspires to be a global leader in architectural education and Christian service."[29]

The architecture students and faculty I spoke with on a visit to Judson are aware that their architecture school is unique in the sense that religious belief is infused throughout the program. Few are shy about talking about the role of spiritual belief in architecture, whatever the building's function. Architecture department chair

Keelan Kaiser estimates that a majority of students chose Judson, where the predominant faith is Christianity, because of its orientation toward creating a Christian architecture. While a profession of belief is not required of the architecture students (faculty, however, must profess their Christian faith), Kaiser estimates that at least half of them are "serious about their faith," and are seeking to merge their beliefs with their professional education.[30] Although there are students of other faiths (such as Islam), Judson architecture Dean Curtis Sartor notes that they have not yet expressed themselves as vocally as Christian students, but he believes many chose Judson because they wanted to study architecture at a school where personal faith was valued. (A similar situation exists at Catholic University among Islamic students, according to Julio Bermudez.)[31]

While the connection between faith, architecture, and spirituality might not be surprising at an architecture school such as Judson, it can manifest itself in a secular institution, albeit in covert ways. Two years ago, a group of students at the Yale School of Architecture, hungry to discuss some of the same issues considered by students in faith-based institutions, began to meet to explore how their faith connects to architecture. The student-led YSOA Christian Fellowship numbers about a dozen students and meets weekly. Yale Ph.D. student Kyle Dugdale, who is interested in architectural education in a Christian context, noted that a similar group exists at the Harvard Graduate School of Design.[32] The YSOA "Conversations on Faith and Architecture" started as a way for students to read and talk about the bible, and has since flowered into a weekly exchange on a variety of topics: what does it mean to be a Christian studying architecture, how can faith be expressed through design, how does one balance personal spiritual belief with the rigors of architecture school (for example, is it possible to observe the Sabbath, to have "a day of rest" in an architecture program?). "The culture of architecture school is strong, demanding, and dominant; it takes over," explained one student, who described how a practicing Christian can "become lost."[33]

Michael Benedikt writes that believers are hard to find in the halls of academe, that faith has no place, but this is not really the case. Anyone who has spent even a short time in architecture school discovers that it has a robust reservoir of true believers, disciplined adherents, and observant devotees of the "religion of architecture." Novices are routinely challenged by the keepers of the flame (or "The Seven Lamps") to demonstrate their commitment to the faith (initiation, long hours, grueling deadlines, humiliation before one's peers). Traveling saints visit on occasion to speak in tongues, a language of faith is cultivated, and the newly ordained are set forth back into the world to preach the Gospel and hold tight to the faith. The Yale students described how architecture school can become a serious distraction to one's faith. The focus of the group is to encourage fellowship, to discover others having the same struggle, and to help each other to hold on to Christian values and belief.[34]

The Yale students have explored such issues as living one's faith through architecture; how one might define a "Christian architecture" beyond building program; what a Christian system of critique of architecture would be (that might operate in ways similar to a Marxist critique, or a gendered critique); what a syllabus for the education of a Christian architect might look like; why conversations about faith are forbidden in studio and how a design problem for combined religious and secular uses might create a space for discussion; and how one approaches concepts such as truth, or beauty, or the sacred in architecture.[35]

Is the Taboo Lifting?

The evidence regarding the presence of the spiritual or the sacred as topics of discussion in architectural education is at this point cursory, and demands continued attention and investigation. However, there seems to be a thawing of the "freeze" on openly considering such topics in architectural education, design, and practice, and the taboo of using the "S" word, whether "sacred" or "spiritual," appears to be lifting. The generation under 30, in particular, is not willing to censor themselves when it comes to discussing and considering religious values and concepts that matter to them, or they are simply curious about, even if it makes their mentors squirm a bit. The result might be architecture, secular as well as sacred, that is more expressive of, and responsive to, the full range of human experience.

Such a development reflects the larger culture and the growing interest in the spiritual dimension of human existence, particularly outside of organized religion. People are turning away from institutions—particularly religious ones—that they perceive as too rigid, too authoritarian, too coercive.

There appears to be a wellspring among those who are looking for greater meaning in their lives and striving for experiences that are more genuine, authentic, and multi-dimensional. There is more emphasis on the mind/body connection, on healthier living and eating, on food that is not processed, is organic, and is flavorful without relying on additives. There is an explosion of interest in meditation and "mindfulness," on exercise and yoga. Voluntary simplicity in lifestyle is gaining more attention in the culture, as many reject the distractions and pressures of industrialized culture, which they believe is moving just too fast. There is a longing for more balance in lives that have become over-scheduled, frantic, and numbing. More people are striving to live more gently upon the land, and to nurture their spiritual lives. This is true not only for younger people in the demographic described above (which is rejecting organized religion) but for people throughout the culture. Within this search for a spirituality that is more personal and authentic, the consideration of such topics are open for discussion. More books are being written on the inner spiritual life and more people are more willing to share this dimension of themselves, how it might affect their careers, and how it might shape their decisions as professionals.

It could be argued that this development is a product of living in a world where we are exposed to more people of different cultures, value systems, and religious beliefs. As our tolerance of and interest in each other grows, we look for a broad base to appreciate differences and to celebrate them. Spirituality is a common ground, which transcends the particular belief systems of the world's organized religions. Jürgen Habermas observed, "… each from its own viewpoint, must accept an interpretation of the relation between faith and knowledge that enables them to live together in a self-reflective manner."[36] Habermas's insight can be interpreted as recognizing the role of spirituality in advancing human knowledge, understanding, and co-existence. This opens spirituality to a mode of questioning human experience that can be shared with others. In this way, spirituality becomes a new way of asking questions and learning what is common across all human experience and all forms of religious belief around the world.

The ways of exploring knowledge in the modern world have traditionally been through the sciences, the humanities, and the arts. Spirituality represents a fourth way, which asks its own questions, and might be able to arrive at answers not accessible through other modes of exploration. This is the reason why the sacred dimension in architecture is important and worthy of our engagement and discussion. It is a dimension of human experience and inquiry that needs to be studied, explained, shared, and debated in architecture. When it comes to the "S" word in architecture, we must finally speak up.

Endnotes

1   American Religious Identification Survey, Trinity College, March 2009, http://faithandform.com/wp-content/uploads/2009/12/ARIS_Report_2008.pdf (accessed June 20, 2014).
2   'Nones' on the Rise. Pew Research Center, October 2012, http://www.pewforum.org/2012/10/09/nones-on-the-rise/ (accessed May 3, 2014).
3   Crosbie, Michael J. (2012). The 'S' Word. *Faith & Form* 45(1), p. 4.
4   Benedikt, Michael (2008). *God, Creativity, and Evolution: The Argument from Design(ers)*. Austin, Texas: Centerline Books, p. 8.
5   Geva, Anat (2012). *Frank Lloyd Wright's Sacred Architecture: Faith, Form, and Building Technology.* London and New York: Routledge, p. 4.
6   Ibid.
7   Britton, Carla Cavarra (ed.) (2010). *Constructing the Ineffable: Contemporary Sacred Architecture*. New Haven: Yale University Press, p. 13.
8   Ibid.
9   Le Corbusier (1948). *New World of Space.* New York: Reynal & Hitchcock, p. 8.
10 Britton, pp. 13–14.
11 Ibid., p. 110.
12 Ibid., p. 159.
13 Ibid.
14 Ibid., p. 176.

15 Bergmann, Sigurd (ed.) (2009). God's Here and Now in Built Environments. *Theology in Built Environments.* London: Transaction Publishers, p. 20.

16 Ibid., p. 113.

17 Ibid., p. 228.

18 Ibid., p. 64.

19 American Religious Identification Survey.

20 'Nones' on the Rise.

21 Britton, Karla (2012). Sacred Spaces in Institutions of Higher Learning. October 25, unpublished manuscript.

22 *Religion & Ethics Newsweekly*, Harvey Cox Extended Interview, September 25, 2009, http://www.pbs.org/wnet/ religionandethics/2009/09/25/september-25–2009-harvey-cox-extended-interview/4342/ (accessed June 16, 2014).

23 Kazanjian, Victor and Stephen Kieran (2009). Design From Dialogue. *Faith & Form* 42(3), p. 6.

24 Interview, Randall Ott, March 8, 2014.

25 Interview, Julio Bermudez, June 6, 2014.

26 Cultural Studies/Sacred Space. Catholic University, http://architecture.cua.edu/degree-programs/cultural-studies-sacred-space-overview.cfm (accessed June 20, 2014).

27 Interview, Duncan Stroik, May 9, 2014.

28 Ibid.

29 Department of Architecture, Judson University, http://www.judsonu.edu/SOADA/ (accessed June 19, 2014).

30 Interview, Keelan Kaiser, March 20, 2014.

31 Interview, Curtis Sartor, April 4, 2014.

32 Interview, YSOA Christian Fellowship group, March 28, 2014.

33 Ibid.

34 Ibid.

35 Ibid.

36 Habermas, Jürgen. Notes on a Post-Secular Society. June 18, 2008, http://www.signandsight.com/features/1714.html (accessed June 12, 2014).

Chapter 6

An Aesthetic and Ethical Account of *Genius Loci*

Hyejung Chang

Introduction: Spirit of Place

The term "place" is hard to define with intelligence and clarity, even if it is used mostly in a generic sense in ordinary conversations. A place appears on the "scene" as a concrete reality in our mind when it is retrieved from personal memory or feelings affiliated with specific or dominant features of an environment. Place is often conceived as the perceptual and existential space and as a center of meanings within the lived-space of the everyday social world.[1] It also is rendered with individually secretive and intimate stories, but at the same time, it is related and responsive to its physical and social context.

"Sense of place" has been thereby an important concept broadly used in an inter-disciplinary context from interior design, architecture, landscape architecture, to urban design, and environmental planning, and cultural studies. At the same time, it has been an overused concept and can mean much nowadays. J.B. Jackson, an American landscape writer notes that "it [sense of place] is an awkward and ambiguous translation of the Latin term *genius loci*—the guardian divinity of a place or protective spirit of a place … We now use the current version to describe the atmosphere to a place, the quality of its environment."[2]

For most environmental designers maintaining the genius loci of a place has become not only a common aspiration for place-making but also a practical claim for the goodness of a place they envision to embody. The concept has also emphasized the importance of restoring the "identity" of landscapes that are inevitably associated with routines, rites, habits, customs, and histories of community.[3] This is because identities of place express human qualities, especially those qualities that lead us to anthropomorphize the particularities of a valued place. The cultural geographer Yi-Fu Tuan shares this view by stating that space is given a personality of place when people and object(s) come together as the embodiment of their feelings, thoughts, and symbols.[4] Architectural theorist Christian Norberg-Schulz writes that *genius loci* represents the sense people have of a place, and that it can be recognized by four thematic levels in the environment: the topography of the earth's surface; the cosmological and natural conditions such as light and the sky; buildings; and symbolic and existential meanings in the cultural landscape.[5]

However, "the sense" people have of, or attach to, their place appears to be elusive, confusing, and subjective, and thus remains an uncritical concept in contemporary design discourse.[6] This can be in part ascribed to the Latin origin of *genius loci*, "spirit of place," because the notion of spirit is usually regarded as an esoteric term that is intangible and unapproachable from the outside, and mostly related to meditative or contemplative states. This general (mis)conception may also be traced to a long-held intellectual belief of binary oppositions of mind and body, soul and matter, and spirit and flesh, and perhaps to the Greek conception that spirit is ranked above all of the three fold distinctions: body, mind, and spirit.[7] The abstruseness embedded in ideas of Sprit, Place, and Identity therefore demands further accounts that are both analytical and holistic.

Norberg-Schulz makes a distinction between perceptual and existential space by stating that the former is essential to one's identity as a person; while the latter makes him or her belong to a social and cultural totality.[8] Needless to say, the identity of a person cannot be formulated independent of the total belief system and life of a community where he or she belongs. To re-paraphrase Descartes: I perceive (in context), therefore I am; meaning, the identity of a person is re-cognized and described with a full perceptual awareness as the accrued meanings of his or her life. This awareness of the meanings of life resonates with the social reciprocity between personal activities and communal life within a particular history of community. By the same token, to examine identities of place, we need to articulate how we perceive what is experienced in a particular place, how we make sense of it, and why the wholeness of the place has a positive effect on the community.

If the "spiritual" nature of place (i.e., *genius loci* or spirit of place) is purely an arbitrary phenomenon or a subjective and uncritical individual experience, as often depicted scientifically, why should we even bother to recognize, restore, and rationalize its presence in our conscious and empirical act of design? This begs the core question: what are the essence and the conditions for *genius loci*? How does a place exhibit a human "spirit" or "humanizing qualities" in its form and features? In this essay I attempt to demystify the concept of "Spirit of Place" by giving more attention to our shared humanity embodied in place. Three questions are posed relating to the central question:

- What makes a place spiritual? To state it differently, what makes a place meaningful and fulfilling? (This concerns the existential dimension of place);
- How does spirituality originate and operate in our experience of place? (This concerns the aesthetic dimension of place);
- How can it inform the goodness of community and our morals of place-making? (This concerns the ethical dimension of place).

In order to answer these questions, this essay puts forward three propositions. First, Spirit of Place is essentially a fuller engagement of the self in place. I will elaborate on this below, but suffice to say that the term "self" is here not limited to individual-centric consciousness. Second, Spirit of Place is inevitably associated with an aesthetic experience of place. Third, Spirit of Place ultimately transcends the moral accountability of the individual to include his or her community and broader environment. By bringing together John Dewey's and Abraham Maslow's thoughts related to the subject of Spirit of Place in a comparative way, this essay illuminates the role of aesthetics and ethics in both the understanding and creation of places.

A Conjunction between Dewey's and Maslow's Thoughts

Spirits are believed to be intelligible and find embodiment in matter, people, events, and places, as presented in folk tales, legends, myths, and religious practices. Natural philosophers or humanistic psychologists have been studying these phenomena for a long time. For example, natural philosophy, a distinct area of study in the arts faculties of most medieval universities, examined the phenomena of the natural or physical world in relation to "invisible" or "internal principles" of change, place, and time.[9] According to George Santayana, who conducted a passionate quest for finding philosophy in "naturalism,"[10] natural philosophers have the tendency "to describe the world from its beginning (if it had a beginning), tracing all its transformations analytically, not pictorially—that is, not in the sensuous language of some local observer composing a private perspective, but in terms of the ultimate elements (if there are ultimate elements) concerned in the actual evolution of things."[11] Natural philosophers conceived the image of the natural world framed by common sense and science, yet at the same time allowed for non-scientific beliefs about existence, such as religious feeling, mythical thinking, or fanciful imagination. They believed that only in observing spiritual perspectives would one endeavor to trace the evolution of these intuitions as alternatives to traditional philosophical reasoning.[12] Santayana continues,

> Naturalism is a primary system, or rather it is not a special system at all, but the spontaneous and inevitable body of beliefs involved in animal life, beliefs of which the various philosophical systems are either extensions (a supernatural environment, itself natural in its own way, being added to nature) or interpretation (as in Aristotle and Spinoza) or denials (as in idealism) … Children are interested in their bodies, with which they identify themselves; they are interested in animals, adequate playmates for them, to be bullied with a pleasing risk and a touch of wonder … It is the world of naturalism … A naturalist may distinguish his own person or self, provided he identifies himself with his body and does not assign to his soul any fortunes, powers, or actions save those of which his body is the seat and organ. He may recognize other spirits, human, animal, or divine, provided they are all proper to natural organisms figuring in the world of action, and are the natural moral transcript, like his own feelings, of physical life in that region.[13]

On the other hand, humanistic or existential psychology—sometimes called integral, transpersonal, or personality psychology, and pioneered by Carl G. Jung and Abraham Maslow—incorporated human subjectivity and spirits to explore questions about what makes life fulfilling or meaningful, a challenge to traditional, positivistic methods in science.[14]

In a similar vein, landscape theorist Ervin Zube argues that the "humanist" approach to landscape perception has shown two trends: one is phenomenological and transactional; the other is historical and cultural.[15] The transactional and phenomenological approach attempts to probe the fundamental meanings of our common experiences, and to provide universal vocabularies for planning and design practice. The cultural and historical approach, on the other hand, concerns itself with interpretive and cultural peculiarities relying on diverse and rich resources. Although there has been a controversy regarding which approach is more humanistic than the other, both types of analyses in the study of landscape perception—phenomenological and historical or conceptual and empirical—recapture and revisit the environment through presenting how meaning is discovered latent in individual experience and in the shared experience with others.

The insightful perspectives of John Dewey and Abraham Maslow provide additional frameworks of observation. These two influential thinkers do not appear to hold similar world views at first glance: Dewey is usually considered a pragmatist in philosophy, while Maslow is often described as a naturalistic realist in psychology.[16] Taking a closer look, however, it is notable that both Dewey and Maslow challenged traditional scientific methods and explored common themes on human nature, as well as on essential aspects and phases of the self and spiritual experience. Moreover, both recognized the vital importance of human experience as they relate to the social and cultural contexts of environments. This principle of continuity in experience underlies a conjunction in Dewey's and Maslow's thoughts: that spirituality is a unified faculty of experience gained through a full participation of the self within a place.

What Makes a Place Spiritual?

> Spirit shares the contingency of existence but surveys it morally.
>
> George Santayana[17]

I began this chapter positing that Spirit of Place is essentially a fuller engagement of the self in place. We all have many experiences in our lives, perhaps concentrated more on individual relationships or stories than anything else, but they all "take place" in places with different depths and scales, such as my house, garden, street, neighborhood, town, community, and country. Many are experiences of now and then, of here and there, but also are related to, and alive in, our memories. Dewey writes that great experiences involve a sense of a wholeness wherein, "perception [that] occurs for its own sake is full realization of all the elements of our psychological being,"[18] and he continues,

> Happiness and delight ... come to be through a fulfillment that reaches to the depths of our being—one that is an adjustment of our whole being with the conditions of existence. In the process of living, attainment of a period of equilibrium is at the same time the initiation of a new relation to the environment, one that brings with it potency of new adjustments to be made through struggle. The time of consummation is also one of beginning anew. Any attempt to perpetuate beyond its term the enjoyment attending the time of fulfillment and harmony constitutes withdrawal from the world.[19]

However, not every experience is deemed good. Dewey also stresses that changes in the continuity of experiences are the necessary conditions for growth. Healthy growth is possible not so much through pure enjoyment as through struggle and critical and creative reflection. Dewey elaborates further that the quality of the experience has two aspects: one is an immediate aspect of agreeableness or disagreeableness that is obvious and easy to evaluate, and the other is its influence upon later experiences.[20] Moreover, this sense of continual growth is related to a place and one's identity. Dewey writes:

> Whenever the bond that binds the living creatures to his environment is broken, there is nothing that holds
> together the various factors and phases of the self. Thought, emotion, sense, purpose, impulsion fall apart, and
> are assigned to different compartments of our being. For their unity is found in the cooperative roles they play
> in active and receptive relations to the environment.[21]

Before moving forward, we need to distinguish "self" from such concepts as "psyche" and "soul" for the purpose of understanding the notion of "spirit." I will use Santayana's definitions as they most appropriately match the spiritual dimension of Dewey's thoughts. Dewey does not talk directly about the word spirit, but rather expresses it as "aesthetic" or "consummatory experience," whereas Santayana's writings often highlight Dewey's quest for the spiritual nature of an experience between organism and environment.

Santayana defines the psyche as the biological aspect of the soul and the soul as the moral expression of the psyche. He says, "Psyches take on the character of souls when spirit awakes in them."[22] In turn, the self is a historical person that conceives his or her individuality and is realized through social relations and moral qualities by re-attaching the soul to the world. Spirit, on the other hand, is "in fact involved in feeling and knowing life from the inside: not that spirit is then self-conscious, or sees nothing save its own states, but that it is then the medium and focus for apprehension, and imposes on its objects, categories, and qualities of its own."[23] Santayana elaborates further on the idea of spirit,

> The birth of spirit caps a long growth … Life follows the seed, through long periods of unconsciousness and
> moral nonexistence; whereas spirit lives in the quick interplay of each sensitive individual and the world …
> Yet the intensity and scope of this moral illumination, as well as the choice of characters lighted up, the
> order of the scenes and how long each shall last, all hang on the preparations nature may have made for this
> free entertainment.[24]

We now move to Maslow's humanistic psychology to further advance our empirical understanding of the self and identity.[25] He asserts that logical positivism in psychology, particularly dealing with personality, has been a failure because its treatments of human motivation are more about techniques to get rid of our discomfort (e.g., motivated behavior, goal seeking, and stimulus-responses) using deterministic animal behaviorism rather than addressing their true nature and origin.[26] In order to better define the essence of man's life-span personality and thus resolve the psychological reality of human beings, Maslow borrows an existentialist view of the human mind from phenomenology. Maslow's growth motivation (or self-motivation) theory considers the fundamental impulses of wanting, desiring, and yearning for pleasure as "basic needs." These basic needs interact with other social and personal needs in a hierarchical order, and thus the gratification of one need brings into consciousness other higher needs or pleasures and so on.[27]

In this way, Maslow argues, personality grows from childhood to maturity in the form of interactive and progressive gratification from immediate and basic needs to ultimate and sophisticated states: a process of self-actualization. Self-actualization is defined as an "ongoing actualization of potentials, capacities, and talents, as fulfillment of mission, as a fuller knowledge of, and acceptance of the person's own intrinsic nature, as an unceasing trend toward unity, integration or synergy with the person."[28] In his terms, the self realizes its own identity when it becomes actualized through the process of growth; which leads to more mature and spiritual goals that an individual mind aims to achieve for its own healthy and balanced personality.

In contrast with Santayana's lucid definitions (i.e., of the self, psyche, and spirit), there is no distinction between the self and the psyche in Maslow's terms. Carl G. Jung's work may be useful to clarify our discussion on the self, as it elaborates on the functions of the psyche and its relation to the self. Both Maslow and Jung share a humanistic or existential view in psychology, yet have slightly different definitions on matters of the self and ego: Maslow's definition of the self is rather loose, often expressed interchangeably with the term "ego," whereas for Jung the self is specifically defined as the spiritual goal of the psyche and different from the individual mind of the ego.

Jung argues that the goal of the psyche leads a growing child to maturity by pursuing its ontological development directed to the archetype of "the Self." In other words, the self is an unfulfilled core of the psyche that needs to be realized through the process of individuation, that is, by integrating one's personality and life experiences.[29] The self signifies the coherent whole, the unified consciousness and the unconscious being of a person, and has an inner "tendency to form various representations of a motif without losing their basic pattern."[30] Jung conceives of this basic pattern of the self as an Archetype, the wholeness of mind and body, that is "common to the whole of humanity."[31] His conception of the self is congruent with the conjunction of Dewey and Maslow's ideas of the self—the biological, psychological, and social meaning of the whole being.

In summary, I reasoned on the first proposition of this essay that Spirit of Place occurs essentially from a fuller engagement of the self in place, because the development of the self moves from individualistic concerns to harmony with other beings as it grows in wholeness (i.e., maturity, spirituality). This sense of whole being grows toward the realization of the self at the center of one's mind-and-body, and yet extends within and without one's surroundings. Therefore, Spirit of Place can grow toward the fullest sense of being in the environmental, social, and personal context with other existences. It results in biological, psychological, and social meanings coming together in a complimentary way, creating a sense balance and unity in a place.

How Does Spirit of Place Originate and Operate in Our Experience of Place?

> To perceive, a beholder must create his own experience
>
> John Dewey[32]

I have stated that Spirit of Place is inevitably associated with an aesthetic experience of place. This proposition demands a discussion about whether or not we can consider a spiritual experience to be aesthetic, and vice versa. In connection with our earlier discussion, the argument is whether or not the fullest sense of being—a consummatory sense of place—is an aesthetic experience. For some this proposition may sound intuitively obvious, but it is not easy to reason or verify its value by scientific empirical methods.

The difficulty concerning judging aesthetic matters of place is not in a lack of data or sophistication in technical means, but rather in the inherent nature of environmental phenomena, including the inexplicable nature of our total experience of landscapes.[33] Thus it is more reasonable to investigate what it means to have an aesthetic experience and how we experience a thing, a work of art, or a place aesthetically.

In fact, an aesthetic experience is circumscribed by descriptions of emotional states like satisfaction, joyfulness, pleasure, attraction, beauty, delight, poetic inspiration, or sometimes with such values as excellence, wholeness, perfection, meaningfulness, balance, unity, and others. The fact that there are multiple ways of describing aesthetics experiences proves that they are fundamentally qualitative events. Dewey contends that an experience is aesthetic when it has unity, that is, when a single quality pervades the entire experience. Dewey exemplifies aesthetic quality:

> In a work of art, acts, episodes, occurrences melt and fuse into unity, and yet do not disappear and lose their own character as they do so, just as in a genial conversation there is a continuous interchange and blending, and yet each speaker not only retains his own character but manifest it more clearly … The experience itself has a satisfying emotional quality because it possesses internal integration and fulfillment reached through ordered and organized movement. This artistic structure may be immediately felt. In so far, it is aesthetic.[34]

However, for Dewey this "Is-ness" as a whole quality is not a sum of different characteristics but exhibits two aspects: emotional and intellectual (immediate and reflective), and these two merge dialectically into one integral quality, the aesthetic. As previously stated, a spiritual experience is mostly intuitive and associated with an integrated sense of human faculties. Similar to Santayana's definition of spirit,[35] Dewey describes intuition this way:

> Intuition is that meeting of the old and new in which the readjustment involved in every form of consciousness is effected suddenly by means of a quick and unexpected harmony which in its bright abruptness is like a flash of revelation; although in fact it is prepared for by long and slow incubation.[36]

If we agree with Dewey's notion an aesthetic sense functions in the dialectic between feeling and thinking, merging into one integral aesthetic quality, then we can argue that an aesthetic experience is a sufficient, although not a necessary condition for a spiritual experience. The reason for this distinction becomes apparent in that the natures of an aesthetic experience and a spiritual experience of a place overlap: both experiences happen in the common perceptual fields that bind the subject (the perceiver) and the object (the perceived). However, how to judge evaluate a thing or a place would vary according to the properties, features, and social or environmental contexts of the object, as well as the knowledge, intellectual ability, or personal history of the subject: the former forms an objective substance; the latter makes all experiences unique, different, and individually subjective. In the end, however, no subject or object differentiation remains in a true aesthetic experience. As Dewey says:

> For the uniquely distinguishing feature of aesthetic experience is exactly the fact that no such distinction of self and object exists in it, since it is aesthetic in the degree in which organism and environment cooperate to institute an experience in which the two are so fully integrated that each disappears.[37]

Therefore, an aesthetic quality (is-ness) does not belong to whoever experiences a thing, a person, or a place, but to the experience itself. Everyday places and landscapes can acquire a richer and newer aesthetic quality when experienced, just as "a work of art is re-created every time it is aesthetically experienced."[38]

Similarly, Maslow's theory of motivation and self-fulfillment shows its relationship to an aesthetic need in an interactive hierarchy. It is defined as a state of finding self-fulfillment and of realizing one's creativity, by an awareness and exposure to the experience that develops from basic needs, including physiological and social needs. The satisfaction of basic needs, from physiological and biological needs to socialization—e.g., such feelings as safety, love, belongingness, respect, and self-esteem—involves a progressive interaction with the physical environment in a quest for safe survival; likewise, the satisfaction of socializing needs involves a comprehensive interaction with other human beings in society and culture for a more self-fulfilling understanding of life. For Maslow, the comprehensive interaction involves "two significant types of needs of the self-actualized person: cognitive and aesthetic needs."[39]

The cognitive need includes perceptual desires to know, to understand, and to explain, and entails the intellectual demand or will to acquire knowledge and systemize the universe. In Maslow's view, our cognitive capacities (perceptual, intellectual, learning) are also activated to seek higher values such as truth, wisdom, and understanding the cosmic mystery, all of which, if not satisfied, may become problems that threaten basic needs.[40] In this sense, the cognitive is the adjustive tool to satisfy both our basic needs and the expression of self-actualization. This supports Dewey's understanding that an aesthetic experience includes both intellectual and emotional dimensions.

Similarly, the aesthetic need, substantiated by overlaps with conative and cognitive needs, has an intermediate function as a tool to gratify basic needs and as a catalyst to activate the center of the self toward self-actualization. According to Maslow, the aesthetic need is a universal drive that can be identified in all healthy people in every culture and in every age.[41] There is a congruency in characteristics of both life's peak experiences (that are abstract) and descriptions of the daily experiences of self-actualizing people (that are practical), as Maslow writes:[42]

> The term peak experience is a generalization for the best moments of the human being, for the happiest moments of life, for experiences of ecstasy, rapture, bliss, of the greatest joy. I found that such experiences came from profound aesthetic experiences such as creative ecstasies, moments of mature love, perfect sexual experiences, parental love, experiences of natural childbirth, and many others. ... My own boiling down and condensation of the ... many description of how the world looked to them, from perhaps a hundred people, during and after peak experiences would be: truth, beauty, wholeness, dichotomy-transcendence, aliveness-process, uniqueness, perfection, necessity, completion, justice, order, simplicity, richness, effortlessness, playfulness, and self-sufficiency... These words are highly abstract. How could it be otherwise?

Maslow argues that this descriptive list of characteristics has empirical features acceptable to positivistic science, as they have public and measurable dimensions. He continues,[43]

I want to stress that these are claimed to be descriptive characteristics; the reports say these are facts about the worlds ... They are the descriptions of what the world appears to be, what it looks like, even, they claim, of what it is ... They are not "ought" or "should" statements, nor are they merely projections of the investigators' wishes.

"This list of characteristics is also simultaneously what the great religionists [theologians] and philosophers have valued, and this is practically the same list that most serious thinkers of mankind have agreed upon as the ultimate or highest value of life."[44] Maslow's identification of universal characteristics of self-actualizing persons informs us of what spirituality is:[45]

- They accept self, others, and nature. They respect and esteem themselves and others.
- They are not externally motivated or even goal-directed—rather their motivation is an internal one of growth and development.
- They have a sense of responsibility. They are mission-oriented, often on the basis of duty, or obligation rather than personal choice.
- They are capable of a continued freshness of appreciation. They repeatedly experience awe, pleasure, and wonder in their everyday world.
- They have mystic experiences, an oceanic feeling. They have experiences of ecstasy, awe, and wonder with feelings of limitless horizons opening up, followed by the conviction that the experience was important and had a carry-over into everyday life.
- They have a deep feeling of empathy, sympathy, or compassion for human beings and other forms of life in general.
- They have deep interpersonal relations with others.
- They are philosophical and creative.

To sum up, a peak or mystical experience is aesthetic.[46] This confirms that a spiritual experience is a sufficient condition for the aesthetic, whereas an aesthetic experience is a necessary condition or quality for spirituality. It follows that Spirit of Place is inevitably associated with an aesthetic experience of place and depends on possessing a phenomenological unity from a single quality, and subsequently allows for a fuller and richer experience of being in place.

How Can Spirit of Place Inform the Goodness of Community and Our Morals of Place-making?

What is perceived is charged with value

John Dewey[47]

In response to the third question that I named the "ethical dimension" of place, I articulated that Spirit of Place demands that the moral accountability of the individual be extendeded to encompass their community and its broader environment. This premise not only sounds intuitively true but also has a long tradition that goes back to the ancient Greek philosophers. For instance, Aristotle saw the word "spirit" as connected to the good, virtue, or unity because the nature of an organism stands at the base of life's hierarchy or *Telos*—the organizing principle in itself which directs the growth, development, and characteristic of that organism.[48] To put it differently, Spirit of Place connects the aesthetic sensibility (i.e., perceptual Is-ness) with moral accountability (i.e., Ought-ness) by making the individual transcend themselves in view of the larger whole (community, environment). This transcendental nature of Spirit is probably what makes a spiritual experience appear to be most esoteric and inaccessible.

In the previous section I argued that all spiritual experiences are aesthetic but not all aesthetic experiences are spiritual. At first sight, it would appear that the views shared by Dewey and Maslow that cover only descriptive values and characteristics (i.e., qualities) of the peak or consummatory experience would be insufficient to address ethical questions related to spirit of place. In general, a descriptive account of "being (and becoming) in place" is about how the world "is"; by contrast, a normative account of being (and becoming) in place is to prescribe the standards that we "ought" to live by to meet certain behavioral or other ways of being.[49] This suggests that genuine *genius loci* demands that we go deeper than the aesthetic, which raises a question about transcendental aspects residing in both aesthetic and ethical experiences. We do find three premises that overlap the transcendental aspects of both aesthetic "Is-ness" and ethical "Ought-ness" in Dewey and Maslow's views which are:

1. Both aesthetic Is-ness and moral Ought-ness allow us to view the environment experientially (not instrumentally), and toward respecting the values of a place in its own terms, rather than as a means for human use.
2. Both aesthetic Is-ness and moral Ought-ness involve emotional characteristics (on a biological and physiological base) and intellectual attitudes (on a cognitive and rational basis), such as our "feeling" of appreciation, reverence, and mystery toward a place that are universal, transcendent, and ultimate.
3. Both aesthetic Is-ness and moral Ought-ness contain symbolic meanings expanded to other beings, place, and nature in general.

The first premise concerns an ontological worldview of spiritual experience. Dewey and Maslow counter the traditional dualistic aesthetic argument, which views the good or beauty as residing either in the perceiver or in the perceived, and propose instead that it is a transaction between the subject and the object. In a traditional world view, moral accountability has been mostly considered as the right of the subject (i.e., anthropocentric), whereas the aesthetic attitude or stimulus has been focused on the object, not on the transactional quality of life, which is experience-centric and therefore bio-centric or eco-centric. For instance, a person who appreciates or treats a cow both aesthetically and ethically in its own right will never perceive her as a mere meatloaf. Similarly, my cat may appear to have a spirit because I love her for the way she is, not because she is useful. Love has been always our trans-personal-cultural quest for beauty and truth. It allows two organisms to become one, but can never be reduced to a mere pursuit of one's pleasure or self-interest.

Moreover, Dewey interprets the essential moral nature of the human mind as a way of being and becoming for its own sake, by connecting it with the cosmos.[50] Maslow's view, on the other hand, confirms that peak-experiences occur in the course of transforming and of transcending biological, social, and personal meanings of a developing being (or the self). Self-transcendence as an aesthetic state thus becomes a moral state of mind that allows the self to connect to something beyond itself and attain self-fulfillment without direct gains.

The second premise points to Dewey and Maslow's thoughts on aesthetic experience. Both share the view that the qualitative dimensions of aesthetic experiences vary from affective and rational, to sensuous and spiritual, and ultimately are associated with our moral stand toward the environment and community. Dewey says that "nature" has a meaning that includes the whole scheme of things, which includes the force of the imaginative and emotional word "universe," and that this emotional quality of the world in which and by which we live is a primary force for an aesthetic experience.[51] He rejects an "Ivory Tower" view of spiritual experience by connecting the higher experience with basic vital roots, and argues that a distinctive aesthetic experience such as mutual love and respect, reverence, and wonder occurs within morality.

Maslow defines some of our aesthetic terms, such as the experience of appreciation, wonder, zest, connoisseurship, mystery, and admiration as end-experience, by which he means "the ultimate biological pleasure (zestful experience) that is an automatic, non-instrumental, unsought-for, unmotivated by-product of being alive and healthy."[52] He names it "the feeling of being."

> There were the same feelings of a limitless horizon opening up to the vision, the feeling of being simultaneously more powerful and also more helpless than one ever was before, the feeling of great ecstasy and wonder and awe, the loss of placing in time and space with, finally the conviction that something extremely important and valuable had happened, so that the man is to some extent transformed and strengthened even in his daily life by such experiences.[53]

Both Dewey and Maslow emphasize "feeling" as a fundamental, trans-culturally inherited and symbolic aspect of the self, beyond a biological need for survival. Maslow explains that such basic needs, as safety, security, belongingness, love, respect, and self-esteem are integrative feelings which move upward to consciousness.

These feelings transcend the self toward others, and are essentially biological, emotionally universal, and ultimately spiritual —the vital moral quality of Maslow's peak experience.

Finally, the third premise marks a symbolic dimension of spiritual experience that exists in both aesthetic sensibility and moral accountability. It is a primary and imaginative force in aesthetic experience, according to Dewey, because it reveals, extends, and regenerates its sympathetic and meaningful associations with the self, others, and place. Dewey describes the primacy of imagination and art in the good as follows,

> Imagination is the chief instrument of the good. It is more or less a commonplace to say that a person's ideal and treatment of his fellows are dependent upon his power to put himself imaginatively in their place. But, the primacy of the imagination extends far beyond the scope of direct personal relationships ... The historic alliance of religion and art has its roots in this common quality. Hence, it is that art is more moral than moralities.[54]

Symbolic transformation is the basic mode of analogy and our metaphorical thinking and enables us to recognize the importance of expressive forms for all human understanding and intellectual activities in both science and art, myth and spiritual experience.[55] "We see images, we reproduce images, we retain images in our memory,"[56] says philosopher Gaston Bachelard. The various images are derived from the liberties that our mind takes with nature, and this image or the imaged value does not designate the nature of the mind but transcends all the premises of sensibility.[57]

This symbolic function of being and becoming (i.e., the self) is the essence of Maslow's peak experience and of spirituality.[58] The transcendental liberty and the imaginative power of spiritual experience become manifest through the work of art, the mind of a painter, or in the soul of a poet. Poetry is a symbolic voice of life. A poetic image captures the very depth of our being and a poet's word strikes the very meaning of our life in place. Both Dewey and Maslow argue that a spiritual person is a morally healthy person who does not depend on the definite dichotomy of good and evil,[59] because s/he does not create or value the way we live, but lives the way we create or value. This is why a great moral and spiritual leader always has a highly symbolic and poetic voice.

In summary, Spirit of Place transcends aesthetic experiences toward moral actions. It glues "Is-ness" with "Ought-ness" of place through aesthetic exploration that is both emotional and intellectual, and through symbolic projection to all dimensions of an environment. To put it metaphorically, the environment gives us soil that provides the embryonic potentials, the seed for our self-growing, and society and culture act as sun and water to foster our aesthetic needs for a fuller moral being.

Conclusion

Beginning with the premise that the existence of *genius loci* is real and connected to our spirituality, and therefore as something to strive for in place-making, this chapter describes and explains the aspects of spirituality that relate to our existential, aesthetic, and ethical relationship to our environment. The underlying premise is that spirituality is an ongoing process of achieving a sense of wholeness inevitably associated with a deeper identification with the transpersonal, social, and environmental values of a place. Supported by a critical analysis of perspectives shared by Dewey and Maslow I have advanced that *genius loci* is (1) essentially a fuller engagement of the self in place; (2) fundamentally an aesthetic experience of place; and (3) ultimately transcends the moral accountability of the individual toward the community and its broader environment.

Such an expansion of the concept spirituality toward a more general concept of the self, aesthetic, and moral experience suggests that spiritual experience can be seen as a more all-embracing and place-bound type of experience. This permits a more descriptive, environmental, value-oriented, and therefore clear and useful translation of such concepts and ideas into place-making. A good design of place could then motivate us to have a fuller sense of the self in a place, enliven our meaningful associations with all of its elements, features, and patterns, and inspire us to transcend our narrow notion of self-bound aesthetic delight and moral fulfillment so that we may encompass the whole world.

Endnotes

1   Relph, Edward (1976). *Place and Placeless.* London: Pion Limited.

2   Jackson, John B. (1994). *A Sense of Place, a Sense of Time.* New Haven, CT and London: Yale University Press, p. 158.

3   Ibid.

4   Tuan, Yi-Fu (1977). *Space and Place: The Perspective of Experience.* Minneapolis, MN: University of Minnesota Press.

5   Norberg-Schulz, Christian (1980). *Genius Loci: Towards a Phenomenology of Architecture.* New York, NY: Rizzoli.

6   Jivén, Gunila and Peter J. Larkham (2003). Sense of Place, Authenticity and Character: A Commentary. *Journal of Urban Design* 8(1), pp. 67–81.

7   Dewey, John (1958). *Experience and Nature.* New York, NY: Dover Publications, p. 251.

8   Norberg-Schulz, Christian (1971). *Existence, Space, and Architecture.* London: Studio Vista, p. 11.

9   *The Routledge Encyclopedia of Philosophy*, http://www.rep.routledge.com (accessed July 19, 2014).

10   Santayana, George and Martin A. Coleman (2009[1936]). Dewey's Naturalistic Metaphysics, in *The Essential Santayana: Selected Writings.* Bloomington, IN: Indiana University Press, pp. 609–21.

11   Santayana, George and Martin A. Coleman (2009[1930]). The Scope of Natural Philosophy, in *The Essential Santayana: Selected Writings.* Bloomington, IN: Indiana University Press, p. 174.

12   Ibid.

13   Ibid., p. 610.

14   Rathunde, Kevin (2001). Toward a Psychology of Optimal Human Functioning: What Positive Psychology Can Learn from the "Experiential Turns" of James, Dewey, and Maslow. *Journal of Humanistic Psychology* 41(1), p. 135.

15   Zube, Ervin H., Sell, J.L. and J.G. Taylor (1982). Landscape Perception: Research, Application and Theory. *Landscape Planning* 9(1), pp. 1–33.

16   Lawrence, Dennis J. and J. Francis Powers (1974). Dewey, Maslow, and Consummatory Experience. *Journal of Aesthetic Education* 8(4), pp. 51–63.

17   Santayana, George and Martin A. Coleman (2009[1940]). The Nature of Spirit. *The Essential Santayana: Selected Writings.* Bloomington, IN: Indiana University Press, pp. 346–56.

18   Dewey, John (1934). *Art as Experience.* New York, NY: A Perigee Book, p. 256.

19   Ibid., p. 17.

20   Dewey, John (1938). *Experience and Education.* New York, NY: Touchstone, pp. 27–8.

21   Dewey (1934). *Art as Experience*, p. 252.

22   Santayana and Coleman. The Nature of Spirit. *The Essential Santayana: Selected Writings*, p. 355.

23   Ibid., pp. 355–6.

24   Ibid.

25   Maslow, Abraham H. (1954). *Motivation and Personality.* New York, NY: Harper & Row Publishers.

26   Maslow, Abraham H. (1968). *Toward a Psychology of Being.* New York, NY: Van Nostrand Reinhold, p. 10.

27   Ibid., p. 30.

28   Ibid., p. 25.

29   Jung, Carl Gustav (ed.) (1964). *Man and His Symbols.* New York, NY: Dell Publishing, p. 40.

30   Ibid., p. 58.

31   Jung, Carl Gustav (1940). *The Integration of the Personality.* London: Routledge & Kegan Paul Ltd, p. 50.

32   Dewey (1934). *Art as Experience*, p. 54.

33   Ibid., p. 54.

34   Ibid., pp. 37–8.

35   See note 25.

36   Dewey (1934). *Art as Experience*, p. 266.

37   Ibid., p. 249.

38   Ibid., p. 256.

39   Lawrence and Powers (1974). Dewey, Maslow, and Consummatory Experience, p. 58.

40   Maslow (1954). *Motivation and Personality*, p. 47.

41   Ibid., p. 51.

42   Maslow, Abraham H. (1971). *The Farther Reaches of Human Nature.* London: Penguin Compass, pp. 101–2.

43   Ibid., p. 102.

44 Ibid., p. 104.

45 Maslow (1968). *Toward a Psychology of Being.*

46 Maslow (1954). *Motivation and Personality.*

47 Dewey (1934). *Art as Experience*, p. 256.

48 Lear, Jonathan (1988). *Aristotle: The Desire to Understand.* New York, NY: Cambridge University Press, pp. 21–5.

49 Fox, Warwick (2006). *A Theory of General Ethics: Human Relationships, Nature, and the Built Environment.* Cambridge, MA: The MIT Press, p. 3.

50 Sartwell, Crispin (2009). Dewey and Taoism: Teleology and Art. *Journal of Aesthetic Education* 43(1), pp. 30–40.

51 Dewey (1934). *Art as Experience*, p. 333.

52 Maslow (1954), *Motivation and Personality*, p. 236.

53 Ibid., pp. 164–5.

54 Ibid., p. 348.

55 Langer, Susanne K. (1942). *Philosophy in a New Key.* Cambridge, MA: Mentor Books with Harvard University Press, p. vii.

56 Bachelard, Gaston (1969). *The Poetics of Space.* Boston, MA: Beacon Press, translated by Maria Jolas, originally published in French under the title La poétique de l'espace, 1958, Presses Universitaires de France, p. xxxiv.

57 Ibid., pp. xxxiv–xxxv.

58 See note 45, universal characteristics of self-actualizing persons.

59 Dewey (1934). *Art as Experience*, pp. 348–9.

Chapter 7

Neophilia, Spirituality, and Architecture

Paul Tesar

> Things are such, that someone lifting a cup, or watching the rain, petting a dog or singing, just singing–could be doing as much for this universe as anyone.
>
> Rumi[1]

Introduction

Rumi's words, suggesting that something as seemingly inconsequential as "watching the rain" or "petting a dog"—a simple act of communion with an event of nature or another living creature—could have significance far beyond the specific moment, act as an apt reminder of the foundation from which many of our higher aspirations for meaning grow: the rich field of beings, things, activities, and events that we encounter in the course of our everyday existence. While they may merely constitute the body of our unquestioned quotidian experience—often on the margins of our awareness and simply taken for granted—they at the same time offer us the opportunity to dignify the ordinary, the repetitive, and the familiar with our mindful attention and in doing so perhaps gain a glimpse of their potential for deeper meaning.

Human experience is inevitably suspended between the familiar and the new. We remember, recognize, and anticipate things we have experienced, and we also constantly confront things that are unfamiliar to us. The familiar is generally connected with feelings of security, predictability, contentment, and comfort, the new with feelings of curiosity, stimulation, excitement, and adventure. The familiar makes us feel safe; the new makes us feel alive. Pushed out of balance with each other, however, the all too familiar may give rise to feelings of stagnation, idleness, complacency, and boredom—and to an increased desire for change—the ever new to feelings of confusion, uncertainty, danger, and anxiety, and to a longing for a modicum of continuity in our daily existence. While we certainly can observe significant variations and fluctuations in our situational need or tolerance for familiarity or novelty—individually, socially, culturally—there nevertheless seems to be a kind of "mental homeostasis" at work that tries to keep the proportions of familiarity and novelty in our experience within an acceptable range.[2] It is as perilous to our mental health to be overwhelmed by an avalanche of the new, as it is to feel suffocated by pervasive and unchanging familiarity.[3] Life happens on the constantly moving threshold between the familiar and the new.

Both, the two dogs in the doorway of a bar and the children on the stoop of their house, have their backs turned toward their home, the place they know and trust, where their days start and end, where they are fed and where they sleep, and—quite predictably—their noses toward the street, where "interesting" new things are likely to happen. The familiar always is the dominant "ground" behind us, the point of departure for grasping the "figures" of the new in front of us. The existential value of familiarity lies in the fact that the recurrence of familiar persons, things, places, and events in the stream of life makes them predictable and our environment safe. Predictability allows us to anticipate and therefore to react through already established habitual patterns. Being able to create an environment that allows us to relegate recurring life-situations to the realm of the familiar in turn liberates our limited mental and emotional capacity for other tasks,[4] whether it is to explore new things that interest us or to dwell longer on familiar ones in order to get them to know better and deeper.

Neophilia

For reasons too many and too complex to entertain here in any detail, this systemic balance between the familiar and the new has become increasingly more lopsided in favor of a disproportionate supply and avidity for the new in our contemporary world. It is probably not too much of an exaggeration to say that we seem to

Figure 7.1   On the Threshold between the Familiar and the New: a) Two Dogs in Paris b) Two Children
               in Bergen, Norway
Source: Photographs courtesy of Paul Tesar.

live in an age dominated by neophilia: the ubiquitous supply and concomitant compulsive need for constant novelty that seems as pathological as its opposite extreme—neophobia—the persistent and abnormal fear of anything new. The possible culprits for this development could be many. Several of Konrad Lorenz's *Civilized Man's Eight Deadly Sins*[5] come to mind. For example, in the chapter on *Man's Race Against Himself* Lorenz reminds us that our competitive greed for material goods, as well as our enervating haste, not only lead to a progressive escalation of ever new wants of mankind, but more importantly to a resulting atrophy of the human faculty for reflection, the nourishment of our conscience, and the development of a responsible morality. In the chapter *Entropy of Feeling* Lorenz points to the systemic interdependence of pleasure and pain (cessation of pain will register as "pleasure," for instance), and to the fact that our increasing intolerance for unpleasant experiences—as well as our success in finding ever new ways to avoid them—is connected to our decreasing sensitivity for pleasant ones ("saturation"), and to the constant pursuit of ever new stimulation in the futile hope to offset a growing sense of emotional emptiness. Similar issues have been raised by other voices since Lorenz, focusing mainly on the causes and the environmental and social consequences of the overproduction and overconsumption of material goods.[6] But it is particularly the environment of information overconsumption in which we live today—the realm of our immaterial exchanges with the world—which seems to accelerate our appetite for incessant novelty and change and at the same time leads to our incapacity to digest and to make sense of it. The more we live in an environment of chronic restlessness and distraction, surrounded by ever more irrelevant "noise," the more we tend to lose the inclination of doing or thinking something again: in other words to devote attention to what we already know, to keep it alive and relevant.

    Few will dispute the fact that we have been wasteful for too long with our limited resources of matter and energy, pushing many fragile ecosystems of our natural environment to the verge of collapse and thereby threatening our physical survival. What is sometimes overlooked, however, is that we are equally wasteful when we mindlessly discard beliefs, ideas, insights, and values that we developed over long periods of time and that were an important foundation for living in harmony with the unseen order of things around us. Though perhaps more elusive, the consequences for the survival of the human race are equally dire: a loss of our sense of origin, of continuity, of identity, of attachment, and belonging—a sort of cultural amnesia that is spread by our unhealthy diet of overindulgence with the ever new and unprecedented.

Spirituality

Against the backdrop of this systemically unbalanced cultural environment, it should not be surprising that we can observe a renewed and rising desire for a counterbalance, particularly in the over-producing and over-consuming capitalistic consumer societies of today: a perceived need for slowing down, for "voluntary simplicity,"[7] for the re-discovery and re-affirmation of "old knowledge," for contemplation, reflection, and meditation, and generally for a more mindful connection to nature and to other human and non-human beings. In other words, for many things we tend to associate with some notion of spirituality.

In this context "spirituality" refers less to its intense and focused forms—sacred, transcendent, exalted—but rather to its more profane and secular manifestations as they arise from everyday and repetitive encounters with the ordinary and familiar things that are often not regarded as "spiritual." Moreover, the argument is more focused on some of the necessary surrounding conditions of spirituality that would increase the chances of its re-emergence as a significant cultural presence, particularly as these conditions relate to the expressive and communicative dimensions of architecture.

In considering the balance between familiarity and novelty as part of the human condition, it becomes obvious that the success of so many things in our individual or collective existence depends on repetition: our cognitive development, the sustainment of memory, the notions of improvement and refinement, the mastery of skills and abilities (we will never become a master of anything if we do it only once), our desire to penetrate the nature of something, and ultimately the whole idea of cultural evolution would not be possible without repetition. Therefore, we cannot be content only to think, to generate, to invent, and to create the new, we also need to perpetually re-think, re-generate, re-invent, and re-create what we already know if we want to retain, expand, differentiate, and strengthen our understandings.

In this context it is worth noting that the predominance of the repetitive and the familiar is particularly pronounced in the life of virtually all major spiritual and faith communities, pursued through the written codification of long-established fundamental beliefs and their perennial re-enactment in rituals and ceremonies, as well as through the typification of the places of worship: the fundamental spatial and symbolic characteristics of churches, temples, synagogues, shrines, and mosques tend to adhere to established and predictable architectural patterns over long periods of time. Similarly, monastic communities prescribe and regulate not only the layout and symbolism of their physical environments, but also the sequence of daily activities—when and how to pray, work, eat, sleep—and even how to dress ("habits"). It is probably fair to assume that this execution of repetitive and habitual acts contributes to the ability of the members of the community to broaden their spiritual horizons by bringing mindful attention to the repetitive tasks of everyday life and thereby revealing the depth of meaning available in the ordinary.

Perhaps too much of our renewed contemporary interest in the nature, purpose, and value of spirituality in human affairs tends to approach it as something that we experience in a realm that lies somewhere beyond ordinary existence: as extra-ordinary places, activities, and events, often seen as an escape from the relentless grind of profane life and as a refuge for renewal to compensate for what is missing in our spiritually vacuous quotidian experience. Generally more by default than by design, this notion of spirituality, particularly if pursued primarily as an individual quest, runs the risk of acquiring a tinge of elitism and self-indulgence, and may be one of the reasons why we still can observe a certain amount of social skepticism towards its validity and cultural relevance beyond the benefits it may bring to the individual who engages in its practices.

In distinction to traditional cultures, where everyday community life tended to be infused with spiritual meanings, the intimate connection between spirituality and the larger cultural context no longer exists in most Western cultures, and a predominant focus on its exultant aspects may actually exacerbate this trend and separate it even more from life as we know it. This raises the question whether there is a way of thinking about spirituality in a less exalted way so that it again could be seen as a more natural and integral part of our daily lives.

An analogous concern was raised about the cultural function and significance of aesthetics. In the introductory chapter of his seminal 1934 book *Art as Experience* John Dewey takes the position that we need a different attitude toward art and aesthetics if they are to have a more significant role to play in society. He observes:

> A primary task is ... to restore the continuity between the refined and intensified forms of experience that are works of art and the everyday events, doings, and sufferings that are universally recognized to constitute experience. Mountain peaks do not float unsupported; they do not even just rest upon the earth. They are the earth in one of its manifest operations.

> In order to understand the meaning of artistic products, we have to forget them for a time, to turn aside from them and have recourse to the ordinary forces and conditions of experience that we do not usually regard as esthetic. We must arrive at a theory of art by means of a detour.

> The factors that have glorified fine art by setting it upon a far-off pedestal did not arise in the realm of art nor is their influence confined to the arts. For many persons an aura of mingled awe and unreality encompasses the 'spiritual' and the 'ideal' while 'matter' has become by contrast a term of depreciation, something to be explained away or apologized for. The forces at work are those that have removed religion as well as fine art from the scope of the common or community life.[8]

If in the preceding quotes we substitute "art" or "esthetic" with terms such as "spirituality" or "spiritual," Dewey's argument decrying the social isolation of art may characterize an analogous situation of spirituality in today's society as well. Applied to the context of architecture the question then becomes: how should we think about the nature of its phenomenal dimension so that it could facilitate the possibility of more integral and mindful, even if maybe not quite "spiritual" connections, with our human-made environment?

Architecture

Architecture has always been predestined to create environments that "mediate"[9] effectively between "heaven and earth" and that promote our connection to the spiritual realm through phenomenal means in special sacred places. But due to its ever-present utilitarian basis, material reality, and its function as a stage for our public life, architecture has also been equally connected and continuous with our communal quotidian existence. While affected by neophile tendencies as the rest of our culture, architecture nevertheless also has by its very nature the more fundamental opportunity to act as an effective form of resistance to this trend. By reintegrating the familiar with the new and re-establishing a productive balance between the two, it has the means to re-cultivate the cultural substrate from which a spiritual dimension of our quotidian experience would be more likely to grow again naturally, like blossoms on a healthy tree.

Types

The all-but-abandoned notion of types—for millennia the predominant framework within which architecture was produced and experienced—may have an important role to play in all of this, because types have acted as effective frameworks of continuity *as well as* vehicles for change. They epitomize the notion of the threshold. They allow the simultaneous perception of familiarity and novelty: of the familiar in the repetition of the underlying essence of the type, and of the new in each particular and specific instantiation and transformation, filling it with new meaning and keeping it alive. Types, in architecture and in general, may be among our most important shared frames of reference, the contexts within which we experience and understand the identity and meaning of things, places, and events as well as their changes over time. Types fulfill an important cognitive function because everything we experience we experience in what social phenomenology calls "Sinnzusammenhang" and "Erfahrungszusammenhang" (the relevant contexts of meaning and of experience respectively).[10]

Their recurrences are the connective tissue that makes our experiences "hang together" in time and allow us to interpret something not as an isolated event, but in a pre-existing context of relevant past experiences and meanings, activated as we are trying to make sense of something similar that is happening in the present.

The primary un-reflected and "natural" experiential context of a thing, place, or event therefore lies mainly in its relationship to other things, places or events of the same kind. For instance, we typically will experience the character, identity, and ultimately the meaning of houses, columns, or doors as they are similar to or different from other houses, columns, or doors we know from experience. Their meaning—not the meaning they have to me individually, but the one they have for us collectively—emerges from the nature, the direction, and the degree of deviation from an imagined "conflated prototype" we share: we perceive them as part of an inter-subjective "expressive system,"[11] like a theme with variations in music. With every repetition and variation a type becomes more differentiated and more "loaded" with evolving meaning. On the one hand this fact makes types experientially rich and significant, reverberating on many layers beyond the present instance. On the other hand it is exactly this "baggage" that appears to make them stand in the way of progress and innovation, preserving a status quo that some of us want to eliminate and replace, for sometimes legitimate and necessary reasons, and other times for frivolous and idiosyncratic motives.

If change and novelty is what motivates us in our architectural production, then one of the first things we need to do is to debunk, unload, undo, "de-typify" these straitjackets. Once liberated from historic and semantic ballast, ever new and unprecedented forms can be invented and created. They shift the context away from the realm of the socially constructed and shared types we know from experience, to a new dominance of the creative and free imagination of the individual or simply to the specific expression of ever-changing situational necessities and expediencies, both fundamentally inimical to any notion of repetition and typification. This has the sometimes intended and sometimes unintended effect of destabilizing and eventually undermining and destroying a system based on habitual repetitions of underlying essences with their appendant rich spectrum of variations and transformations: in other words the stock of our common and socially shared inter-subjective knowledge of architectural types.

Today many of our biologically and culturally evolved frames of reference have been increasingly pushed aside in favor of others that don't facilitate the development and maintenance of any sense of a communicative community. This trend is particularly tragic in a discipline like architecture, if we understand it as an *inclusive* social and public art—the art of building buildings, places, and communities, as *our* home on earth—rather than as an *exclusive* fine art with the attendant freedom to explore and to express subjective, personal, and maybe even private subject matter presented to pre-selected and informed audiences. Architecture, perhaps more than any other human endeavor, historically has shown an almost unlimited potential to articulate and to manifest our shared values, ideals, aspirations, and memories in the public realm in long-lasting form: as a material frame of reference that we experience together in the act of daily living.

This significant social function of architecture is now increasingly called into question. It does not seem legitimate any more to adhere to types as purveyors of these common denominators as they are deemed to be grounded in specific cultural contexts and therefore unable to act as "shared frames of reference" in a multi-cultural and global environment. But the notion of types—the consequence of the act of categorizing and differentiating—is too fundamental to human nature and to an aesthetically and cognitively engaged relationship to the physical world around us to be simply abandoned as irrelevant and no longer applicable. Architectural types exist on many levels, from those that are specific and unique to a particular culture, to other more general ones that show up in many cultures in different guises, to yet others that seem almost universal to the point that they are sometimes called "archetypes."[12]

The fact that an individual thing belongs to a class or species of things that are unified by certain shared characteristics—that it is a representative of a type—does not only *not* militate against the unique and specific identity and expressiveness of any individual member, but on the contrary, it actually makes it more apparent and stronger by the possibility of a simultaneous perception of identity and difference. The perceived dimension of familiarity—an act of re-cognition—establishes an immediate basis of relevance. More importantly, it simultaneously liberates our capacities for the perception and interpretation of the *specific differences* and characteristics and their meanings: we immediately recognize that this thing is *a* rose, and then can readily devote our whole attention to its unique and specific identity—to *this* rose as we experience it as a presence in the "here and now."

As an example let us look at one of the most familiar of all "types" in human experience: our face. Our faces are all composed of the same components—a forehead, eyebrows, eyes, cheeks, ears, a nose, lips, a chin, etc.—and yet nature has somehow managed to make every one of us new and unique. Do we ever get tired of looking at a new face simply because we have seen so many of them and because they are *essentially* all alike? On the contrary, exactly because we are so familiar with them, we penetrate to the subtleties that carry a myriad of profound and differentiated meanings and associations. Portraits fascinate us because they allow us to dwell on what a painter or a photographer has discovered in a face, in *this particular face*, and in this particular facial expression, among all the many others we have experienced until now. In other words, far from numbing us into a stupor, a significant dimension of familiarity and repetition may actually help to facilitate our *relation to* and a *dialogue with* something. Moreover, relations—to humans, animals, places, or things—usually do not develop out of singular first encounters, but out of repeated experiences and condense themselves over time to a sense of familiarity and intimacy.

In his seminal 1922 book *Ich und Du* (translated into English as *I and Thou*) Martin Buber proposes the basic thesis that the world is given to us in a twofold attitude in accordance with the two basic word-pairs we can speak: *I-You* and *I-It*. There is no *I* in and of itself, but only the *I* of one of these two word pairs. The *I* of the *I-You* encounters the world in a relation. Relation is always mutual: I become an *I* only through *You*. The *I* of the *I-It* perceives the world as experience: its *It* refers to things among other things.[13]

But humans can enter *I-You* relationships not only with their fellow human beings, but also with things, with nature, and with spiritual beings. The difference between "relation" and "experience," between *You* and *It*, is also that between *presence* and *object*, in other words the difference between something that comes to life as a *You* through the presence of my *I*, and something that has an autonomous existence without me. *I-You* is always an unmediated mutual presence. We encounter a being, we experience some-thing. Buber illustrates this difference with a story. An old linden tree once stood along a path that he had walked time and time again. He always accepted it as it was given to him, until he once was overcome by this question: now, that I encounter it, the linden tree is as it is —but how is it before, and how is it after our encounter? What is it when no experience approaches it? Botany could tell him nothing about the properties of this linden tree that he experienced, nothing about the space that it shared with him. But there was a moment when he accepted this It-thing, that had become a featureless and abstract category, as a presence that had waited for him to once again become the blooming, scented, and rustling linden tree of the world of his senses, by speaking Goethe's words: *"Du bist es also!"*—*"So, it's You!"*[14]

Attention

Buber's story is a good example of how something utterly familiar can be experienced in an entirely new way, almost as if for the first time, and at the same time feel like suddenly having found a long lost friend that has always been there "waiting" for him: the familiar and the new become one. Buber does not offer us an account of what may have caused this shift in attention and change in his attitude. It may have been an inexplicable instance of divine grace, but more likely simply had to do with a changed state of mind that was triggered by a momentary unusual constellation of the sensory qualities surrounding the familiar object of perception, focusing his attention on the "here and now," and thus transforming the expected into the unexpected, the ordinary into the extraordinary, "perception" into "relation," and an "It" into a "You."

The dimension of repetition inherent in architectural types has the potential to facilitate comparable dynamics in our experience of the built environment: it increases our ability to focus our attention on what makes the familiar specific, unique, and new—we could say what makes it "strangely familiar" by revealing its hidden wonder and mystery, thus bringing us a step closer to the beginning of a spiritual connection. Such revelations, while seemingly intuitive, sudden, and happening in the present, often have a history of something that was present but obscure in our consciousness. They are not so much the discovery of something new as the "uncovering" of something we have known all along but without actually knowing that we knew it.

Repetition in the form of types is not only of value in reducing the "demand" side of our overstressed attention economy in a neophile environment: it is equally the source of aesthetic delight. It is not too far-fetched a notion to assume that our propensity to experience the repetitious manifestations of like things and their variations, architectural or otherwise, with a certain degree of pleasure is rooted in the evolutionary past of our species:

in our experiences with the vastly repetitive yet always unique forms of life and nature, as well as with the repetitive diurnal and seasonal patterns, over long periods of time. They have deposited themselves in our DNA and are part of the cognitive equipment and predisposition with which we intuitively encounter the world around us.[15]

By contrast, it is probably fair to say that it is one of the unchallenged prejudices of designers and of design education today that our core identity is wrapped up in us being among the primary agents of change in society, and that we somehow have an obligation to be perpetual purveyors of creativity, originality, and novelty. We are almost terrified to repeat something we have done before, probably because we fear that any repetition could be seen as a sign of intellectual laziness, convenience, or complacency, or that we somehow don't have the capability, or simply not the will, to work hard enough to come up with something new.

This disproportionate emphasis on invention and novelty is probably a consequence of architecture's alignment with fine art, from which it inherited the "shock and awe" aspirations of the avant-garde in the 20th century: it has become a status symbol for architects, even if it is in constant friction with their other identity and responsibility as providers of a "professional service," to be an *enfant terrible*, to be innovative, unconventional, provocative, and controversial. This tendency to destabilize our patterns of perception and expectation, and—by design or by default—to undermine the dimensions of familiarity in our environment, has become not only a badge of honor for the "serious practitioners" of the art of architecture, but an economic necessity as well. Professional success today largely depends on the skill of attracting attention to one's work through novelty.

But what may be good for the demand side of the business, where receiving attention through conspicuous production is more and more becoming *the* capital of the trade, is damaging to the supply side of the human attention economy. As long as architecture acts as a major player in this heated competition for our superficial attention it will have difficulty engaging us in any kind of "mindful attention" to the subtlety of something. The alternative of a more differentiated and nuanced approach lies perhaps in strategies that would acknowledge typological precedents not by simply restating them, but by reinterpreting and transforming them in light of changing cultural, social, or technological circumstances, thereby giving our interpretive attention a foothold for the appreciation of subtleties as well as a framework for the acceptance of their new dimensions.[16]

There is much in our environment that beckons for our attention, and receiving our attention is the first threshold to be surmounted if we are to be engaged with something. Attention is one of the most basic gifts we can bestow: a distinction that separates a person, a thing, or an event from the vast sea of the unattended. Our desire to uncover layers that lie beyond the surfaces of things seems to be one of the fundamental conditions for developing a spiritual relationship. It allows our attention not to be ravaged by clamors forced upon us, but to be freely given to something we have discovered, liberated from its former irrelevance, and thus admitted to the realm of the world that truly matters to us.

Conclusion

The perceived identities and meanings of persons, animals, things, and places—how we think about them, how we remember them, how we relate to them, and ultimately why we love them—may tend to reside more in their repetitive and typical characteristics than any singular and unique ones, but they are ultimately dependent on each other.

The realms of the familiar and the new, the forces of continuity and change—historically connected with each other by tugging at the same core of unifying cultural conventions, customs, beliefs, and traditions—have now become largely segregated, compartmentalized, adversarial, and mutually polarizing. In the case of architecture there is on the one hand an often flagrant, unfettered, and self-centered avant-garde, whose protagonists are constantly stumbling over themselves in their breathless pursuit of opportunities to baffle and to confound their fellow human beings with a constant flow of astonishing novelty. At the other extreme this sets the stage for a rather widespread vapid, superficial, and sentimental "traditionalism," an illusionary refuge into an inauthentic make-believe world that never was.

Neither one nor the other is capable of providing the kind of fertile ground in which any spiritual dimension of human experience could gain a foothold again, let alone grow and thrive. What is missing is a connective center, without which both forces become unmoored from one another and spin off into senseless and cartoonish perversions of the legitimate cultural function and purpose they both should have.

It is questionable whether we will ever be able to regain this center with architecture as an important constituent part, but we may more readily find it in the realm of the common, ordinary, quotidian world we share than on its fringes. It is not where the higher reaches of spirituality will reside, but it may well be where we need to begin if we want to recover its significance for our culture.

Endnotes

1 Ladinsky, Daniel with Nancy Owen Barton (2012). *The Purity of Desire: 100 Poems of Rumi.* New York, NY: Penguin, p. 27.
2 See Laszlo, Ervin (1969). *System, Structure, and Experience: Toward a Scientific Theory of Mind.* New York, NY: Gordon and Breach. Laszlo describes the interactions between humans and their environments in terms of their operation as "Self-stabilizing Self-organizing Systems" on the physiological, perceptual-cognitive, and cultural (scientific, aesthetic, and religious) level. Through the simultaneous processes of "manipulative projection" and "adaptive mapping" homeostatically balanced steady states can be achieved.
3 See Selye, Hans (1956). *The Stress of Life.* New York, NY: Mcgraw-Hill. Selye discusses the causes of physical and mental health and illness and identifies desirable versus distressing degrees of stress, or "stress without distress," in this classical study on the subject.
4 Knötig, Helmut (1980). General Interaction Scheme. *Humanökologische Blätter* 9, pp. 71–2. Knötig discusses the "selective advantage" (referring to natural selection) of being able to achieve the "highest degree of predictability of the environment with the least amount of information processing effort," a tendency observable in all higher forms of life.
5 See Lorenz, Konrad (1974). *Civilized Man's Eight Deadly Sins.* New York, NY: Hartcourt Brace Jovanovich. In addition to the two chapters mentioned, Lorenz also discusses such issues as overpopulation, devastation of the environment, the break with tradition, and indoctrinability.
6 See De Graaf, John, Wann, David and Thomas H. Naylor (2001). *Affluenza: The All-consuming Epidemic.* San Francisco, CA: Berrett-Koehler; and Schor, Juliet (1998). *The Overspent American: Why We Want What We Don't Need.* New York, NY: Basic Books.
7 Elgin, Duane and Arnold Mitchell (1977). Voluntary Simplicity. *Co-evolution Quarterly* (Summer), p. 2. The authors characterize this notion as "living in a way that is outwardly simple and inwardly rich ... embracing frugality of consumption, a strong sense of environmental urgency, ... and an intention to realize our higher human potential—both psychological and spiritual—in community with others."
8 Dewey, John (1979). *Art as Experience.* New York, NY: Paragon Books, pp. 3, 4 and 6.
9 See Barrie, Thomas (2010). *The Sacred In-Between: The Mediating Roles of Architecture.* New York, NY: Routledge.
10 See Schütz, Alfred (1981). *Der sinnhafte Aufbau der sozialen Welt.* Frankfurt am Main: Suhrkamp Verlag, pp. 100–105. The title of the English translation is *The Phenomenology of the Social World.*
11 See Tesar, Paul (1991). The Other Side of Types, in *Midgård Monograph 2: Type and the (Im)Possibilities of Convention.* New York, NY: Princeton Architectural Press, pp. 165–75.
12 See for instance Thiis-Evensen, Thomas (1989). *Archetypes in Architecture.* Oxford: Oxford University Press; and Alexander, Christopher et al. (1977). *A Pattern Language.* New York, NY: Oxford University Press. Both Thiis-Evensen and Alexander claim "archetypal," or at least culture-transcending qualities for the patterns and types they discuss and illustrate in both books.
13 Buber, Martin (1974). *Ich und Du.* Heidelberg: Verlag Lambert Schneider.
14 Ibid., pp. 30–31.
15 See Hildebrand, Grant (1999). *Origins of Architectural Pleasure.* Berkeley, CA: University of California Press. Hildebrand discusses such notions as "prospect" and "refuge" in architecture, or our preferences for "ordered complexity" or "complex order," as having essentially biological foundations.
16 See Hubbard, William (1981). *Complicity and Conviction: Steps toward an Architecture of Convention.* Cambridge, MA: The MIT Press. In the chapter "Methods for Making an Architecture of Convention" Hubbard discusses—drawing on terms proposed in Harold Bloom (1973). *The Anxiety of Influence.* New York, NY: Oxford University Press—such methods as "Swerving," "Completion," "Focusing," and "Becoming the Essence" as ways or "rereading" established precedents and thus giving them new meaning and relevance.

PART III
Symbolic Engagements

Chapter 8

A Home in the World:
The Ontological Significance of Home

Thomas Barrie

Introduction

The following chapter presumes that one of the perennial tasks of architecture has been to assist humans in structuring their understanding of the world and their place in it. It begins with a discussion of the human homeless condition, as expressed through religious, philosophical, and literary traditions. Homelessness is termed as an ontological estrangement from a world, in the words of the American poet Wallace Stevens, "that is not our own and, much more, not ourselves." Congruent with Stevens' assertion that from this condition "the poem springs," the roles of architecture in general and the domestic specifically are presented as fundamental ways to explicate the world and ameliorate our homeless condition. Home is argued to be a complex and ephemeral word—typically charged with multifarious and often deeply personal meanings—but essentially the locus for our human, corporal life while providing the setting to transcend it. The essay's subject may appear to be voluminous, but many historical, anthropological and socio-political aspects are, of necessity in a piece of this length, omitted, and the subject further narrowed by its focus on the assigned and assumed ontological roles of home. Lastly, even though home depends on materially defining space for the quotidian activities it encloses, the conclusion suggests that its most compelling and significant aspects may be largely immaterial in nature. Home not only serves to shelter the body but also to house the soul.

The Home, Homelessness, and Homecoming

The condition of homelessness, and the desire for homecoming, for founding and inhabiting a home, define, in part, the human condition. Even though homelessness is often described as a modern phenomenon of alienation, it appears throughout Western philosophic, religious, and literary traditions. Examples from the Pythagorean and Platonic schools include descriptions of human existence as one of exile and imprisonment in incarnate life,[1] as in Plato's "Allegory of the Cave" in Book VI of *The Republic* that describes the isolation of humans trapped in the sensible world. In the Judaic-Christian tradition humans are often characterized as lost and wandering, separated and homesick for an elusive god. In *Psalms*, David beseeches god, "How long wilt thou hide thy face from me?" a plaintive expression of estrangement from the divine.[2] This dislocation is evocatively described in *Genesis* as a lost Eden, where Adam and Eve eat from the tree of knowledge of good and evil, and subsequently are alienated from the paradise garden where such separation does not exist.[3]

Traditionally questions and narratives regarding humanity's relationship with the world were embedded in religion. In the modern era they typically emerge from confrontations with scientific discoveries and the attendant social and cultural displacements. The Christian philosopher and mathematician Blaise Pascal wrote in *Thoughts* (*Pensées*) that in contemplating the universe "The eternal silence of these infinite spaces fills me with dread,"[4] articulating the knowledge, mystery and even terror of a certain type of alienation. The emergence of non-dogmatic thought and recognition of an autonomous human rationality also resulted in the loss of a certitude of belief of our place in the universe typically supplied by religion.

Figure 8.1   Plato's *Allegory of the Cave* describes a type of ontological homelessness
Source: Drawing courtesy of Phillip James Tabb.

Martin Heidegger identified the capacity of humans to view the world from a separate, individual perspective as a source of anxiety, an intrinsic part of the human condition. When one is no longer enclosed within the limits of their world, in the homely (*heimlich*), then broader perspectives are disclosed. Paradoxically, in seeking to understand the world we must stand apart from it, and this separation from the familiar we feel as anxiety. For Heidegger, homelessness was an enduring philosophic theme. "Uncanny homelessness" (*unheimlich*) was the condition of estrangement from the familiar, provoking a mood of homesickness, and a desire for homecoming.[5]

But what do we mean by homecoming? One answer may be to recognize that in some cases the condition of homelessness is redemptive. World mythology contains a panoply of stories regarding hero-redeemer figures, and the necessity of leaving home to gain benefits for oneself and others. The Buddha must renounce the comforts and sensual pleasures of his palaces to achieve enlightenment, Mohammad's solitary sequestration in the cave on Mt. Hino is required to receive the revelations of god, the 17th-century Japanese poet Basho must wander homeless to access the insights he records, and American Plains Indians embark on solitary vision quests to pass from one stage of life to another. The hero's journey is one of separation from the familiar and a journey to the unknown, followed by a return "home" with insights or knowledge gained along the way.[6]

The western literary tradition is replete with ruminations on the ontological condition of homelessness. Many works share a common topic of leaving and returning home, and descriptions of "home" and of "coming home" have a rich literary history. Homelessness is the primary subject of *The Odyssey*, where Odysseus, cast adrift in the world, must wander for 10 years following the Trojan Wars, unable through a range of impediments (attributed to the gods), to find his way home, poetically describing the disorientation and terror of being "homeless." But, even upon returning home he must appear as a stranger, symbolizing the degree of his estrangement from home.

Figure 8.2   Uncanny homelessness defines, in part, the modern condition. Casper David Friedrich,
              Wanderer Above a Sea of Fog, 1817
Source: Hamburger Kunsthalle, Hamburg, Germany. Photograph by Elke Walford, Art Resource, New York.

However, not all journeys are redemptive, (in fact more are not), as Orpheus' journey to the land of the dead conveniently illustrates. Another example is Oedipus who, born into the Royal House of Thebes, lives his life as a wanderer, his antidote to the Delphic Oracle's prophecy that he will kill his father.[7] In Robert Frost's *The Death of the Hired Man*, Silas is reluctantly taken in by Mary and Warren when he returns to die at the only place he considers home. He writes, "home is the place where, when you have to go there, they have to take you in."[8]

Home is typically described as a refuge from the vicissitudes of the world and a place of stability, safety, and nourishment (or, in Frost's poem, as a last resort), but this is not always the case. Hansel and Gretel from *Grimm's Fairy Tales* expect succor in the old women's house while she sees them as sustenance. And in Nathaniel Hawthorne's *House of the Seven Gables*, the house itself is as malevolent as the evil characters it admits. An equally sinister house is the setting for the psychological disorder depicted in Edgar Allen Poe's *The Fall of the House of Usher*. More unsettling (and instructive) than evil is Rainer Maria Rilke's description in *The Notebooks of Malte Laurids Brigge* of a Parisian townhouse whose rooms are revealed by the demolition of its adjoining building. "The tenacious life of those rooms" and the ephemerality of human existence were revealed by its exposed surfaces, layers, structure and services in a manner that, Rilke admitted later, elicited feelings of dread such that he fled in horror.

Figure 8.3   Homelessness is a predominant subject of *The Odyssey*. *Harbor with Fog (The Embarkation of Ulysses)*, Claude Lorrain, 1646
Source: Louvre, Paris, France. Erich Lessing/Art Resource, New York.

Some writers describe the quest for home, and all that it implies, as a rather futile enterprise. Thomas Wolfe famously stated, "You can't go home again" in the novel of the same name. The novel's protagonist George Webber asserts,

> You can't go back home to your family, back home to your childhood, back home to romantic love, back home to a young man's dreams of glory and of fame, back home to the father you have lost and have been looking for, back home to someone who can help you, save you, ease the burden for you, back home to the old forms and systems of things which once seemed everlasting but which are changing all the time—back home to the escapes of Time and Memory.[9]

Wolfe's pronouncement has become a common expression but essentially means once we have left our childhood home, the knowledge and perspectives gained reveal our lives as constituent of larger contexts. Consequently, we cannot return home and find the singular meaning and comfort it once offered.

Wolf more compellingly describes the condition of dislocation at the beginning of *Look Homeward Angel*,

> Naked and alone we came into exile. In her dark womb we did not know our mother's face; from the prison of her flesh have we come into the unspeakable and incommunicable prison of this earth. Which of us has known his brother? Which of us has looked into his father's heart? Which of us has not remained forever prison-pent? Which of us is not forever a stranger and alone? O waste of loss, in the hot mazes, lost among bright stars on

this most weary unbright cinder, lost! Remembering speechlessly we seek the great forgotten language, the lost land-end into heaven, a stone, a leaf, an unfound door. Where? When?[10]

Other writers ascribe a special role of the arts to address the human condition outlined by Wolfe. The American poet Wallace Stevens writes;

The first idea was not our own.
The clouds preceded us
There was a muddy centre before we breathed.
There was a myth before the myth began,
Venerable and articulate and complete.
From this the poem springs: that we live in a place
That is not our own and, much more, not ourselves
And hard it is in spite of blazoned days.[11]

These examples express a certain type of irreconcilable homelessness congruent with the human story of the recognition that we inhabit a world that is not of our own making and is often capricious and indifferent to our needs. But, as Stevens explains, this recognition is also the birth of poetry, of the myriad of creative compulsions and activities whose aim is to create some semblance of place—a home in the world. Similarly, according to Vitruvius in his observations on the origins of the dwelling house, it was the unique human capacity to stand "upright and gazing upon the splendor of the starry firmament," to realize and consider our place in the universe, that was, in part, the impetus for the birth of architecture.[12] In other words, the recognition of a certain kind of estrangement from the world was catalytic of the impulse to create one of our own making. Consequently, humans have demanded that architecture not only shelter them from the storms of the environment but the storms of existence as well.[13] Karsten Harries (referencing the Stevens poem) argues that poetry and myths (and by extension other art forms such as architecture) serve to "re-present the world that it no longer seems indifferent to our needs, arbitrary and contingent, but is expressed as a place we call home."[14] According to Harries, architecture has a special and perhaps preeminent role, which "answers to the human need to experience the social and natural world as a non-arbitrary meaningful order."[15]

All of which to suggest that one of the functions architecture has been asked to serve is to ameliorate our homeless condition. Wallace Stevens, in the poem "Anecdote of the Jar," describes how even a simple object, once placed in the "slovenly wilderness" that surrounds it, brings a particular kind of order, rendering it "no longer wild."[16] Norman Crowe argues that the perennial quest for order and stability in an often capricious and unpredictable world produced the need for a "new nature" of the "domicile and the settlement;"—what Cicero described as "a second world within the world of nature."[17] "With Eden left behind" humans needed a "new garden, one permanently positioned in the world of time and place."[18] Harries and others have suggested that the domestication of our environment served to recover the Eden or paradise we had lost. But, conversely, acts of appropriation, congruent with the making of architecture, promise not so much a return to paradise, but a making of our own.[19] However, even though the simplest of domiciles and settlements may have served as a "new nature" they were also positioned as part of nature, with alignments to cardinal points, celestial bodies, and environmental features that served to link them to the order of the world around them. The houses of American Indians often served as cosmograms, where the roof represented the sky, the smoke hole the sun, and the walls boundaries of the cosmos. The Navaho Hogan, given by their god as described in the Blessingway Myth, represented the world and ordered their lives. Architecture in replicating nature also served to explicate it. Other examples from world traditional dwellings, such as the Sakalava houses of Madagaskar that are organized according to positions of astrological signs, evidenced similar ontological agendas.[20] And so, the realization of human homelessness and the need to ameliorate it leads to particular architectural responses potently materialized in the home.

Figure 8.4   Architecture has often served to ameliorate our homeless condition. Avebury, Wiltshire,
               UK, Neolithic
Source: Photograph courtesy of Thomas Barrie.

The Special Roles of Architecture

Herman Hertzberger writes about the special capacity of art to change our understanding of a particular
place and our relationship to it. "Not only do painters succeed in rendering the space of our reality, the
opposite is also true, that reality is a rendering of the painter's space. We also experience space as we know
it from images given by painters."[21] What does he mean by this? Isn't it about the transformative potential
of art to change how we see the world? Hans Georg Gadamer argues that creative artifacts have an enduring
capacity to engage and even positively change us, and that art and design can be a means to articulate and
provide new perspectives to life's most important questions. He states, "We do not encounter the work
of art without being transformed in the process."[22] In a similar manner, the embodied and experiential
capacities of architecture and the built environment can subtly or provocatively affect us in ways that are
instructive, even life changing.

   Throughout the history of human culture architecture has materialized ontological meaning and
communicated symbolic content, to elucidate, inspire, convince, and even coerce. However, even though
assessing what architecture *does* may be a fruitful enterprise, it is problematic due to its largely subjective
nature. It is perhaps more reliable to consider what we *ask* architecture and the built environment to do.
As it turns out throughout history we have *asked* architecture to do quite a lot. As a predominant cultural
artifact architecture has often been tasked with embodying and articulating what a culture values most, and
its material evidence is both a mirror and a lamp, reflecting and illuminating the culture that produced it.[23]
This is particularly evidenced by sacred architecture, which can be comparatively understood as serving to
recreate and reveal a world that otherwise, it was believed, would have remained hidden. From the earliest
of works the media of architecture served as an intermediary between humans and the gods they worshiped
or the knowledge they sought. They are both heroic and heartbreaking in their expressions of the perennial
human quest for understanding and meaning.[24] That said, architecture *per se*, doesn't actually mean anything
at all—we assign it meaning as part of the roles we ask it to play.[25] In these contexts we can conceptualize
architecture as an active agent, engaging its users in a variety of perceptual and experiential ways.[26] We come
to understand architecture and construct its meaning through our daily and episodic, individual and collective,
engagements with it.

Figure 8.5   Architecture has often been tasked with materializing ontological meaning and
                communicating symbolic content. The Cathedral of Christ the Light, Oakland California,
                Skidmore, Owings and Merrill, San Francisco/Craig Hartman, 2005
Source: Photograph by Timothy Hursley, courtesy of Skidmore, Owings & Merrill LLP.

The tasking of architecture to replicate or reveal the world and situate our place within it can be understood as a quest for making a home in an inherently unstable world. Acts of building have served to connect us with ourselves and our place in the cosmos, while simultaneously revealing the vast contexts of which we are a part. This double mediation—individual to architecture and architecture to the world—describe the essential roles that architecture has been asked to play generally, and has often materialized specifically. However, one could equally argue that architecture doesn't have any special providence to help humans explicate the world and facilitate our homecoming. The capacity of architecture to articulate the human condition and render it more comprehensible and meaningful, is limited at best (in part, because of the enormity of the task), and it does so problematically and inadequately. But, similar to Winston Churchill's statement that "Democracy is the worst form of government, except for all those other forms that have been tried from time to time,"[27] it is perhaps one of the better means we have—even our best hope. In particular, architecture may have the most promise of materializing and eliciting the collective aspects of the human condition, and of transcending the depressing and erroneous concept of separate individuality and human exceptionality.

The Ontological Function of Home

In our lives we inhabit and pass through a number of houses, beginning with the first "house" of the womb. We live in the house or houses of our parents or guardians, and eventually move out (but never completely), to live with roommates or alone as we find our way in the world. Finding and creating the first home we can truly call our own is typically an important milestone. Then there are the houses we rent or own and the homes we make as we move to new jobs or opportunities, cohabit with a partner, marry or divorce, raise or adopt children, and eventually where we grow old. At some point we may live with our children or move to specialized care facilities, before the inevitable death of our bodies. All are temporary and impermanent (and indeed humans are distinguished from most other animals in that we often live in dwellings previously occupied by others), but, throughout our lives, are considered "home."

Home is the center of our lives, the place from which we depart but to which we always return. As a bulwark against the uncertainties of life it serves as the hub of our personal world, and its safety and stability are essential to our sense of wellbeing. All of which explains why descriptions of home and its value, dating from early history, have enjoyed preeminent status in the arts. In *The Odyssey* Odysseus states, "There's nothing better in this world" than a "happy peaceful home." Home is the place of our most intimate relationships, as expressed in the Burt Bacharach and Diane Warwick song, "A house is not a home, when there is no one there to hold you tight." But home is not simply a physical place to contain our lives, but one we appropriate and through which we express ourselves. We may rent or buy a house or housing unit, but it is through our occupation and personalization that the house becomes our home.[28] Through inhabiting our home we establish our identity in the world, while communicating this self-definition to others.[29]

Figure 8.6   Home is the setting for our life while providing the setting to transcend it. Farmhouse, UK
Source: Photograph courtesy of Thomas Barrie.

Figure 8.7   In Jungian psychology the house typically symbolizes the self. Jung House, Bollingen,
               Switzerland, 1923–55
Source: Photograph courtesy of Thomas Barrie.

Phenomenology has had an enduring interest in the ontological significance of home, beginning perhaps with Heidegger's philosophical construct of "dwelling." Christian Norberg-Schulz, who was primarily an interpreter of Heidegger, equated "dwelling" with a "return to things" and his arguments are often illustrated by domestic examples.[30] Gaston Bachelard described the "oneiric house" as a place saturated with memories, dreams, and symbolic meaning. For Bachelard, home is deeply connected to the "unforgettable house" of childhood, and that the "house is one of the greatest powers of integration for the thoughts, memories and dreams of mankind."[31] Referencing the Swiss Psychiatrist Carl G. Jung, he attributes the different places and vertical layers of the house to the structure of the psyche.[32] Claire Cooper Marcus similarly argues, "the unconscious often chooses houses, buildings, and secret rooms as symbols. The basement or cellar is often a metaphor for the unconscious, of something hidden that needs to be explored, whereas the attic of roof or opening to the sky often reflects a desire to explore transpersonal realms or spiritual dimensions."[33] In Jungian psychology when the house appears in dreams or psychoanalysis it typically symbolizes the self, and it was Jung himself who built a highly symbolic house at Bollingen that at its completion became a "symbol of psychic wholeness."[34]

The feeling of "being at home" describes a condition of ease, support, and comfort, and so it is not unusual that we often tell our guests to make themselves "at home." According to Thomas Moore, "Home is an emotional state, a place of the imagination where feelings of security, belonging, placement, family, protection, memory, and personal history abide. Our dreams and fantasies of home may give us direction and calm our anxieties as we continually look for ways to satisfy our longings for home."[35] For Moore, feelings associated with truly being "at home" are among the most significant and meaningful. Being at home is associated with "enchantment," of being connected, centered, even rapturous and ecstatic. One is literally under the "spell" of the numinous, the mysterious and the meaningful, paradoxically accessed, experienced and appreciated, in an Epicurean sense, through the everyday activities of life.[36]

And yet for Moore, the "emotional sickness" of contemporary society (and its built environment), is emblematic of our alienation from the places we inhabit, and that "our society is suffering from profound homesickness."[37] According to Moore, even though the home may possess the capacity for enchantment, engaging our soul in profound and meaningful ways, we are disenchanted with our culture and its artifacts.[38] Christopher Reed, in his introduction to *Not at Home: The Suppression of Domesticity in Modern Art and Architecture*, discusses the cultural forces that have produced the domestic environments Moore finds so deficient. For Reed, even though a home dedicated exclusively to domesticity is a modern phenomenon, modern art did not tend to celebrate it, and that modernism's preoccupation with the *avant garde* "imagined itself away from home, marching towards glory on the battlefields of culture."[39] The 17th-century Dutch were among the first to create what could be considered a modern home, and often celebrated the domestic environment in the art of their time. However, according to Reed, beginning with the favored subjects of the Impressionists—landscapes and city scenes—modern art had "no time to spare for the mundane details of home life and housekeeping," and that the home was eventually positioned "as the antipode to high art."[40]

However, the 20th-century architectural *avant garde* did not so much abandon the domestic environment but sought to rehabilitate it. Influential theoreticians such as Adolf Loos dismissed decoration and ornament as both superfluous and degenerate, an attack directed in part at the favored domestic interiors of his time. The moralizing tone of much of the treatises of early modernism often conflated architecture and morality. Le Corbusier opens his discussion of the ideal house by citing "a question of morality," and the need for "truth." Referencing the primordial nature of the house as the "first tool that (man) forged for himself," he argues that the current "out of date tool" should be relegated to the "scrap heap." Le Corbusier insists that his contemporaries "should be pitied for living in unworthy houses, since they ruin our health and our *morale*," before turning to the virtues of the "pure" and the "abstract," epitomized by the eponymous engineer.[41] Le Corbusier's acerbic and prolonged polemic regarding "home" has actually very little to say about domesticity, and is emblematic of modernism where "the domestic, perpetually invoked in order to be denied, remains throughout the course of modernism a crucial site of anxiety and subversion."[42]

It was in the post-modernism of the early 1960s that terms and subjects associated with home and domesticity were rehabilitated and a renewed interest in the domestic appeared. Charles Moore shares Thomas Moore's sentiments about home when he states "You bind the goods and trappings of your life together with your dreams to make a place uniquely your own. In doing so you build a semblance of the world you know, adding it to the community that surrounds you."[43] Feminism in particular had an interest in repositioning the domestic as a means to reclaim its suppressed histories and challenge its agency as an enforcer of gender roles and social hierarchy. During this time, phenomenology was also put in service of validating the value of the quotidian nature of life and the sensuality of domesticity. Thomas Moore, whose descriptions of home are phenomenological in spirit,[44] invokes Heidegger when he characterizes the earth as our home and argues, "we are always making a house for the heart and always looking for the house of divinity."[45]

The Spanish writer Vicente Verdu reflected that the house is "between reality and desire, between body and dream, between what is possible and what remains to be longed for."[46] It is where we orient ourselves in the world and which, through the quotidian rituals of domesticity, we are oriented. The Navaho considered the building of one's Hogan to be a prerequisite to navigating the world. One had to build the "home place" before one could proceed with the next stages of their lives.[47] In Japanese literature of the Medieval Period the hermit scholar's hut held a preeminent position as a place that both centered one while providing connections to the larger world. The title of Kamo no Chomei's *The Record of the Ten-Foot-Square Hut* refers to a room of these dimensions where the Buddhist sage Vimalakirti was said to have accommodated a multitude of devotees.[48] For the author, his austere mountainside retreat similarly grounds him in a place while revealing a vaster world beyond it.

Henry David Thoreau's philosophical discussions regarding the building and inhabitation of his simple hut on Walden Pond similarly positions it as a threshold to other worlds. In many ways *Walden* is not about a house at all, but traverses a broad territory, encompassing practical, economic, social, political, psychic, spiritual, sensual, quotidian, metaphysical, and cosmic realms. Thoreau argues that "every man is tasked to make his life, even in its details, worthy of the contemplation of his most elevated and critical hour,"[49] and systematically describes the virtues of an authentic life, as facilitated, materialized, and symbolized by his self-built dwelling.

Figure 8.8   Thoreau's house at Walden Pond materialized and facilitated his philosophy
Source: N.P. Santoleri, 1991. Courtesy of the artist.

The parable of the Artist of Kouroo that appears in the conclusion illustrates how simple acts of creation lead to vast cosmologies and ontological understandings.[50] For Thoreau, his home served as a means to shed the encumbrances of material life and access a deeper, more authentic consciousness. Throughout his extended essay, he is both bound to a specific place delineated by essential architecture and freed to consider broader ontological questions.

Lastly, to round out our discussion of the ontological significance of home we turn to two specific house types: the temple and the tomb. The attribution of sacrality to the home is commonly found in the religious beliefs and practices of cultures around the world and, as we have previously observed, the house was often employed to materialize a diverse range of symbolic content. However, there is also an entirely different area of domesticity where the home doesn't serve the function of aligning its inhabitants with the divine, but actually houses the god or gods to the exclusion of all others. Descriptions of the 'house of god" commonly appear in Hindu, Jewish, and Christian scripture, with detailed descriptions regarding the locations, orientations, organizations, materials, and proportions required for the god(s) to dwell there. Some present (and replicate) primordial houses as models of the sacred. For example, the holy books of Islam do not describe how god is to be housed, but instead the "original" house of the Prophet in Medina served as the model for early mosques. Others conflate the domestic and the sacred as a means to lend cultural and historical authority to the sacred setting, as in the cultural and political functions of the Greek Prytaneion. All of which illustrate, in a variety of ways, cross-cultural beliefs in the capacity (or promise), of architecture and the domestic, to connect humans with the gods or understandings they sought.

However, the capacity of the home to make metaphysical connections is perhaps most potently illustrated by the traditions of house tombs. Funerary architecture is arguably the oldest of building types and from the earliest of examples utilized domestic symbols to communicate the continuity of the ruler gods and, by extension, the people under their protection. To do so house tombs often included all of the accouterments necessary for the dead's postmortem existence. As illustrated by the elite funerary architecture of Pharaonic

Figure 8.9   Monumental tombs for rulers symbolized eternal domiciles. Humayun's Tomb, Delhi,
                India, 1565
Source: Photograph courtesy of Thomas Barrie.

Egypt, the house of the deified, eternal ruler not only materialized his continued participation in the affairs of his culture but also provided a setting where it was commonly believed he might accessed. The mortuary architecture of cultures as diverse as Neolithic Europe and American Indians also predominantly performed these dual functions, further illustrating the capacity of the house to embody a diverse range of cultural, symbolic, and religious content.

Conclusion

The virgin goddess Hestia was known as the goddess of the home and hearth, and a Greek custom was to carry a newborn baby around the hearth as a symbol of their homecoming. Meal offerings included the following prayer:

> Hestia, in all dwellings of men and immortals
> Yours in the highest honor, the sweet wine offered
> First and last at the feast, poured out for you duly.
> Never without you can gods or mortals hold a banquet.[51]

But Hestia also had a public role as guardian of the sacred hearth of the Prytaneion. And so the responsibilities of her personified divinity ranged from the realms of individual dwelling to the civic— both essential to the preservation of wellbeing. The myth of Philemon and Baucis similarly presents broadened aspects of domesticity. In the story (made famous by Goethe's *Faust*), the pious old couple welcomes into their simple hut the gods Jupiter and Mercury, disguised as wayfarers, after all of the other inhabitants of Phrygia had turned them away.[52] Even though they are very poor the couple welcomes the gods to their hearth and generously feed them. Eventually the wayfarers reveal themselves, and at Philemon and Baucis' request, their primitive hut becomes a temple that they tend until their death—the simple hut now a sacred setting.

In these and other examples previously cited the home serves as a sacred realm, which comprises broader ontological territories that transcend the common assignation of home to the secular. In other words, as has been suggested throughout this chapter, even though the home may be predominantly understood as the prosaic materialization of space for quotidian, symbolic, and ritual activities, it is more completely known according to its poetic capacities. Its metaphysical and ontological aspects render more completely what home represents, reveals, and even means. Of these, homelessness and the home's roles in assisting our ontological homecoming have been of primary concern.

The spiritual path is similarly material and immaterial. Paradoxically, it typically requires leaving home and journeying into the world to find our home. Embarking on this journey has been described by the novelist Peter Matthiessen as prompted by a restless unease. But, it can also be a return. Matthiessen reflects, "Yet one senses that there is a source for this deep restlessness; and the path that leads there is not a path to a strange place, but the path home."[53] Pascal reflected, "Returning to himself, let man consider what he is compared with all existence; let him think of himself as lost in this remote corner of nature; and from this little dungeon in which he finds himself lodged—I mean the Universe—let him learn to set a true value on the earth, its realms, its cities, its houses and himself in their proper value."[54] For Heidegger, true homecoming is through an understanding of our essential homelessness, our being in the world, and our place in finite and infinite space and time. This was (and is), his call for an authentic life, and perhaps one that offers perspectives on the role of home to assist a continuous homecoming to our shared humanity.[55] Both Heidegger and Thoreau upend the common definitions of architecture as more than mere shelter, and suggest that through the domestic act of sheltering, much like Stevens' jar in Tennessee, worlds formerly occluded may be revealed.

So home, as it turns out, is not really so much about how we reflexively conceive and imagine it. It is not so much about a place, as it is finding our place in the world—it is not so much about our physical abode, as it is a home we collectively inhabit. And yet, it is about a place, about placing ourselves in that which we can only truly know, or from which we can come to know. The secular spiritualty of Thoreau needed the cabin at Walden, in all of its physicality, to be able to transcend it and discover what he was compelled to seek, consider, and attain, the reflections and understandings that comprise his philosophy. And it is the latter, paradoxically, that endures.

Endnotes

1   O'Donoghue, Brenden (2011). *A Poetics of Homecoming: Heidegger, Homelessness and the Homecoming Venture.* Newcastle-upon-Tyne: Cambridge Scholars Publishing, pp. 26–9.

2   Psalms 13.1.

3   Harries, Karsten. Building and the Terror of Time. *Perspecta: The Yale Architectural Journal* 19, 1987, pp. 59–69, p. 60.

4   Pascal, Blaise (1995). *Pensées*, translated by A.J. Krailsheimer. London: Penguin Books.

5   Robert Mugerauer explains Heidegger's position, "Insofar as a displacement would be metaphysical, collapsing our grounding and orientation in the world/cosmos, it would seem that a recovery would require, or even amount to, an ontological homecoming." Mugerauer, Robert (2008). *Heidegger and Homecoming: The Leitmotif in the Later Writings.* Toronto: University of Toronto Press, p. 24.

6   The "hero's journey" is a term employed by the religious scholar Joseph Campbell and comprehensively presented in *The Hero With a Thousand Faces*. Princeton, NJ: Princeton University Press, 1949.

7   He does eventually find a home, but, as is well known, it is short-lived and ends in tragedy.

8   Conners Latham, Edward (ed.) (1969). The Death of the Hired Man. *The Poetry of Robert Frost: The Collected Poems, Complete and Unabridged.* New York, NY: Holt, Rinehart and Winston, pp. 34–40.

9   Wolfe, Thomas (1934). *You Can't Go Home Again.* Garden City, NY: The Sundial Press, from the introduction of Book VII, p. 706.

10 Wolfe, Thomas (1929). *Look Homeward Angel: A Story of the Buried Life*. New York, NY: Charles Scribner's Sons, p. 2.

11 Stevens, Wallace (ed. Holly Stevens) (1972). *The Palm at the End of the Mind: Selected Poems and a Play.* New York, NY: Vintage Books, from *Notes Towards a Supreme Fiction*, pp. 209–10.

12 Vitruvius goes on to equate the birth of architecture with the creation of language and the founding of culture. Hicky Morgan, Morris (trans.) (1960). *Vitruvius: The Ten Books of Architecture.* New York, NY: Dover Publications Inc., Book II, Chapter 1. Ovid wrote in *Metamorphoses*, "All other creatures look down toward the earth, but man was given a face so that he might turn his eyes toward the stars and his gaze upon the sky."

13 For Harries, architecture has a particular function of embodying the timeless and consequently ameliorating the reality of the passage of time and its implications regarding mortality.

14 Harries, Karsten (1998). *The Ethical Function of Architecture.* Cambridge, MA: The MIT Press, p. 136.

15 Harries, op. cit., p. 149.

16 Stevens, Wallace (ed. Holly Stevens) (1972). *The Palm at the End of the Mind: Selected Poems and a Play*, p. 46.

17 "We enjoy the fruits of the plains and of the mountains, the rivers and the lakes are ours, we sow corn, we plant trees, we fertilize the soil by irrigation, we confine the rivers and straighten or divert their courses, In fine, by means of our hands we essay to create as it were a second world within the world of nature." Cicero, *De Natura Decorum.*

18 Crowe, Norman (1995). *Nature and the Idea of a Man-made World: An Investigation into the Evolutionary Roots of Form and Order in the Built Environment.* Cambridge, MA: The MIT Press, p. 30.

19 Karsten Harries in his essay "Building and the Terror of Time," suggests that acts of building serve as a "domestication of space," and "every house may be considered an attempted recovery of some paradise." Harries, op. cit., p. 59.

20 Oliver, Paul (2008). *The Vernacular House World Wide.* London: Phaidon.

21 Hertzberger, Herman (2005). *Space and the Architect, Lessons in Architecture 2.* Rotterdam: 010 Publishers, 5th Edition, p. 19.

22 Paraphrased by Robert Bernasconi in the Introduction to Hans-Georg Gadamer, Hans-Georg (1986). *The Relevance of the Beautiful and Other Essays.* Cambridge: Cambridge University Press, p. xiv.

23 Mugerauer, Robert (1995). *Interpreting Environments: Tradition, Deconstruction, Hermeneutics.* Austin, TX: The University of Texas Press, p. xxi. According to Lindsay Jones, architecture can serve as a primary means of deciphering a culture, its assigned meanings revealing a culture's histories, values and self-awareness. "Architecture is a particular sort of cultural production, but it need not, as the disparaging assignation 'mute text' implies, be judged as inherently lower, weaker, or crippled documentary resource to which one retreats only in the absence of the certainty that written texts can provide." Jones, Lindsay (2000). *The Hermeneutics of Sacred Architecture, Experience, Interpretation, Comparison. Volume 1: Monumental Occasions, Reflections on the Eventfulness of Religious Architecture.* Cambridge, MA: Harvard University Press, p. xxv.

24 But, as I have argued elsewhere, their packed agendas included a panoply of elements—from the declarative, didactic and coercive, to the nurturing, instructive and transcendent. Barrie, Thomas (2010). *The Sacred In-between: The Mediating Roles of Architecture.* London: Routledge.

25 Lindsay Jones, op. cit., pp. 29, 36.

26 According to Perez Gomez, "The fundamental thrust of architecture … (is) a poetic representation of significant human action." From Perez-Gomez, Alberto (2006). *Built Upon Love, Architectural Longing after Ethics and Aesthetics.* Cambridge, MA: The MIT Press, p. 125.

27 From a House of Commons speech on November 11, 1947.

28 Karsten Harries reminds us that in contemporary Western culture "home has become a place where one just happens to live," but that "a good home needs to be appropriated." Harries, op. cit., p. 146. As Claire Cooper Marcus states, "A home fulfills many needs: a place of self expression, a vessel of memories, a refuge from the outside world, a cocoon where we can feel nurtured and let down our guard." Cooper Marcus, Claire (1995). *The House as Symbol of Self: Exploring the Deeper Meaning of Home.* Berkeley, CA: Conari Press, p. 4.

29 The house has also been described as a "third skin," an outer layer that, in addition to our bodies and clothes, provides a medium to project our self-image.

30 For example, Georg Trakl's poem, "A Winter Evening," is discussed at length to illustrates Heidegger's positioning of phenomenology as a "return to things" and the ontological significance of home and domestic rituals. Norberg-Schulz, Christian (1980). *Genius Loci: Towards a Phenomenology of Architecture.* New York, NY: Rizzoli, pp. 8–11.

31 Bachelard, Gaston (trans. Maria Jolas) (1969). *The Poetics of Space.* Boston, MA: Beacon Press, p. 6.

32 Bachelard, op. cit., pp. 18–19.

33 Marcus, op. cit., p. 40.

34 See Barrie, *The Sacred In-between, The Mediating Roles of Architecture*, pp. 64–79.

35 Moore, Thomas (1996). *The Re-Enchantment of Everyday Life*. New York, NY: Harper Collins, p. 77. Moore also states "The need for home lies deep in the human heart: when our homeland is threatened we go into action to defend it, and when our family house is violated we are profoundly offended. We spend our lives trying to "make a home"—building, buying, renting, borrowing houses, staying in the old family homestead or moving from house to house according to the winds of fate. Few things are more important than finding a home and working at it constantly to make it resonate with deep memories and fulfill deep longings," p. 42.

36 Moore argues "nothing is more intimate than home, and therefore nothing more proper to the soul. Whatever it takes to call forth the spirits of home, our own lares and penates—ancient Roman household spirits—is worth our effort and expense." Moore, op. cit., p. 85.

37 Moore, op. cit., p. 43.

38 Moore, op. cit., pp. ix–x.

39 Reed, Christopher (ed.) (1996). *Not at Home: The Suppression of Domesticity in Modern Art and Architecture*. London: Thames and Hudson, p. 7. Reed reminds us that the term *avant garde* is a military one, meaning the advance guard that leads the charge against the enemy.

40 Though there is an equally plausible argument that modern art of the 20th century had a preoccupation with themes of homelessness and alienation.

41 Le Corbusier (1960). *Towards a New Architecture*. New York, NY: Holt, Rinehart and Winston, pp. 17–20.

42 Reed, op. cit., p. 16.

43 Moore, Charles, Allen, Gerald and Donlyn Lyndon (1974). *The Place of Houses: Three Architects Suggest Ways to Build and Inhabit Houses*. New York, NY: Henry Holt and Company, p. vii.

44 Like many phenomenological writers he can be exclusive in what he considers pertinent to his subject, generally reserving his arguments for the transcendent nature of domesticity to the exclusion of other important elements.

45 Moore, op. cit., p. 42.

46 Quoted in Zabalbeascoa, Anatxu (1995). *The House of the Architect*. New York, NY: Rizzoli, p. 6.

47 Crowe, op. cit., p. 34.

48 As recounted in *The Vimalakirti Sutra*, an important Mahayana text first translated into Chinese in the 2nd century CE.

49 Thoreau, Henry David (1942). *Walden*. Roslyn, NY: Walter J. Black, Inc., p. 114.

50 It is introduced by his most famous quote, "Why should we be in such desperate haste to succeed in such desperate enterprises? If a man does not keep pace with his companions, perhaps it is because he hears a different drummer. Let him step to the music which he hears, however measured or far away." He goes on to describe an artist who "strives for perfection," through a fashioning of a staff, and as he does so, time and space are transcended, ages come and pass away, and vast cosmologies are revealed. Through the creative act of the fashioning of a staff he creates a new perspective on the world. Thoreau concludes, "The material was pure, and his art was pure; how could the result be other than wonderful?" Thoreau, op. cit., pp. 350–52.

51 Quoted in Hamilton, Edith (1942). *Mythology*. Boston, MA: Little Brown and Company, p. 37.

52 Wayfarers and travelers were under Jupiter's protection.

53 Matthiessen, Peter (1978). *The Snow Leopard*. Toronto: Bantam Books, p. 45.

54 Pascal, *Pensées*, op. cit.

55 Harries, op. cit., p. 213.

Chapter 9

Symbolism and Myth of Mountains, Stone, and Light as Expressed in Sacred Architecture

Anat Geva

This chapter raises the question of how can the designs of mountain places of worship relate to the majestic exteriors of rock formations while also creating a human scaled space that invites the worshiper to experience its desired spiritual solitude. In answering this question I examine two mountain churches in Ticino, Switzerland, designed by Mario Botta to illustrate the challenges and opportunities of mountainous settings: the Chapel of St. Mary of the Angels, built in Monte Tamaro, 1990–96 (Figure 9.1); and the San Giovanni Battista Church, Built in Mogno, 1992–98.

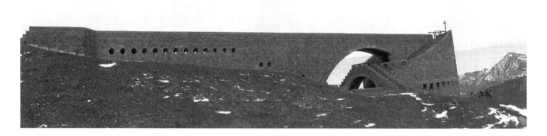

Figure 9.1   Chapel of St. Mary of the Angels, Monte Tamaro, Switzerland, 1990–96, Mario Botta
Source: Photograph courtesy of Anat Geva.

Figure 9.2   San Giovanni Battista Church, Mogno, Switzerland, 1992–98, Mario Botta
Source: Photograph courtesy of Anat Geva.

The immense Swiss Alps of Ticino alone may evoke a spiritual experience, and thus the insertion of even a small object changes the scenery.[1] Therefore, the first design challenge is how to introduce a built form into the majestic landscape and create a worship structure that will enhance the dimension of nature and provide in itself a spiritual experience. Is it by blending the structure with the mountains? Or by erecting a new pillar of a vertical axis that imitates the mountain and builds a new one?

The second design challenge is how to treat light in each house of worship to enhance the relationship with the surrounding mountains while creating a setting that enriches the worshiper's spiritual experience.

This chapter aims to illustrate the interplay of symbolism and myth associated with sacred mountains, spiritual stones, and the holy light in sacred settings as expressed in the targeted churches (Figures 9.1 and 9.2). *Mountains* are perceived as the link between heaven and earth and as God's dwelling. *Stones* expose the earth strata and color, and represent permanence and human longing for eternity. *Light* is associated with the transcendent sky and heaven and symbolizes God's presence. The integration of these three elements in nature conjures a variety of spiritual experiences of God's creation, as mountains are anchored in earth soaring to heaven and are infinite and eternal.[2] Frank Lloyd Wright called to spell nature with capital N since "Nature is all the body God has by which we may become aware of Him [and] understand His process."[3] Thus, the design of mountain temples encourages close observations of the environment and the study of its relation to the built form.

Mountains

Throughout history, and across the world, mountains were and still are perceived as sacred and as manifesting God's existence: "Now Mount Sinai was altogether in smoke, because the LORD descended upon it in fire; and the smoke thereof ascended as the smoke of a furnace, and the whole mount quaked greatly" (Exodus 19: 18). Moreover, mountains symbolize the link between heaven and earth. Confucius in his famous dialogue "The Spring and Autumn Annals" replied to one of his students that mountains are considered the embodiment of the spirit of Chi—the balance and harmony between the world forces of yin and yang, and the cosmic energy of sacred verticality. He stated that in the mountains "wind and clouds grow and communicate Chi between Heaven and Earth."[4] The ancient Chinese believed that the original center of Chi was a sacred mountain, Kunlun, located in the center of the Qinghai-Tibetan plateau. Chinese Buddhism believed that China's four major mountains located at the cardinal points symbolized the human drive to reach heaven while rooted in earth.[5] Many stories and myths were created around mountains. Examples include the belief that the echoes surrounding mountains are the voices of spirits;[6] or the Japanese perception of heavily wooded mountains being the home of their gods;[7] or the various stories about the formation of the sacred Ayers Rock named Uluru by the Aboriginals of the Northern Territory of central Australia.[8]

These spiritual myths and their symbolism inspired humans to erect their own "sacred mountains," as structures to connect heaven and earth and, as such, serve as a means of human transcendence from earth to heaven.[9] The man-made sacred vertical axis is described in the Old Testament when Jacob set the stone up as a pillar and poured oil on its top to establish its sacredness.[10] The definition of such a pillar can be as simple as a visible vertical element that establishes a point on the ground plane creating a space. The establishment of a point on the ground is usually associated with the center of a sacred plan, above which rises the vertical element. This center and pillars/tower combination represents both sacred symbols and a place of orientation.[11] For example, the Canaanite stone pillars at Tel Hazor, Israel from the 13th century BCE may have represented gods.[12] Here the center stone was carved with hands raised to a crescent, a symbol of the moon god or to the circle of the sun.[13] Another example is Stonehenge in the United Kingdom where it is believed that the vertical pillars created circles in reverence of the celestial gods.[14] As such, the sacred vertical axis provides a cosmic pillar(s), spiritual experience, and a greater understanding of form.

History demonstrates that sacred structures either imitated the shape of mountains and rock formations, or were erected on top of a mountain as a "new" top. Examples of sacred monuments such as Ancient Mesopotamia Ziggurats, Egyptian and Pre Columbian pyramids, the three Great Living Chola Temples in Tamil Nadu, India show how these structures generate the axis mundi by imitating the form of mountains. Others, such as the Chapel of the Holy Trinity in Egypt, the Taoist temples on Thunder Sound Peak of Mount Koongtong, China, or Saint-Michel d'Aiguilhe, Le Puy, France, and the Holy Monastery of Saint Nicholas

Figure 9.3   Chapel of St. Mary of the Angels, Monte Tamaro: its cross and bell at the end of the pathway
(bridge) over the chapel
Source: Photograph courtesy of Anat Geva.

Anapausas in Meteora, Greece, were built on top of mountains. These sacred structures define the place by adding a new distinctive cultural color piece to the mountain.[15]

Mario Botta's Chapel of St. Mary of the Angels, in Monte Tamaro (chapel in Tamaro) and the San Giovanni Battista Church, in Mogno (church in Mogno), are good examples for both approaches of imitating the mountain shape or building atop the mountain, and may be understood as part of the continuous attempt of humans to build their cosmic pillars as a link between earth and heaven. The chapel in Tamaro stands on top of the mountain (at an altitude of 4,921 feet),[16] and, as described by the architect, "detaches itself from the mountain to form a new horizon, the starting point of an ideal viaduct [bridge]."[17] As such, the chapel serves as an extension of the mountain (Figure 9.1). Indeed, the horizontal axis on top of this chapel creates a sacred path offering a new glimpse of the mountains as a continuation of the worshiper's infinite pilgrimage path for meditation and thought. At the end of the path you see a metal cross in front of the magnificent background of the mountains, while looking down the mountain you see the bell hanging from the pathway (bridge).

This path on top of the mountain exposes the worshiper to the vast land, the colors of the seasons, and the mountain silhouette, evoking feelings of eternity where humans return to the realm of nature to reach tranquility.[18] However, this realm also creates a tension between man and nature, as the chapel is a marker of human overcoming of the mountain.[19] The chapel itself is located underneath the path, an anchored fortified circle on top of the mountain, which creates a new mountain at the exterior (Figure 9.4). While the exterior pathway has a direct dialogue with the mountain, the interior chapel was designed as a shelter with very small 22 embrasure windows set at the chapel's floor level, and narrow skylights (Figures 9.5a and 9.5b). Mario Botta explains that the chapel concept follows the local traditions where the aim of a structure, in its most profound sense, is to give protection.[20] He was inspired by traditional Alps architecture using local stone to create the "eternal rock."[21] Botta called for stone to help "evoke the

Figure 9.4   Chapel of St. Mary of the Angels, Monte Tamaro: A view of the rear of the chapel as a
              built mountain

Source: Photograph courtesy of Anat Geva.

Figure 9.5   Botta's chapel of St. Mary of the Angels, Monte Tamaro: a view towards the entrance to the
              chapel underneath its exterior bridge (pathway)

Source: Photograph courtesy of Anat Geva.

concept of solidity and protection."[22] Thus, he applies stone in creating a sense of sacred shelter, retreat, and inner sanctum.[23] Botta returns to the basic idea of shelter and manifests a continuation of regional history and traditions. This contrasts Bruno Taut's utopian ideas of alpine architecture (1917),[24] which aspired to plan cities in the mountains expressing a new and modern life. Their design would introduce architectural crystalline forms made only from glass and reject historic precedents and traditional aesthetics. Rather than contrasting the mountain with a modern material such as glass, Botta blends the chapel in Tomaro with the surrounding mountains.

In contrast, the Church in Mogno was designed as a vertical pillar. It is a focal point of the valley's skyline, where the cylindrical form of the church rises above the surrounding village (Figures 9.2 and 9.6). This vertical axis expresses the spiritual *axis mundi* (world axis) of the village, standing "as a bulwark for the village, in defiance of the mountain."[25] Indeed, the church in Mogno was built where an avalanche destroyed almost the entire village including their historic church and caused death and loss. The residents of the village requested that the new church be built in the same place of the old one.[26] Thus, the driving force underlying the project was to maintain the collective memory of the community, their history and culture.[27] Francesco Da Co states that the church is in character with the "image of new ruins," as its goal was to provide a commemorative meaning.[28] Moreover, the axis of new church's central arch is aligned to the nave of the destroyed church[29] (Figure 9.2). However, Botta states that the church is not a memorial, but its design arose from the "determination to resist the mountain, and the need to bear witness to something greater than one's life."[30] He emphasizes the continuation of the age-old struggle between man and the mountain.[31]

Though Botta expressed different approaches in the two buildings' relationships with their surrounding landscapes, both demonstrate his design inspiration and concept of "architecture always roots itself to a specific place."[32] Both houses of worship also manifest human relationship to the mountain. Botta states, "The chapel is a stone nail in the mountain. It was born of the need of man to possess the mountain."[33]

Figure 9.6   San Giovanni Battista Church, Mogno: a view of the church as a vertical pillar
Source: Photograph courtesy of Anat Geva.

Stone

Placing a stone on top of a stone is an ancient act of construction and meaningful statement. In Genesis Jacob erected a pile of stones as a *Gal'ed*, commemorating an event with a permanent monument to God. In other verses in the Bible, piles of stones indicate a burial place—a sacred place. Thus, stone is perceived as a permanent and sacred material.

Mario Botta specifies that building with stone evokes the language of earth and its eternity, and therefore, it "involves the architect beyond the religious sphere."[34] Stone is part of the layers and colors of earth as shaped by forces of nature, and reveals the earth's sacredness. It is part of nature's strata that gleams in its mineral color(s).[35] In a poetic way stone reflects the soul of the earth. Therefore, we should consider stone not only as a geological object, but also as a material that retains our history and culture. Thus, the use of stone in sacred architecture can symbolize this continuity and the religion that created that culture.

The use of locally quarried stones in Botta's two churches expresses their relationship to their locations as well as permanence, and human longings for eternity. This permanency expands stone's spiritual associations.[36] Indeed, in Catholicism, the need for a permanent sacred building allows only stone houses of worship to be consecrated by the higher levels of clergy.

Mario Botta's chapel in Tamaro is constructed from reinforced concrete faced with rusticated and rough porphyry[37] (Figures 9.1, 9.4 and 9.5). Its stone façade makes the chapel blend into the rocks of the mountain while creating a new mountain peak. Furthermore, as stone embodies the concept of endurance, this chapel enhances the principle of gravity inherent in architectural structures.[38] The interior is not clad with stone but uses blackened lime mortar and white outlines in the ceiling. This treatment enriches the interplay of light and shadow and creates an intimate place to showcase contemporary liturgical art (Figure 9.7). Similar to other churches by Botta, this chapel also demonstrates how he designed the sacred architecture to become a piece of art and to also frame sacred art.[39] Botta worked with artist Enzo Cucchi who marked the chapel's interior walls with a collection of symbols of prayers. It became "a leitmotif for the metaphoric illustration of the Madonna"—Santa Maria degli Angeli—to whom the church is dedicated[40] (Figure 9.7). Plastering the interior walls for displaying art recalls the Romanesque churches built of stone and plastered inside to let the artists of the time create their astonishing frescos.

Figure 9.7   Chapel of St. Mary of the Angels, Monte Tamaro: interior
Source: Photograph courtesy of Anat Geva.

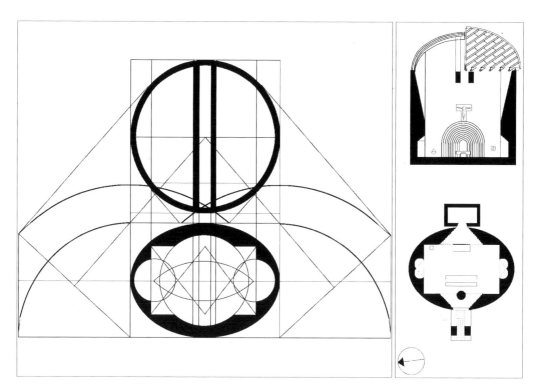

Figure 9.8   San Giovanni Battista Church, Mogno: a) the transformation of its geometry, b) floor plan
                and section

Source: a) and b) From *Architetture Del Sacro*, eds. Mario Botta and Gabriele Cappellato (Bologna, Italy: Editrice
Compositori, 2005) redrawn by Gali Zilbershtein under author's supervision.

The church in Mogno is a double skin of alternating courses of gray *Riveo* granite and white *Peccia*
marble outside and inside. These were quarried locally in the valley similar to historic Tuscan cathedrals
(e.g., Siena Cathedral). As such, it continues a tradition of church construction and creates a statement of
permanence, stability, and gravity. Moreover, "by superimposing the new volume onto the ruins of the old
[destroyed] church, Botta programmatically forsakes the idea of recovering its essential characteristics."[41]

The interior stone walls demonstrate the transformation of the geometry of the building from
"a rectangle inscribed within an external ellipse that ultimately changes into a circle at roof level. Botta,
thus orients the church space by means of the minor axis of the ellipse, which becomes a circle at the
conveniently sloped roof"[42] (Figures 9.8a and 9.8b).

This requires the cut stones to adapt gradually, layer by layer, to the changes in geometry, and eventually
reach the circle form of the roof to frame its shape (Figure 9.9). Thus, they can be associated with the sacred
since they reach the climax of the sacred space, the circle.

Rudolf Schwarz in *The Church Incarnate* (1958) states that the circle (ring) is the richest of all
geometrical forms since it represents the endless and infinite form of eternity.[43] Furthermore, Nader Ardalan
and Laleh Bakhtiar in *The Sense of Unity* claim that the circle is the symbol of truth, the way, and the law.[44]

Botta studied the nature and techniques of cutting stone so it could transform the geometry and the
shape of the building. He claims that he focused on the technique as an architectural invention rather than
an ecclesiastical one.[45] Still, the transformation of the stone according to geometry in the church in Mogno
received numerous interpretations from scholars and visitors alike. Judith Dupre (2001) sees it as a metaphor
for potential spiritual transformation.[46] Rudolf Arnheim (2005) examines the philosophical and theological
interpretations of an ellipse controlling a rectangular space within the sacred realm of a circle[47] (Figure 9.8a).

Figure 9.9   San Giovanni Battista Church, Mogno: interior view towards the sky
Source: Photograph courtesy of Anat Geva.

Some find symbolism in the axis of the circled roof, which appears in the middle of the two powerful arched buttresses of the interior, and is aligned with the point where the stone curved crucifix is attached to the wall (Figure 9.10). The apse below is interpreted as the passage of time, and its 12 concentric arches as representing the 12 apostles (Figure 9.10). Although Botta's primary concern in the design of this church was technical (cutting the stone), his design created myth and symbolism that enhance the worshiper's spiritual experience.

Figure 9.10   San Giovanni Battista Church, Mogno: the crucifix, the apse, and the altar
Source: Photograph courtesy of Anat Geva.

Light

While stone construction in sacred architecture represents earth and permanence, light expresses heaven and contributes to the connection of the human with a higher order of things, with the essential, and with the immutable truth.[48] Mircea Eliade states, "Even before any religious values have been set upon the sky it reveals its transcendence. The sky symbolizes transcendence, power and changeless-ness simply by being there. It exists because it is high, infinite, immovable, powerful."[49]

Light enhances the experience of materials, forms, lines, colors and texture in a manner that represents beauty. Botta believes that light creates the temporal ambience of the sacred since it is "the visual sign of the relationship that exists between the architectural work and the cosmic values of the surroundings."[50] Moreover, scholars such as Giovanni Pozzi declare that architecture starts with the design of light.[51] However, darkness is necessary to complete the experience of light.[52] The relationship between light and darkness creates the dramatic visual and spiritual experiences in a sacred setting and links the celestial body with spiritual and mystical transcendence.[53] We can find the cosmic forces of this relationship already in the first chapter of Genesis: "Then God said let there be light and there was light—God saw how good the light was … evening came and morning followed—the first day."[54] Thus, light in sacred settings illustrates the divine presence and is perceived as an attempt to enrich the inner spiritual experience of God as Light.[55] This in turn fulfills the human aspiration to be closer to the divine and offers "a hopeful sanctuary in a shadowy void, a safe-haven in the ontological night, a friendly harbor in the cosmic sea."[56] Manipulating light and shadow in sacred architecture is to rediscover the symbolism of sacred architecture beyond the functional imperatives of worship.[57]

Interestingly, Botta treated the relationship of light and the cosmos differently in the two houses of worship. The Chapel in Tamaro, which is located below the outdoor crucifix, under the exterior pathway on top of the mountain, is dimly lit like a grotto (Figure 9.7 and section in Figure 9.11). Although the circular space of the interior seems like one area, it is actually divided into a nave with a vaulted ceiling and two aisles with stepped ceilings (Figure 9.11). The central space is defined by its linear axis initiated by two columns at the entrance. The axis directs the worshiper towards the small apse where a large image of the hands of Mary is placed (Figure 9.7, plan in Figure 9.11). This line is accentuated by the black paint on the nave's ceiling that continues from the exterior linear ceiling underneath the pathway (bridge) (Figures 9.5 and 9.7). Similar to the interior of the church in Mogno, Botta's design leads the eye toward the focal point of the sacred space (e.g., the apse, the crucifix, or a liturgical image). As such the central line defines the main volume of the chapel recalling traditional processional ways in Catholic churches (Figure 9.7). The white outlines of the ceiling help reflect the light admitted by very small windows in the bottom of the walls and through the narrow skylights (Figure 9.7). The exterior stair's risers that descend to the chapel from the upper path create the chapel's skylights (section in Figure 9.11). Each riser is indented and made from opaque glass. To diffuse the light, the ceilings on both sides of the major vaulted arch (the nave) were designed as white-washed steps and light bounces off them to reach the interior.

The light treatment in the Tamaro Chapel continues the long tradition of Italian Romanesque churches where dim light frames the liturgical art. The light effect and the space's strong linear path within the circular volume draw one's attention to the artwork in the apse, while the light that bounces off the small windows onto the interior highlights Cucchi's paintings above the tilted windows (Figure 9.7). Similar to the light penetration in historic churches, the light in the chapel comes from very small windows and narrow skylights and therefore the interior is always dimly lit. While in Romanesque churches the monumental large space allows the art to blend with the sacred space, this chapel is too small to allow this effect and creates the feeling of visiting an art gallery rather than a sacred chapel. Therefore, it diminishes the invitation for meditation inside a protective "cave" in the mountains, or its religious symbol of a crypt.[58]

In the Mogno Church, Botta introduced the ever-changing patterns of light and the relation to the cosmos through a circular glass roof (Figures 9.2 and 9.9). This roof frames the sky to bring the worshiper closer to the divine. Botta recalls the richness of the relationship between sunlight and shadow, and shadow within shadow, by orienting the building and its congregation to the sun (north arrow in Figure 9.8b). He experimented with these relationships in his drawings, which suggest a geometric instrument like a sundial. Through these studies Botta discovered a sense of gravity, light, and the sun's movement during the day.[59]

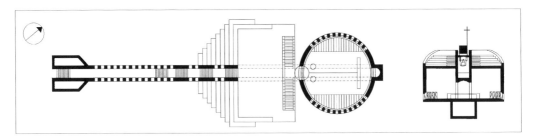

Figure 9.11   Chapel of St. Mary of the Angels, Monte Tamaro, Switzerland: floor plan and section
Source: From *Architetture Del Sacro*, eds. Mario Botta and Gabriele Cappellato (Bologna, Italy: Editrice Compositori, 2005) redrawn by Gali Zilbershtein under author's supervision.

The glass roof serves as the only source of light in the church—a window to heaven collecting infinite views to the sky—recalling the sentiments of Su Shi from the 11th century, "This pavilion has nothing in it, yet sitting here, one could collect a thousand views and obtain the whole Heaven."[60]

Two granite buttresses pierce the envelope of the building arch over the interior (Figure 9.9) and create an east–west axis that aligns with the axis of the destroyed historic church (Figures 9.2 and 9.8b). The light coming from above highlights this connection to the past, the present, and eternity. It also contributes to the interpretations and symbolism of the interior. Furthermore, the relationship of light and shadows illustrates Botta's transformational geometry and the interplay of the special stone coursing (Figure 9.10). In this church Botta used light to capture the passage of time and to establish our relationship with the solar and seasonal cycles, and the eternal. Through light Botta opened the secluded stone shelter to the sky, creating a place for praying, meditating, and reflecting.

Summary and Conclusion

The integration of mountains, stone, and light illustrates how mountain temples may represent the link between heaven and earth since "Mountains allow man to make the connection between Heaven and Earth in this physical world."[61] As such, designers may employ the vertical axis to mirror this link while embracing the mountains' horizon, their panoramic views, contours, and aura of mystery and magic.[62]

The analysis of Botta's two churches attempts to answer the chapter's question of the relationship between the design of mountain temples and their majestic surroundings while also creating a human scaled space for spiritual solitude This study shows different architectural approaches to the relationship with mountains. The chapel in Tamaro was built on top of the mountain creating a new peak, while the church in Mogno was built as a pillar soaring upward resembling a mountain. The analysis also illustrates that the experience of the spiritual transformation between the sacred building and nature—God's creation is at times associated with the exterior (the chapel in Tamaro) and at times the interior (the church in Mogno).

The sacredness of the chapel in Tamaro is experienced while walking on the horizontal path on top of the chapel and the mountain **where** the sacred path and the vertical axis of the mountain **coincide**. It leads the worshiper to the edge of the "built" new top of the mountain, where the mountains' horizon dominates the vista, while a metal cross and a bell are placed close by (Figure 9.3). This design is as grand as the mountains and follows Botta's claim that the landscape dictates his architectural solution (Figure 9.1). While the exterior of the structure evokes spirituality and a feeling of awe, the interior, designed as a cave or grotto, diminishes the outside experience. Still, the chapel can be viewed as a shelter that corresponds with traditional alpine architecture and with the sacredness associated with caves.[63] Botta states that his design attempted to extend beyond protection from the elements, it intends to serve as a place of sanctity and to offer solitude and tranquility, as a shield against human anxiety and stress. However, it seems to be alienated from the mountain context becoming a small art gallery rather than a sacred space. One can see how the iconography of grace and Mary created by Enzo Cucchi may lift the human spirit and encourage a dialogue with God. Yet, this artwork does not necessarily transform the interior space into a holy place. Although the architectural design framed the art, it did not support this transformation since the place is too dim and small.

Looking at the church in Mogno as part of the village skyline (Figure 9.2) one can sense a resemblance to the mountains' lines in the background, while it serves as the vertical focal point of the village (Figure 9.6). The church stands more as a sacred pillar, suggesting to the inhabitants that they possess the mountains. Furthermore, as pillars and cosmic axis are bound up with ideas about the composition of the universe and represent on one hand earth and on the other heaven, the verticality of the church links earth and heaven. However, the building does not seem to rise from the earth and to represent the specifics of the site. In other words, it does not effectively "adopt natural forms derived from the context."[64] Indeed, the formalism of the cylinder and its tilted circular glass roof more reflect Botta's unique style, which he used in other sacred and secular projects in different locations.

Instead, the holiness of the Church in Mogno is created in the interior—an enclosed small space washed with light penetrating from the glass roof—"aspires to meet the basic demands of a temple of worship" using the symbolism of geometrical transformation.[65] The scale, proportions, geometry, and light make the interior a sacred space, a shelter for spiritual meditation, uplifting the spirits of worshipers and visitors. It leads them to experience the inner light combined with the outer light that pours into the church through the glass roof. The upper source of light frames the sky (heaven) and the changes of light by the hour and seasons bring one to admire the universe—God's creation. While the interior of the church does not relate to the surrounding mountains and does not seem to grow out of the earth, one can obtain the whole heaven by looking to the sky in this remote place of solitude.[66]

In conclusion, even though the two churches express different architectural approaches to the design of mountain houses of worship, they also demonstrate several common design aspects, which can be applied to other designs of mountain temples: both sacred buildings illustrate essential aspects and characteristics of mountain temples that suggest a certain type of historical symbolic continuity while introducing modern forms and innovative techniques of stonework; both utilize local stone to emphasize the permanence of the place and links to its history; both designs were influenced by the relationship/no relationship to the mountains surrounding their place and evoke various spiritual interpretations; and both buildings introduce the notion of shelter and protection from the surrounding environment corresponding to traditional mountain architecture and to the idea that manmade caves or grottos may serve as a sacred place. In both, geometric transformation served as the basis or his sacred architecture; in both, the construction details and execution are impressive and contribute to the spiritual experience; and in both sacred artwork is to be understood after experiencing the sacredness of the buildings themselves. As Louise Pelletier states, "only by receiving true emotion from architecture will man be able to consider art."[67]

Acknowledgments

I would like to thank the editors of this volume for the opportunity to publish my chapter in this book. Special thanks to Tom Barrie whose insightful comments and editorial notes strengthen the chapter; to Gali Zilbershtein for redrawing the churches' plans and sections; and to Nehemia Geva who helped with the photography.

Endnotes

1   Dupre, Judith (trans.) (2011). *Churches.* New York, NY: Harper Collins, pp. 12–13.
2   Shunxun, Nan and Beverly Foit-Albert (2007). *China's Sacred Sites.* Honesdale, PA, p. 19.
3   Lloyd Wright, Frank (1900). A Philosophy of Fine Art, unpublished speech, reprinted in Pfeiffer Bruce (ed.) (1992). *Frank Lloyd Wright Collected Writings*, vol. 1. New York, NY: Rizzoli, pp. 39–44.
4   Shunxun and Foit-Albert, *China's Sacred Sites*, p. 19.
5   Ibid., p. 4.
6   Hale, Elizabeth (2007). *Sacred Space, Sacred Sound.* Wheaton, IL: Theosophical Publishing House, p. 52.

7   Frampton, Kenneth and Kunio Kudo (1997). *Japanese Building Practice: From Ancient Times to the Meiji Period.* New York, NY: Van Nostrand Reinhold, p. 3.

8   Brockman, Norbert (1997). *Encyclopedia of Sacred Places.* Santa Barbara, CA: ABC-Clio Inc., pp. 292–3; Layton, Robert (2001). *Uluru: An Aboriginal History of Ayers Rock*, 2nd edition. Canberra, Australia: Aboriginal Studies Press.

9   Shunxun and Foit-Albert, *China's Sacred Sites*, p. 4.

10   Genesis 28:18.

11   Geva, Anat (2011). *Frank Lloyd Wright's Sacred Architecture: Faith, Form, and Building Technology.* London, UK: Routledge, p. 140.

12   Tel Hazor was declared a UNESCO World Heritage site in 2005.

13   Mirsky, Jeanette (1976). *Houses of God.* Chicago, IL: The University of Chicago Press, Phoenix ed., p. 6.

14   Geva, *Frank Lloyd Wright's Sacred Architecture*, p. 141.

15   Shunxun and Foit-Albert, *China's Sacred Sites*, p. 52.

16   You can reach the chapel located 5,141 feet above sea level only by cable car or by a one-and-a-half-hour journey on foot.

17   Mario Botta, http://www.botta.ch/ (accessed November 2014).

18   Shunxun and Foit-Albert, *China's Sacred Sites*, p. 7.

19   Mario Botta, in Dupre, *Churches*, p. 12.

20   Ibid., p. 8.

21   Oechslin, Werner (2005). Mario Botta: Sacred Architecture, Expression and Stone, in Mario Botta and Gabriele Cappellato (eds), *Architetture Del Sacro: Prayers in Stone.* Bologna, Italy: Editrice Compositori, p. 91.

22   Botta and Cappellato, *Architetture Del Sacro*, p. 192.

23   George Michell in his book: (1977). *The Hindu Temple: Introduction to its Meaning and Forms.* London: Elek, p. 69, addresses the idea of a cave serving as a retreat and occasionally as habitation of gods.

24   Taut, Bruno (2004). *Bruno Taut, Alpine Architektur: eine Utopie = Bruno Taut, Alpine Architecture: A Utopia*, translated by Matthias Schirren. New York, NY: Prestel.

25   See endnote 18.

26   Dupre, *Churches*, pp. 12–13.

27   Ibid., p. 12.

28   Dal Co, Francesco (2005). Church of San Giovanni Battista, Mongo Fusio, Canton Ticino, in Mario Botta and Gabriele Cappellato (eds), *Architetture Del Sacro*, pp. 37–41.

29   Dupre, *Churches*, p. 13.

30   Mario Botta in Dupre, *Churches*, p. 12.

31   Mario Botta in Botta and Cappellato (eds), *Architetture Del Sacro*, p. 32.

32   Mario Botta in Dupre, *Churches*, p. 12.

33   Ibid.

34   Mario Botta in Botta and Cappellato (eds), *Architetture Del Sacro*, p. 191.

35   Lloyd Wright, Frank (1928). In the Cause of Architecture III: The Meaning of Materials—Stone. *Architectural Record* 63(4), pp. 350–56; Tabb, Phillip (2007). Semantic Cosmologies of Ronchamp and Rothko Chapel, in K.C. Eynaten, Kate Hutchins Don Quaintance (eds), *Not Seen: Search for Understanding: The Rothko Chapel Art Series.* Houston, TX: A Rothko Chapel Book, pp. 89–99; Geva, *Frank Lloyd Wright's Sacred Architecture.*

36   Geva, *Frank Lloyd Wright's Sacred Architecture*, p. 167.

37   The roof of the chapel in Monte Tamaro is also constructed from reinforced concrete faced with rusticated and rough porphyry.

38   Mario Botta in Botta and Cappellato (eds), *Architetture Del Sacro*, pp. 191–2.

39   Geva, Anat (2014). Architecture as Art and Frame for Art. *Faith & Form* XLVII(1), pp. 6–8.

40   Dupre, *Churches*, p. 15.

41   Dal Co, Church of San Giovanni Battista, p. 40.

42   Mario Botta, http://www.botta.ch/ (accessed November 2014).

43   Schwarz, Rudolf (trans.) (1958). *The Church Incarnate: The Sacred Function of Christian Architecture.* Chicago, IL: H. Regnery Co.

44   Ardalan, Nader and Laleh Bakhtiar (1973). *The Sense of Unity: The Sufi Tradition in Persian Architecture.* Chicago, IL: The University of Chicago Press.

45 Mario Botta in Dupre, *Churches*, p. 13.

46 Dupre, *Churches*, p. 13.

47 Arnheim, Rudolf, "Notes on Religious Architecture" in Botta and Cappellato (eds), *Architetture Del Sacro*, pp. 32–6.

48 Geva, *Frank Lloyd Wright's Sacred Architecture.*

49 Eliade, Mircea (1996 [1958]). *Patterns in Comparative Religion.* New York, NY: Sheed and Ward Inc., 1996 edition published by University of Nebraska Press, Lincoln, Nebraska; Eliade, Mircea (1985[1992]). Sacred Architecture and Symbolism, in Mircea Eliade and Diane Apostolos-Cappadona (eds), *Symbolism, the Sacred, and the Arts.* London and New York, NY: Bloomsbury Academic.

50 Botta, Mario in Gabriele Cappellato (ed.), *Mario Botta: Light and Gravity, Architecture 1993–2003.* Munich, Germany: Prestel.

51 Pozzi, Giovanni "The Origin of the Church" in Botta and Cappellato (eds), *Architetture Del Sacro*, p. 93.

52 Mukherji, Anuradah (2001). The Holy Light: A Study of Natural Light in Historic Hindu Temples in The Southern Region of Tamilnadu, India (MS Thesis, Texas A&M University; Lechner, Norbert (2001). *Heating, Cooling, Lighting: Design Methods for Architects*, 2nd edition. New York, NY: John Wiley & Sons Inc.

53 Geva, *Frank Lloyd Wright's Sacred Architecture*, p. 189.

54 Genesis 1:35.

55 Anat Geva, Anat (2009). Light and Darkness in Sacred Settings. *2A—Architecture and Art Magazine*, Quarterly 12, Autumn, pp. 56–9.

56 Plummer, Henry (1987). Poetics of Light. *Architecture and Urbanism* December, pp. 8–11.

57 Petitt, Jean, Space and Form of the Invisible, in Botta and Cappellato (eds), *Architetture Del Sacro*, p. 42.

58 Michell in *The Hindu Temple* states that the Hindu faith considers human's caves or grottoes as sacred as the natural sacred cave.

59 Mario Botta in Dupre, *Churches*, p. 13.

60 Su Shi, *The Void Pavilion* (1036–1101).

61 Shunxun and Foit-Albert, *China's Sacred Sites*, p. 4.

62 Shunxun and Foit-Albert, *China's Sacred Sites*, p. 18; see examples in Shunxun and Foit-Albert, *China's Sacred Sites*: the Zhao Gao Memorial, p. 45, and the flying immortal pavilion in Mount Dochuan, p. 72.

63 See endnotes 24 and 57.

64 Dal Co, Church of San Giovanni Battista, p. 38.

65 Arnheim, Notes on Religious Architecture, pp. 32, 34.

66 Su Shi, *The Void Pavilion.*

67 Pelletier, Louise (2008). Modeling the Void: Mathias Goeritz and the Architecture of Emotions. *Journal of Architectural Education* 62(2) (November), pp. 6–13.

Chapter 10
Narrating Chichén Itzá:
Storytelling, Disagreement, and Second Naïveté at the "City of the Sacred Well"

Lindsay Jones

The pre-Columbian pilgrimage destination and now archaeological-tourist site of Chichén Itzá owns innumerable distinctions. Not the largest of ancient Mayan sites nor, by any assessment, the most architecturally beautiful, Chichén Itzá is, and has been for the past several hundred years, the most high-profile and oft-visited of Mayaland ruins. Forever located on a main Yucatan thoroughfare, the long-abandoned city figures large in the accounts of 16th-century conquistadors and priests, 19th-century antiquarians, and 20th-century archeologists, including those who, from the 1920s through to the 1940s, made this the base of operations for a huge Carnegie Institution of Washington initiative to explore the entire Mayan zone. More recently and at present, the great Maya capital, the least pristine and most "Disneyfied" of Mesoamerican ruins, continues to be the object of on-going excavations and major reconstruction efforts in parts of the ancient city that remain hidden from all but the most intrepid tourists.[1]

All this activity has likewise had irreparably destructive effects so that, ironically enough, the Maya site that has received the greatest outlay of resources and attention remains among the most poorly understood and thus most hotly contested. Still there is disagreement about even the basic outline of Chichén Itzá's history, and the current literature suggests a growing disparity of views rather than anything like an emergent consensus.

Not surprisingly, then, among all Mesoamerican sites, these built forms have also inspired by far the richest, and still-fast-growing, *oeuvre* of stories. Indeed, arguably, a foremost attribute of the monuments of Chichén Itzá—as the very quintessence of what I've termed "the autonomy and superabundance of architecture"[2]—is their enduring proclivity to *evoke narrative*. In this case, persistent historical uncertainties have the sometimes salutary, invariably revealing effect of opening space for creative story-telling and/or myth-making. That is to say, virtually every visitor to the ruins—Mexican or foreign nationals, casual or seriously studious, spiritually inclined or simply on a holiday furlough—feels inclined and entitled to pick out, or maybe make up, a story that accounts for the enormous and distinctive monuments. The primary means of "making sense" of these pre-Columbian buildings nearly always entails proposing a plotline about them. And though stories of Chichén Itzá are enhanced by a sense among both tellers and listeners that the narrative more or less matches actual past events, it becomes clear fairly quickly that, among this ever-unfolding catalogue of creative compositions, historical accuracy is far more an exception than the rule.

Departing from that basic premise, this essay has an asymmetrical three-part agenda.[3] First, I briefly narrate a heartfelt story about the pivotal role that this place and these buildings, the focus of my Ph.D. dissertation, have played in shaping my own scholarly and personal outlooks. The second part, which will constitute the lion's share of this written version, is a roughly chronological inventory of a whole series of what might be termed Chichén Itzá "meta-narratives" insofar as these are stories about the stories that many others have told about this place. Additional contenders for inclusion on that list are abundant in the extreme, and students of the site may find mine a somewhat eccentric collection of usual suspects along with a few less likely voices. Nonetheless, these different renditions of Chichén Itzá's past represent, in a sense, competitors for the approval of contemporary visitors to the site, the great majority of whom operate without the technical knowledge that would enable a rigorous evaluation of the competing accounts. And thus by showcasing the very wide range of alternative accounts, and providing a little back-story on the respective narrators, I set a stage for the third section, which presents some tentative reflections on two sorts of illusions that, I contend, are required for a rewarding visit to the so-termed City of the Sacred Well.

Figure 10.1   For decades, the ruins of Chichén Itzá have been the Mayaland's foremost tourist
attraction, and thus a quintessential venue for the creative storytelling of guides, scholars,
and visitors

Source: Photograph courtesy of Lindsay Jones.

Fictive and/or Real Conquests: From Pre-Columbian History to the On-going History of Ideas

In the 1980s, when, as a graduate student, I first began to take a special interest in Chichén Itzá, I, like so many others, accepted with little skepticism the very widely-circulated notion that the site, located in the northern Maya zone, owed its oddly Mexican architectural style to a historical circumstance that was variously termed "the Toltec Conquest of the Maya" or "the Mexicanization of Yucatan."[4] Permutations on the storyline of this infamous invasion (a handful of which I will mention below) are abundant in the extreme.[5] Nonetheless, in the simplest scenario, at some point, maybe around the 10th century, the Toltecs—who were third-rate artists but first-rate warriors—came marauding out of central Mexico, perhaps led by a great priest-king named Quetzalcoatl, into the Yucatan Peninsula where they encountered the Mayas—who were first-rate artists and religious thinkers, but diffident warriors. Given this great disparity in talents and dispositions, the bellicose Toltecs bullied and bashed the gentle and cerebral Maya and, so the story goes, forced them to build in the north sector of Chichén Itzá a bigger and better version of their home capital at Tula.

This narrative frame, albeit fleshed out in innumerable different ways, appears in nearly every 20th-century synthesis of Mesoamerican history. And though (or actually *because*) the ballyhooed resemblance between Tula and Chichén Itzá was one of the most heavily trafficked topics in the field, as a historian of religions in training, I set for myself the task of extracting and examining what Mircea Eliade would term "the specifically religious dimensions" of the Toltec Conquest. It was, then, to make a very long meta-story short, a matter of no small consternation when, following a couple of years of reading and thinking about this celebrated old problem, it became increasingly—if, in hindsight, much too slowly—apparent to me that the infamous Toltec Conquest of the Maya had, in fact, never happened!

This seeming deathblow to the dissertation project, wherein the Toltec Conquest was exposed for the fiction that it is, marked the end of my "first naïveté" or face-value assessment of the stories about Chichén Itzá as though they were literal or even figurative accounts of historical events.[6] But instead of disillusionment and disappointment, just as quickly I awakened to, in Paul Ricoeur's term, a "second naïveté" appreciation of the enormously rich collection of (re)construction narratives that the ruins of Chichén Itzá has evoked.

In other words, at that point, the focus of my inquiry switched from a quest after the "religious dimensions" of a historical Toltec Conquest to the no less fascinating set of questions concerning why so many people, top-tier scholars included, have been so persistent in representing this apocryphal tale as though it were an actual historical event. If this conquest narrative—which scholars have by now largely dismissed, but that one can still read in countless books and still hear retold countless times every day at Chichén Itzá—is not really an account of events that had happened, then what is that story about? Where did this tale of a confrontation between mean Indians and mystical Indians come from? What forces were at work in its construction? And what, besides the history of Chichén Itzá, are these stories about? Moreover, if the appeal of these stories has *not* been primarily contingent on their faithfulness to the sequence of pre-Columbian events, then to what do they owe their impressive endurance? Why have so many, for so long, and in so many venues told these stories with such enthusiasm and interest?

Elsewhere I provide fuller replies to these questions about both the tangled origins of this gaudy tale wherein the fierce Toltecs smash the erudite Mayas, as well as the myriad of forces that account for the story's exceptional endurance and appeal.[7] But, for present purposes, suffice it note that, as I eventually replaced my initially incautious assumptions about the historicity of the so-termed Toltec Conquest of the Maya with a more critical contextualization and deconstruction of the same narrative, I came to two larger and interrelated realizations. For one, the prospect of discovering anything like the "specifically religious dimension" of the military adventuring that had given rise to Chichén Itzá's great monuments vanished and was replaced by an interest in the still-unfolding history of ideas—or the succession of storytelling—about those monuments. And, for two, that shift in emphasis reaffirmed my ideas about the "superabundance" of sacred architecture in ways that redirected my attentions away from a quest after the definitive, once-and-for-all meanings of Chichén Itzá's monumental architecture (secure meanings that I maintain never existed) and onto an appreciation of the fabulous diversity of significances—and stories—that have emerged from the site's ongoing "architectural reception history."[8]

In short, problematizing and thus "seeing through" the dominant narrative of Chichén Itzá, if at first a shock and disappointment, had the fortuitous, indeed career-altering effect of opening the way to a fuller appreciation of the cacophony of discordant attitudes and explanations, unsurpassed at any other Mesoamerican site, that continues to make this place so fascinating.

A Sampling of Chichén Itzá Storytellers: Alternate Enthusiasms for the Same Old Sacred Place

With that brief rendition of my own story of Chichén Itzá and the profound effect that the site has had on my thinking about the more general workings of sacred architecture, I turn now to a roughly chronological, staccato-like inventory of 13 alternate storytellers. A few were leading proponents for some version of the Toltec Conquest story, but others either reject or ignore that view. A mélange of intriguing personalities and fascinating characters, most are ostensibly scholars but others are deliberately (or inadvertently) anti-academic. Most are published authors and many are subjects of biographical works, which is to say, all deserve much fuller treatment; the sketchy bibliographic references are, then, intended only to initiate a wider search.

Be that as it may, I assemble this oddly eclectic cast in hopes of representing 13 decidedly different ways of engaging these architectural ruins—with a special emphasis on their respective means of assessing the supposed "sacredness" of the place; and thus I assign each a descriptive, if distressing elliptical title. That is to say, while most belong to long by-gone eras, I would wager that the respective attitudes they bring to the Maya capital are temperaments one could still encounter among similarly eclectic constituencies of present-day visitors to Chichén Itzá. And, to that extent, prospective visitors are encouraged to assess them either as alternative models worthy of emulation or anti-heroes whose attitudes toward the ruins ought to be fastidiously avoided.

Figure 10.2   Since the 1980s, Chichén Itzá has attracted more than 30,000 visitors each spring equinox
                and on December 21, 2012, a day that many associated with a dubious prophecy of
                apocalypse, the crowd was estimated at more than 45,000
Source: Photograph courtesy of Lindsay Jones.

The Reverent: Colonial-era (and Present-Day) Mayas

Numerous accounts of colonial-era sacrifices at the Sacred Cenote in times of drought, some probably
exaggerated by Spanish priests wanting to demonstrate the persistence of "heathen" practices, nonetheless
provide strong evidence that, for many Mayas of that time, the largely overgrown site of Chichén Itzá, which
had centuries earlier ceased to be a place of habitation, remained a much-revered pilgrimage destination.[9]
Though devoid of any reliable empirical information about the history of the ancient city, these Mayas surely
had abundant stories to account for the creation and abandonment of the ruins, which were always considered
by the indigenous locals a place of special access to their deities. The copal offerings that one can still
frequently find in the outlying portions of Chichén Itzá, usually at the base of some ruined structure, evince
continued reverence for these old structures even among present-day Maya Catholics.

The Strictly Pragmatic: Francisco Montejo the Younger (born c. 1507)

Among the earliest Europeans to visit Chichén Itzá, this Spanish conquistador, a member of the infamous
Montejo family who spearheaded the much-resisted conquest of Yucatan, established a military base at the
largely abandoned site in 1532.[10] That the local Mayas continued to regard this as a sacred place was, it seems,
entirely incidental. For Montejo the Younger, who mounted a cannon atop the Castillo pyramid, the appeal
of the site and its monumental architecture was its central location and ready-built fortifications. This strictly
pragmatic irreverence may persist, though to rather different ends, among the many commercial interests or

their visitor-clients for whom the ruins, by far the most intensely commodified of any in Mesoamerica, are attractive first and foremost as a venue for selling and buying.

The Religiously Intolerant: Diego de Landa (1524–79)

Paradoxically, this Spanish Franciscan Bishop of the Roman Catholic Archdiocese of Yucatán who is infamous for his wholesale burning of Maya codices is also responsible for the *Relación de las cosas de Yucatán*, the most thoroughgoing account of colonial-era Mayan life, which also includes the most extensive descriptions of the status of Chichén Itzá during this era as well as a then-current story about how the city had been founded by three brothers.[11] For Diego de Landa, that local populations held the place in such high esteem was of crucial importance—but largely because that devotion signaled their continued investments in a wholly unacceptable "pagan" religion. Deeply committed to this own Christian faith and just as deeply intolerant of others' religious orientations, Landa, one suspects, might have conceded that Chichén Itzá and its Cenote do provide privileged access to some supernatural agents, but of the unsavory, demonic sort. Nowadays, though the vim of Landa's intolerance may be difficult to duplicate, there are, nevertheless, visitors who are either quietly condescending or openly antagonistic toward the proposition that Chichén Itzá is a sacred site on a par with their own places of worship.

The Eminently Reasonable: John Lloyd Stephens (1805–52)

In advance of any reliable methods to date the ruins, many 18th- and 19th-century visitors to Chichén Itzá and other sites, ventured wild guesses about both the extreme antiquity of these overgrown buildings and their foreign-born builders, attributing them variously to Phoenicians, the Chinese, or perhaps refugees from the lost continent of Atlantis. By contrast, this American explorer, author and diplomat, who visited Chichén Itzá and numerous other sites in the 1840s, avoided any such brash speculation, and instead correctly concluded that the ancestors of the local Mayas had built these monuments a few hundred years ago.[12] John Stephens' evenhanded journalistic style provides first-rate stories of travel and excellent descriptions of the ruins, but very little in the way of a narrative designed to account for the pre-Columbian construction or use of these buildings. Moreover, Stephens' tempered views likewise display a version of cultural relativism that remains the prevailing attitude among most subsequent visitors, today's tourists included, insofar as he could appreciate that, *for the Mayas*, these were sacred places; but his positivistic leanings exempted him from believing that there really was anything intrinsically powerful about Chichén Itzá's Cenote or buildings that might apply to him.

The Eccentrically Diffusionist: Augustus Le Plongeon (1825–1908)

Living in Yucatan from 1873–85, this French antiquarian and his wife were highly accomplished photographers and even more exuberant storytellers. Their accounts—wherein the builders of Chichén Itzá are eventually responsible Egyptian civilization!—are, these days, usually deployed as comic relief rather than as a consideration-worthy alternative.[13] Much more over-determined, more fantastic, and less grounded in the archaeological and ethnohistorical sources than his more mainline counterparts, Le Plongeon's ruminations about "a lost continent of Mu" secure his status as an outsider.[14] Sometimes seemingly resentful that he was shunned by the scholarly establishment of his day and sometimes celebrating his independence from the stuffy strictures of academe, Le Plongeon's outlook also includes investments in mesmerism and other metaphysical movements of the time, which embolden him to acknowledge Chichén Itzá's intrinsic sacrality in ways that others did not. He, then, provides an heir to the abundance of deliberately anti-establishment "New Age" authors currently writing about Mesoamerica.

The Paternalistic Amateur: Edward Herbert Thompson (1857–1935)

American diplomat, self-trained archaeologist and owner from 1894–1926 of the hacienda that included Chichén Itzá, E.H. Thompson, often termed "the last great amateur," is subject to particularly mixed assessments.[15] In one view, he is a daring explorer and forward-looking caretaker of the site at a time

Figure 10.3   At present, a visit to the pre-Columbian pilgrimage destination of Chichén Itzá, requires
               navigating an ineludible gauntlet of souvenir stalls and the ceaseless din of cheap
               jaguar whistles
Source: Photograph courtesy of Lindsay Jones.

when Mexican antiquities were seriously neglected.[16] From another view, he was more treasure-hunter than researcher, a condemnation based especially on the contentious legal proceedings that required him to forfeit his hacienda and return to Mexico many of the objects he had recovered from the Sacred Cenote and shipped to the USA. That controversy, in any event, illustrates another sort of visitor who still frequents Chichén Itzá, namely, the condescending American connoisseur who finds ways to appreciate pre-Columbian antiquities—for artistic rather than religious reasons—while denigrating Mexico and Mexicans. The purported sacredness of the place is, according to this less gracious version of cultural relativism, primarily a consequence of naivety; wiser minds know better.

The Fully Professional: Alfred M. Tozzer (1877–1954)

This American anthropologist, archeologist, linguist and Harvard professor, the dominant university-based Mayanist for the first half of the 20th century, adopted the "Toltec-Maya Problem" as his life's work. He first visited Chichén Itzá in 1902, and thus was forced into a relationship with Edward Thompson, the keeper of the keys in that era, with whom he stands in stark contrast. On the one hand, like Maudslay and Holmes in his insistence on scholarly rigor, the incomparably well-informed Tozzer, ironically enough, deserves credit for the most convoluted of all versions of the Toltec Conquest of the Maya story. Albeit with a much more measured (or duller) prose, Tozzer's grand synthesis depends heavily on the interpretation of ethnohistorical documents, in this case a reference in the poetical *Books of Chilam Balam* that reads, "three times it was, they say, that foreigners arrived …"[17] Correlating the apparent duality in Chichén Itzá's art and architecture to that arcane line, Tozzer drafts a labyrinthine scenario wherein, following each of the first two incursions by Central Mexicans, the Yucatan Mayas win back control of the Sacred Cenote, only to lose it again in a third Mexican invasion, after which the once great city eventually fades into obscurity.[18]

Derided as a veritable "Virginia reel of alternating Maya and Mexican regimes"[19] or, in my own work, as the premier instance of "irreconcilable Maya-Mexican polarity" wherein the prospect of bi-ethnic mixing is distressingly ruled out,[20] Tozzer's serpentine saga is too complicated for subsequent Mayanists to endorse fully or for tour guides to repeat. Nonetheless, it is noteworthy that even the consummate scholar, writing primarily for other scholars, seems to share the view that, to be rewarding, the ruined city's dates and data need to be fashioned into a plausible plotline.

The Famously Exuberant: Sylvanus G. Morley (1883–1948)

This American archaeologist, epigrapher and director of the enormous Carnegie Institution of Washington's Chichén Itzá Project (1922–40) deserves singular credit for bringing the site to the attention of the American public, especially via *The National Geographic Magazine*, which was the ideal venue for his popularizing narrative style.[21] In part a deeply serious Mayanist scholar, the energetic Morley, who spent much of his time at Chichén Itzá from 1910 through the 1940s, was even more fully devoted to publicizing the remarkable accomplishments of the Classic Mayas, and, to that end, presented a series of simpler renditions of the Toltec Conquest of the Maya story.[22] The leading proponent of what I've termed "popular Maya-Mexican polarity," Morley experiments with several different scripts, but in all cases depicts the Yucatec Maya as thoroughly benign, apolitical, peaceful, and fully preoccupied with astronomy and calendrical pursuits; the invading Central Mexicans, by contrast, are their diametrically opposed antagonists who account for human sacrifice and anything else unsavory that one might encounter in the oeuvre of Chichén Itzá.[23] Though more fully academic contemporaries like Tozzer were bemused by the sometimes ridiculously extravagant praises that Morley heaped on his beloved Mayas, excesses that contemporary Mayanists fully reject, the fact that the majority of present-day tourists continue to arrive at Chichén Itzá with gushy expectations of an encounter with "the mystical Maya" reaffirms Morley's great skill and influence as a storyteller. His legacy is very much alive.

The Brilliantly Romantic: J. Eric S. Thompson (1898–1975)

The more accomplished scholar, this field-dominating British archaeologist and epigrapher joins Morley as the other author most responsible for the enduring images of the Classic Maya as largely peaceful astronomer-priests whose preoccupations with the worship of stars, nature and time superseded any interests in political domination or contestation. A similarly avid storyteller, who spent lots of time at Chichén Itzá from 1926 through to the 1960s, Eric Thompson provides renditions of the Toltec Conquest story that, unlike Tozzer's or Morley's, feature "symbiotic Maya-Mexican polarity" insofar as the erudite Maya and aggressive Mexican protagonists, while diametrically opposed, nonetheless find ways to commingle and merge their respective talents into a whole—namely, the Great Plaza of north Chichén Itzá—which is greater than the sum of their parts.[24] Though a scenario in which the great Castillo pyramid and plaza eventuate from the collaborative efforts of very different ethnic groups might seem to have appeal for Americans, Thompson's intricate accounts of fortuitous cultural mixing never enjoy the popular currency of more plain plots in which the wonderful Mayas are simply bullied by mean Mexicans. Nonetheless, careful listeners can detect the continued influence of Eric Thompson, particularly regarding Maya calendrics, in the creative pastiches of most on-site guides.

The Independent Minority: George Kubler (1912–96)

In the wake of Désiré Charnay's initial recognition in the 1860s of a special resemblance between Chichén Itzá's northern plaza and the 800-mile distant Toltec capital of Tula—an uncanny semblance that no one denies[25]—virtually all accounts are predicated on the assumption of a west-to-east movement of central Mexicans into the Maya area, where they built or forced others to build a bigger and better replica of their former home base. In rejecting that nearly unanimous assumption, then, this eminent art-historian adopts a radically unorthodox view.[26] Determined to build his opinions directly on the basis of the actual art and architecture (rather than ethnohistorical sources), Kubler emerges in the 1960s as the most articulate voice for the minority view that contends, contrary to entrenched opinion, that the principal cultural migration was east-to-west, and thus that Chichén Itzá was the original and Tula the copy. He, moreover, powerfully demonstrates that Chichén Itzá was a vigorously eclectic site, whose art and architecture resemble not just Tula but innumerable other Mesoamerican sites. Rejecting the old view that the city juxtaposed just two main styles—Toltec and Maya—Kubler argues instead that this is the most truly cosmopolitan of all pre-Columbian ceremonial centers, a provocative claim that provides the point of departure for the creation of all sorts of new and different stories of Chichén Itzá (mine included).

The Normalizing Iconoclast: Charles E. Lincoln (1960–)

The long-prevailing view of a west-to-east Mexicanization of the Yucatec Mayas, which few besides Kubler contest, is, moreover, predicated on the similarly timeworn assumption that the southern section of the site, commonly known as "Old Chichén," was the original Maya portion of the city that had been built in advance of the northern Toltec portion, which is still labeled on countless maps as "New Chichén." Taking issue with Alfred Tozzer's inclination to separate every feature of the site into either Maya versus Toltec—i.e., a "no overlap model"—Charles Lincoln, as a graduate student, undertakes new excavations and reinterprets old ones in ways that lead him to the iconoclastic stance of "total overlap," which is to say, that both the south and north sectors belonged to a single urban settlement that was continuously occupied through its history.[27] A giant, if overdue, change in thinking about the site!

With respect to storytelling, ironically, Lincoln's seemingly subversive agenda, which does nullify most previous plotlines, actually has a normalizing effect insofar as it deprives Chichén Itzá of its unique standing as a weirdly Mexican site in the Maya area, and transforms it instead into a more typical classic Maya city. Many scholars, long dubious of the Toltec-Maya bifurcation of the site, are persuaded; archaeologists less fully impressed by Lincoln's momentous modification respond with various sorts of compromise proposals for "partial overlap;" and, in more popular venues, Lincoln can be entirely ignored in favor of older Toltec Conquest stories that, despite their scholarly disrepute, still comport more favorably with most visitors' exoticizing expectations.

Figure 10.4   Large portions of the ancient city, including major buildings that have been recently reconstructed such as this archway in the Initial Series Group, are in areas that are restricted from normal tourist traffic

Source: Photograph courtesy of Lindsay Jones.

The (Over-)Corrective: Linda Schele (1942–98)

During the 1980s and 1990s, endorsing the "total overlap" model and keying on then-new breakthroughs in the decipherment of Maya hieroglyphs, which had played little role in earlier stories of Chichén Itzá, this epigrapher and her collaborators are vehement in their rejection of Morley's and Eric Thompson's images of the peaceful, time-worshipping Mayas.[28] Initiating a kind of renaissance in imaginative storytelling about all Maya sites, Chichén Itzá included, Linda Schele recasts the supposedly ethereal Maya as worldly political operatives who are relentlessly concerned with grisly blood-letting ceremonies, with besting their adversaries on the battlefield, and with ceaseless disputes over dynastic succession. Accordingly, there is no reason to invoke foreign invaders (e.g., Toltecs) as the perpetrators of the violent imagery that one observes in the Great Ballcourt and elsewhere at Chichén Itzá. Alternatively, the site's "truly cosmopolitan style" is, in her view, the result of an aggressive and deliberate appropriation of styles and images from other areas of Mesoamerica, which was designed to serve the imperialist ambitions of the Maya lords of the City of the Sacred Well.[29] For many, the glyph-derived stories of Schele and others present a much needed corrective, made especially appealing by the introduction of unprecedented amounts of information about specific Maya rulers and events; but for others, this drastically different vision of the not-nice Mayas replaces one set of exaggerations with another. In either case, the outcome is a (re)construction of Chichén Itzá that is both excitingly detailed but also so profoundly different from previous accounts that is it difficult to imagine discerning readers embracing the stories and characterizations of both Schele and her heirs.

The New Age Daykeeper: Hunbatz Men (1941–)

On the one hand, circling back to head of the list, the perspective of this Yucatan-born Maya elder, shaman, day-keeper and author confirms that contemporary Mayas continue to regard the ruins of Chichén Itzá as a sacred site of the highest order. On the other hand, this widely traveled, self-described "New Age" holy man, who has conducted countless workshops in the USA—and who was once allied but then parted ways with controversial artist, poet, philosopher, visionary and "time traveler," José Argüelles (1939–2011)[30]—finds his largest and most devoted following not among fellow Mayas, but rather American enthusiasts of the Mayas. In any case, Hunbatz Men, who founded and works out of the Lol Be Yok'Hah Maya Ceremonial Center and Cosmic Initiatic University near Merida, Yucatan, maintains that the monuments of Chichén Itzá, most notably the geometric Castillo pyramid, were designed according to, and thus remain repositories of, an esoteric wisdom, which mainstream scholars have wholly failed to appreciate, but which he has acquired via years of initiatory training.[31]

Attendees to Men's seminars encounter explanations that connect Chichén Itzá architecture to various "ancient mysteries," flows of energy, healing techniques and prophecies as well as to Crystal Skulls, which are, of late, a special focus of his commentaries. That all these ideas bear faint resemblance to "establishment scholarship" is, for him, a sign of just how impoverished academic understandings of Maya archaeological sites are. In short, Hunbatz Men and his abundant followers exemplify a perspective that accounts, in large part, for the crowds at Chichén Itzá of more than 30,000 each spring equinox and more than 45,000 on December 21, 2012—namely, that to reduce the "sacredness" of the site to a matter of opinion or cultural perspective skirts the crucial issue that the City of the Sacred Well is truly powerful in permanent and objective ways. Visitors who deny that miss a life-altering opportunity.

Figure 10.5   In the outlying sections of Chichén Itzá, where few tourists tread, it remains common to find
copal offerings, usually at the base of some ruined structure, that evince continued reverence
for these old structures among present-day Mayas

Source: Photograph courtesy of Lindsay Jones.

The Rewards of Illusion:
Evading the Tourist Experience and Embracing the Diversity of Chichén Itzá Stories

Certainly this inventory of Chichén Itzá storytellers and attitudes could be much longer. Absent, for instance, is that large constituency of Mexican officials, educators, students and citizens for whom a visit to the great Maya capital is most of all an occasion to feel a sense of pride—which verges on the spiritual—in one's Mexican national identity. For them it is a happy coincidence that the spring equinox that brings tens of thousands of visitors to Chichén Itzá happens to coincide with the national holiday celebrating the birth of Benito Juárez, Mexico's famed Indian president. Or likewise missing from the list is that even larger contingent of Cancun vacationers who are dragged by their spouses or friends to a half-day junket in the ruins, an outing that summons equivocal memories of school fieldtrips and teacherly injunctions to take an interest in things that one does not find very interesting. For these reluctant day-trippers, the experience of Chichén Itzá is an obligatory component of a well-rounded vacation, perhaps a token exercise in continuing education, but hardly a spiritually rewarding occasion.

Others, however, I am very happy to observe, bring to their encounters with the City of the Sacred Well much higher aspirations for an experience of depth and "authenticity."[32] Decades of interaction with these ruins persuade me that success in that regard (usually) depends on holding in place two highly vulnerable illusions.

First, amid the ineludible gauntlet of souvenir stalls and the din of cheap jaguar whistles, serious visitors must persuade themselves that they are not, after all, mere photo-snapping tourists like the rest—an anti-tourist's self-deception that is, according to scholars of tourism, nearly omnipresent among meaning-seeking travelers.[33] Specially invested visitors, perhaps most notably those who imagine themselves "pilgrims" rather

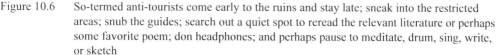

Figure 10.6   So-termed anti-tourists come early to the ruins and stay late; sneak into the restricted areas; snub the guides; search out a quiet spot to reread the relevant literature or perhaps some favorite poem; don headphones; and perhaps pause to meditate, drum, sing, write, or sketch

Source: Photograph courtesy of Lindsay Jones.

than sightseers, but also those who claim a scholarly rather than recreational status, must take steps (usually inadvertently) to persuade themselves they truly are exceptions to the vacationist crowds. According to this illusion, *they* are tourists, but *I* am not. Anti-tourists come early to the ruins and stay late; sneak into the restricted areas; snub the guides; search out a quiet spot to reread the relevant literature or perhaps some favorite poem; don headphones; dress differently; pause to meditate, sketch, write, drum or sing. In short, one observes at Chichén Itzá a myriad of tactics whereby these serious-minded excursionists undertake to set themselves apart from the tourist herd, to resist and subvert the processes of commercialism in which they find themselves unwilling participants, and thereby to afford this "sacred place" the respect that they consider it deserves. The arguably futile efforts of anti-tourists are, I think, well worth a try.

And second, regarding the challenge to which this essay speaks more directly, a rewarding experience of the ruins (usually) requires that visitors also hold in place the illusion that the story of Chichén Itzá to which they are being treated is largely consistent with actual pre-Columbian peoples and events—a sense of historical veracity that is, I hope to have demonstrated, almost assuredly *not* the case. The mainstream tourist experience reminds one, in fact, of existential philosopher Leszek Kolakowski's musings on the ubiquitous "presence of myth" wherein he argues, on the one hand, that people have an urgent need for some explanation of the world that myths alone can provide;[34] and yet, on the other hand, in order to be fully functional and rewarding, those need *not* be correct explanations of the world, only explanations that are adequate to sustain "trust."[35] By the same token, nearly all visitors to Chichén Itzá, on the one hand, demand, it seems, some narrative explanation of the ostensibly historical circumstances that gave rise to these big buildings; even causal tourists who suspect they are being subjected to the "made-up" renditions of unreliable guides feel cheated. Though making their evaluations on decidedly uncritical grounds, visitors need to "trust" that they have gotten a straight story. And those travelers who can escape with this illusion intact—those who continue to enjoy a kind of "first naïveté" experience of ruins, which affords them (false) confidence that they have encountered a true story of the ruins—are likely to have had a rewarding experience of the ruins.

But what of the others? What happens to those who encounter something like the present discussion, which accentuates the diversity of Chichén Itzá narratives, and thereby forces to attention the disturbing realization that, based on what we now know of the pre-Columbian past, virtually all of the most widely circulated stories of the ancient city are historically untenable? While we remain uncertain about "what really happened," there is, at this point, enough certainty about what did *not* happen to conclude that every generation of Chichén Itzá enthusiasts—including the very best scholars of their respective eras—has labored and lived, apparently quite happily, with historically *in*accurate stories of the ancient city's emergence, development and decline. If historical veracity is the sole criterion, then the renditions not only of Le Plongeon and Edward Thompson, but also Tozzer, Morley, Eric Thompson and, one has to suspect, all the newer versions as well, come up short.[36]

Is this essay, then, an exercise in debunking, myth-busting or Santa-slaying, as it were, which destroys any hope of an "authentic" or rewarding experience of the ruins of Chichén Itzá? To be sure, this more critical perspective on the convoluted history of storytelling about the Yucatan ruins (admittedly, another meta-narrative of its own) can be, as it initially was for me, dismaying, even profoundly disappointing; and more than one audience of these comments has accused me of robbing them of the beguiling images of the ancient Mayas that had prompted their trip to this region in the first place. That vexation is to be expected. As noted, the great appeal of the stories that one hears at Chichén Itzá depends, in very large part, on a lack of self-consciousness concerning their fictive nature; and to lose one's "first naïveté" appreciation of those stories and this place is jarring. Here we are reminded what of Kolakowski terms "the fragility of myth" and the inevitable disillusionment that ensues when trusted narratives are contextualized and exposed.[37]

But rather than an intellectual elitism that ridicules visitors for their incautious enthusiasms—and rather than an aspiration to replace their preferred stories of the Maya capital with my own—I hoped instead to engender among thoughtful visitors something of the "second naïveté" perspective that keeps this place so fascinating to me. Appreciating these famed pyramids and palaces—this quintessentially superabundant sacred architecture—as inexhaustible evocateurs of meanings and narratives is an awareness that, for me anyway, enriches rather than wrecks one's experience of Chichén Itzá.

Endnotes

1   For a review of archeological work at Chichén Itzá since the 1990s, see Schmidt, Peter J. (2007). Birds, Ceramics, and Cacao: New Excavations at Chichén Itzá, Yucatan, in Jeff Kowalski and Cynthia Kristan-Graham (eds), *Twin Tollans: Chichén Itzá, Tula, and the Epiclassic to Early Postclassic Mesoamerican World*. Washington, D.C.: Dumbarton Oaks.

2   See Jones, Lindsay (2000). *The Hermeneutics of Sacred Architecture: Experience, Interpretation, Comparison*, vol. 1. Cambridge, MA: Harvard University Press, chapter 2.

3   Very special thanks to Julio Bermudez and Robert Hermanson for organizing the fourth symposium of the Architecture, Culture and Spirituality Forum, which included an extended visit to Chichén Itza, and for including me in the program.

4   See Jones, Lindsay (1995). *Twin City Tales: A Hermeneutical Reassessment of Tula and Chichén Itzá*. Niwot, CO: University Press of Colorado, especially chapters 1 and 2.

5   Jones, Lindsay (1997). Conquests of the Imagination: Maya-Mexican Polarity and the Story of Chichén Itzá, Yucatan. *American Anthropologist* 99(2) (June), pp. 275–90.

6   Paul Ricoeur used the oft-cited terms "first naïveté" (or "primitive naïveté") and "second naïveté" sporadically, without ever writing an essay specifically on the topic. See, for example, Ricoeur, Paul (1967). *The Symbolism of Evil*. Boston, MA: Beacon Press, p. 351ff.

7   Jones, Conquests of the Imagination.

8   Regarding "architectural reception histories," see Jones, *The Hermeneutics of Sacred Architecture*, vol. I,, chapter 12.

9   See, for example, Lopez Medel, Tomas *Relación* (1612). Concerning the False Religion and Idolatry of the Occidental Indians …; reprinted as Appendix B to Diego de Landa, *Relación de las cosas de Yucatán* [originally 1566], translated and edited by Alfred M. Tozzer (1941). Papers of the Peabody Museum of Archaeology and Ethnology #18. Boston, MA: Harvard University.

10 See Chamberlain, Robert S. (1948). *The Conquest and Colonization of Yucatán, 1517–1550.* Washington, D.C.: Carnegie Institution of Washington, chapter 7.

11 See Landa, in Tozzer (ed.), *Relación de las cosas de Yucatán.*

12 See Stephens, John Lloyd (1841). *Incidents of Travel in Central America, Chiapas and Yucatan*, 2 vols. New York, NY: Harper Brothers; and Stephens, John Lloyd (1843). *Incidents of Travel in Yucatan*, 2 vols. New York, NY: Harper Brothers.

13 See Le Plongeon, Augustus (1886). *Sacred Mysteries among the Mayas and Quiches, 11,500 Years Ago.* New York, NY: R. Macoy; and Desmond, Lawrence and Phyllis M. Messenger (1988). *A Dream of Maya: Augustus and Alice Le Plongeon in Nineteenth-Century Yucatan.* Albuquerque, NM: University of New Mexico Press.

14 See Le Plongeon, Augustus (1896). *Queen Móo and the Egyptian Sphinx.* New York, NY: by the author.

15 See Thompson, Edward H. (1932). *People of the Serpent: Life and Adventure among the Mayas.* Boston, MA: Houghton Mifflin Co.

16 For a particularly glowing assessment, see Willard, T.A. (1926). *The City of the Sacred Well: Being a Narrative of the Discoveries and Excavations of Edward Herbert Thompson in the Ancient City of Chi-chen Itzá.* New York, NY: Century.

17 Roys, Ralph L. (trans. and ed.) (1967[1933]). *The Book of Chilam Balam of Chumayel.* Norman, OK: University of Oklahoma Press, p. 84.

18 See Tozzer, Alfred M. (1957). *Chichén Itzá and its Cenote of Sacrifice: A Comparative Study of Contemporaneous Toltec and Maya*, Memoirs of the Peabody Museum, vols 11 and 12. Cambridge, MA: Harvard University.

19 Thompson, J. Eric S. (1959). Review of Alfred M. Tozzer. *Chichén Itzá and its Cenote of Sacrifice*; *American Journal of Archaeology* 63, pp. 119–20.

20 Jones, Conquests of the Imagination, pp. 282–3.

21 See Morley, Sylvanus G. (1925). Chichén Itzá, An Ancient American Mecca. *The National Geographic Magazine* 47 (January), pp. 63–95; and Morley, Sylvanus G. (1936). Yucatan, Home of the Gifted Maya. *The National Geographic Magazine* 70 (November), pp. 590–644. Also see Morley, Sylvanus G. (1947[1946]). *The Ancient Maya.* Stanford, CA: Stanford University Press.

22 See Brunhouse, Robert L. (1971). *Sylvanus G. Morley and the World of the Ancient Maya.* Norman, OK: University of Oklahoma Press; and Harris III, Charles H. and Louis Sadler (2003). *The Archaeologist was a Spy: Sylvanus G. Morley and the Office of Naval Intelligence.* Albuquerque, NM: University of New Mexico Press.

23 Jones, Conquests of the Imagination, pp. 281–2.

24 Jones, Conquests of the Imagination, pp. 283–4, works to point out similarities and differences between the respective stories of the Mexicanization of the Maya that appear in Thompson, J. Eric S. (1954). *The Rise and Fall of Maya Civilization.* Norman, OK: University of Oklahoma Press; and Thompson, J. Eric S. (1970). *Maya History and Religion.* Norman, OK: University of Oklahoma Press.

25 See Charnay, Désiré (1887). *The Ancient Cities of the New World: Being Voyages and Explorations in Mexico and Central America from 1857–1882.* London and New York, NY: Chapman & Harper Brothers.

26 See Kubler, George (1961). Chichén Itzá y Tula. *Estudios de Cultura Maya* 1, 47–9; Kubler, George (1984[1962/1975]). *The Art and Architecture of Ancient America: The Mexican, Maya, and Andean People.* New York, NY: Penguin Books; and Kubler, George (1958). The Design of Space in Maya Architecture. *Miscellanea Paul Rivet*, 1 (Mexico).

27 See Lincoln, Charles E. (1990). Ethnicity and Social Organization at Chichén Itzá, Yucatan, Mexico. Ph.D. dissertation, Department of Anthropology, Harvard University; and Lincoln, Charles E. (1986). The Chronology of Chichén Itzá: A Review of the Literature, in Jeremy A. Sabloff and E. Wyllys Andrews V (eds), *Late Lowland Maya Civilization: Classic to Postclassic.* Albuquerque, NM: University of New Mexico Press.

28 See Schele, Linda and Mary Ellen Miller (1986). *The Blood of Kings: Dynasty and Ritual in Maya Art.* Fort Worth: Kimbell Art Museum; and Schele, Linda and David Freidel (1990). *A Forest of Kings: The Untold Story of the Ancient Maya.* New York, NY: William Morrow and Company, Inc., which, on p. 497, n. 6, supports the view, as argued by Charles Lincoln, that Chichén Itzá was a single city continuously occupied through its history.

29 See Freidel, David, Schele, Linda and Joy Parker (1995). *Maya Cosmos: Three Thousand Years on the Shaman's Path.* New York: William Morrow Paperbacks; and especially Schele, Linda and Peter Mathews (1998). *The Code of Kings: The Language of Seven Sacred Maya Temples and Tombs.* New York, NY: Scribner, chapter 6.

30 As a point of entry into the work and influence of José Argüelles, see, for instance, South, Stephanie (2009). *2012: Biography of a Time Traveler: The Journey of José Argüelles.* Franklin Lakes, NJ: Career Press.

31 See Men, Hunbatz (1990). *Secrets of Mayan Science/Religion*. Sante Fe, NM: Bear & Company Publishing; and Men, Hunbatz (2010 [1983]). *The 8 Calendars of the Maya*. Sante Fe, NM: Bear & Company.
32 Regarding travelers' much-discussed aspirations to "authenticity," the usual starting point is MacCannell, Dean (1999). *The Tourist: A New Theory of the Leisure Class*. Berkeley, CA: University of California Press.
33 Regarding the pervasive tendency for tourists to persuade themselves (if no one else) that they are not really tourists, see ibid. or Culler, Jonathan (1981). Semiotics of Tourism. *American Journal of Semiotics* 1(1–2), pp. 127–40.
34 See Kolakowski, Leszek (1989). *The Presence of Myth*, translated by Adam Czerniawski. Chicago, IL: University of Chicago Press, chapter 3. The considerable extent to which the stories of Chichén Itzá discussed here qualify as "myths" is a fascinating question that lies beyond the scope of this paper.
35 Ibid., p. 119ff.
36 Students of Mircea Eliade would counsel us to suspect that this preoccupation with the (supposed) historical veracity of the stories of Chichén Itzá is actually a modern Western preoccupation rather than a universal one.
37 See Kolakowski, *The Presence of Myth*, chapter 10.

PART IV
Sacred Landscapes

Chapter 11
Space, Object, and Encounter

Rebecca Krinke

Introduction

In this this chapter I discuss three recent participatory public art projects: *The Table for Contemplation and Action (A Place to Share Beauty and Fear)*, *Unseen/Seen: The Mapping of Joy and Pain*, and *What Needs To Be Said?* as vehicles to discuss new types of objects, spaces, and encounters that engage our emotional lives. *The Table for Contemplation and Action (A Place to Share Beauty and Fear)* and *What Needs To Be Said?* offered temporary, physical environments and opportunities for ritual-like writing. Although they were conceived as secular activities in a secular settings, some participants told me that their writings were directed to various definitions or ideas of beyond the ordinary—"the Universe," "God," or other possible meanings. *Unseen/Seen: The Mapping of Joy and Pain* was a temporary, outdoor environment that traveled to several parks in Minneapolis and St. Paul and invited the public to map where in the Twin Cities they had experienced joy and pain. A shared space of emotional engagement and catharsis was created as many participants talked as they mapped and shared intense stories of pain and joy with others present. These projects reveal that there is an opportunity (some might say necessity) for new types of objects, spatial typologies, and engagements to address wider ranges of human emotion and need.

There are threads that underpin all this work. The first is work as an artist and designer (designing landscapes and sculpture) and represents my research into contemplative landscapes.[1] I am broadly interested in place and emotion, especially through exploring ideas and experiences of opposites such as pain/joy and contemplation/action. I am also interested in the beneficial effects of contact with nature on human health and well-being (both physically and psychologically).[2] The beneficial effect of writing about thoughts and emotions, especially stressful ones, and its effects that have been demonstrated by recent research,[3] is also at work in my projects. You will see this thread of contact with nature/natural elements and writing in these projects.

The Table for Contemplation and Action (A Place to Share Beauty and Fear)

The Table for Contemplation and Action (A Place to Share Beauty and Fear) was a work of public art that offered the opportunity for ritual-like writing (2007–10).[4] Located in the interior public courtyard of Rapson Hall on the University of Minnesota campus, the *Table* was in continuous use by students for three years. It was 6-foot square (1.8 meters), of two types of wood, with a central copper box containing a changing, single, unusual element from the outdoors, and a blown glass vessel (Figure 11.1a). The *Table* provided participants the opportunity to write about their fear/stress/hopes/wishes (Figure 11.1b), and deposit these writings into the glass vessel (Figure 11.1c), which when full, was emptied and the papers burned without reading. Writing was completely voluntary and a small book on the tabletop functioned as a comment book. Anyone could also use the *Table*: for studying, meeting, and eating.

The information/comment book briefly described recent research from contact with nature and writing about emotions on the beneficial effects on physical and psychological health. This project was extremely successful, meaning participants understood, used, and benefited from the *Table* as I had intended. Some of the many positive responses written in the comment book included: "A wonderful place to sit and study. Sight, texture, smell, lovely. [*sic*] The opportunity to write something down and let it go is very freeing and I am thankful for it." And another comment: "Thanks for the opportunity to jettison extra thought baggage. I like the smell of the pine in my hands." (There were fresh pine needles in the copper box at one point.)

Figure 11.1   *The Table for Contemplation and Action (A Place to Share Beauty and Fear)*: a) the *Table*,
                b) the writing, c) submitting the writing
Source: Photographs courtesy of Rebecca Krinke.

What I didn't expect was that the comment book began to collect some writings referencing Christianity and Jesus, as well as quotes by Camus and Thoreau. One visitor to the *Table* was inspired to leave a small vase of flowers. A small book of *Psalms* was also left by another visitor.

After reading the comment book, seeing the *Table* "in action," discussing it at an open forum event, and taking a trip to Japan, I began to see my *Table* project in a new light. Could correlations be made between the ritual-like writing at *The Table for Contemplation and Action* and ritualized writing found in religious practices? Shintoism, Zen Buddhism, and Judaism include practices of writing to the transcendent, in sacred settings, open to all, and done directly by the worshipper (with varying degrees of officiating).

For example, at Shinto shrines one can purchase wooden prayer plaques called *ema*, where an individual can write prayers, wishes, or messages of gratitude. These plaques are then hung on open racks by the worshipers so that the *kami* (gods) will receive them. If your prayer is answered, you can remove your plaque, and/or you can hang a new prayer plaque if desired. A shrine may be known for its focus on facilitating certain types of prayers, such as success at work or healing, although, many shrines have no specific focus.[5]

At Zen Buddhist temples in Japan, visitors write on prayer sticks which can be purchased for a few hundred yen (a couple US dollars). At Sanjusangendo Temple in Kyoto, signs in Japanese and English invite you to write your prayer and leave it on the altar, and they explain that the priests will burn the sticks. The burning releases the prayer to the transcendent. In this tradition, an officiant is needed as an intermediary between the individual and the divine.

Jerusalem's Western Wall is Judaism's most sacred site which, after the Second Temple was destroyed, became a place of pilgrimage. Today there is a large plaza in front of the wall that functions as an open-air sanctuary, with separate sections for men and women as is common with Orthodox traditions. At the Wall, many write prayers on slips of paper, fold and place them into crevices between the stones. These communications to the divine can even be sent by fax, email and Twitter for placement in the Wall. It might be noted that there is no charge for these services, but rather one is invited to make an online donation. Advances in technology have made it possible for an individual's prayers to be placed in the Wall while not being physically present, raising interesting questions about the role of physical presence in relation to the actual sacred setting, and the secular officiating of prayers.

Twice a year, at Passover in the Spring and the Jewish New Year in the Fall, the Wall's workers, under the direction of the rabbi, clear out the accumulated notes, which, in accordance with Jewish law, must be buried. Those responsible for removing the prayers treat them with great respect: including, a *mikveh* (ritual bath) before beginning the holy work of removing the notes. The writings are removed without the use of metal bars or utensils—which stand for warfare and the taking of life—but rather are removed with wooden rods.[6]

These examples influenced the way I thought about the *Table*. I designed (a customized wooden rod) to collect the writings from the glass vessel (Figure 11.2a). It also reinforced my decision that the writings should be burned, and consequently, I made the burning of the writings a public event. A student asked to carry the copper bowl containing the messages, and several people accompanied us outdoors for the burning—saying that the act of watching their writings burn was important to them (Figures 11.2b and 11.2c).

Figure 11.2   *The Table for Contemplation and Action (A Place to Share Beauty and Fear)*: a) collecting the messages from the glass vessel embedded in the *Table* and placing into the copper bowl, b) a student carries the copper bowl outdoors, c) the messages are burned
Source: Photographs courtesy of Rebecca Krinke.

The way *The Table for Contemplation and Action* was embraced raises provocative questions about the role of private contemplation and action in a shared public space. The success of the project suggests that there is a strong potential for new types of spaces and objects that address the emotional, psychological, and possibly even spiritual issues of contemporary life, especially if we think of the term spiritual as it is often broadly defined in contemporary life: "the deepest values and meanings by which people live."[7] And, in the case of the projects described in this chapter—these new spaces and objects can be realized as temporary overlays/additions to existing buildings and landscapes.

Unseen/Seen: The Mapping of Joy and Pain

After I had launched *The Table for Contemplation and Action (A Place to Share Beauty and Fear)*, I knew that I wanted to continue exploring my long held interest in "sharing beauty and fear." Creating a *Table* for visitors to map where they found "fear and beauty" in Minneapolis-St. Paul was my initial idea. However, that didn't feel quite right, so I decided the pairing of "joy and pain" would be a more useful and clear way to invite the public to map, and my new project, *Unseen/Seen: The Mapping of Joy and Pain* was begun. I knew that where I sited the project and its duration would have a major impact on how it was experienced. I thought about it being in a public library, and the mapping as a relatively private, contemplative activity. But I was also interested in being present with this new project and its visitors, and the idea of bringing it as a temporary, traveling, participatory work of public art to Twin Cities, parks emerged via the support of Diane Moe, who was then Cultural Arts Administrator for the Minneapolis Park and Recreation Board. The project launched in the summer of 2010, and featured a unique table-like object containing a custom, laser-cut wooden map of Minneapolis-St. Paul. This created the setting and the opportunity for the participants to map where in Minneapolis/St. Paul they experienced joy and pain (Figure 11.3).

The wooden map has streets clearly labeled, and is to scale, providing easy orientation for the mapping process. Visitors had the opportunity to literally add colors to this map—gold where they have felt joy and gray for pain. Participating in mapping was voluntary, free and open to everyone. The project was always facilitated, meaning that I was present at all the mappings, along with one-or-two students who worked with me on the project. We set it up at times and places announced in advance, typically for four-hour time periods. We spoke with anyone interested about the project and invited them to add their experiences to the map. We did not define joy or pain—that was up to each participant.

I thought the mapping would be a rather silent process. Instead, most people talked as they mapped, and I was especially surprised by the depth of personal stories that participants shared with others and me around the map. Conventional maps tell you where you are or where to go—this one recorded these two aspects of one's emotional life. Joy was quickly colored in along the Mississippi River, and the Minneapolis lakes and parks.

Figure 11.3   *Unseen/Seen: The Mapping of Joy and Pain*, Coloring the very first marks on the map;
                gold and gray sculptures provide a landmark for the project and reference the "joy and pain
                colors" of the mapping process
Source: Photograph courtesy of Rebecca Krinke.

Interestingly, Lakewood Cemetery was also colored in gold very early on. The map was additive—meaning that all the coloring remained from each mapping session—so, for example, people could add gray to someone else's gold. As we took the project from park to park, the coloring built up, and sometimes symbols, drawings and words appeared (Figure 11.4). Visitors speculated on others' mapping, and asked me if I knew the stories behind them. Some people had made an "appointment with the map" after learning through the media that it was going to be at a certain park. Some even had personal symbols and language prepared in advance. Most people however, found the project set up in parks, and out of curiosity came over to see what was going on. Almost everyone participating, even those who said they would not map, ended up mapping. Most people stayed quite a long time; 20–30 minutes or more was common. Using the parks as our setting was a perfect match for the project being launched in a Minnesota summer. Park-goers are already in a leisurely mode and this frame of mind brought many visitors to the map.

    Sometimes one person's mapping triggered a response from another. A powerful example of this was when a participant was mapping and talking about where he overdosed on heroin, and would have died were it not for a drug paramedics who came right away. Then another participant said, "That same thing happened to me" and they looked at each other with a kind of "we made it" and a "not alone, no shame" shared moment. Many people heard this unusual and potent exchange; it is something I still think about.

    Another experience that continues to live on in me is a powerful story of joy. The map was set up at Como Park in St. Paul, and a man walking his dog came over to take a look. We invited him to map.

Figure 11.4   *Unseen/Seen: The Mapping of Joy and Pain*, close up of the map and participants mapping
Source: Photograph courtesy of Rebecca Krinke.

He said that he was so happy that he had moved to this neighborhood, and he talked about how wonderful his new neighbors were—giving examples of their welcoming him with food, invitations, and garden plants. He colored a deep gold over his neighborhood and went on with his walk. Perhaps a half hour later he came back and said to us, "I've been thinking about joy the whole time I walked around the lake, and I want to map more joy."

A third story contains both joy and pain. Two women were both adding color to a hospital on the map, one gold, one gray. The woman coloring gold said, "I'm mapping where my daughter was born." The woman coloring gray said she was mapping where her daughter died. They looked at each other with tears in their eyes and one woman said, "Maybe we are here to balance each other out."

These are just a few of the many, many stories I heard of joy and pain. I did not expect this sharing of deeply personal memories in public; I had no idea so many people held such intense stories. I met people who lived in the parks, and learned about homelessness and shelters. I even received emails from people who were no longer living in Minnesota, but who wanted me to add color to the map for them. A soldier stationed in Iraq at the time sent a message that talked about the joy he felt running along the lakes—and he gave us his route so that we could map it for him.

Unseen/Seen: The Mapping of Joy and Pain created a temporary, shared, social experience for emotional engagement, empathy, remembrance, and even a kind of healing. The project created "new publics": people that would not have met otherwise (Figure 11.5). There were times when I felt a strong sense of my listening becoming deeper, as if I was becoming a "witness," and being entrusted with intensely personal stories. One particular event at the map comes to mind. It was just as we were starting to pack up the project at a St. Paul park.

Figure 11.5   *Unseen/Seen: The Mapping of Joy and Pain*, a temporary community of mappers
Source: Photograph courtesy of Rebecca Krinke.

A man walked towards us, and we invited him to take a look at the map, and we told him about the project. He said, "I would just want to color all of St. Paul gray." We invited him to do that. He said that he didn't want to take over the map, but that he would color the courthouse dark gray. He told us that he was essentially being "run out of town" and described difficulties with housing, and unpaid fines and tickets. We listened and again saw a window into a person, his life, that perhaps we could not have imagined. This man closed by shaking our hands and saying, "No one ever asks me how I feel. Thank you for that."

This story brings up an important aspect of the project: no one can tell you what you feel, and no one's mapping is "better" or more "accurate" than anyone else's. Kids understood this very well. They mapped pain and joy at their schools and other places. One mother and son had an in-depth discussion about fear at the map. The project was transformative for my students, and I suspect for others as well. I know I have a much broader sense of warmth, empathy, and respect for my fellow citizens. It also has changed me and my art practice.

Unseen/Seen: The Mapping of Joy and Pain invited people to think about pain and joy in their lives, and the places in which they dwell. Pain and joy are a dialectic, but also a continuum, and people mapped this way. It was an emotional mapping—something that seems so forgotten when we think of maps, but not when we remember: in memory, space intertwines powerfully with emotion. The whole sculptural environment with the table, along with the map and nearby participants all contributed to providing a powerful setting of an emotional opening up, letting go, sharing, and release. A story of joy triggered joy in others and myself. Hearing stories of pain triggered compassion. The project also served as a place for private reflection and offered a contemplative moment—an invitation to step outside the familiar and mull over personal connections of emotion and place.

Figure 11.6   *What Needs To Be Said?* a) Writing Room in the St. Paul vacant storefront, b) inside the
              Writing Room with the writing desk visible
Source: Photograph courtesy of Rebecca Krinke.

Unseen/Seen: The Mapping of Joy and Pain challenged conventional ways of seeing the Twin Cities by
creating a temporary setting for memory, speculation, imagination, and transformation.

What Needs to be Said?

What Needs To Be Said? was a work of participatory public art installed in an empty storefront in St. Paul
for a week in August 2012, and also at the Nash Gallery in Minneapolis for six weeks, later in the same year.
The project provided the setting and opportunity for participants to say what "needs to be said"—however
one chose to define that. I created a unique "Writing Room" for this project and purpose.

The Writing Room is made of materials that engage sight, sound, smell, and touch. You step up onto a
low black platform made of charred wood to enter a small cube-like, ceiling-less room. The doors are made
of charred cedar and hold a trace of this fragrance. A sliding door moves with a distinctive low rumble
from one end of the room to the center. As you enter the space, you see a small black writing desk and
chair—also of charred wood. There is a pale wood writing surface affixed to the desk, with inset laser cut
text that states: "What Needs To Be Said? You are invited to write on the paper provided, and if you'd like
to keep your writing private, place it in the vessel attached to the inside wall, or if you choose to make your
writing public, pin it to the gallery walls. Thank you" (see Figures 11.6a and 11.b).

Taking a seat at the desk, you can select a pen or pencil from a glass container embedded in the
surface—and write—or simply relax and enjoy the unique space. The room is made of screen doors fitted
together—with crumpled blank lined pages (like the paper you are being invited to write on) placed between
the screens and the semi-transparent mylar that clads the outside of the room. Light interacting through
the mylar, the screens, and the paper make for beautiful gradations of color ranging from white through
a deep palette of grays. It's unusual and captivating while also having a tranquil effect. From outside the
Writing Room, visitors experience a more pure white version of the paper and mylar due to lighting and
the layering of the materials in reverse from inside the room. Both on the storefront and gallery walls are
narrow wooden dowels where the public messages are attached for everyone to read.

What Needs To Be Said? continues the exploration of writing begun in *The Table for Contemplation and
Action (A Place to Share Beauty and Fear)*, but added the public display of messages, and added the social

Figure 11.7   *What Needs To Be Said?* in a St. Paul vacant storefront, showing the Writing Room and the
                public messages on the wall
Source: Photograph courtesy of Rebecca Krinke.

interaction of *Unseen/Seen: The Mapping of Joy and Pain*. At the storefront setting, I was always in attendance, oftentimes with the two students who helped me build it. We invited people to enter the Writing Room, and were drawn into many powerful conversations. (However, at the Nash Gallery, the project was not facilitated, but visitors to the gallery used the project as it was intended and the private and public messages accumulated.)

Asking "what needs to be said," (even if a visitor chose not to write) had the impact of this question resonating in their mind. Should something long kept to oneself be unburdened? Should a joy be celebrated out loud? Is there something you wished you had said and now that person is gone? What do we as individuals, and/or as part of larger groups feel needs to be said? Or is it being said—but not being heard or believed? It can be cathartic to "speak up" and share in public, and this artwork offered a compelling physical setting for this activity. *What Needs To Be Said?* was deliberately differentiated from blogs and message postings that are virtual, linear, and forever present on the Internet. Instead this project offered the possibility for writing and reading others' writings in a random, physical, visceral way. New "temporary publics" were created around the project, who read and talked about the messages (Figure 11.7).

Some of the conversations at the *What Needs to Be Said?* project included discussions of the Writing Room itself: one visitor to the project, an undergraduate student I knew, went into the room, shut the door and spent almost 30 minutes inside. He came out and exclaimed that I was "asking people to contemplate, to slow down—that's not American!" I asked him why he had spent so much time in the Room then, and he said that he had never experienced a room like that before—both in its form and in its singular function—and that he had enjoyed it.

For several visitors, the crumpled papers conjured notions of thoughts discarded or leftover, or signaled an overflow of creativity or re-connecting to secrets. One of the first participants in the project was a woman who came in and said, "I've been waiting for this project to open!" She went inside the Room and quickly came out with a message that read in large, all capital letters, "You owe me an apology!" She went back in and as she came out said that she had also written some private messages. This was something many people did—they wrote both privately and publically, although there were about twice as many private messages as public ones. The wall of public writings contained messages that ranged from the very personal to others that were pointed more toward ideas of the public good, such as urging people to vote. Many of the public messages had to do with communication between people in general and started many conversations about face-to-face interaction versus social media.

The question, "*What Needs to Be Said?*," in large letters was also placed across the storefront windows (and we left the lights on all night for our week in the storefront). One man came in as we were closing to tell us that he had driven by the project—and had seen that question in the windows along with something mysterious inside—and his curiosity was such that he wanted to find out what it was about. He told us he was a local carpenter, and went inside the Writing Room, when he came out he said that we should take the project to a cemetery; there are so many things that could be said about the dead, which were unsaid when the person was alive.

One of the most poignant responses to *What Needs to Be Said?* arrived in an email from someone who had visited the project. What follows is the first paragraph of his message: "The installation charged myself as well as the space that it occupied. What Rebecca did not know is that my father died a few weeks prior to seeing her work (this is notable because I am currently 28 years old, and of course, because my Dad is no longer with us). Anyway, what I'm getting at is that there are therapeutic qualities of art, and not just by being the artist, more importantly by being the viewer. Rebecca was markedly able to give me something to elevate myself upon—her room was a vessel of self-realization."[8]

The email was extremely humbling and powerful to receive. I felt deep empathy for the writer and also a sense of confirmation that artists can make spaces, objects, and encounters that can embody an aura or quality that removes us from the everyday world, and allows unexpected events to unfold.

This writer described his experience, "There I was, in a wonderfully lit cubical-esc [*sic*] structure that was straight from a Japanese tea garden or what my imagination pictured as a room where the dalai lamas [*sic*] of the world's history must've sat in order to write down all those cleverly brief, and generationally transcendent teachings. Oh, wait, that's the past. Okay, let's focus on the present (Buddhists rejoice). Seriously though, all my senses were salivating. I smelled the aroma of fiery lit lumber, consumed the smokiness that my nostrils brought to my taste buds, heard the voices of the other viewers lifting my intellect, saw the crumpling of paper that preceded my personal letter, and I felt."[9]

In conceiving the project, I had indeed been thinking of Japanese tearooms and philosophers' huts, and also, perhaps, scriptoriums—the cells in monasteries where monks copied manuscripts. *What Needs to Be Said?* was a place apart from the everyday: a contemplative space. It was an enclosed, somewhat primordial place that and invited one to sit still, reflect and journey inward. It was an overlay to an existing space; a "hut" inside a building, in the city, and invited both dreamers and a crowd. *What Needs To Be Said?* invited all the voices from the community to speak, and to speak their truth.

Heterotopias, Third Places, and Thin Places

The philosopher Michel Foucault, presented the concept of "heterotopia" as the counterpoint of "utopia," and described it as a place that juxtaposes in a single real place several kinds of space.[10] The projects that I have discussed in this chapter could perhaps be described in this way; for example, the projects are temporary, they conjure memories, which accrue as writings or marks on a map, which then may disappear through burning, becoming a new memory. Edward Soja in *Thirdspace*, expands on Foucault's work and others to posit a theory of what he calls a "thirdspace" that contains spaces both real and imagined. (Conventionally, a "third space" is considered a place that is neither home nor work). Soja's thirdspace is a "transcendent concept that is constantly expanding to include 'an-Other,' thus enabling the contestation and re-negotiation of boundaries and cultural identity."[11] "Thin places" are a term from the Celtic tradition—defined as places "where the distance between heaven and earth collapses and we're able to catch glimpses of the divine, or the transcendent."[12]

While not setting out intentionally to make a heterotopia, thirdspace, or thin place, I do think that in some ways these three participatory projects could be understood through these ideas. Unpredictable things happened to the participants and facilitators of these projects—perhaps contributing to an experience of "otherness," which may suggest a correspondence with heterotopia, thirdspace, and thin place.

As Eric Weiner wrote recently in the *New York Times* (2012), "Thin places relax us, yes, but they also transform us—or, more accurately, unmask us. In thin places, we become our more essential selves. Thin places are often sacred ones—but they need not be, at least not conventionally so."[13] *The Table for Contemplation and Action (A Place to Share Beauty and Fear), Unseen/Seen: The Mapping of Joy and Pain*, and *What Needs to Be Said?* created new spaces, objects, and encounters that addressed, engaged, and even transformed our emotional lives, and for some participants, facilitated a connection to the transcendent. The three participatory public art projects provided opportunities for ritual-like writing, personalized mapping of joy and/or pain, and expression of things unsaid, helping facilitate meaningful experiences and personal revelations.

Acknowledgments and Credits

Imagine Fund, Institute for Advanced Study, and Undergraduate Research Opportunity Grants; University of Minnesota.
Minneapolis Park and Recreation Board and St. Paul Parks and Recreation Starling Project.
"Space, Object, and Encounter" was the name of a 2011 workshop given by Skewed Visions Studio of Minneapolis that I participated in. I thank them for the inspiration and have borrowed it here for my chapter title.

Student, Staff, and Consultant Teams

The Table for Contemplation and Action (A Place to Share Beauty and Fear)
Kevin Groenke, Justin Kindlespire, Peter Zelle, Michael Boyd, McGrath Architectural Sheet Metal.

Unseen/Seen: The Mapping of Joy and Pain
Michael Dorfman, Jamuna Golden, David Kerber, Eric Maass, Joseph Cronick.

What Needs to Be Said?
Miss Emily Lowery, Michael Richardson.

Endnotes

1   Krinke, Rebecca (ed.) (2005). *Contemporary Landscapes of Contemplation*. London, UK: Routledge.
2   Contact with nature, especially vegetation, has a beneficial effect on physical and psychological health, including lower blood pressure, less muscle tension, elevated mood, among others. For a good overview summary of this research, see Louv, Richard (2011). *The Nature Principle*. New York, NY: Algonquin Books.
3   See for example, the work of James Pennybaker Ph.D., and the results of his 1997 controlled clinical research in *Opening Up*. London, UK and New York, NY: Guilford Press.
4   A version of *The Table for Contemplation and Action (A Place to Share Beauty and Fear)* portion of this chapter appeared as: (2010). Writing Toward the Transcendent, in *2A: Architecture and Art* Winter, pp. 43–5.
5   Japanese Religions Website: http://www.travel-around-japan.com/j06-religion.html (accessed August 2014).
6   Fendel, Hillel (2009). Western Wall Cleared of Prayer Notes, March 31. https://groups.yahoo.com/neo/groups/EZEKIEL33/conversations/topics/9069 (accessed August 2014).
7   Sheldrake, Philip (2013). *Spirituality: A Brief History*. Chichester, UK: John Wiley & Sons Ltd., pp. 1–2.
8   Personal email to the author, August 29, 2012.
9   Ibid.
10   Foucault, Michel (1984). *Of Other Spaces: Utopias and Heterotopias*. Architecture/Mouvement/Continuité October; Des Espace Autres, March 1967. Translated from the French by Jay Miskowiec. http://web.mit.edu/allanmc/www/foucault1.pdf (accessed August 2014).
11   http://en.wikipedia.org/wiki/Edward_Soja (accessed August 2014).
12   Weiner, Eric (2012). Where Heaven and Earth Come Closer. *New York Times*, March 9. http://www.nytimes.com/2012/03/11/travel/thin-places-where-we-are-jolted-out-of-old-ways-of-seeing-the-world.html?_r= (accessed August 2014).
13   Ibid.

Chapter 12
Regarding Sacred Landscapes and the Everyday Corollary

Dennis Alan Winters

Introduction

Making my way through woods in a part of the Canadian Shield, a vast billion-year-old igneous rock formation, on a path navigating an island surrounded by shrub swamp and shallow marsh, through a grove of mature hemlocks named "The Cathedral," I was attentive to a profoundly, mysterious and intimate relationship to something present both within and around me, a luminous familiarity with this place; surrender and embrace. This island grove of beauty and majesty, unmarked on any topographic map, was neither designated nor implied as a special place. Yet surely, here was a landscape connected to the sacred fabric of the universe.

My experience there elicited insights: designated sacred landscapes provide both a foundation and qualitative index by which to design and evaluate landscapes in everyday life, and where people can experience spiritual renewal. This led to three vital questions: 1) What distinguishes sacred landscapes from other landscapes? 2) How does one's relationship with landscapes make spiritual experiences viable in everyday life? and, 3) what qualities of sacred landscapes are a corollary, and therefore, applicable to landscapes of daily life?

Figure 12.1   The Cathedral, Canadian Shield
Source: Photograph courtesy of Dennis Alan Winters.

Designating the Sacred Landscape

Seemingly, with magical and mysterious qualities, sacred landscapes are places that captivate and move us to increased awareness, energizing feelings and thoughts about the spiritual dimensions of life. According to classical Buddhist perspectives, a sacred landscape is a medium for pilgrims' devotional practices, where spiritual experience becomes tangible as form and space. But, except for its extraordinary features, physically apparent or esoterically subtle, a landscape is otherwise considered everyday space, unrecognized unless officially acknowledged.

> Certainly there are many places in Tibet that are power places by geomantic definition, but unless they have been consecrated by tradition they lack the association with Buddha-mind that endows them with particular sanctity. When both geomantic and human factors are optimized the result will be a great power place, a sacred place.[1]

There are a number of aspects regarding the transformation of place to sacred landscapes in Tibetan Buddhism known as the four-fold ordination process. First, the landscape arises through geological, atmospheric and ecological forces—orogeny, tectonics, glacial morphogenesis, mass-wasting, fluvial erosion—producing distinct physical qualities and characteristics. Certain landscapes reveal the essence of these natural forces, where people acutely sense landscape's power and are drawn to it for spiritual renewal, not unlike celestial moments of transformation when people became acutely aware of time.

Second, Buddhas and Bodhisattvas empower these particular landscapes with sacrality by purifying the landscape of physical, mental, emotional and spiritual afflictions and delusions. Esoteric Shingon Buddhism posits the Buddha as inseparable from nature, and having the ability to manipulate the operations of nature so that a natural landscape is transformed into a sacred landscape.[2]

Third, a spiritual teacher discovers the sacred landscape and consecrates the lands, waters and skies by their personal presence and purification practices. Tibetan Buddhist texts refer to this blessing as, "opening the sacred landscape," whereby the natural sacred landscape is designed as an embodiment of spiritual teachings.

Fourth, continued reverence by pilgrims and disciples maintain the sacred landscape. Although the landscape produced by the awakened mind is considered a permanent phenomenon, its presence is dependent upon its reception by disciples; the Buddha's teachings last only if disciples cultivate karmic predispositions to receive them.[3]

How would such a place be identified? In Japan, a sacred landscape is designated with *a shimenawa*, a straw rope tied with paper around the sacred precinct. At Shinto shrines and Buddhist temples a gate, or *torii*, marks a transition between "sacred" and "profane." In Tibet, prayer flags and *laptche*, piles of stones carved with mantras, conspicuously acknowledge homes of protectors and the presence of deities at mountain peaks and passes, ends of ascents, stream crossings, and caves where revered teachers have meditated.

The Everyday Corollary

As noted above, regardless of its spiritual qualities, a landscape not officially established to be sacred is considered ordinary. However, the everyday corollary, a landscape endowed with physical characteristics that accord with ordination's phase one, has the potential to contravene orthodoxy, transforming into a place that provides for spiritual engagement. According to both Christian and Mahayana Buddhist views, this everyday corollary appears through virtuous relationships and qualities of interaction between individual (and community) and landscape. But, how?

The first is the quality of relationship. In contrast to a purely objective view that identifies a person here and landscape over there, philosophers of many traditions questioned the seemingly hard edge between thoughts and substances. Kobo Daishi, founder of Japanese Shingon Buddhism, said:

Differences exist between matter and mind, but in their essential nature they remain the same. Matter is no other than mind; mind is no other than matter. Without any obstruction, they are interrelated. The subject is the object; the object is the subject. The seeing is the seen, and the seen is the seeing. Nothing differentiates them.[4]

H.H. the Dalai Lama says that of inhabiting the landscape, as well the landscape we inhabit, that all evolve, abide and dissolve through the operation of five elemental forces: solidity of Earth, fluidity of Water, heat of Fire, movement of Wind, and unobstruction of Space. Furthermore, no difference is to be found between the actual particles that compose our physical body and the environment. Investigating the relationship among very subtle, internal and external elemental forces reveals an understanding of the interaction between mental events and external matter—the relationship between inhabitant and landscape.[5]

> I came to realize clearly that mind is no other
> than mountains and rivers and the great earth.[6]

Paul Brunton wrote, much as he tried, he couldn't hold existence and the perception of existence apart from each other. He concluded that mental experiences were the visible things that he took to be outside himself, but in reality were not two but indissolubly one.[7] John Blofeld recalled what the young Assistant Taoist Abbot named Wu told him:

> You see, dear friend from the Western Ocean, mind is all! Eliminate thought and the mind is no longer to be differentiated from the formless Tao, in which all things and processes originate, however ordinary or extraordinary.[8]

The second is the quality of interactions, the recognition of beauty and spirituality in the everyday corollary is dependent upon the cultivation of virtues in one's mind. Seventh-century Indian Buddhist scholar Chandrakirti wrote in his *Guide to the Middle Way* that an undisciplined state of mind gives rise to delusions, projecting an individual into negative actions, and produces a negative environment in which that person lives; a disciplined and virtuous mind however, gives rise to insight, projecting positive actions, and produces a pleasing environment.[9] Concerning the interaction of spirituality and landscape beauty, the *Avatamsaka Sutra* states:

> Teaching how to strengthen spiritual practice, Buddha Shakyamuni caused the landscape of Jetavana Monastery to appear as an emanation of the awakened mind; garlands of jewelled trees and radiant flowers, rivers of fragrant waters, cloud-palaces of music and song, and flower ornaments pervaded all of space. Although they sat before the Buddha, disciples had not cultivated virtues enabling them to see the landscape as a Buddha Field.[10]

In a *Vimalakirti Sutra* parable, Buddha Shakyamuni was asked, "How can anyone create and inhabit a beautiful landscape?" The Buddha replied, "The magnificent landscape you witness is none other than an expression of Buddha's mind, with qualities developed through pure action, compassion and wisdom: physical manifestation of the Six Perfections of Bodhisattvas: Giving, Ethics, Patience, Effort, Concentration and Wisdom."[11] Teachers of Neo-Platonic and Christian traditions also regarded the experience of landscapes' beauty as no less a spiritual engagement. In *Enneads*, Plotinus stated:

> All the Beauty and Good of this world comes by Communion with Divinity as Ideal-Form. Communicating in thought (reason and logic) that flows from the Divine is how material becomes beautiful; and the Soul, heightened to Intellectual Principle, expression of Divinity, makes beautiful to the fullness of all things it grasps and moulds, attained as the Good.[12]

Referencing *The Divine Names*, Divinity was seen to have certain qualities, such as Goodness, and Dionysius the Areopagite celebrated Goodness as Beautiful—the cause of harmony and splendor in all things.[13] Furthermore, William Blake profoundly exclaimed in his "Vision of the Last Judgement:"

> When the sun rises, do you not see a round disk of fire somewhat like a guinea?
>
> O, no, no, I see an Innumerable company of the Heavenly Host crying, "Holy, Holy, Holy is the Lord God Almighty."[14]

The empowerment of the landscape with spirituality arises from the core of every sentient being, the subtlest faculty of mind. Buddhists call it the Spark of Awakening, or "Buddha-nature" (Skt: *Tathagathagarbha*). Indistinguishable from the Buddha's mind, the Spark of Awakening is an individual's source of wisdom and virtuous activities, the source of happiness, kindness and love, and the capacity to cry at the sight. And, like the Buddha, the Spark of Awakening is the source of the ability to produce beauty in artistic expression, promoted in everyday life through spiritual practice. It is comprised of two parts: the natural and potential spark.[15]

Accordingly, just as an individual's outer appearance reflects his inner spaces, the designated sacred landscape is an expression of one's positive thoughts and actions. Just as cultivation of body and mind has the potential to alter the qualities of the landscape in which one participates, so can the everyday corollary assume qualities of designated sacred landscapes. And just as an individual has the potential to transform landscape, so does the everyday corollary have the reciprocal potential to alter the state of one's body and mind. They mirror each other. Ralph Waldo Emerson wrote in his *Essay on Nature*:

> Every natural fact is a symbol of some spiritual fact. Every appearance in nature corresponds to some state of the mind, and that state of the mind can only be described by presenting that natural appearance as its picture.[16]

A Qualitative Index for the Everyday Corollary

Does the everyday corollary already possess qualities of sacred landscape or does it assume these qualities in accord with the individual (or collective) cultivation of body and mind? Owing to geological, atmospheric and ecological forces, the first phase of the four-fold ordination process, not all landscape is produced equally. Just as the potential for individual and collective cultivation varies, so will a landscape's capacity to be accorded with the qualities of sacred landscape.

A qualitative index for the everyday corollary describes potential states of mind and the qualities of sacred landscape, and the capacity to turn ordinary landscape into sacred landscape according to the development of an individual's mind. Giving language to the quality of sacred landscape is equivalent to giving language to an individual's character and their capacity for full awakening. Likewise, in evaluating sacred landscape for its ability to facilitate spiritual awakening, it is possible to assign a qualitative index to evaluate characteristics of landscapes in everyday life where people can experience spirituality.

But, what would a qualitative index of sacred landscape characteristics consist? During my initial investigations of this question, I explored four criteria that reflected well-established standard landscape design procedures for siting, organization, composition and format. However, drawing from historical references, was necessary to develop a point-by-point correspondence of sacred landscape and states of mind, modes of attainment or levels of consciousness, including, perhaps, inquiry into the nature of phenomena. In this context, Prasangika Buddhism divides phenomena into two classes: an afflicted class of 53 phenomena and a pure class of 55 phenomena, called "one hundred and eight bases of commentary." The 53 afflicted phenomena include the five aggregates, six senses, six consciousnesses and objects of consciousness, six contacts and feelings of experience, six elements and 12 links of dependent arising. The 55 pure phenomena include the six perfections, 18 emptinesses, 37 yogic paths, paths of calming, paths of special qualities, paths of effect, five actualizing beings and three final fruits.[17]

I soon discovered that working index of 108 criteria was unwieldy. However, a significant, and less expansive list of landscape qualities appear in the "First Avalokita-sutra" of *The Mahavastu*, a 4th-century CE Buddhist Mahasanghika text:

From the moment that bodhisattvas become completely endowed with steadfast activities of body, speech and mind they go to that spot of earth where they sit to overcome all hindrances. That spot of earth (the Diamond Throne) where Bodhisattvas go to overcome all hindrances has sixteen characteristics.

At the end of the world it is the first to be burnt. At the beginning it is the first to be established and stands there conspicuously in the centre. It is not situated in the outer provinces but in the central province. It is level, with good proportions and even like the palm of the hand. In its pools, bright lotuses of various colours grow. It is renowned and is used by powerful people. It is impregnable and is invincible. It has no evidence of afflictive emotions. It is favoured by devas. It is known as a throne. It is like a diamond. It is covered with soft grasses. It is the only place chosen for such renown.[18]

Each of the16 characteristics implied a correspondence between mind and landscape. In a similar, and much simpler enumeration, Thomas Aquinas stated:

God is Beauty, and Beauty and Good are grounded in Form. Three things are necessary for Beauty: first, integrity or perfection, for things that are lacking in something are for this reason ugly; second, proportion or consonance; and third, clarity, for we call things beautiful when they are brightly coloured."[19]

These three corresponded to Aristotle's qualities of beauty in "Metaphysics," "The chief forms of beauty are order and symmetry and definiteness, which the mathematical sciences demonstrate in a special degree." In "Poetics," he wrote:

A beautiful object, whether it be a living organism or any whole composed of parts, must not only have an orderly arrangement of parts, it also must be of a certain magnitude; for beauty depends on magnitude and order.[20]

In the correspondence between mind and landscape, Buddhist teachings enumerate 10 stages, or grounds of awakening (Skt: *Bhumi*) from which hindrances are overcome; each abides in its respective landscape, and based on the cultivation of *Ten Perfections*. The perfections of generosity, ethical application, patience, creative resolve, concentration and wisdom comprise the foundational six; followed by the perfections of method, intention, power and exalted wisdom are components of Highest Yoga Tantra (Skt: *Annutarayoga-tantra*).

The *Prajna-paramita Sutra* and *Vimalakirti Sutra* refer to a landscape cultivated by the purity of mind as a field of perfection itself, and is called a Buddha-field. Each cites to the ability of landscape to awaken, equivalent to the ability of a person to be awakened; each abides as the foundational the Perfections.

How does a bodhisattva purify the Buddha-field? A Bodhisattva, from the first thought of enlightenment onward, purifies their landscape by coursing in the Six Perfections. The Six Perfections are the great vehicle of a Bodhisattva.[21]
Six Perfections and the four-fold boundless mind are the Bodhisattva's pure land –
Giving is a Bodhisattva's Buddha land;
Keeping precepts is a Bodhisattva's Buddha land;
Forbearance is a Bodhisattva's Buddha land;
Exertion with energy is a Bodhisattva's Buddha land;
Deep thought in concentration is a Bodhisattva's Buddha land;
Wisdom is a Bodhisattva's Buddha land.[22]

By enumerating landscapes of the *Six Perfections*, these texts offer a viable basis to evaluate both sacred landscapes and those of the everyday corollary. Additionally, these landscapes correspond to six degrees of subtlety in both design and procedures of meditation. Furthermore, the 16 characteristics of "The First Avalokita-sutra" could be condensed neatly into six, and even could correlate to an expanded six-part procedure of Aristotle's *Poetics*.[23] Giving tangibility to the relationship between person and landscape, I call these *Six Signs of Sacred Landscapes*.

Regarding Sacred Landscapes and the Everyday Corollary

Signs	Fields – Perfections	Procedures in Meditation	Procedures in Design
Favorable Context	Field of Generosity	Locating and selecting the sacred grounds	Selecting the location
Contained	Field of Pacifying Ethics	Formulating the relationship; cleaning the place	Analysis of relationship with physical and social environment
Coherent	Field of Patience	Arranging the meditation grounds, implements, texts	Organizing the framework
Composed	Field of Joyous Effort	Formulating the meditation procedure	Creatively designing the focus
Clarity	Field of Concentration	Focus, luminosity of the meditation	Illuminating design intent
Artistic Expression Contemplation	Field of Wisdom	Insight	Conveying the narrative with the design vocabulary

Figure 12.2   Chart: six signs of sacred landscapes and the everyday corollary
Source: Courtesy of Dennis Alan Winters.

Six Signs of Sacred Landscapes

1. **Favorable Context** –Locating and selecting the sacred grounds; a Field of Generosity.

Of Favorable Context –
This place of refuge, nestled in the embrace of the landscape
Embodies balance and harmony of the universe
Accepting gifts offered by earth, waters and skies;
Sited to absorb auspicious life forces and mitigate negative ones –
Seeking transactional grounds for spiritual renewal,
a universe is offered in its entirety.

In addition to standard analytical environmental procedures, Buddhist teachers seeking landscapes for spiritual engagement adopted esoteric techniques of divination and geomancy like *feng-shui*, processes to reveal auspicious sites. Literally meaning wind-water, *feng-shui* refers to the evolution of landforms through the operations of nature. *Feng-shui* accords with the belief that the balance and harmony of the cosmos is expressed through the interaction of shapes and patterns in the landscape. Creating a favorable relationship with surrounding landforms, environmental conditions and celestial events offers greater potential to benefit from the site's attributes because proper siting integrates human life with the natural and cosmic process. Certain places meet these criteria and are considered suitable for physical and spiritual renewal; many are not. Referring to an index that speaks to both states of mind and qualities of sacred landscape, Plato said:

The goddess herself chose the well-placed site with a well-tempered climate, the site most likely to produce people most resembling her. In her home territory, the Greeks, resembling the perfection of the goddess, surpassed all others in every excellence.[24]

The Japanese monk Ekai Kawaguchi wrote that the location of Pretapuri on the Sutlej River in Western Tibet, one of the 24 sacred sites of the Chakrasamvara mandala, constituted one of nature's best essays on landscape.

Figure 12.3   Favorable context: liminal landscape of Pretapuri, Tibet
Source: Photograph courtesy of Dennis Alan Winters.

He amplified the importance of auspicious landscapes where sages chose to undertake meditation retreats and disciples constructed temples, shrines, and chortens in which to strengthen their connection to these places.

Pretapuri is a liminal landscape; a point of conjunction between distinct and disparate forms and spaces. Its liminality accentuates the positioning and relationship of landscape formations within their environmental context—where they meet and speak with one another. Here, topographic configurations dramatically reveal fundamental qualities and characteristics of geological structures and processes over time where the influence of one assemblage of elemental forces or operations of nature contrasts with another.

At such places, people acutely sense and effectively engage with the spiritual wonder of nature, becoming most in touch with the deepest values of landscape within themselves: where female landform meets male landform, stratigraphic conformity meets outcrop or recumbent fold, river flows over precipice, mountain meets plateau, rising meets descent, motion meets repose, and space meets form.[25]

Accordingly, Japanese Shinto, or "way of the *kami*," refers to a sense of the mystic rules of nature, and shrines are constructed where *kami* are revealed at these auspicious liminal landscapes. Also revered for its natural beauty, the site of a shrine is generally the most beautiful and auspicious place in the landscape. Consequently, *kami* worship is associated with a keen sense of the beautiful.

These are the transactional grounds where pilgrims make sacred pacts with divinity—charging the atmosphere with the power of those pacts, absorbing the energy of the landscape, breathing it—and as it flows through their veins, strikes chords in their hearts to make them to sing.

2. **Contained**—Formulating and analyzing the relationship with the physical and social environment, cleaning the meditation place; a Field of Pacifying Ethics.

Contained –
A distinct form in space, or a distinct space surrounded by form
Silence cradled by sound, light cradled by night;

Visually uncomplicated and easily identifiable
In contrast with chaotic or nebulous surroundings
A harmonious relationship supporting virtue and justice.

The sacred landscape speaks to a harmonious and virtuous relationship through wholesome and respectful standards between people and the surrounding landscape. Assigning distinction to the landscape and meditation space, cradled as a thought in one's heart, the sacred landscape stands formidably, held in esteem by its supporting theatrical cast, in distinct contrast to chaotic or nebulous forms, spaces, and activities. An expression of security not dependent upon egoism and the negative thoughts and actions it fuels, such a landscape offers a cradle to view others with compassion and kindness. What is the cradle's achievement? The 14th-century Tibetan Buddhist teacher, Je Tsong Khapa, referred to "The Three Principle Aspects of the Path" of: a) recognizing the actual nature of human existence; b) altruistically cultivating the awakening mind; and c) knowing the nature of reality and the reality of nature.

During the second week after attaining full awakening, Buddha Shakyamuni sat in meditation facing the Bodhi Tree to show respect for the landscape integral to his awakening. Pabongka Rinpoche taught in his concise discourse on the path to enlightenment that cleaning the meditation place before practice is a necessary preparatory rite to demonstrate respect for teachings and teachers invited into one's heart in the meditation space.[26]

Mt. Kailas in Western Tibet is one of the most revered sacred places for a billion people, and a place of pilgrimage for Hindus, Buddhists, Bon-po and Jain. Rising high above the Tibetan Plateau, Mt. Kailas is bounded on all sides by steep escarpments and narrow river valleys on the west, north and east, with the Barkha Plains to the south. Each facet of Mt. Kailas seems to bathe the surrounding landscape with light, like jewels of the four sides of Mt. Meru—crystals on the west, gold on the north, silver on the east, and lapis on the south. Discovered more than 3,000 years ago, Mt. Kailas was invested with the power of Mt. Meru, the physical embodiment of the center of the cosmological universe from which four celestial rivers flow in the four cardinal directions. Similarly, the landscape surrounding Mt. Kailas is the headwaters of the four major rivers of the South Asian

Mt. Kailas Inner Kora: 1994

Figure 12.4   Contained: Mt. Kailas, Tibet
Source: Photograph courtesy of Dennis Alan Winters.

Figure 12.5   Coherent: gateways of Tanukidani Fudo-in, Kyoto
Source: Photograph courtesy of Dennis Alan Winters.

continent—Brahmaputra to the east, Karnali to the south, Sutlej to the west and Indus to the north. Tibetan people call Mt. Kailas, *Kang Rinpoche*, Precious Jewel of Snow, and hundreds circumambulate the mountain each day.

Kobo Daishi established Koya-san mountain monastery in the early 9th century as the center of Esoteric Shingon Buddhism in Japan. Returning to Japan from China, stories say, he threw a small ritual implement into the sky, prayed for guidance, and discovered a landscape like the mandala of Mahavairocana. A wooded mountain 2,640 feet (805 meters) above sea level in the center of the Kii Peninsula, Koya-san is contained by two circles of eight mountain peaks, like petals surrounding the center of a flowering celestial lotus.

3. **Coherent**—Organizing the framework, arranging the meditation grounds, implements and texts; a Field of Patience.

Coherent –
Defined and organized to help the spiritual journey make sense, comprising:
a) Enclosure, a refuge where busyness and confusion can be left outside;
b) Gateway, the transition marking entry into sacred space;
c) Paths, directing guided, focused movement –
Slowly, slowly, every step a prayer
Right here, right now.

With its orderly arrangement of constituent parts a sacred landscape helps a spiritual journey make sense. The coherence of the landscape helps clear the mind from confusion caused by apprehension and uncertainty, debilitating companions to suffering. Suffering is experienced when wishing that circumstances were other than at present. Coherence helps to cultivate presence and patience; having arrived, right here and right now, this landscape is all there is; nothing else to want or to not-want, to need or to not-need. Consequently, the coherence of one's mind helps clear the landscape from suffering.

Pabongka Rinpoche noted five benefits of proper preparation and organization: "One's mind becomes clear, others' minds become clear, one cultivates the karma for physical and spiritual beauty, one will be reborn in celestial realms and the deities are pleased."[27] Coherence also corresponds to Aristotle's Definiteness in "Metaphysics" and Harmony in "Poetics;" and Thomas Aquinas' Integrity.[28]

Tucked into a narrow valley near the village of Ohara, respecting the spiritual beauty of nature within the mountains north of Kyoto, is the Pure Land temple Amida-ji, inspired by remote mountain Chinese Taoist retreat places. The surrounding mountains define the temple precincts, affording the sacred landscape a setting distinct from the outer populated environment. Refuge within these boundaries, more so than habitation outside, offers the opportunity to clear the mind of inner turmoil and cultivate intimacy with nature. The gateway identifies the threshold where the potential for absorption with impending depths of the mind brushes with the temporarily jettisoned exterior world. Paths through temple grounds are clearly arranged, enabling focus on a guided movement through a clear sequence of experiences and manipulating the sense of time and space: a rite of passage through a place of stillness.[29]

The path surrounding sacred structures and landscapes of Tibet is called the *kora*, meaning "going without arriving." Chanting the mantra, *OM MANI PADME HUM,* with prayer beads and prayer wheels in hand, pilgrims circumambulate the landscape (50 miles (80 km) around Mt. Kailas) by walking or prostrating the circumscribed path, expressions of their intimate relationship with the intense spiritual power of the landscape. Where significant milestones have been reached along the *kora*, pilgrims erect mani walls and *laptche*, piles of stones on which mantras are carved—punctuation marks along the spiritual path. They identify places of significant natural activity, where their revered teachers camped and meditated, and deities appeared: in front of meditation caves, at rivers and streams, tops of mountain passes, and ends of ascents. By setting stones on the mani wall, one creates causes and conditions to cultivate a landscape of the Buddhas and Bodhisattvas. A field of spiritual energy, like the overhead prayer flags blowing in the winds, the landscape sends forth vibrations of wisdom and compassion. Other pilgrims passing into this landscape absorb the energy, the music of the awakening mind.

4. **Composed**—Creatively designing the focus, formulating the meditation procedure; a Field of Joyous Effort.

Composed –
An intentional arrangement of form and space
In nature's lyrics: flora, earth, water, fire, wind and space
And architecture's scores: ordering principles, balance and sacred geometry;
Features, patterns and operations of nature telling one's story –
Paying attention with joyous effort,
Awakening the Mind, opening the Heart.

From Buddhist points of view, the ordinary mind and its ordinary landscape both flit like a monkey; weak and distorted because of delusions and emotional afflictions, twisted by neuroses and preconceptions that justify and solidify a sense of self-preservation. What kind of landscape produces such a mind? What kind of mind produces such a landscape? The composition of analytical and stabilizing meditation practices helps dissolve negative thoughts and actions, to enable one to become familiar with the Spark of Awakening, the source of wisdom and virtuous activities, the source of beauty in artistic expression. Thomas Aquinas wrote that "Beauty consists of due proportion, for the senses delight in rightly proportional things as similar to themselves." Composed corresponds to Aristotle's 'Symmetry' in "Metaphysics" and 'Rhythm' in "Poetics;" and Thomas Aquinas' Proportion. Centuries earlier, Plotinus wrote:

From what does Beauty draw its grace, showing itself in material form: Symmetry of parts towards each other and towards a whole. What of symmetry in noble and abstract thought? All the virtues are a beauty of the Soul. Where is the symmetry here? What standard of measurement can be used? The Soul, by the Truth of its Nature, when seeing its kin, thrills with delight.[30]

Figure 12.6   Composed: Daisen-in, Kyoto
Source: Photograph courtesy of Dennis Alan Winters.

An abstraction of nature, a story rich with unfolding symbolism, a metaphor for the span of human experience, the gardens at Daisen-in Temple in Kyoto is a collection of tales along a stream of granite pebbles that reveals one's intimate nature through the "River of Life." Springing from the heights of the *Immortals*, its "waters" plunge impulsively down cascading torrents of youth towards maturity muttering, "What is life about anyway?" Rocks in the river's path symbolize the hard lessons of life and trials of adulthood, the broadening of human experience and eventually the expansive "Great Sea of Meditation."

The temple of Saiho-ji is a large woodland garden at the base of Mt. Arashiyama in Kyoto. A stone path meanders around a pond originally conceived as an expression of the Western Paradise of Amida. Covered with 120 species of moss, the garden arose from the belief that fundamental balance and harmony, health and well-being innate to each individual are most dramatically revealed in nature. The garden serves as the link between the physical and the spiritual worlds. The composition produced in nature itself, revealing the intricate weaving of solidity, wetness, heat, cold, atmosphere and space over time, is the setting of a walking meditation along its path.

5. **Clarity**—Illuminating design intent, luminosity in meditation; a Field of Concentration.

Clarity –
A simple format, cultivating concentration and insight
Pointing to less in order to see more
With unwavering attention to just one thing,
A single story in one design vocabulary –
Present and mindful in each moment.

When fueled by lifetimes directed to cultivating the Spark of Awakening, a moment of clarity in concentration almost feels instinctive. In actuality, extensive training has been undertaken to achieve what teachers call the calmly settled mind of deep concentration. Clarity in meditation progresses through stages:

Ryogen-in: 1994

Figure 12.7   Clarity: Ryogen-in, Kyoto
Source: Photograph courtesy of Dennis Alan Winters.

from fixing the mind on an object, to developing continuity, to a ninth stage called single-pointed concentration.[31] Zen practitioners call that moment *satori*, when all the forces of the universe conspire to make sense, pieces fit together, and truth is no other than a truth coming to the mind. As a sign of sacred landscape, clarity corresponds to Aristotle's "Order" in "Metaphysics" and 'Language' in "Poetics;" and Thomas Aquinas' "Clarity," as well as Plotinus' "Charm of Colors."

Such is the instinctive sensation felt by the clarity of the presence of stones at the temple of Ryoan-ji in Kyoto. For good reason, its dry mountain-waterscape garden is the most famous in Japan. A weathered stucco wall in the background once tied the garden to the distant Kyoto mountains, now hidden from view by a stand of cryptomeria and maple trees. Within the wall, in a rectangular bed of gravel-sized granite, 15 stones are set in five circles of moss. The relationship among the five circles is geometrically configured through golden mean proportions.

Considered the essence of Zen wisdom, scholars have written speculative commentaries about the meaning of the 15 stones. Many have intensely analyzed the geometric relationship of scalene triangles among the five stone groups. The garden has been called "Islands in the Sea," "Mountains Poking through the Clouds," "Garden of Tiger Cubs Crossing a Stream to Follow their Mother," "Five Great Mountains or Monasteries of Zen Buddhism," and "Garden of Emptiness."

Having had the appearance of a *satori* moment, seemingly coming alive, the landscape of 15 stones expressed all that possibly could take place at that moment; nothing more, nothing less.

6.   **Artistic Expression of Contemplation**—Conveying the narrative with a deliberate design vocabulary, insight; a Field of Wisdom.

Artistic expression of Contemplation –
Poetic image of profound wisdom and compassion, pure abode of divinity;
Unique dialect of subtle design

Figure 12.8   Contemplation: stone nun at Pretapuri, Tibet
Source: Photograph courtesy of Dennis Alan Winters.

Mandala, pure land, paradise, nature, breath, God, silence
Presented with the glory of awakening,
How will you inhabit this divine sacred space

The grassy woodland bank of the Nairanjana River at Bodhgaya was not merely an inconsequential background for the scene of the Buddha's awakening. Nor were the scriptural descriptions of the landscapes embellishments or mere academic technicalities of subtle details. The Buddha purposefully sited and designed the landscapes in which he taught as inseparable and integral components of his discourses, blessed with qualities in which to most effectively present them, making them clues to the artistic expressions produced by the fully awakened mind. The keynote landscape of awakening at Bodhgaya, the "Middle Way" landscape of Deer Park, Veluvana bamboo garden of impermanence, Vulture's Peak as the Perfection of Wisdom, Vajrayana mandala landscape of Jetavana—were intentional.

Because of their relationship with landscape, integrating both states of mind and qualities of sacred landscape, designs by Buddhist teachers were like their own skin and bones, part and parcel of their purified five aggregates. Not only sources of inspiration, their landscapes revealed how teachers learned to do what they did. In Japan, mind took form as mandala and Pure Land Gardens like Koya-san and Byodo-in; meditations on the natural process like Saiho-ji and Tenryu-ji; Chop Wood, Carry Water Gardens like Entsu-ji and Daisen-in. Muso Soseki said:

> There are people for whom a landscape sustains their search for truth. This must truly be called noble. If one draws a distinction between landscape and a search for truth, one really cannot be called a seeker after truth. For the seeker of truth, this is the true way to love a landscape.[32]

Envoi

Sacred landscapes are places that energize feelings and thoughts attending the spiritual dimensions of life. Traditionally designated through ordination rituals, sacred landscapes are believed to differ from ordinary places of everyday life.

In spite of their lack of official acknowledgment, the everyday corollary landscape offers the potential for spiritual engagement. Endowed with distinct physical qualities and characteristics, its viability to perform as a sacred landscape operates through the instruments of virtuous relationships and qualities of interactions with individuals and/or communities whereby landscape and individual mirror each other. The fuel empowering individuals with spirituality arises from the core that Buddhists call the Spark of Awakening.

Designated sacred landscapes provide both a foundation and qualitative index by which to design and evaluate landscapes in everyday life where people can experience spiritual renewal. A qualitative index of characteristics for the experience of spirituality speaks to both landscape and individual. What I've named the *Six Signs of Sacred Landscape*: are Favorable Context, Contained, Coherent, Composed, Clarity and Artistic Expression of Contemplation. Corresponding to Mahayana Buddhist Six Fields of Perfection, they also refer to six procedures in meditation and six procedures in design. The everyday corollary, like sacred landscape, is endowed with these Six Signs.

Offering an example of the everyday corollary, my Tibetan Buddhist teacher told me a parable of his grandfather's long-term imprisonment in Tibet. Although distant from any designated sacred landscape, it was in that confined and isolated space that his grandfather experienced his most profound spiritual epiphanies. He had so much devotion to his Buddhist practice that revelations came from within, rather than despite, his cell, and his grandfather established a profound interaction with that prison cell. Because the cell had the potential, my teacher's grandfather transformed the cell—the everyday corollary.

Endnotes

1   See Dowman, Keith (1997). *The Sacred Life of Tibet*. London, UK: Thorsons, pp. 147–50.
2   However, the power of Buddha is equal to the collective karma of sentient beings.
3   See Winters, Dennis Alan (2014). *Searching for the Heart of Sacred Space*. Toronto: Sumeru Press, p. 144.
4   See Hakeda, Yoshito (1972). *Kukai—Major Works*. New York, NY: Columbia University Press, p. 90.
5   Public Talk: Teachings by H.H. The XIVth Dalai Lama, University of Toronto, September 1990.
6   See Dogen (1994). The Voices of the River-Valley and the Form of the Mountains, *Shobogenzo*. Woking, UK: Windbell.
7   See Brunton, Paul (1977). *The Hidden Teaching beyond Yoga*. New York, NY: Samuel Weiser.
8   Blofeld, John (1973). *The Secret and Sublime, Taoist Mysteries and Magic*. New York, NY: E.P. Dutton, p. 97.
9   Oral teaching by His Holiness the XIV Dalai Lama on Chandrakirti's *Guide to the Middle Way*.
10 See Cleary, Thomas (1987). *The Flower Ornament Scripture: A Translation of the Avatamsaka Sutra*, vol. III. Boston, MA: Shambala.
11 See Thurman, Robert (1976). Vimalakirti Nirdesa Sutra. Pennsylvania State University, http://huntingtonarchive.osu.edu/resources/downloads/sutras (accessed January 2005).
12 See Plotinus (1991). *The Enneads*, translated by Stephen MacKenna. London, UK: Penguin, pp. 45–7.
13 See Dionysius the Areopagite (1980). *The Divine Names*. Fintry, Surrey: The Shrine of Wisdom, p. 34.
14 See Frye, Northrup (1947). *Fearful Symmetry: A Study of William Blake*. Princeton, NJ: Princeton University Press.
15 See Obermiller, E. (trans.) (1984). *Uttaratantra: The Work of Arya Maitreya with a Commentary by Arya Asanga*. Talent, OR: Canon Publications.
16 Stephen, Whicher (ed.) (1960). Nature. *Selections from Ralph Waldo Emerson*. Boston, MA: Houghton Mifflin Company.
17 See Hopkins, Jeffrey (1983). *Meditations on Emptiness*. London, UK: Wisdom Publications, pp. 201–12.
18 See Jones, J.J. (trans.) (1952). *The Mahavastu*, vol. II. London, UK: Luzac and Company, pp. 247–8.
19 See Eco, Umberto (1988). *The Aesthetics of Thomas Aquinas*. Cambridge, MA: Harvard University Press.
20 See Aristotle, *Metaphysics XIII, Part 3* and *Poetics Part VII*, http://classics.mit.edu/Aristotle.html (accessed January 2009).

21 See Conze, Edward (trans.) (1979). *The Large Sutra on Perfect Wisdom*. Delhi: Motilal Banarsidass, p. 618.

22 See Thurman, Vimalakirti Nirdesa Sutra.

23 Choice of theater location, staging, organization, integrity, clarity and performance.

24 See Kavanaugh, Leslie Jaye (2007). *The Architectonic of Philosophy: Plato, Aristotle, Leibniz*. Amsterdam: Amsterdam University Press, p. 19.

25 See Winters, *Searching for the Heart of Sacred Space*, pp. 202–4.

26 See Rinpoche, Pabongka (1991). *Liberation in the Palm of Your Hand*, translated by Michael Richards. Boston, MA: Wisdom Publications, pp. 131–2.

27 Ibid.

28 The next three signs also refer to the tripartite evaluation of beauty and nature by Aristotle and Thomas Aquinas.

29 See Nitschke, Günter (1993). *From Shinto to Ando*. London: Academy Editions, p. 32.

30 See Eco, *Aesthetics*; Plotinus, *Enneads*.

31 See Rinpoche, Serkong (1982). *Teachings on the Meaning of the Profound Mahamudra*, translated by Alex Berzin. Barnet, VT: Milarepa Centre, pp. 159–68.

32 See Soseki, Muso (1989). *Sun at Midnight*. San Francisco, CA: North Point Press.

Chapter 13
Sacred Landscapes:
The Threshold between Worlds

A.T. Mann

Introduction

If we are fortunate in our lifetime we visit certain places, whether near to home or far away, that evoke the sacred in us. These places differ from our usual environment in some magical, powerful and often inexpressible way because they resonate with something in our deeper self, and challenge our beliefs by their mere presence. They create such awe that we come away feeling that we have glimpsed something very special and unique, and by extension, this experience may even restore our sense of wonder in the world.

There are places in the world that are considered sacred, but our experience of them is often out of this world, in the sense that while they exist in time, our experience of them may temporarily take us outside of time. Most sacred landscapes were created in the distant past, well before modern humans walked on the earth, so when we gaze at these sublime terrains, it is as if we are transported to a timeless realm, revisiting the creation itself. It is therefore appropriate that many of these were considered places of the origin of the world to the so-called "primitive" peoples all over our planet. The earliest myths and stories are the narratives of sacred places, as they attempted to describe how the world, their gods and goddesses, and they themselves came into being or existence.

But what exactly is the sacred? There are many varying and sometimes contradictory interpretations of what the sacred is and also what the sacred means, and of course many people do not believe that "the sacred" exists at all. Indeed since these "sacred" qualities cannot be measured, they are ignored by the positivist scientific worldview. The sacred isn't the property of any particular belief system, although each religious system claims to own them or at least articulate them.

According to the psychologist Carl Jung, the sacred is an ethereal quality that has roots in the life of the soul and spirit rather than in any formal religious association. Spiritual qualities are dynamic aspects of the human psyche that are independent of forms, but that find expression through the world of form.[1] A special quality possessed by a sacred landscape is that it triggers spiritual recognition in us when we experience it, independent of whether or not it is familiar to us or consonant with our beliefs.

Australian Aborigines describe the earth's sacred power as the "Dreaming" of a place, because anything that occurs in a particular sacred location "leaves seeds, myths or images, unseen vibrations that provoked the place into being in the first place."[2] Certain Aboriginal art is a map of this interaction between the spiritual realm and the physical place. If we are awake, present, open, and engaged, we can pick up these energies and the resultant information inherent in and stored in the dreaming of the place. The Aborigines navigate through the world using such places as markers and guideposts between the worlds. In their view, everything in the world is alive with sacred symbolism, imbued with spirit, and pregnant with possibility.

In Vajrayana Buddhism, the sacred isn't beyond thought or supernatural in some vague way, but "rather it has to do with things being so true, so real, and so direct."[3] The great Tibetan Buddhist master Chögyam Trungpa knew that the sacred is a matter of truth and that "the magic is simplicity."[4]

The sacred is also a component of spirituality—that transcendent quality so integral to people of all persuasions in our present world, some of who are scientists or even self-ascribed atheists. Spirituality, being both intensely personal and universal, is inclusive of but not necessarily limited to religious beliefs.

Figure 13.1   Wave Rock, Hayden, Western Australia, 1991. The natural weathering of the sandstone
               shows the principle of flow in the landscape
Source: Photograph courtesy Lynn Davis.

   The Forum for Architecture, Culture, and Spirituality (ACS) uses the following definition: "the spiritual refers
to a heightened or alternative state of mind in which one is overcome by, or perceives the presence, insight, or
action of forces beyond self-limited consciousness. Spiritual experiences are realized individually and although
possible to articulate, they cannot be completely conveyed due to the limited nature of our symbolic language.
More specifically, spirituality addresses the human need for transcendence ...."[5] Essential to experiences of the
sacred is a break in our normal perception of the world. Moments of transcendence impel us to abandon profane
or chronological time, which is linear and composed of the hours, days, and years of our life. As philosopher
and historian Mircea Eliade remarked, "by its very nature sacred time is reversible in the sense that, properly
speaking, it is a primordial mythical time made present."[6] Because sacred landscapes are typically created by the
evolution of nature over millions of years, they evoke the pure original state of earth and sky. Such places are
wild and chaotic, revealing their history to us in profound ways that we may not understand on a conscious level.
In sum, experiencing sacred landscapes is like being present at primordial realities that occurred at the beginning
of time and that continue to repeat ad infinitum, if only in the collective imagination and our psyche.

The threshold between worlds is where we offer sacrifices to the divinities at rites of passage such as births, deaths, and the brink of adulthood. These thresholds are a boundary, like consciousness, protecting us from the wildness of nature while allowing us a glimpse of the higher, spiritual realms. Whether it is a church or temple, a mountain or grove of trees, a pyramid in the jungle or expanse of northern ice, there is a profound difference once we cross the symbolic gateway into such sacred territory and allow ourselves to open up to the experience of pure spirit. Many of these passages are attended by protective deities that take the form of crosses, lions, dragons, Buddhas, and demons, to name a few, as well as symbols or signs that speak their potency. We don't have to accept or believe any religious or spiritual doctrine in order to feel the power of these landscapes, however, because they precede all human made structures and, by evoking some ancient occurrence recorded in our collective psyche, strike us at our true core.

In physics resonance is a phenomenon by which a pair of atoms, objects, waveforms, or bits of information that oscillate in a similar fashion and at a common frequency instantly communicate information over large distances. This information flows both ways and happens at speeds faster than light travels. We recognize it as the natural but exceptional process of "being on the same wavelength" as someone else, like seeing someone we perceive as familiar across a room full of strangers. In music, resonance is when a sympathetic vibration intensifies or prolongs an initial sound, as demonstrated by some Eastern musical instruments with strings inside the body of the instrument that vibrate with the outer strings. Resonance psychologically enriches the apparent significance of things and evokes spontaneous, deeply emotional experiences.

Sacred landscapes also act in this way, so that when we come to a sacred place it might be that we resonate with its energy fields, the density of its material, the play of light and shadow, the look of certain angles or curves, or even the field of experience that the landscape has carried through millions of years. When monuments or sacred buildings are constructed in or on these places, they may act as a kind of focus for these resonant dynamics, and thus the building or object acts as a sounding board for deep feelings evoked by the landscape, centering it and bringing it into a more sensible form. In this sense, the resonance of sacred places may be a transition point between heaven and earth, above and below, unconscious and conscious. We pass between worlds in such places because the environment contains a sacred presence, and if we are willing to "go there," we can enter the spirit of these landscapes and receive their profound messages.[7]

In Search of the Sacred

When we experience a sacred landscape, we resonate inwardly with its power, whether or not it conforms to our education, beliefs or knowledge of the world. This may be why people travel to the ends of the earth to visit such places, even though they may not be aware of what they are experiencing. Indeed, what they experience in sacred landscapes may not necessarily conform to their formal religious, scientific, or philosophical beliefs. This is because the sacred is a ritual process, a journey where we often begin at these evocative places, and once we participate, we remain on the quest for the rest of our lives.

The myriad definitions of the sacred are applicable to ancient as well as modern sites, ranging from pure, vast landscapes to specific intimate localities. Most often, they date from before human history, although many sites have since attracted religious markers, pilgrimages, buildings, or settlements. Sacred landscapes are manifestations of nature and places possessing power, with the ineffable capacity to confer this potency to those who behold them. They recharge our spiritual energy, and purify the soul.

Essential to our understanding of sacred landscapes are the myths, stories, and beliefs that early inhabitants associated with them. Sometimes they involve mythic places that we cannot find in our modern world, such as the central Asian kingdom of Shambhala, Camelot the British site of King Arthur's palace, the Australian aboriginal Dreamtime, the Three Underworlds of the Navaho, and the mythic island kingdom of Atlantis. Whether or not they ever existed in the material world, sacred sites and their accompanying myths fire our imaginations and continue to exist in our minds as we search for traces of them in our journeys across the globe.

For early nomadic peoples, the history from which we all carry within us thanks to our DNA, the dwelling of their divinities were imprinted in the vault of the heavens above. This vast dome overhead, with its infinite stars, seemed to center around them and moved with them on their travels. They observed planetary and other celestial movements and created mythologies to identify, explain and worship them.

Figure 13.2   Temple of Athena, Delphi, Greece, 2008. This temple was open to the sky and the vault of
               the heavens above

Source: Photograph courtesy Lynn Davis.

The first temples, including Stonehenge and the other stone and forest circles, as well as burial mounds, across Europe and the Americas, were in the open, framing the heavens. When humanity developed agriculture, animal husbandry, settled, and created cities and temples, pyramids became sacred mountains, while their vaults and domes were recreations of the sky. These early monuments were observatories, sacred sanctuaries, and cult centers. Monuments such as Newgrange and other passage tombs in the Boyne Valley in Ireland and throughout Europe contained stone passageways that also aligned to the rising and setting of the sun, moon or stars. They were where humanity met the divine and where observations necessary to the development of astrology, navigation, and calendar making took place. The Solstice solar rays interacting with the recumbent stones within the mound were deemed a fertility rite of heaven and earth.

To the earliest cultures, the earth was considered the center of the world/universe and was viewed as being entirely sacred. Their deities created Mother Earth and Father Sky, the rivers and oceans, mountains and valleys, woods, trees and all growing things, and the abundance of animals, and they were at one with their world. Indeed, these deities *were* derivative of the land and its creatures as well as having created them, embodying spirit on Earth and in life. All the various domains and species were part of the family of the divinities, and consequently, all were sacred.

Early religious rituals celebrated the creation of the world out of primal chaos, during which participants relived the mystery of this great birth, stepping out of ordinary time to achieve a new beginning, transcendence, healing, or contact with their ancestors and primeval gods and goddesses. The same process appears in holy texts, where mysteries of sacred origin are revealed to prophets, always within a particular sacred setting—Mecca, Mount Sinai, Delphi, Bodhgaya, Jerusalem, Mount Meru, Palmyra—all of these holy places continue to function as symbolic gateways for origins. Thus, religious revelations and myths transmit the power of our common origins to subsequent generations.

The traditional Abrahamic religions enforced a separation of their followers from the spirits and symbols of the natural world, as well as separating male from female in their congregations, a reality that remains to this day. The "pagan" reverence for the earth and its plants and creatures was seen as a subversive force to be rooted out and eliminated, and this viewpoint persists among large numbers of the current world population—particularly Christian, Islamic, and Jewish fundamentalists. The fact that the world population is striating into those for whom science and atheism are supreme and those with blind belief in religion as a worldview makes the whole situation infinitely worse, because neither scientists nor fundamentalists respect the sacred places of earlier times, deeming them impious, pagan, useless, and even oppositional to the needs of modern society. For example, the expression "tree hugger" is used as a negative connotation by a large percentage of our population who consider ecology, nature and species preservation to be antithetical to commercial and industrial development, including the ever expanding global corporate world.

The irony is that the Abrahamic religions have often built atop the ruins of earlier sacred places and incorporated their remains, symbolism, and rituals into their own religious observances. Thus, we find groves of trees sacred to the early Middle Eastern fertility goddesses like Ishtar and Isis incorporated into temples, churches, or mosques as columns decorated with floral imagery and carved with vertical flutes like stems and spiraling vines. The earliest places of nature worship were prototypes and even site-specific locations of later sacred pyramids, temples, mosques, stupas, churches, and holy cities. The natural world becomes an adjunct to the human made world, where it exists as an abstraction, artistic convention, or decoration. However, these original symbols of the sacred continue to exert power over us, albeit within rather than without.

The Evolution of Sacred Symbolism

The Old Testament is a mythic history of the early Jewish tribes, which emerged from, and then continually struggled against, much earlier Middle Eastern "pagan" nature cults that worshipped "graven images" such as winged deities, animals like bulls or rams, and plants—especially trees. Their cultures emerged from nomadic herders and farmers, and it was natural for them to worship such natural beings in their environment, and also this remained well after the patriarchies took hold in the Middle East. Henceforward, in times of stress the people reverted to their polytheistic earth-worship. The later patriarchies eventually neutralized this tendency by condemning any such objects of worship, but also incorporating early ritual places and objects as symbols, sacred implements, and influences affecting their choices of sacred landscapes. Sacred mountains, which are where revelations and communication with God occur, became symbols, like the tent-like triangular roof of Solomon's Temple, and the Tree of Knowledge in the Garden of Eden became a menorah. In both cases, the form of the object reminds the worshipper of origins, of beginnings, and of divine revelations achieved through direct contact with God, but all the while partaking of and integrating earlier symbolism, which evoked different pantheons of gods and goddesses.

Few understand the natural transformation from early sacred places to formal religious precincts where the symbolism is present. This is because many have lost the capacity to understand the "symbol" that is so integral to understanding the sacred. Often the original symbols have been appropriated for religious purposes. A *sign* has a specific meaning that does not vary, like a corporate logo or a stop sign, while a symbol expresses an inner truth that carries multiple meanings according to one's level of understanding of it. The psychologist Carl Jung defined a symbol as an "expression of the inner unconscious drama of the psyche which becomes accessible to man's consciousness by way of projection—that is, mirrored in the events of nature."[8]

Figure 13.3   Great Pyramid of Giza (Dynasty IV), Egypt, 1989. The Great Pyramid is a sacred mountain,
                has inner caves, and a guardian protector in the Sphinx
Source: Photograph courtesy Lynn Davis.

Sacred landscapes are symbolic in that the elements that make them powerful—mountains, rivers, sky
and stars, oceans and lakes, majestic trees and jungles, deserts and plateaus—function on many levels
simultaneously. They are natural and tangible, yet they also carry deep symbolism that is either evident to
those who behold them, or they are associated with myths or legends that make them numinous places once
occupied by gods or goddesses.

     Although we tend to think of the cross as a Christian symbol, it appears in virtually all earlier
cultures—thousands of years before Christianity—for example, the equal-arm cross was a symbol of the
cardinal directions of the compass, the meeting between heaven and earth, within a circle as the original
astronomical symbol of Earth, and is prominent today on top of the Basilica of San Francesco in Assisi,
Italy. Ancient symbolism is thus inseparable from our experience of sacred places, as we resonate with
these underlying symbols wherever we encounter them. The sacred landscape is beautiful and powerful
in its own right, but it also carries a numinous light-bringing quality that we can't help but notice and
respect, whatever one's religious beliefs. These are sometimes places of natural wonders that have been

seen as special for many generations, or are places where the world began. Creation mythologies are often associated with specific places in the landscape, such as Aphrodite and the ocean at Cyprus, or the Psychro Cave on Crete where the goddess Rhea hid the infant Zeus. It is valuable for us to learn how to recognize what constitutes a sacred place, so we can begin to identify the sacred in our local world and also replicate these sacred principles in our own work. We are not returning to the ancient ways, but simply utilizing them to further our connection to the earth and other natural forces. When sacred forms are recognized and integrated into made landscapes, they resonate on deeper levels beyond mere beauty.

In his book *The Re-Enchantment of Everyday Life*, psychotherapist Thomas Moore talks about new definitions of the increasingly common word "ecology" that give it more potent moral and ethical overtones. Sacred Ecology describes one "who has an ethical concern for all living creatures and for the earth as a living system."[9] This is in direct opposition to the prevailing profane and scientific view of the earth as an inert body available for exploitation. When we understand the earth as an organism, we rediscover ancient concepts such as "cosmos" and "world soul" from a time when the gods and goddesses were still valued and known by direct experience. I am not suggesting we revert to ancient practices, but it is important to understand that they constitute valid underpinnings that have an ever-increasing relevance today especially for our values and our inner life.

Restoring the Sacred

Many of the patriarchal religions of the past defined the precinct or land around a church or temple or mosque as "sacred," inferring that the surrounding land was non-sacred. Thus, in this division, we fail to recognize the holistic nature of the entire natural world, demeaning all of nature by assigning it a subsidiary role as a mute backdrop to our more important lives. Unfortunately, humanity continues to abuse the memory of the spirits by desacralizing the earth, using it as raw material for our vision of dominance through materialism and further desecrating it to the extent that we are making our only home nearly inhospitable to all living species. In order to restore the natural world to its proper place in the order of things, we must encourage the view that all nature is sacred. This is not a religious issue, but rather a moralistic and sensible issue.

There are many manifestations of the sacred landscape, such as mountains, boundaries, gateways, caves, flowing waters, springs, spectacular views, vast jungles and trees. Many of the most powerful sacred sites contain more than one natural feature, if not many or even all of these characteristics. Of course, it is often the case that human-made monuments have been constructed in such sacred landscapes, to take advantage of them, to place mark them, or simply to respect them. It is also important to remember that in earlier times ordinary sites were also considered sacred because the entire earth was treated as sacred. For example all small rivers and streams in India were seen to resonate with the Ganges. Pyramids, for instance, mark important points in the landscape, are oriented toward the cardinal compass directions, evoke sacred mountains in their shape, have inner passageways like caves, and are protected by guardians like the Sphinx. In this case, the sacred monument functions on many different levels of perception while evoking earlier stages in the development of the sacred. The evolution of architecture, particularly sacred architecture, grew from this principle. We know that many Christian churches and cathedrals were sited near or above underground springs, rivers, fissures, and other natural places that had been considered sacred in the pre-Christian era. As identified in my book *Sacred Architecture*,[10] many sacred buildings throughout history exhibit literal or abstract representations of natural elements, such as column capitals echoing reeds or foliage, floors showing water patterns, or ceilings that show the sky and heavens.

Although pyramids, stupas, sanctuaries, churches, temples, and mosques were built in sacred landscapes, it is the landscape itself that evokes the sacred. Formal religions had the sense to recognize and attempt to capture the sacred quality that the landscape possesses and to willfully dispose it. Let us therefore rediscover our ancient roots in these sacred landscapes and bring their wisdom into a world that sorely needs it. The following pages will introduce some of the key characteristics of sacred landscapes as we experience them, both as physical places and the processes they represent.

Figure 13.4   Monument Valley Navajo Tribal Park on the border of Utah and Arizona,
                United States, 1991
Source: Photograph courtesy Lynn Davis.

Ascending the Sacred Mountain

Heaven and earth meet atop the highest mountains, which early humans believed housed the divinities and supported the heavenly vault of the sky. Mountains evoke a need to climb them, surmount them, and feel their power, which is an expression of their sacredness. They provoke rituals and journeys that are both physical and also spiritual. Their impact is visual, visceral, intensely physical, and tangible—and even more so when they are high enough to penetrate the clouds, are explosively volcanic, or are covered with ice and glaciers.

Jung says that "the mountain stands for the goal of the pilgrimage and ascent; hence it often has the psychological meaning of the self."[11] The actual sacred world mountains, like Ararat, Sinai, Fuji, Olympus, and Kailas, are places of origin because the gods and goddesses that abide there created the world, according to their local cultures. Our ancestors celebrated creation as a continuous process, revered the creators, and made continual sacrifices to maintain equilibrium. They were aware that change was inherent in reality. The mountains marked sacred places on earth that protected humanity from the abyss of the underworld and acted as pathways to the profound world of spirit. It is not surprising that later cultures designated mounds, natural hills, and high plateaus as sacred and later recapitulated them through the forms of pyramids, domes and stupas.

Figure 13.5   Petra, Jordan, 1995. The carved rock entrance evokes the mystery of the sacred cave
Source: Photograph courtesy Lynn Davis.

In the creation myths of early cultures, the earth's revolving axis is the navel of the world (*axis mundi*) because the stars and planets in the night sky appear to revolve around the North Pole Star. This "divine tent pole" links above and below and is the path by which gods descend to earth, and by which humans ascend to the realm of deities. Mountains are thus revered because they appear to provide access to the axis of the world above. Characteristics of sacred mountains appear in myths from all over the world   as twins, containing mysterious caves, surrounded by rivers or a body of water, and, in the case of fiery, volcanic mountains, providing access to the core of the world or the hell-fires of the underworld. Above all, however, mountains are places of revelation. The sacred mountain is where Moses was given the tablets of the law and where Zen, Hindu, and Buddhist sages meditate. Likewise, many European cultures make references to the "magic mountain."

Machu Picchu in Peru is an archetypal sacred mountain; it has layers of symbolic and ritualistic architectural elements. Its discoverer Hiram Bingham named the building he found there the "Temple of the Three Windows" because its trapezoidal openings echoed the three ceremonial caves of the primary Inca creation myth, the central window representing the cave from which the Inca people emerged at the beginning of the world. Many small temples in Machu Picchu echo the shapes of the surrounding sacred mountains, as do the pitched roofs of many houses in this astounding city. The Inca accepted that Mother Earth held great power manifested in the sacred places (*huacas*), such as caves, springs, lakes, and mountains.

The ultimate symbol of the sacred mountain is ascent, showing the quality of rising higher and attaining the heights, and is similar to the symbol of fire, with its upward pointing triangle, hence its association with pyramids, stupas, the pitched roofs and pediments of Greek and Roman temples, as well as churches and mosques.

Sacred Cave Mysteries

Among the earliest sacred places were caves. It was natural for our nomadic ancestors to discover, take shelter in and revere these hollowed sanctuaries in the landscape. They found the bones of bears and other animals, and considered these animals totemic and magical. Caves were the site of cult rituals and stored imagery that carried the early generative histories of a people or tribe. Some renowned examples include the Upper Paleolithic caves of Lascaux, in France, and Altamira, in Spain, both of which contain paintings of totem animals and the hunt; the oracular cave at Delphi, in Greece, where the priestesses of Apollo sat to receive divine prophecy; the cave in which Zeus was allegedly born, on Crete; and also the many Himalayan caves where hermits obtained profound wisdom.

Figure 13.6   Cave Tombs of the Achaemenid Kings, Naqsh-e Rostam, Iran, 2001
Source: Photograph courtesy Lynn Davis.

Most sacred caves around the world are appropriately located in sacred mountains, and there is a naturally strong relationship between the two. Mountains are masculine and phallic, ascending up to the sky, while caves are feminine and burrow into the earth, have huge underground pockets full of mysterious waters, and are the natural domain of the Earth Mother goddesses and the underworld. If the landscape above ground is the land of the living, it is only natural to locate the land of the dead below ground.

To the Maya, the geography of the entire world was sacred, but this sacredness was particularly concentrated in more arresting geological phenomenon such as mountains and caves—channels through which one could pass to the starry heavens above and the darkness of the underworld below. These gateways between dimensions commanded great respect and fear while also determining the siting and other aspects of their jungle pyramid complexes. Thus, humans created their own power points, which integrated and resonated with the god-made power points inherent in the world.

The Mayan temples that reach up into the sky in Central America were conceived as sacred mountains, and the entrances into their interior spaces represented caves leading to the heart of those mountains. Inside the cave grew the sacred World Tree—the Mayan cosmos—which united the underworld and the "Skyworld" with the world of men and which completed the sacred trilogy of mountain, cave, and tree.[12] Much like the ancient ancestor and nature worship of the Balinese people, the surviving Maya Indians still re-create the sacred landscape of the cosmos in miniature out of leaves, vines, flowers, and with indentations in walls or hills.

Flow

Water is the substance of life both in the physical world and in our bodies. Its benevolent phase allows the growth of crops, it determines our climate and weather, and its movements are essential for transportation of goods around the planet. We must drink water and bathe in it to maintain a healthy life. Water is also a mysterious and magical substance associated with the feminine, emotions, and tidal changes. Additionally, it symbolizes the amniotic fluid of the womb, and its flow is analogous to our dream life and soul.[13] When we live on or near the water, we can't help but be deeply affected by its rhythms, sounds, and overall presence. As water moves, so does time, and we talk about the inexorable flow of time, one of life's greatest mysteries and a governing principle of our lives. And, its destructive phase is something to be feared.

Eastern philosophies such as Hinduism, Taoism, Confucianism, and Buddhism regard flow (especially of spirit) as a central component of spirit and health, as do Native Americans, shamanic religions and many other spiritual creeds. In sacred landscapes, flowing water is an activating substance. Every continent has a major mountain chain that gathers water and sends it toward distant seas, through a series of rivers that permeate the land and feed the great oceans. These rivers are the agricultural lifeblood of the continents—blood vessels of the earth, essentially—bringing vitality as they wash away toxicity and waste.

Water signifies regeneration, a washing away of sinful wrongs, and the ultimate mystery of death and rebirth. At the Castalian spring above Apollo's oracular shrine at Delphi, ceremonies were held in veneration of nymph goddess Castalia. The spring, located in a deep ravine near the sacred spot where Apollo killed the Python, was used for the purification of the pilgrims who came to the site. The immersion of newborns or the newly converted in water in the later Christian rite of baptism similarly represents a purifying cleansing as well as a return to a purer state—perhaps even an intrauterine state before birth in the world. Taking the metaphor further, myths about a great flood (such stories exist all over the world) imply a collective regeneration—more explicitly, destruction by water of a prior generation of humanity and other life forms, leading to a fresh start.[14] Once again sacred mountains, caves and the springs, rivers and waterfalls that emanate from them are linked by their sacredness.

Some early traditions focus on the generative properties of great, standing bodies of water. In Buddhist legends, the Kathmandu Valley in Nepal was a vast lake, and at the center bloomed a resplendent lotus. From this thousand-petaled lotus shone a light that illuminated the entire valley.[15] This luminescence was called the *Swayambhu*, or "self-sprung." This magnificent lotus did not escape the notice of the bodhisattva Manjushri, who vowed to serve humanity by draining the lake and thus making the lotus accessible for worship. He flew through the air and landed on a Himalayan mountain peak at the edge of the lake. Holding aloft his sword, which symbolized wisdom, he cut a gorge through the mountain range that separated Nepal from India. After the original lake drained away, a fertile valley remained, and is considered sacred to this day.

Figure 13.7   Iguaçu Falls, Brazil, 2008
Source: Photograph courtesy Lynn Davis.

Sacred Trees

We tend to underestimate the tangible value trees have for the world, even as they provide us with houses, books, furniture, ships to sail the oceans, implements to work in the fields or garden, axe handles, gunstocks, baseball bats, newspapers, and the oxygen we breathe. It is therefore not surprising that trees are among the most sacred living things and an essential component of virtually all early creation myths, legends, and folk tales. They inhabit our inner world and unconscious mind simultaneously and are potent symbols of the living contents of the personality and a prototype of the self.[16]

Since a sacred mountain is considered an axis of the world (*axis mundi*), trees perform the same function in creation myths. Balancing their visible upper halves with the invisible root systems that hold them firmly in the soil, the leafy canopies symbolically reach up to the heavens as the roots penetrate down into the underworld. Thus, it is not surprising that the mythic "Tree of Life" remains with us today as a powerful esoteric symbol of this connection.

Rediscovering the Sacred

Over millions of years, the forces of time and nature have worked their powerful ways on earth to create myriad of places considered sacred. Even today, there are still sacred landscapes to be discovered in undiscovered and remote places. Not long ago, the ancient Buddhist temple at Borobudur in Java was rediscovered a thousand years after its creation because some Javanese people mentioned to then–colonial governor Sir Thomas Raffles that there was a mountain in eastern Java that had heads emerging out from it. When he finally explored the place he realized that these Buddhas were part of the gigantic temple that has now been restored to its former glory. Similarly, the tale of Hiram Bingham discovering Machu Picchu echoes the romance and adventure of finding a hidden city in the mountains. We can experience this romance in our own lives by exploring the Great Pyramid and the Sphinx, or the exotic and forbidden Mayan temples in Central America, which take us back into the mists of time to an era when the world was pure and the gods and goddesses reigned.

In our time of environmental crisis, we have demystified and de-sanctified our sacred landscapes. However we have seen that such landscapes are alive, that they flow, that they produce a deep and powerful resonance that can be felt, and above all that their power is often encoded in myths or stories that tell of ancient origins—mysteries that precede and influence the major world religions. There is no one true story, but rather a matrix of interrelated tales and myths that attempt to explain particular elements of a sacred place, or its coming-into-being, or the perceptions of various generations of inhabitants who lived in and experienced the place when it spoke directly to them. In this sense, these magnificent landscapes and their associated mythology represent an older and deeper layer of connection we share with our world.

Stories are the primary way that we communicate who we are and what we value, so it is important that we learn the stories that are embedded in our landscapes. It is also essential that we encourage these stories to remain in the common language and that we pass on their magic and mystery to our children and their children. Facing the daunting reality of rising oceans and the extinction of entire species, we must reanimate our landscapes and renew our understanding of their sacred qualities. Only when we achieve this universal, fundamental change in the way we relate to our environment can we hope to preserve the tenuous ecological balance of our only planet earth.

It is more necessary than ever that we understand how profound and wide is the symbolic sacred that surrounds us. Every continent has its own mountains, rivers, lakes, oceans, trees, gardens, gateways, and boundaries that define the sacred. There is no one view about what constitutes the sacred, but rather many. Consequently, we can dedicate the sacred to the entire world that surrounds and sustains us.

Endnotes

1   Jung, C.G. (1969). *Archetypes and the Collective Unconscious*, translated by R.F.C. Hull. London, UK: Routledge & Kegan Paul, p. 6.

2   Lawlor, Robert (1991). *Voices of the First Day*. Rochester, VT: Inner Traditions, p. 1.

3   Trungpa, Chögyam (1994). *Illusion's Game: The Life and Teachings of Naropa*. Boston, MA: Shambhala, p. 133.

4   Ibid., p. 33.

5   Part of the statement of purpose by John Graham, an early Serenbe resident in 2008, of the Forum for Architecture, Culture and Spirituality Statement. Their website is: http://faculty.arch.utah.edu/acs.

6   Eliade, Mircea (1959). *The Sacred and the Profane*. London, UK: Harcourt Brace and World, p. 68.

7   In the New Physics there is a process called Entanglement, which Einstein predicted, and it essentially suggests that two subatomic particles can become entangled and inextricably linked so that even if they are separated by being in different universes, a change in one particle would instantly be reflected in the other. The same could be true of information. See Aczel, Amir D. (2001). *Entanglement*. New York, NY: Four Walls Eight Windows.

8   Jung, C.G. (1969). *Archetypes and the Collective Unconscious*, translated by R.F.C. Hull. London, UK: Routledge Kegan Paul, p. 6.

9   Moore, Thomas (1997). *The Re-Enchantment of Everyday Life*. New York, NY: HarperPerennial, p. 41.

10 Mann, A.T. (1993). *Sacred Architecture*. London, UK: Element Books.

11 Jung, C.G. (1983). *Memories, Dreams and Reflections*. London, UK: Collins, p. 83.

12 Schele, Linda and David Freidel (1990). *A Forest of Kings*. New York, NY: Quill, p. 67.

13   Moore, Thomas. Ibid., p. 14.
14   Mann, A.T. (1986). *The Divine Plot*. London, UK: Allen & Unwin, pp. 38–9. This book lists 39 cultures around the world that have flood legends.
15   The lotus is also a symbol of the crown chakra at the top of the head, a place of enlightenment.
16   Jung, C.G. (1967). *Alchemical Studies.* London, UK: Routledge and Kegan Paul, p. 194.

PART V
Spirituality and the Designed Environment

Chapter 14

Secular Sacredness in Place Creation: A Case Study and Analysis of Serenbe Community

Phillip James Tabb

Introduction

In the built environment, placelessness and its vapid character, dysfunction, alienation, and disconnectedness, has become alarmingly pervasive. Moreover, contemporary discourse and applications in response to these conditions and to rampant urban growth seem to be dominated by uncontrolled suburban sprawl, continued automobile dependency, and stylistic/historicist approaches each offering short-term alternatives rather than long-term solutions. In some instances there is what urban planner Nan Ellin calls "razzmatazz" or a hyper-modernity born from a cynical and even desperate urbanism.[1] And even popular media is filled with depictions of dystopian visions of a dire urban future. This chapter, rather, provides new paradigms that intend to raise the integrity, inclusiveness and quality of experience of the built environment by applying sacred principles and patterns, all of which are in service of not only a more humane, environmentally sensitive and spiritually enriched architecture, but are especially applicable to the urban design scale.

Secular-sacred architecture, and secular-sacred communities are not purposed specifically for religious functions, but are designed for higher and more integral, transformative, and inclusive everyday experiences. These places usually manifest in sensitivity to the land and nature, in relationships among community members, in special activities made available to residents, and in embodied qualities in the physical design. The secular-sacred is evident in spiritual values and sensitivities set in a secular environment that provides daily contexts and opportunities for them to occur. The integration of secular and sacred follow similar ideas put forward by psychologist William James' proposition of natural theology (2009), philosopher Robert Sardello's perspectives on spirituality, soulfulness and everyday consciousness (2012), psychotherapist Thomas Moore's arguments for the re-enchantment of everyday life (1997), and Frederic and Mary Ann Brussat's spiritual perspectives on everyday experience (1998). Additionally, Paul Oliver suggests that indigenous communities are also important sources for demonstrating correspondences with sacrality of nature, stewardship of the land, and an intrinsic understanding of the importance of changes of the seasons as well as the sky and cosmos in everyday experiences (1987).[2]

Several secular-sacred examples illustrate these concepts: Auroville in India, Findhorn Community in northern Scotland, Järna Community near Stockholm, Sweden, New Harmony, Indiana, and Damanhur, Italy. Auroville is an experimental trans-national township in the state of Tamil Nadu, India. It was founded by the French teacher Mirra Alfassa in 1968, and designed by architect Roger Anger. The master plan was intended to foster unity and progressive harmony, conceived using the geometry of a spiral nebula with the Matrimandir, in Sanskrit for *Temple of The Mother*, at its center (Figure 14.1a). Auroville aspires to be a site of material and spiritual research for an actual living embodiment of human unity.

Findhorn was established in the early 1960s by Peter and Eileen Caddy, and grew into a community because of a remarkable garden they first created there. They prepared the ground upon the sandy barren soil of coastal Scotland, planted with care and phenomenal success, and became wonderful stewards of the place that evolved from a garden to an eco-community (Figure 14.1b).[3] Within a year of its planting, the garden grew to 65 different types of vegetables, 21 kinds of fruits and 42 different herbs, and was overflowing with life. Today the community is a constantly evolving demonstration of the spiritual, social, ecological and economic dimensions of life. Findhorn is the largest intentional community in the United Kingdom. The community extends also to individuals, businesses and organizations within a 50-mile (80 km) radius of The Park and to the islands of Iona and Erraid on the west coast of Scotland.

Figure 14.1   Secular sacred communities: a) Auroville, India, b) Findhorn Eco-Community, and c) New Harmony, Indiana

Source: a) Photograph courtesy of Flicker, b) Photograph courtesy of Findhorn Community, c) Photograph courtesy of Wikimedia Commons.

Järna is described as a constellation of businesses and social activities, organized with concepts developed by the philosopher Rudolf Steiner. At the beginning of the 20th century, Steiner founded, *Anthroposophy*, an esoteric philosophy growing out of European transcendentalism and with links to Theosophy. Järna is considered the center of the anthroposophical movement in Sweden. The community is nestled beside a coastal inlet of the Baltic Sea; the landscape interweaves the Södermanland forest, and open plains punctuated with organic farms. Buildings within the community were designed by Danish architect Erik Asmussen using Steiner's principles. The community also employs biodynamic agriculture, and composting with a network of farms using these practices.[4]

Other notable intentional communities include New Harmony in Indiana, which was established in 1814 as a utopian experiment to advance education, scientific research and governance models. Originally, the German immigrant George Rapp led the New Harmony Society. In 1825, it was purchased by Scottish industrialist Robert Owen, but soon became unsustainable due to several factors including the lack of individual sovereignty and private property. Socialist programs quickly transformed into individualism by 1828. Today New Harmony has nearly 800 residents (2010 census), and is considered a historic town that is viewed as a vacationers' and researchers' dream place (Figure 14.1c).

Another example of designed communities with a search for the spiritual dimension is Damanhur, Italy that is a United Nations Award-winning intentional and sustainable community. Considered a Federation of communities, it is situated in the Piedmont region of northwestern Italy in the foothills of the Alps. Founded in 1975 by Oberto Airaudi based on neo-pagan beliefs, it presently has approximately 900 residents. It is known for its spectacular underground worship or meditation space called the "Temples for Humankind," which was constructed by the residents themselves without formal plans, where nine ornate temples on five levels, narrate the history of humanity.[5]

Numerous contemporary places of contemplation and renewal have been created all over the world throughout time, and provide what anthropologist Martin Gray has termed a network "planetary acupuncture," where he observed a global landscape of more than 1,000 interconnected places of light, power, geomantic energies, and mystery.[6] While there are numerous examples of intentional sacred places, there are few examples of agendas to create secular sacredness by promoting health and wellness, sustainability, interactions with nature, sense of community, urbanism, and what Rudolf Otto referred to as "the numinous experience."[7] These places support William James' suggestion that they are "ineffable, noetic and pluralistic transcendences, occurring in everyday life."[8] Their goals echo Henri Lefebvre's words: "it is the transformation of life in its smallest detail."[9]

Furthermore, according to geographer Peirce F. Lewis, four "axioms" describe the cultural landscape of the sacredness of place. One, sacred places are not determined by human-centered perspectives or in deterministic ways, but are chosen by the land, genius loci or a higher presence. Two, sacred places are ordinary places ritually made extraordinary. Three, sacred places can be tread upon without being entered. And four, sacred places include both centripetal (local) and centrifugal (universal) energies.[10] Sacred-secular communities and emergent faith communities are distinguished by sacred acts and relationships, similar to qualities explained by these axioms, that enable their inhabitants to experience wholeness, the divine, or the transcendent. These same intentions and spirit informed the design and realization of Serenbe Community located in Chattahoochee Hills, Georgia, USA.

Serenbe Community

Serenbe Community is an intentional development located southwest of Atlanta, Georgia, and was founded by Steve and Marie Nygren in 2000 and designed by the author. The name, *Serenbe*, derives from a portmanteau or the blend of two root terms: *serene* or *serenity* and *be* or *being*.[11] So embedded in the very name is an affirmational or intentional quality that has guided the development process and created a unique community. Serenbe received the Inaugural Sustainability Award from the Urban Land Institute in 2008, and is considered an exemplar of land preservation, creative mixes of use, density, agricultural urbanism, connectivity and walkability, wellness and active living, green architecture and construction practice, as well as associations to the sacred.

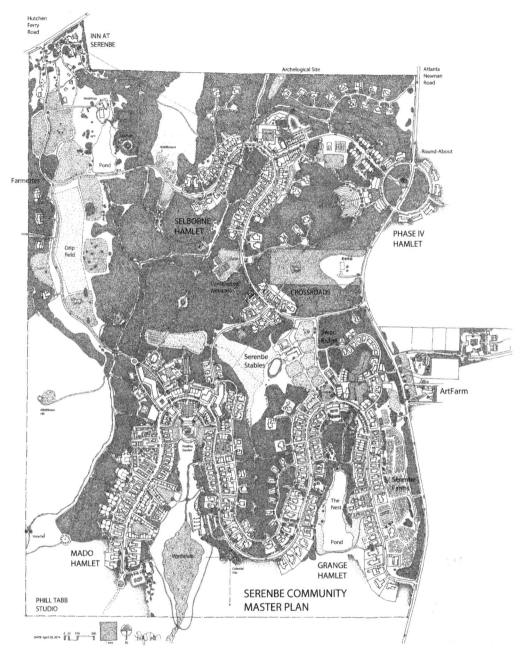

Figure 14.2   Serenbe Community Master Plan (2014 Version)
Source: Designed by Phillip Tabb.

The development program, defined as the right balance between the natural and urbanized portions of the design, evolved through an iterative land planning process. The zoning allowed for one dwelling unit per acre (2.5 dwellings per hectare), but it was felt that a total build-out would either be too land intensive or too dense given the reduced buildable area caused by the undulating character of the land. An intuitive "*sieve mapping*"[12] was implemented to determine the optimal place(s) to urbanize the land and guided the design for the master plan (Figure 14.2). The first three hamlets and crossroads cluster can clearly be seen in the master plan along with the connecting serpentine networks. A large percentage of land was dedicated to openspace: the developed portions of the master plan use only 30% of the land, leaving 70% as open space comprising various uses, including agriculture.

The developed portions of the plan are situated on the land where sets of interconnected hills and valleys form natural interfaces between valley floors and surrounding slopes. A network of omega-shaped hamlets emerged rather than a low-density, single-use, and spaghetti-form development scheme imposed on the land. While each hamlet is visually and physically separated from one another, they are in very close walking proximity either through the connecting omega-shaped roads or paths through interstitial spaces. The result is a composition of four hamlets blended into the place-defining characteristics of the natural environment.

By 2014, approximately 90% of the residences in Selborne Hamlet (North) were built, 80% in the Crossroads Cluster (center), and another 30% in Grange Hamlet (Southeast). Mado Hamlet (Southwest) began construction in spring 2015. The four hamlets are themed or given particular non-residential land-use mixes designed to create and reinforce certain character, amenities, and sustainable life-enriching functions. Selborne is planned around the arts, Grange around agriculture, Mado around wellness and the Phase IV hamlet (Northeast) around education and sustainable commerce.

Two primary ideas were reinforced at Serenbe Community: first was placemaking, and the second was the geometry of place. These two ideas were given form through sacred moments reinforced throughout the plan, and sacred processes occurring in everyday experiences. They go hand-in-hand as the former, placemaking, is a phenomenal consequence of the qualities of the latter, the geometry that organized Serenbe. Indeed, derived from the land is a powerful geometric configuration of form—the omegas. Each has an inherent shape-grammar with place-defining characteristics and community form.[13] The multiple hamlets connect within inter-dependent automobile and pedestrian networks, resulting in an agglomeration of individual landform identities, thematic landuse mixes of activities, and close proximity and connectedness among the hamlets. The resulting constellation is a combination of the spirit of the place and a network configuration that represents the whole of Serenbe.

Systemic Constellation Theory, originally developed by psychotherapist Bert Hellinger for family dynamics, suggested that independent yet interconnected parts of a system create a combination of actions affecting the collective whole.[14] For Serenbe, this means that the interrelated hamlets, and the individual placemaking practices they employ, can support even greater constellating, synergetic and programmatic relationships. The Gestalt Effect is the experience of the entire community as a self-organizing unity or coherent place. On a physical level the *constellation* of the settlement parts is meant to respond to specific site contexts that are naturally related; while at a social level it is meant to help create multiple opportunities for participatory gatherings and social interactions, healthy-living practices, and a broader network for community. The combination of the four hamlets and the crossroads cluster evolve as proximate urban areas creating the entirety of Serenbe Community. Taken together these concepts form the tenets of sacred urbanism largely from a place-oriented point of view.

The individual qualities of the four hamlets provide place diversity, and taken together, they support a synergy of non-residential activities with different mixes that are intended to support broader commercial, sustainable and community functions. While each accommodates differing thematic foci, they comprise similar housing typologies: from large detached estate houses, cottage homes and townhomes, to condominiums, live-work units, and independent and assisted living. Each hamlet is located around a different natural feature including intimate forested valleys, streams, ponds and wetlands. Primary road circulation typically occurs on common contours partially encircling the small valleys, and each hamlet incorporates density gradients, which grow to a climax at the zenith of the serpentine road where there is a concentration of higher density housing, commercial, and other non-residential activities. As can be seen in Figure 14.3, at the ends of the omegas, lots are larger, density is lower, and houses are more nested into the forest.

Figure 14.3   Aerial Photographs: a) Selborne Hamlet, and b) Grange Hamlet
Source: Photographs courtesy of Serenbe Development Corporation.

The diverse land uses of Serenbe contribute to generating individual settlement functions and unique, individuated evolving character. The *omega* form derives from a double-loaded, linear serpentine organization that combines two village form characteristics common to most English villages: the linear spatial roadside form and the nucleated form. According to Thomas Sharp, "The road may curve gently away from the straight or it may take a sharp turn; in either case the village is thereby transformed into a *place*; a place with a way in and a way out and not merely an incident on the roadside."[15] The combination of the linear and nucleated forms along with the semi-containing omega shape creates an increased potential for placemaking.

Selborne Hamlet in Serenbe, with the same name as a linear village located in the south of England, originally was referred to as the "Artist Hamlet" with a focus on the visual, performing and culinary arts. Two restaurants, the Saturday Farmers' and Artists' Market, and shops and galleries support these functions and identity. Architects Mack Scogin and Merrill Elam designed the town center—a critical regionalist U-shaped building surrounding a center green. When built-out, Selborne will have about 180 dwellings of varying type and size.

The second hamlet is called Grange and is oriented to more pragmatic matters of the land. It features the 25-acre (10 hectares) Serenbe Farms and the Farm Market, Serenbe Equestrian Center, a small food store, the Bosch Center, Montessori School, and shops. In the center of the hamlet is a 5-acre lake that provides a focus of activity and a tranquil view. Opposite the commercial area at the apex of the omega form is a small neighborhood green with a common mail pavilion that serves as an urban gathering place for the local residents of Grange Hamlet.

The third hamlet is "Mado," from the Creek Nation word meaning "things in balance," a fitting name for the hamlet's focus on health and wellness.[16] Rather than concentrating and separating these activities, they are dispersed and woven throughout the fabric of the hamlet so that they are more integrated and accessible. This unique land-use strategy assimilates the activities that include a spa, recuperative hotel, independent and assisting living, east-west pharmacy, fitness center, therapeutic swimming pool, healing gardens, medical offices, and vegetarian restaurant.

The fourth hamlet, which is located along Atlanta Newnan Road in the northeast section of the master plan, is planned for more commercial activities with a small bank, grocery store and office space, and is oriented toward education, especially higher education. The master plan indicates a small campus aligned next to the roundabout that would house study-away programs from various university programs in planning, urban design, landscape architecture, architecture and construction, and provide facilities for executive retreats.

The hamlet sizes vary from 180 to around 340 dwelling units, and are composed of attached and detached dwellings, and varying mixes of commercial use. When complete, Serenbe Community will comprise approximately 900 homes and a population of several thousand residents. The demographics of Serenbe are composed of a diversity of residents that vary in age, stages of life, family sizes, income levels, occupations, political affiliations, and spiritual or religious orientations. In 2014, the population was 400 residents, which included nearly 100 children. There is a mix of singles, couples, small and large families, working, retired, and same sex households. Employment occurs within Serenbe, in nearby communities and towns as well as in Atlanta. Housing costs vary from the mid $200,000 to $3,000,000 (as of 2015). Unlike some intentional communities, to become a resident of Serenbe Community, there are no additional vetting processes beyond those normally related to the purchasing of property, homes or businesses found in most locations.

Sacred Moments at Serenbe

Serenbe's sacred experiences can be found in various places and at differing times, and it is not necessarily important that they be overtly stated or obviously expressed. Rather, the sacred design moments are integrated into the fabric of the secular place, contributing to a process of revelation. They are to be discovered and experienced through a self-reflective consciousness enhanced by the ensouling qualities of the place. There is, in Edward Casey's terms, "a refractory survival of the hidden presence of the sacred in certain spatial oppositions"—ordinary versus special places or urban versus rural.[17] There was an intention from the very beginning to integrate the sacred in significant and ordinary ways. Sacred or intelligible geometry was an informing part of the master plan with instinctual, symbolic and natural emplacement of the urban design elements. Strategic ceremonies and community gatherings were also an integral part of the Serenbe's development and manifestation process.[18]

The sacred finds expression in Serenbe in several ways. First, and foremost, is the reverence toward the land, and the ways in which residents can participate with nature fostering recreational, contemplative and transcendent experiences. Serenbe's special qualities are informed by the earth, forests, meadows, streams and lakes, animal farm, wildlife, wildflowers, gardens, rock outcrops, bonfire site, archeological sites, and the day and night skies. The natural features are all important especially in contrast to generic urban areas found throughout metropolitan Atlanta. Other very special places found within the interstitial spaces between hamlets include two intimate waterfalls, the celestial observation site adjacent to Mado Hamlet, the Interfaith Chapel site, the Labyrinth, childrens' tree-houses, the Secret Garden, and the wild areas adjacent to Cedar Creek. And hidden throughout Serenbe are other, yet to be discovered, places.[19]

Second is the presence and function of the omega form and constellation of hamlets. The *omega* (Ω) or horseshoe shape is rare as a settlement pattern, but has been used before, such as Pueblo Bonito in northern New Mexico, many sea cove towns found around the world, and curving English linear villages. For Serenbe the omega shape came from a twin-phenomenal response to the landforms, more specifically the natural contours of the curvilinear valleys, and to the objective of creating place-oriented development

Figure 14.4   Sacred moments: a) Selborne tree-house, b) Yoga in the woods, c) Child and baby piglet, d) Breakfast on the farmhouse porch, e) Serenbe playhouse, f) Serenbe farms, and g) Interfaith gathering at the Blue Eyed Daisy

Source: d) Photograph courtesy of Steve Nygren. All other photographs are courtesy of Carla Royal.

configurations. The unique qualities and interesting properties or shape grammars include the linear, nucleated and transected characteristics, along with the power of circularity. The omega geometry is singularly strong but, because it lies on the land, is a more integrated element of the topography and landscape, and becomes an important spatial and functional organization for the urbanized areas of the hamlets. From a designer's point of view, geometry is an interesting immaterial aspect of place as the everyday sacred is experienced in the patterns of daily life that it organizes.

The omega is a symbol for the last or 24th letter of the Greek alphabet and means the completion of a sequence. It also suggests the volume of an object and the containment of an open-loop system. Therefore, the geometry related to this form has two qualities. The first is the creation of a sense of place through its embracing nature where center, boundary and domain are clearly given form. The shape is not a "U," but it is an "Ω," which supports greater containment. The second occurs with the open end of the omega, which allows for a natural ecological flow—solar energy, water, clean air, resident animals and people. That which is contained is also allowed to escape and refill. In the ancient I-Ching, The *Chinese Book of Changes*, the omega may be equated to the caldron, or a bronze-cooking vessel called the *ting*, as it provides nourishment and transformative powers.[20]

Third is the creation of the labyrinth that was constructed in the woods over a weekend by family and friends of Serenbe. Made with stone and gravel, the Serenbe labyrinth is modest in its materiality, but its presence in the woods is powerful. The center was formed with six-fold, rosette geometry, containing five large marble slabs positioned in the very center. At a normal pace, walking the labyrinth takes about 15 minutes to get to the center. The participant meanders through each of the four quadrants several times before finally reaching the short path into the center. Many who have experienced the labyrinth found it to be quieting, reflective and renewing. Adjacent to the Serenbe labyrinth is a small refectory structure for spiritual restoration overlooking the adjacent pastoral pond. It was designed by one of Serenbe's founders, Ryan Gainey for spiritual restoration.

Fourth is the integration of Serenbe Farms into the fabric of the community. *Integrated Agriculture* or *Agrarian Urbanism* is a planning approach applicable to both architecture and urban design scales. According to Janine de la Salle and Mark Holland, it is an emerging design framework for integrating a wide range of sustainable food and agricultural systems into communities. In other words: "it is a way of building a place around food."[21] For Serenbe, the 25-acre (10 hectare) farm provides not only certified organic food, but also another opportunity to interact with the land and each other. The farm produces over 300 varieties of vegetables, herbs, flowers and fruits. In addition the seasonal and growing cycles are reinforced through participation with the lifecycles and husbandry of the nearly 100 farm animals. According to Professor John Ikerd, "we can begin reclaiming the sacred in food and farming by acknowledging, up front and without compromise, the spiritual nature of sustainability."[22]

Serenbe's sacred moments are punctuations within the secular landscape and help provide greater depth of experience, discovery and meaning to patterns of everyday life. Several sacred moments include the Serenbe secluded tree-houses (Figure 14.4a), yoga on the grounds at Serenbe (Figure 14.4b), a young Serenbe resident with a newly born piglet (Figure 14.4c), a quiet morning breakfast on the Farmhouse porch (Figure 14.4d), the summer Serenbe Playhouse performances held in the Selborne live-work courtyard (Figure 14.4e), Serenbe Farms (Figure 14.4f), and a photograph in the Blue Eyed Daisy of Interfaith members after a Sunday meeting (Figure 14.4g).

Archetypal Principles and Ectypal Patterns

There can be a powerful and inextricable relationship between a settlement's form and its ability to create place, which correspondingly affects its function, use, dwelling and its structure for patterns of behavior. Consequently, as a settlement becomes more place-oriented, its potential for livability, health, community, sustainability, and inculcation of the sacred increases. Place can further be described by three different dimensions.

According to Lawlor (1982), Platonic archetypes are part of a triad of concepts—*archetypal* energies, *ectypal* exemplifications and *typal* concrete examples.[23] Archetypes represent the nature, intentions and energetic qualities of a principle. They are the action-force emanating from a (the) spiritual source. Ectypes are portrayals, models or patterns associated with archetypes. Similar to Joseph Campbell's *"The Masks* [ectypes] *of God* [source of archetypes]" (1991), ectypes are external depictions of the inner spiritual dimensions.[24] Types are physical and specific examples reflecting archetypes and ectypes. Lawlor suggests that five principles from Plato's *Timaeus*, derive meanings related to the intrinsic significances embodied in the first numbers 1, 2, 3, 4, and 5.[25] And according to Robin Waterfield in *Theology of Arithmetic*, numbers were seen as divine principles, and by extension they were allegorical with inspirational powers.[26]

The number "1" corresponds to the *Unity Principle* and describes two alternating actions—the outward emergence and division of unity into harmonic parts and the inward dissolving of parts into a comprehensible whole. The number "2" relates to the *Generative Principle* and describes duality and organic growth within a place and the organization for its natural multiplication and proliferation. The number "3" relates to the *Formative Principle* and describes varying ordering systems with geometric characteristics and structures of form. The number "4" relates to the *Corporeal Principle* and grounds placemaking into pragmatic, substantive and material realities. And the number "5" relates to the *Re-generative Principle* and describes transformative and mutable qualities of place.

1. Unity Principle—*wholeness, harmony and proportional integration.*
2. Generative Principle—*duality, diversity, multiplication and proliferation.*
3. Formative Principle—*form, structure and order of space.*
4. Corporeal Principle—*concrete volumetric, material and pragmatic realities.*
5. Re-generative Principle—*temporality, transformation and qualities of rebirth and renewal.*

An archetype of the Unity Principle, for example, is the energy of wholeness experienced through common unity, and singularity of focus, or the attracting energy of centeredness. It dissolves parts into an aggregate totality, which is both coherent and inclusive. An *ectype*, in this instance, can be described by circularity and the circle's shape where its circumference is uniformly equidistant from the center point. That which exists between the center and perimeter is contained or considered the domain experience of circularity. Taken together, they become a whole. Archetypes and ectypes are essentially non-physical, where *typal* examples are physical and tangible actualizations with a specific nature and character, as the dome and oculus at the Pantheon in Rome is a unique and distinct expression of Unity.

A placemaking pattern is an ectypal model and a guide that embodies both principle ideas and the representational means by which to express that idea. According to Christopher Alexander, it is a "design language network" and is organized in a sequence from larger to smaller patterns.[27] In a series of works by the architect and architectural educator Michael Brill and his architectural students at State University of New York at Buffalo, a set of place patterns were identified as being present at sacred sites (Brill 1985). Brill and his students believed that a sacred, or in their words, "charged" site, could contain a common set of fundamental characteristics by which the sacred was revealed. In, *Using the Place-creation Myth to Develop Design Guidelines for Sacred Space*, they identified a series of patterns that routinely accompanied sacred places.[28] Research by the author (1990) focused on English villages, archetypes, and similar placemaking patterns at the small settlement scale.[29]

In *Chambers for a Memory Palace*, by Lyndon and Moore, certain patterns like "axis that reach," "gardens that civilize," "light that plays," "shapes that remind," and "borders that control" were illustrated.[30] Similarly, Vitruvius in his *De architectura*, discussed patterns such as containment, direction, elemental and physical materiality, celestial references, and order and proportion to name a few.[31] For the work at Serenbe, the principles and patterns were initially used as a pre-design set of design guides, and later used for post-occupancy analysis. Patterns utilized in the design of Serenbe's hamlets, derived from Vitruvius (15 BC), Alexander (1977), Brill (1985), Tabb (1990),[32] and Lyndon and Moore (1994), and were primarily used to enhance the place-defining characteristics, especially with the hamlets' omega forms.

Subsequent to the design, a literature search and comparative analysis of published place patterns was conducted by M(Arch), MS and PhD in Architecture students at Texas A&M University and a redux of placemaking patterns were re-generated forming a basis for the current 20 patterns and analysis

(Joseph 2006,[33] Rodrigues 2008,[34] and Shafer 2012[35]). Following is the complete pattern listing and a set of diagrammatic icons for each pattern (Figure 14.5):

1. Centering, making location
2. Connections, reaching outward
3. Bounding with differentiation
4. Domain, internal order
5. Orientation and direction
6. Descent, grounding
7. Reaching upward, levity
8. Multiplication, proliferation
9. Geometric order
10. Nature within
11. Social spatial structure
12. Celestial order
13. Scaler order, anthropomorphism
14. Functional order
15. Economical order
16. Physical materiality
17. Elemental materiality
18. Passage and thresholds
19. Light, ether and illumination
20. Consecration and ceremonial order

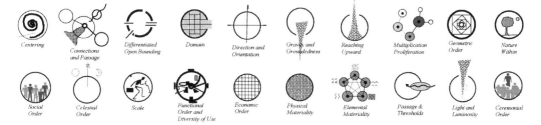

Figure 14.5   Selborne Hamlet ectypal diagrams of the post-occupancy place patterns
Source: Courtesy of Phillip James Tabb.

Application of the ectypal patterns evolved directly from the five principles to form an ordered and comprehensive list of characteristics (Figure 14.5). *Bounding*, Pattern 3, for example, describes place-containing forms typically found in community-oriented designs. Patterns, such as *Grounding*, Pattern 6, relate to the forces of gravity and connections to the earth as demonstrated by the way the road lays on the land or with the design of a building's foundation, and Pattern 10, *Nature Within*, is a natural land-use found in each hamlet center. Pattern 18, *Passage* and *Thresholds*, provides a transect where experience between profane environments can transition into the domain of sacred places—an essential pattern in creating intentional communities, such as Serenbe. *Ceremonial Order*, Pattern 20, is an important pattern in that it describes the interactions between the built place and the ritual and ceremonial experiences organized by it. It should be noted that both the list of guiding principles and corresponding place patterns within this study do not represent exclusive lists.

Table 14.1   Selborne Hamlet placemaking pattern matrix

#	PATTERN (as ectype)	PRINCIPLE (as archetype)	PRESENCE (quantitative)	EXPRESSION (qualitative)	EXEMPLIFICATION (as type)
1.	Centering	Unity Principle	4.0	4.5	Omega centers, special natural areas and concentration of commercial zones
2.	Connecting		5.0	5.0	Roads, drives, sidewalks, trails, bridle paths, greenways, streams and visual axis
3.	Bounding		5.0	4.25	Hills, natural contours, forested areas, the curved-shaped omega road and built form
4.	Domain		4.5	3.75	Valleys, area contained by omega organization, and hamlets constellation
	Average		4.5625	4.375	
5.	Finding Direction	Generative Principle	4.5	4.0	Omegas oriented to south and to natural centers within 'U-shape'
6.	Grounding		4.5	4.0	Terraced sites and buildings, agriculture, unique natural features of the land
7.	Reaching Up		3.0	3.0	Hamlet urban centers, hills surrounding hamlets, trees, Selborne hotel
8.	Multiplying		5.0	4.5	Hamlet replication in naturally formed valleys, housing duplication, fenestrations
	Average		4.25	3.875	
9.	Geometric Order	Formative Principle	5.0	4.5	Strong serpentine geometry (omega), Aligned along parallel contours
10.	Nature Within		5.0	5.0	Nature within and surrounding, 100 farm animals, Serenbe Farms, forest, meadows
11.	Social Structure		4.25	4.0	Urban spaces/activities, structure of omegas, privacy in interstitial space
12.	Celestial Order		3.0	3.5	Solar orientation of hamlets and houses, solar technologies, celestial site
	Average		4.325	4.25	
13.	Scale	Corporeal Principle	4.5	4.5	Residential with diverse mixes of use and building type, street section and furniture
14.	Functional Order		4.0	3.5	Omega, transect and commercial mix-use, ArtFarm, functional arrangement, density
15.	Economic Order		4.0	3.5	Smaller variable plot sizes, higher densities, attached housing, the Nest
16.	Materiality		4.25	3.5	EarthCraft construction, vernacular and diversity of materials, transect materiality
	Average		4.1875	3.75	
17.	Elemental	Regenerative Principle	4.25	4.5	Hills, valleys, rock outcrops, red earth, water falls, streams, ponds, and bonfire
18.	Passage		5.0	4.5	Rural-to-urban transect, many paths leading into the hamlet and urban center
19.	Light/ illumination		3.0	3.0	Filtered through the forest, natural daylight, night sky light and lamps
20.	Ceremonial Order		5.0	5.0	Sense of community, labyrinth, market, 5K race, theater, rituals and ceremonies
	Average		4.3125	4.25	
	Total Average		4.33	4.10	

Source: Drawing courtesy of Phillip James Tabb.

Placemaking Analysis

The placemaking patterns, applied to the Serenbe design and physical construction of Selborne Hamlet, formed the basis of the analysis. Visits to the project site broadened the analysis to include, a photographic record, field notes and behavioral maps, resident testimonials, a questionnaire, and data represented in the matrix (Table 14.1). The matrix indicates the listing of the patterns, the principles through which the patterns function, numerical ratings for both the presence and quality of expression of each pattern, and finally a brief description of the physical or typal characteristics of the pattern as specifically found in Selborne Hamlet. The Likert scale, originally developed by psychologist Rensis Likert (1932), was used in this study to determined values by two methods—master plan analysis and in-situ observations.[36] It is important to realize the presence (quantitative) and the quality of expression (qualitative) impacts of each of the patterns as they constitute the properties and attributes of a charged or sacred place.

1. *Pattern Presence*—is a quantitative emphasis on entities, measurements, amounts, and frequency. For Serenbe it is the identification and description of the existence of the various patterns, a detailed geometric analysis, and a measure of their magnitude. Was the pattern discernable?—a positivists/post-positivist viewpoint.[37]
2. *Quality of Expression*—is a qualitative dimension emphasizing relationships, socially constructed reality, and situational constraints. For use in the context of Serenbe, it is the value-laden measure of the placemaking patterns. What is the experience of the pattern and how is it valorized?—a naturalistic proposition.[38]

Serenbe's hamlets are comparable in form, and therefore an analysis of each of them would produce similar results. Some differences do exist, such as the hamlet's natural centers and non-residential functions. For example, Selborne's center is forested without an identifiable place-marker and is oriented to the visual, performing and culinary arts,. In contrast, Grange's center has a large pond that is highly visible and difficult to reach and is oriented to equestrian and agrarian uses. Therefore, analysis was limited to one hamlet, Selborne as it was the most built out and analyzed physically. Pattern presence was determined by several site visits to Selborne with direct experience of the hamlet, including photography of examples of the various place patterns. In addition there was a detailed analysis of the physical or formal characteristics indicated on the master plan. Each pattern was identified and evaluated.[39] For example, Pattern 1, *Centering*, was examined within the omega on the master plan, and verifying the presence of the center within the omega hamlet was done while visiting the actual site.

Pattern quality was more difficult, requiring direct experiences of the place, which were made into general observations and perceptions reinforcing the patterns while in-situ. Methods also included discussions with residents and a questionnaire that focused on each of the placemaking patterns. The Likert scale values were then determined through cross-examination of these methods. In this regard, *Centering* quality was evaluated in the center of the hamlet by sensing and recording its qualities by personal experience and comparing to resident testimonials. For Selborne, the center of the hamlet was the forested area with the small stream running through it. An exact center was not discernable, but the experience of this area had a distinctive sense of place, and was commonly viewed as serene, picturesque and aesthetically pleasing. Therefore, the quality of expression was experienced as being high on the Likert scale. Table 14.1 includes evaluation and comments of the 20-ectypal patterns according to the five-archetypal principle sets. Each pattern is assigned a numerical value on the Likert Scale of 1 (lowest) to 5 (highest) assessing both the presence (quantitative) and the quality of expression (qualitative) separately.

The analysis was directed to Selborne Hamlet as it represented the most developed portion of the masterplan, rather than the other under-built hamlets. As a guide for identifying values for both pattern presence and quality, Likert scale numbers of 1 or 2 meant they were not discernable or the quality was poor. A value of 3 suggested that the pattern was present, but not remarkable. Scores of 4 and 5 meant that the patterns were quite visible with a strong experiential impact and charged content.

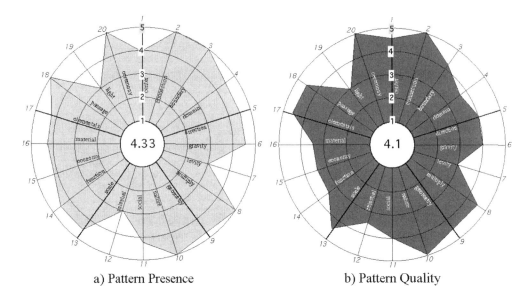

a) Pattern Presence   b) Pattern Quality

Figure 14.6   Placemaking pattern analysis: a) Pattern presence, and b) Pattern quality
Source: Diagram courtesy of Phillip James Tabb.

Findings of the Analysis

Data from the matrix in Table 14.1 were applied to create the spiderweb diagrams, seen in Figure 14.6. Spiderweb diagrams, originally developed by Georg Van Mayr in 1887, are graphic methods for organizing multivariate quantitative variables in radial and concentric systems of values. Starting at the top of the diagram is pattern number one—*Centering* with the rest of the patterns following in a clockwise direction, with the star-like shapes indicating the results of the variable values. In the case of the Selborne analysis (Figure 14.6a), the Principle with the highest value for presence is the Unity Principle; the one with the lowest value for presence is the Corporeal Principle. The Generative, Formative, and Regenerative Principles all received ratings in-between these two. For pattern quality (Figure 14.6b), the highest is the Unity Principle, and the lowest is the Corporeal Principle. Pattern presence received slightly higher values than pattern quality of expression.

Both spiderweb diagrams can be analyzed together and their relative impacts compared. As can be observed from diagrams in Figure 14.6, all but a few of the place patterns are strongly present within Selborne and the quality of the expression of these patterns is nearly as high. The Selborne analysis revealed that the patterns contributing the most to placemaking include: *Centering (1)*, *Bounding (3)*, *Multiplying (8)*, *Geometry (10)*, *Nature Within (11)*, *Passage (18)* and *Ceremonial Order (20)*. Only *Centering (1)* and *Elemental Materiality (17)* scored higher in quality than with presence. Patterns, such as, *Reaching Upward (7)*, *Celestial Order (12)* and *Light/Illumination (19)* were not as expressive in Selborne, probably due to the multiple building scale and horizontal territory of the hamlet that do not emphasize the vertical or axis mundi within the built form of the place. This, of course, is not necessarily the case in denser urban areas with larger or multiple-story buildings and architecture with more vertically exaggerated spatial designs.

Figure 14.7 shows patterns receiving the highest score of 5.0—*Connections*, with 7 miles (11 km) of trails and the network of serpentine roads throughout Serenbe; *Bounding*, with the stands of trees, topography and circular omega form; *Multiplication*, with the repetition of the hamlets, individual houses, and building elements (porches, dormers, windows and doors); *Geometric Order*, with the strong omega serpentine road form, transect and geometrically significant sites; *Nature Within*, with the stand of woods and stream in the center; and *Ceremonial Order*, with the Serenbe Saturday Farmer's and Artists' Market, theatrical productions, weddings, various seasonal parades, Halloween, Easter egg hunt, May Day,

Figure 14.7   Placemaking patterns with the highest scores a) Connecting, b) Bounding, c) Multiplication, d) Geometric order, e) Nature within, and f) Ceremonial order

Source: Photograph b) is courtesy of Phillip James Tabb. All other photographs are courtesy of Steve Nygren.

Interfaith meetings, and 5K race organized around the omega roads.[40] While single patterns are certainly fervent, it is the consummatory effect of all principles and patterns that fully contribute to the nexus of placemaking, and provide a context for secular-sacredness.

> Serenbe is marked by an extraordinary sense of community. What has contributed to this remains something
> of a mystery: The founder's vision, the inculcation to the sacred, and the commitment to the principles of
> sacred geometry in physical design, have resulted in a strong sense of place that attracts residents sharing a
> commitment to the land, the environment, and to each other.[41]

Conclusions

Serenbe represents the on-going development of an experimental community that is designed as a model to counteract the negative effects of suburban sprawl and placelessness. The hamlet-focused design affords an incremental approach to deepening into greater levels of placemaking over time. Serenbe is an in-progress investigation on how to envision, design, and sustain a secular-sacred community today. In other words, it is a reflection that shadows the process of construction along with growing occupation and increasing numbers of residents. It is anticipated that the place patterns provided planning guides not only for greater levels of sacredness, but also for a healthier and more livable place in which to live.

The placemaking analysis for Selborne indicates a relative consistency and balance among the five principles and 20 patterns. There is a slight difference between the presence and quality, which is in part due to the rural character and emphasis on vernacular architecture that are normally less refined compared to more urban languages and materials. The patterns with the greatest values seem to support the initial intentions, as Serenbe offers a laboratory in which to test these assumptions and designs, creating a language where community, health and wellness, sustainability and sacred placemaking, converge.

With the sustainability measures, integrated agriculture, and embodied place patterns, it is hoped that there is a transfer of knowledge that might inform future development projects, particularly at the urban edge of metropolitan regions or with re-structuring of existing suburban areas. Many researchers of placemaking theory may be skeptical of the development of essential traits and formal structures of place, and would posit something more indeterminate and less causal. Instead, this analysis of Serenbe is what Edward Casey might call "place at work" with the dynamic ingredient of "something else." Serenbe suggests that both in fact coexist—an unchanging archetypal essence and mutable and evolving phenomenology of place. It is the ceremonial order of Selborne that blends the physical characteristics with community participation and the dynamic behavioral patterns of everyday living—secular-sacred in place creation.

The forms of new secular-sacred communities, like Serenbe, typically seek to preserve land for future generations and provide diverse kinds of spatial experiences, both urban and rural, that reflect evolving contemporary needs and opportunities for varying sacred experiences. The geometry of Serenbe provides an explicit structure, spatial order, a context for reverence in everyday living, community ceremonial events, and a strong sense of belonging.[42] Socially, community is expressed by resident gatherings, it can also be experienced in immaterial ways as a felt sense of belonging or in the dissolving solitude found in omega centers. In these regards, community members are sharing a similar place-centered style of living and are part of the larger collective of residents. The social environment also creates the place through which a living Serenbe thrives in a biotic community of inclusiveness, interdependence and participatory interaction. Serenbe, with its sensitivity to sacredness, represents a next generation small settlement planning approach in a linage that began with suburbs and counter urbanism and later with sustainable and agricultural urbanism.

This secular-sacred relationship helps to actualize Serenbe's purpose, which is to engender a serene place with the numinous experience of being—being with nature, being in community, being more human, and being with an ineffable higher presence. The Biblical message found embedded in a concrete slab in the ground next to the small waterfall near Selborne Hamlet is a hopeful outlook and fitting conclusion for the study and analysis of this remarkable place.

Be still and know that I am God.
Be still and know that I am.
Be still and know.
Be still.
Be …[43]

Endnotes

1   Ellin, Nan (2006). *Integral Urbanism*. London, UK: Routledge.
2   These authors have investigated the relationship of spiritual ideas relative to expression in everyday experience from philosophical, theological, and psychological points of views. William James (see endnote 9 below); Sardello, Robert (2012). *Power of Soul*. Goldenstone Press; Moore, Thomas (2012). *Re-enchantment of Everyday Life*. London, UK: Harper Perennial; Brussat, Fredric and Mary Ann Brussat (1998). *Spiritual Literacy: Reading the Sacred in Everyday Life*. New York, NY: Scribner; and Oliver, Paul (1987). *Dwellings—The House Across the World*. Austin, TX: University of Texas Press.
3   Findhorn Community (1975). *The Findhorn Garden: Pioneering a New Vision of Man and Nature in Cooperation*. New York, NY: Harper and Row.
4   Coates, Gary (1997). *Erik Asmussen, Architect*. Stockholm, Sweden: Byggforlaget.
5   Airaudi, Oberto (2007). *The Book of Synchronicity: The Game of Divination*. Berkeley, CA: North Atlantic Books.
6   Gray, Martin http://www.gainesville.com/article/20021109/NEWS02/211090319 (accessed October 15, 2014).
7   Otto, Rudolf (1958). *The Idea of the Holy*. Oxford, UK: Oxford University Press.
8   James, William (2009). *The Varieties of Religious Experience*. CreateSpace Independent Publishing.
9   Harris, Steven and Deborah Berke (eds) (1997). *Architecture of the Everyday*. Princeton, NJ: Princeton Architectural Press.
10 Lewis, Peirce F. (1979). Axiom for Reading the Landscape. *The Interpretation of Ordinary Landscapes: Geographical Essays*. Oxford, UK: Oxford University Press, pp. 11–32.
11 The word *Serenbe*, while initially created by co-founder Marie Nygren, is now a common or more general term used to describe the entire community at Serenbe. This includes the land, the inn, the hamlets, the crossroads, interstitial spaces and functions, activities and residents. Serenbe is the broader whole or constellation that comprises the larger place.
12 *Sieve mapping* is a landscape analysis technique developed by landscape architect Ian McHarg in the 1970s. This method functions by articulating layers of an environment into separate screens which serve as ecological zones and reveal the relationships between them. In the context of this work the mapping identifies the place patterns and their interrelationships.
13 *Shape Grammar* for the omega form is interesting as it is a combination and integration of several geometric curves designed for different purposes. The slightly closing semi-circle found at the top of the omega is designed to frame and contain the inner natural area, and create a sense of place. The next mirroring set of curves open outward in a gesture of openness and receptivity.
14 Systemic Constellation Theory: The combination of the four hamlets and crossroads clusters evolve as proximate urban areas creating the larger development whole and sphere of influence, which is referred to as Serenbe Community. The idea of a *constellating urbanism* can have both literal and symbolic presences. Preiss, Indra Torsten (2012). *Family Constellations Revealed: Hellinger's Family and other Constellations Revealed (The Systemic View, Volume 1)*. CreateSpace Independent Publishing.
15 Sharp, Thomas (1946). *The Anatomy of the Village*. Hammondsworth, UK: Penguin Books. There are three primary village form structures in Great Britain—the linear village, nucleated village and the random or poly-nucleated village.
16 *Mado* is the name of the Health and Wellness Hamlet and derives from the Creek Nation meaning "things in balance." This name was given by one of the Serenbe residents, Karen Reed. In the context of this work "health" was seen as a relative state of the physical, mental, and social condition of a person. While "wellness," was seen as being in a relative state of positive health.
17 Casey, Edward S. (1997). *The Fate of Place—A Philosophical History*. Berkeley, CA: University of California Press.
18 Sacred geometry derives from either natural orders (Earth-based geometry), from celestial orders (time-based geometry), or from intrinsic orders (number and mathematics).

19 A *sacred moment* exists, but is not necessarily initially revealed. It may take on a natural form or human-made design, but when present, it can have transformative effects. At Serenbe this occurs at special places along the streams or in the woodlands. It can be a wildflower meadow or a piece of poetry found on the grounds somewhere. It can also occur through community-based activities in the urban areas of Serenbe.

20 The I-Ching is the Book of Changes and expresses 64 hexagrams or patterns that describe certain energies and phenomena. The Caldron is Hexagram 50 and describes the nature of sacred containment and nourishment, symbolic of the preparation of food.

21 de la Salle, Janine and Mark Holland (2010). *Agricultural Urbanism: Handbook for Building Sustainable Food & Agricultural Systems in 21st Century Cities*. Winnipeg, Canada: Green Frigate Books.

22 Ikerd, John E. "*Reclaiming the Sacred in Food and Farming*," University of Missouri, http://web.missouri.edu/~ikerdj/papers/Sacred.html (accessed August 12, 2014).

23 Lawlor, Robert (1982). *Sacred Geometry: Philosophy and Practice*. London, UK: Thames and Hudson, p. 6.

24 Campbell, Joseph (1991). *The Masks of God*, vol. 1. Hammondsworth, UK: Penguin Books, Primitive Mythology.

25 Archetypes are part of a triad of concepts—*archetypal* energies, *ectypal* exemplifications and *typal* concrete examples. The five principles used here derive from semiotics related to the significance of the numbers 1, 2, 3, 4, and 5. All but the number 4 have immeasurable square roots [Pi, $\sqrt{2}$, $\sqrt{3}$ and $(\sqrt{5}+1)/2$]. The source is Plato, *Timaeus*, Focus Publishing, 2012.

26 Waterfield, Robin (1988). *The Theology of Arithmetic*. Grand Rapids, MI: Phanes Press, pp. 22–3.

27 Alexander, Christopher et al. (1977). *A Pattern Language*. New York, NY: Oxford University Press.

28 Brill, Michael (1985). *Using the Place-creation Myth to Develop Design Guidelines for Sacred Space*. Self-published. Patterns included: making location, succession of spaces, differentiated bounding, verticality, celestial order, discriminating views, light from above, and consecration.

29 Tabb, Phillip (1990). The Solar Village Archetype. London, Architectural Association: Ph.D. Dissertation.

30 Lyndon, Donlyn and Charles Moore (1994). *Chambers for a Memory Palace*. Cambridge, MA: The MIT Press.

31 Vitruvius, Pollio Marcus (2013). *The Ten Books on Architecture*. Architecture Classics.

32 The relationship between the five Platonic principles and 20 place patterns was part of research and a publication prepared for the Dallas Institute for Humanities and Culture. Tabb, Phillip (1996). *Sacred Places: The Presence of Archetypal Patterns in Place Creation*. Boulder, CO: self-published.

33 Joseph, Melanie (2006). A Pattern Language for Sacred and Secular Places. College Station, TX: MS Architecture Dissertation.

34 Rodrigues, Arsenio (2008). The Sacred in Architecture: A Study of the Presence and Quality of Place-Making Patterns in Sacred and Secular Buildings. College Station, TX: Ph.D. dissertation.

35 Shafer, Cristina (2012). Serenbe Place Analysis. College Station, TX, A&M University: Master of Architecture Directed Studies.

36 Likert, Rensis (1933). A Technique for the Measurement of Attitudes. *Archives of Psychology* 140, pp. 1–55.

37 Groat, Linda and David Wang (2002). *Architectural Research Methods*. New York, NY: Wiley & Sons.

38 Denzin, Normak K. and Yvonna S. Lincoln (2000). *Handbook of Qualitative Research*, 2nd edition. Thousand Oaks, CA: Sage Publications, Inc.

39 The Pattern Matrix was developed over several years beginning in 2008 with several visits to Serenbe, a questionnaire sent to the residents living there at that time, and graphic analysis of the master plan.

40 Ceremonial order suggests a high degree of participation and engagement with the place that is enhanced through the geometry, spatial structure, and the character of the physical place. It suggests stewardships, ritual and ceremonial interactions.

41 Statement given to the author by John Graham, an early Serenbe resident (2008).

42 Tabb, Phillip (2009). *Placemaking as a Sustainable Planning Strategy: Serenbe Community*. San Antonio, TX: ARCC Conference, April 17; and Tabb, Phillip (2010). *Serenbe and the Geometry of Place*. College Station, TX: self-published.

43 Located in front of a bench in a contemplative site and adjacent to the small waterfall is the Biblical reduction of this poetic phrase to simply "Be still and know that I am God, I will be exalted in the earth," which is at the very heart of Serenbe. It is from Psalms 46, Verse 10.

Chapter 15

Experiencing the Architecture of the Incomplete, Imperfect, and Impermanent[1]

Rumiko Handa

Introduction

For some time now architects have operated with the notion that the building is *complete* when construction is finished. They strive to make the building *perfect* and wish to keep it so *permanently*. Seen from this point of view, any subsequent alterations seem to degenerate the original. And yet, buildings never stay the same as they take part in politics, economics, and religion through the course of time. Their changes may be caused by natural forces or artificial means, and may manifest physically or in meaning. For example, immediately after the inauguration of the Colosseum in Rome, structures were added beneath the arena's floor in order to accommodate gladiators and beasts. Since then, its meaning has changed from a place for spectacles to a temple of the sun god, a Christian site of martyrdom, and a romantic ruin, until it became a site of archeology, tourism, and entertainment. It has served as a source of building materials, a backdrop for squatter houses and fortresses, a specimen of classical architecture, a medium for growing flora, and a stage for Fascist propaganda. Lightning started a fire, which burned the upper levels of the amphitheater's interior in 217AD, and a number of earthquakes damaged the building, including one in 1349, which destroyed a substantial portion of the stadium at the south side. This portion still remains missing with a reinforced concrete wall to prevent further damage.[2]

If changes are the norm rather than exception of buildings, is it not better for architects to find ways to accept and incorporate them into their work as assets than to consider them outside of their realm? This chapter will examine how incomplete, imperfect, and impermanent pieces of architecture engage their visitors and inhabitants in a manner that demonstrates their ontological significance. The study is intended as a first step toward critiquing the long-held assumption about the perfection, completeness, and permanence of architecture and constructing an alternative paradigm of aesthetics and ethics. The following is divided into three categories: synecdoche; palimpsest; and *wabi*. These three divisions roughly correspond to the incomplete, the impermanent, and the imperfect respectively, but the three are not necessarily mutually exclusive.

Synecdoche

Synecdoche is a term in linguistics that refers to a figure of speech meaning the whole, of which it is a part, or vice versa.[3] Close to synecdoche is metonymy, but they are in strict sense different as a metonymy refers to a thing or a concept by association, not by part-whole relationship. For example, "White House" is a metonymy used to mean the President of the United States (a particular person) or the presidency (a more abstract concept). Synecdoche in this study refers to a part of a building invoking the whole or a larger area of the building in the visitor's imagination. In particular, at a site of ruins a surviving or missing portion (part) of a building inspires a visitor to imagine the building in its prime (whole).

Author Sir Walter Scott, with his sharpened sensitivity to the environment, took the ruins of Kenilworth Castle as inspiration for *Kenilworth: A Romance* published in 1821.[4] The story revolves around three historical individuals: Queen Elizabeth I; Robert Dudley, Earl of Leicester and the Queen's favorite; and Amy Robsart, Dudley's wife. Amy visits Dudley at Kenilworth Castle, while Elizabeth is on a royal visit. Amy encounters the queen but cannot reveal her relation to Dudley in order to maintain his position at court. Amy eventually is murdered on Dudley's orders because he suspects her of disloyalty.

Figure 15.1   Kenilworth Castle: a) Leicester's Gatehouse, south wall, b) Leicester's Gatehouse, west
            wall, c) Wall adjacent to Keep
Source: Photographs courtesy of Rumiko Handa.

The piece is a historical fiction in the sense that many details of the story, including the Queen's visit to
Kenilworth Castle and Amy's premature death, are historical facts while the murder is Scott's fiction.
Scott's intention was to tell an intriguing story of ambition and love surrounding Queen Elizabeth I, and by
doing so, to give a vivid and alluring portrayal of the past, and its settings.

  Similarly, Scott incorporated historical and fictional building descriptions, inspired by antiquarian
documents and his own observations of the ruined buildings. Kenilworth Castle, which lay in ruins in
Scott's time is located between Warwick and Coventry, and has been an important site of English history
because of its close relation to the royal household. It was first constructed in the early 12th century by
Geoffrey de Clinton, the royal chamberlain to King Henry I (r. 1100–1135). Major additions were made by
King Henry II (r. 1154–89); King John (r. 1199–1216); John of Gaunt (1340–99), son of King Edward III
and Duke of Lancaster; and Robert Dudley (1532–88), Earl of Leicester, and damages incurred during the
19th century Civil Wars. In the present day, English Heritage manages the property, which it has done since
1984, dubbing it "one of England's most spectacular castle ruins."[5]

  When he visited Kenilworth Castle for the second time in 1815, Scott is said to have asked searching
questions and spent several hours in contemplation at the castle ruin. Comparing what Scott saw at the site

to his narrative will reveal what some details of the ruinous architecture afforded his imagination.[6] First, Scott expanded the range of heraldic symbols on the buildings as far back as to the 12th century, while the only remaining ones were those from Robert Dudley's time. Here, limited physical presence within the incomplete architecture prompted the viewer to imagine similar instances elsewhere in the compound. On the south façade of Leicester's Gatehouse is a shield of a *fess* between six cross-crosslets (a horizontal band between six crosses with each arm crossed) (Figure 15.1a), and on the west are cinquefoils, ragged staffs, and letters "RL" from Robert, Earl of Leicester (Figure 15.1b). Also, the wall immediately west of the Keep are the remains of ornamental carvings, including "70," which refer to the construction of this portion of the castle in 1570 (Figure 15.1c). Above these are cinquefoils and the letter "R" with its vertical stroke made of a ragged staff. These symbols all point to Dudley, who adopted them from his ancestors and predecessors, e.g., Richard Beauchamp, Earl of Warwick and Dudley's ancestor through paternal grandmother, and Simon de Montfort, old Earl of Leicester.

Secondly, Scott imagined the complete workings of doors for a number of key locations, while at the site only parts or traces of opening mechanisms were discernible. One instance is an opening on the ground level of the western wall of the Great Hall block, which likely was used to reach the entryway in the outer wall nearby, and still exists in the ruins Scott sometimes calls it a "sallyport or secret postern," and is an important setting, especially in the final chapter when Amy is removed from the castle.[7] In the opening of the Great Hall the remains of a portcullis can be observed (Figure 15.2a), with grooves for the door that was suspended and operated by a pulley from above, which Scott may have taken as an inspiration. Another instance is the door of Mortimer's Tower. Its upper-story and most of the ground-level structure are gone, as they were in Scott's time, but the remains of the stone hinges existed for Scott's observation, and are still visible today (Figure 15.2b).

Figure 15.2   Kenilworth Castle: a) Great Hall, the remains of the portcullis, b) Mortimer's Tower, the remains of the great door

Source: Photographs courtesy of Rumiko Handa.

Figure 15.3   Kenilworth Castle, Great Hall, and roof detail
Source: Photograph courtesy of Rumiko Handa.

Third, Scott imagined a "highly-carved oaken roof" along with a splendid interior space magnificently decorated for the queen's reception.[8] In the ruin, where the Great Hall existed, the roof had vanished completely by the early 18th century. What remain are some fragments of ornate perpendicular-style pointed arches, fireplaces, and window-side benches. In addition, only discernible to observant eyes, are notches in the uppermost position of stone walls, regularly placed above the solid portions of the walls between the arched openings, which would have held the hammer beams (Figure 15.3).

These and other descriptions of the castle in its glory were generated Scott's synecdochic imagination. The vivid descriptions of the building in Scott's novel attracted many visitors to the ruined castle, who were eager to experience in their own ways what Scott created out of his imagination. Among the visitors were Charles Dickens (1838), Queen Victoria (1858), and Henry James (1870s). Scott's imagination is influential even today. English Heritage is reported to have consulted, in addition to antiquarian documents, his narrative in recreating Elizabethan gardens at the castle. I would contend that the synecdochic nature of ruins, which we have observed in Scott's case, is not limited to the 19th century but instead is still with us, in some cases. Otherwise, we would not have contained feelings toward ruins, nor would we see the value in adaptive reuse projects.

Palimpsest

A palimpsest is the layer of writing on a writing surface that has been reused by erasing the original. This was a common practice in medieval times when parchment of animal hides, that were durable but costly. The existing script was often washed from the surface to allow overwriting, but the passage of time, however, the earlier writing resurfaced. By presenting multiple layers of writing simultaneously on a singular surface the palimpsest gives physical presence to the past, which otherwise has been obliterated.

Figure 15.4   Leon Battista Alberti, Palazzo Rucellai, and façade detail
Source: Photograph courtesy of Rumiko Handa.

Writing, like drawing and painting, is a physical trace of bodily movements. The palimpsest requires a prior act of erasure, and therefore carries three layers of time: the past perfect or the time of the original writing; the past simple or the time of the original writing's erasure and overwriting; and the present or the time after the original has reappeared on the parchment's surface.

One example of an architectural palimpsest that has three distinct layers of time is the façade of Palazzo Rucellai in Florence, designed by Leon Battista Alberti. Palazzo Ruccelai's façade qualifies as a palimpsest as explained by Marco Frascari through its contrasting notions of "apparent" vs. "actual" joints.[9] Channels cut into stone blocks *appear* as if they were joint lines of mortar placed between the adjacent stone blocks. In reality, however, they are mere grooves, and the *actual* joints between stone blocks are much narrower and do not always coincide with the channels.[10] With the strong shadow cast by the channels that are wide and deep, the much finer and shallower actual joints must have been almost completely invisible when the building was newly constructed. Today, however, the actual construction joints have emerged (Figure 15.4). Erosion has taken away sharp corners of stone, both at the actual joint line and at the corners of the channels, and weathering on the stone's surface has happened unevenly from one stone to another, revealing the blocks that used to make a smooth surface of a singular unit. The Ruccelai façade therefore is comparable to a palimpsest on parchment, both in the intentional obliteration of the traces of the original deeds and the unintended resurfacing of them in the passage of time.

At Palazzo Ruccelai the traces of the construction, which were originally concealed, have been revealed drawing attention of today's observers, who then imagine the act of construction that took place more than half a millennium ago. Today we hide the traces of construction. This applies not only to exterior and interior finishes, like the Ruccelai case, but also to structural, mechanical, electrical, and plumbing systems. It is as if, in order for a building to be complete, we need to hide its construction, but in doing so, we are taking away opportunities for the visitors and inhabitants to experience and appreciate the construction process of the building, and placing the architect on the passive side of the architectural palimpsest at the mercy of the erosion of building materials.

A good case of an architect actively involved in the production of the palimpsest, is Carlo Scarpa as evidenced by the Castelvecchio Museum, in Verona. The history of the castle itself dates to 1354 when the Lord of Verona, Cangrande II della Scala, began building a fortified residence inside the old Roman city walls in the center of the town.[11] Three systems of walls had been constructed as Verona expanded each: the oldest and innermost one by the Romans, a subsequent one from the 12th century when the city was an independent state ("Commune"), and the newest and outermost one completed early in the 14th century. Cangrande located the new palace where the Commune wall met the Adige River. After Cangrande, a succession of alterations were made to the castle. The Venetian Republic, which subdued the Scaligeri, used the castle for a military academy, but otherwise kept the building fairly unaltered. It fell to Napoleon's forces in 1797; the French forces took down the top portions of the existing walls and towers and built a defensive wall along the river against Austrian forces stationed on its opposite side of the river. They connected the courtyard to the upper-level battlements of this north wall by building an exterior staircase along the Commune wall. They then built an L-shaped building block on the north and the east sides of the courtyard along the walls for use as military barracks.

In the 20th century, under Antonio Avena's directorship of the city's art museums, the Castlevecchio was designated as a place for a centralized collection. In the 1920s the building underwent what was at that time considered "restoration" to create the illusion of a historical palace, much of which caused negative rather than positive effects on the historical building.[12] The battlements of the walls and the upper portion of the towers were rebuilt, but not in an historically correct manner. Interiors were decorated and painted after the 16th- and 17th-century domestic styles. False fireplaces and chimneys built inside closed the narrow openings on the riverside fortification. The courtyard façades received door and window frames that had been salvaged from a Gothic palazzo demolished in 1886.

Scarpa was hired by its new director Licisco Magagnato in 1957, and worked on it until the museum's reopening in 1964 and again between 1964 and 1973.[13] Not all design aspects of Scarpa's work at Castelvecchio fit into the architectural palimpsest, but, this study will focus on the aspect of Scarpa's Castelvecchio design in which the architect is an agent that reveals the physical traces of past deeds and events that had been concealed or obliterated.

In 1958, a year after Scarpa began his undertaking; Morbio Gate was discovered in the Commune wall and an inner moat shortly afterwards.[14] Subsequently, Scarp's work focused on what would become the Cangrande space of the present museum. In Avena's time, the arched opening at the western end of the Napoleonic block was closed with a set of wooden doors. Contemporary photographs show how the archway, once these doors were opened, revealed another arch further west, and at the much lower level. Once, the Morbio Gate was a connection between the two sides of the Commune wall. With this connection revealed, Scarpa and Magagnato determined to recover it for the museum's circulation purposes (Figure 15.5a), and with this decision, they went on to demolish the exterior grand staircase from the Napoleonic era. The inner moat was also excavated (Figure 15.5b). While it is not evident to the contemporary visitors that the gateway had once been concealed and was revealed later, the number of round rocks, which used to be among the materials that closed up the gateway, were left at the site to suggest this history.

Another act of revealing was the stripping off of the stucco on the courtyard-side façade of the Napoleonic block. Another contemporary photograph shows a man working on the main, south-facing façade, stripping off the existing stucco. What is revealed is the construction, which is a mixture of the Napoleonic one and those at the time of Avena's "restoration." Bricks, stones, as well as a concrete beam from Avena's intervention can be seen. Scarpa decided to keep this trace of past construction visible in a number of spots on the building's façade when he applied new layers of stucco (Figure 15.5c).

At the Castelvecchio, then, the architect literally is the one who reveals the physical traces of the past, showcasing them in such a way that they are clearly apparent, regardless of the public knowledge of the building's past. In doing so, Scarpa allowed the impermanent aspects of architecture to act as a palimpsest.

Figure 15.5   Carlo Scarpa, Castelvecchio Museum: a) Morbio Gate, b) Moat and the bridge,
              c) Façade detail

Source: Photographs courtesy of Rumiko Handa.

Wabi

In 16th-century Japan, we find an artist who relied on the properties of the imperfect, which in Japanese are called *wabi*, in order to create physical objects that induced participatory interpretation in the viewer. The artist is the famed tea master Sen no Rikyū (1522–91), who consecutively served Japan's two military generals in the turbulent feudal era.

The drinking of tea, which originated in China, can be a mundane act of sustenance. But, in Japan it developed into an art form and ethical practice. Japan's history of tea goes back to the 8th century when the imperial court dispatched missions to the continent to bring back various cultural artifacts and practices, among which were those related to tea. In the 12th century, tea spread among Zen monks as an everyday beverage to fight drowsiness during meditation. In the same century the governing warlord overcame his hangover by following a Zen monk's suggestion to drink tea, and proclaimed tea as "this world's healthful divine medicine" and drinking tea as a "special art of extending man's life span."[15] Soon tea gained popularity among aristocrats and warlords, but was an expensive undertaking since tea and tea wares had to be imported from the continent. Eventually, the tea "ceremony" became an activity of high culture, and an occasion for the host to show off an impressive display of imported artifacts. In this context, some attempted to make the practice less exclusive. In particular, Zen Buddhist monk Murata Jukō (or Shukō 1423–1502) promoted the blurring of the distinction between domestic tea-ware and expensive imports, and Takeno Jōō (1502–55) built a small tearoom of four-and-a-half tatami mats (approximately 9 square feet) for drinking tea. Jukō and Jōō's practice, however, still remained primarily an expensive enterprise. Jukō did not approve of a tea setting comprised only of domestic articles. Jōō, who was born in one of the richest merchant families of Sakai, was himself famous for his collection of imports.

The term *wabi* may be translated into "imperfect" or "impoverished," but is often elusive, escaping definitive interpretation. Jōō is believed to have initiated the term "*wabi* tea," finding a parallel between the tea ceremony practiced in inexpensive settings and the philosophy of *renga*, a type of poem-writing in which a number of poets gathered to compose lines in succession, of which he a master. Engaged in the challenges not only to bestow one's own creative twist to the poem handed by the preceding poet, but also to leave the poem with imaginative possibilities when passing it onto the succeeding poet, Jōō and his contemporaries came to value the insufficient and unfulfilled state of things. But it was Jōō's disciple Sen no Rikyū who synthesized *wabi* tea into ethics and aesthetics by applying it to every aspect of the tea ceremony, from the tea setting to the physical environment, and from the manner of making and drinking tea to the way of interacting with the environment.[16]

Tai-an Tearoom, located at Mhyoki-an Temple, Kyoto (1582), is the only extant building designed by Rikyū (Figure 15.6a).[17] It consists of a tearoom of two tatami mats (6 square feet), an approximately one-half mat to konami recess to the north, the anteroom of one mat to the west, and the preparation space of another mat to the north. While the tea ceremony can be practiced in a space of any size, Rikyū was reported to have set 4.5 tatami mats as the largest possible limit of the ideal tearoom. Such a restricted space, where even a slight change in breathing was detectable, may have been construed as imperfect, as any careless maneuver by either the host or the guest would have spoiled the proceedings of the ceremony. But Rikyū preferred it because the inconvenience and discomfort put the participants in a state of acute sensibility, making them attentive to the tea rituals. To compare, a larger space, while perhaps providing perfect dimensions, would have relaxed them and dulled their senses.

Rikyū also stayed away from perfect alignments in his design. For stepping-stones of the garden path, he chose individual stones that were imperfect and placed them in an irregular formation. For window arrangements he also avoided perfection. The eastern wall of Tai-an has two windows that are of different sizes and without any regular alignment (Figure 15.6b). As a result, Rikyū's design features look as if they had been found in nature rather than heavy-handed. For Rikyū it seems that an imperfect setting would induce the disciples' contemplation more than tea equipment. It is reported that at one tea ceremony water was leaking from a flower vase made of bamboo by the tea master himself and the raised floor was getting wet. It had developed a crack, which naturally happens to bamboo when it dries. To the guest who pointed this out Rikyū replied, "This dripping water is the life."[18]

Rikyu developed, in collaboration with his potter Raku Chōjiro, a type of pottery called Raku, which is created by hand-molding clay (as opposed to turning it on a potter's wheel), and by firing it at low temperatures, which results in a porous body.[19] Rikyū preferred this process because the potter has to surrender to the forces earth, fire, and water, which are beyond his control. As a consequence, the pottery never achieves a perfect circle, uniform thickness, or smooth texture. Subtle irregularities to make the guests focus on the cup occurred during the tea ceremony. The host offers the tea by placing the cup on the floor with its "front," or the side combining superior features, facing the guest. The guest then picks up the cup from the floor in both hands, with the left palm supporting its weight and the right palm rounded to feel its curvature and texture. The guest then turns the cup in the hands, caressing the irregular surface, such that its "front" faces back to the host, before drinking the tea. The guest's interactions with the cup therefore involve not only the eyes but also the entire body as the guest bends over the floor, the palms as he/she feels the weight of the cup as well as its form and texture, and the mind as he/she is careful to take care of the "front" of the cup.

By producing artifacts and environments that clearly showcased the imperfect nature of their physical aspects much like the bamboo vase, Rikyū succeeded in guiding tea participants to the ontological contemplation of their own imperfect and transient existence. If Rikyū's guests were to look for beauty in imperfect objects, they needed to be readied for these types of experiences and appreciation.

Figure 15.6   Temple and replica: a) Sen no Rikyū, Tai-an, adjacent to Myōki-an Temple, b) Heisei no Tai-
              an, replica of Rikyū's Tai-an built in Daitoku-ji Temple Kohō-an, eastern wall
Source: Photographs courtesy of Rumiko Handa.

Rikyū stated that the principle of tea is only to boil water, make tea, and drink it. The *Roji*, or the garden path leading to the tearoom, was a place for guests to rid themselves of their desires and wills in anticipation of the pure experiences of tea. As such, the *tsukubai*, a stone water basin set on the path for the guests to wash their hands, has an important role. Rikyū designed water basins in such a way that the guests had to bend over to wash their hands. In a similar manner the entrance to the tearoom, the *nijiriguchi* (from the Japanese *nijiru* meaning crawl), also required humbling postures intended to induce humility and openness. The proceedings of the tea ceremony have specific moments when the guests are expected to observe particular objects. For example, Tai-an's raised floor is situated directly opposite the *nijiriguchi* entrance so that when the guests crawl in, their eyes go directly to the flowerpot or the calligraphy displayed there.

Both *tsukubai* and *nijiriguchi* are important features in the film *Rikyū*, directed by Teshigahara Hiroshi and based on the popular novel by Nogami Yaeko, who in turn had referred to an anecdote reported in one of the written records of oral transmissions produced several generations after Rikyū's death.[20] Elements of the story of the Rikyū, Hideyoshi and the morning glory indicate that Toyotomi Hideyoshi, the powerful warlord who Rikyū served as a tea master, hearing of the beauty of blooming morning glories in the garden of Rikyū's house, demands a visit. Hideyoshi arrives early in the morning, but no flowers are to be found. Puzzled, he enters the tearoom and understands. Rikyū has picked one flower for display, destroying the rest. Hideyoshi observed the flower and the cramped entrance that made even him lower his head and body, and could not but concede the sophistication and superiority of his tea advisor and political confidant.

Rikyū eliminated the use of movable display shelves in a room smaller than 4.5 mats, and instead placed tea wares directly on the floor. As a result, all the attention is given to the tea wares, without the shelves distracting the guests' interest. In Tai-an, the interior corner of the two walls is rounded where the hearth is cut; this is where the host makes tea. The same rounded corner treatment is used for the raised floor. Contemporary scholars think these rounded corners were for the purpose of making the small space appear larger. Considering Rikyū's philosophy, however, it is more likely the rounded corners were

Figure 15.7   Heisei no Tai-an, replica of Rikyū's Tai-an built in Daitoku-ji Temple Kohō-an,
                corner detail
Source: Photograph courtesy of Rumiko Handa.

intended to hide the wooden post or beam, which otherwise would have drawn the viewers' attention and distracted from the tea wares near the hearth or the art object over the raised floor.

For Rikyū, the state of imperfection is desirable because it allows the pursuit of the mind's eye, or beyond simply seeing a perfect object. At Tai-an, once the doors are closed, the outer world is shut out, and the tearoom becomes its own world. Rice paper screens cover the windows, creating a subdued interior space to help the guests rid themselves of their earthly desires and willfulness, and to concentrate their minds and spirits on the experience of tea. It does not shut out the outer world entirely, however. One can see the shadows of the window mullions changing by the amount of sunlight and can hear the birds or the leaves in the wind. With this subtle relationship to the outer world, once again, the guest is drawn into the imagined outside world, which may not exist beyond the walls.

Rikyū's philosophy of tea focused not on an artifact for its own sake but on the ways it enticed participants into imaginary interpretations. The same can be said about his style of teaching. Rikyū did not produce a comprehensive treatise; he left behind only letters and brief manuscripts. By not writing down his teaching Rikyū was following the principles of Zen, which teach that the enlightenment of the Buddha can be experienced directly by devoting oneself to the sitting practice of meditation without relying on the scriptures. Even when asked face-to-face by a disciple, Rikyū avoided theorizing his praxis, instead only reciting a well-known classical poem or producing a brief enigmatic statement. Rikyū seems to have been interested in enticing the disciples to contemplate his implied meaning, or what I have called the participatory interpretation. The lack of a written record continued after his death, with his son and grandson following his example. Only after the grandson's death did disciples begin to inscribe the oral transmissions, often in the form of anecdotes, for the benefit of an increasing number of followers.[3]

Rikyū's ethics and aesthetics were aimed at guiding tea participants to the ontological contemplation of the world and the self. Rikyū accomplished this by producing artifacts and environments that clearly showcased the incomplete, imperfect, and impermanent nature of their physical aspects. Rikyū had no quarrel with relegating his control over form and matter. No artist could have been further from the desire to produce beautiful artifacts that were perfectly shaped and made of high-quality materials. Consequently, his objects could be deemed as unremarkable as those found in the commonplace, imperfect scenes of everyday life. Though potentially alike in appearance, however, the differences are crucial. On the one hand, the primary value of objects of daily use would lie in their utility, while their physical properties could easily have escaped the user's notice. These material features, standard at best, were no target of aesthetic appreciation. On the other hand, the physical properties of Rikyū's objects, and expanding the Tai-an tearoom, presented themselves without relying on their functional purpose or historical significance. They engaged the imagination, not *despite* but *because* of their imperfection, incompleteness, and impermanence. The viewers could therefore participate in the appreciation of the objects more deeply and abstractly, not relying on the extrinsic meanings derived from their function or provenance. The viewers even drew parallels between themselves and these objects, contemplating their own imperfect and transient existence.

Conclusion

This chapter has observed particular cases of not-so-perfect buildings, categorizing them into three types: synecdoche, palimpsest, and *wabi*; all to argue that imperfect buildings engage the viewer's imagination, more so than the buildings' purpose, events, construction, or historical significance. Consequently, the viewer engages the object deeper, and beyond mere superficial appearance. Not only that, the viewers can be drawn to employ their imagination, and because they do, they can involve the whole of their being in relating to the object. With incomplete, imperfect, and impermanent architecture some certain existential opportunities are afforded to some participants who engage their imagination. As a result, it seems that in some occasions the physical object transcends its prosaic, matter-of-fact existence to something poetic, which allows the viewers to contemplate their own existence, including the transient nature of existence in time's continuum.

Architects need to acknowledge the nature of viewer involvement when designing structures as the architecture and consider the capacity of the incomplete, imperfect, and impermanent to engage the viewer. Our modern worldviews commonplace events and artifacts as banal, and daily life as impure, uncertain, and instable, governed by chance and happenstance. Thus, nothing about our ordinary lives seems precious or worthy of our attention. The ethics and aesthetics of the incomplete, imperfect, impermanent may provide an antidote, offering instruction on how to find the meaning of our existence in simple acts of creation and participation.

Endnotes

1   Portions of this chapter are condensed versions of two previously published articles: (2012). Sir Walter Scott and Kenilworth Castle: Ruins Restored by Historical Imagination. *Preservation Education & Research* 5, pp. 29–44; and (2013). Sen no Rikyū and the Japanese Way of Tea: Ethics and Aesthetics of the Everyday. *Interiors: Design, Architecture, Culture* 4(3), pp. 229–48. The chapter as a whole is a summary of a section of a book: (2015). *Allure of the Incomplete, Imperfect, and Impermanent: Designing and Appreciating Architecture as Nature*. Abingdon, UK: Routledge.

2   Hopkins, Keith (2005). *The Colosseum*. Cambridge, MA: Harvard University Press.

3   Geeraerts, Dirk and H. Cuyckens (2010). *The Oxford Handbook of Cognitive Linguistics*. Oxford, UK: Oxford University Press, pp. 238–40.

4   Scott, Walter (1821). *Kenilworth: A Romance*. Edinburgh, UK: Printed for Archibald Constable and Co. and John Ballantyne; and London, UK: Hurst, Robinson, and Co.

5   Morris, Richard K. (2006). *Kenilworth Castle*, 2nd revised edition. London, UK: English Heritage.

6   For a detailed comparison between Scott's textual descriptions of the building and what he had available in the historical documents and site observations, please refer to my journal article or book cited above.

7   Scott (1821), vol. 3, p. 54.

8   Scott (1821), vol. 3, pp. 87–8.

9   Frascari, Marco (1984). The Tell-the-Tale Detail. *Via* 7, pp. 23–37.

10   Borsi, Franco (1989). *Leon Battista Alberti: The Complete Works.* New York, NY: Electa/Rizzoli, pp. 62 and 68.

11   Murphy, Richard (1990). *Carlo Scarpa and the Castelvecchio.* London, UK and Boston, MA: Butterworth Architecture.

12   Magagnato, Licisco (ed.) (1982). *Carlo Scarpa a Castelvecchio.* Milan: Edizioni di Comunità.

13   Schultz, Anne-Catrin (2007). *Carlo Scarpa Layers.* Stuttgart: Edition Axel Menges.

14   Murphy (1990).

15   Kobori, Soujitsu [小堀宗実] (2003). *Cha no Yu no Fushigi* [茶の湯の不思議]. Tokyo: NHK Book, p. 14.

16   Tsutsui, Hiroichi [筒井紘一] (1990). Taka Akanuma [赤沼多佳], and Toshinori Nakamura [中村利則], *Rikyū No Chakai.* [利休の茶会]. Tokyo: Heibonsha.

17   Nakamura, Masao [中村昌生] (1993). *Tai-an: Wabi-Suki No Sekai* 待庵—侘数寄の世界. Kyoto: 淡交社.

18   Tanihata, Akio [谷端昭夫] (2011). *Chawa Shigetsushū Kōshin Gegaki* [茶話指月集・江岑夏書]. Kyoto, p. 28.

19   Raku, Kichizaemon [楽吉左衛門] (2007). *Rakuyaki-Sōsei: Rakutte Nandarō* [楽焼創成　楽ってなんだろう]. Kyoto: Tankōsha.

20   Yaeko Nogami, Yaeko [野上弥生子] (1964). *Hideyoshi to Rikyū* [秀吉と利休]. Tokyo: Chūō-Kōronsha.

Chapter 16
Wonder, Wisdom, and Mastery in Architecture

Prem Chandavarkar

Preamble: The Architect's Inevitable Silence

The creative orientation of architects tends to be shaped by discussions that occur within professional circles such as architecture schools, journals, conferences and other peer forums. In all these spaces the voice of the architect can be clearly heard, either explicitly, or reconstructed through critical analysis; and within the discourse this voice has a tangible presence that co-exists with the work. This predisposes the architect to believe that his or her voice is a primary factor in imbuing architecture with significance by articulating the work through compelling conceptualizations of the world or through exciting possibilities liberated by a new architectural language.

While the power of the architect's intentions carries potency within the influential formats of peer review, these contexts are at odds with the prosaic experience of architecture. The discursive protocols of education and journalism tend to presume a freshness of architectural experience. Even if the work being discussed is not new, the singularity with which it enters a relatively short discussion gives it an air that is artificial and detached. In contrast, the actual experience of architecture is inextricably contaminated by mundane repetitive and extended routine, for works of architecture typically have a core group of people who inhabit them regularly over years. Even if one assumes the codes by which an architect's compelling intentions can be interpreted are explicit enough to enable a clear perception (a doubtful proposition), the question remains as to how the power of those intentions is able to survive the boredom that would ensue from the barrage of incessant repetition implicated by the inhabitation of architecture over time.

Inhabitation is a process that begins after the professional task is complete and the architect has stepped away from the work. Unlike the performing arts, such as music or dance, that are most vivid in the presence of the artist, architecture is one of the arts that must be perceived as alive in the *absence* of the artist. When the work is handed over for inhabitation, all the words, thoughts and intentions of the architect are left behind, and all that remains is the presence of the work itself. How can architecture be meaningful despite the architect's everlasting silence? One dimension of this issue is that acts of inhabitation generate memory, and memory breeds meaning, so the architect would need to create spaces that are conducive to the generation of memory. While this is a significant and worthwhile aim that has not received sufficient attention, primary reliance on the inhabitant to generate meaning implies that the quality of architecture has little role to play in imparting significance to architectural experience. And the architect's intentions would quickly lose their charm once subjected to routine and repetitive experience. Creating architecture that is vibrant in the absence of the architect demands an ability to empower architecture with a meaningful voice that does not rely on references that are external to it.

Juhani Pallasma writes, "In the experience of art, a peculiar exchange takes place; I lend my emotions and associations to a space and the space lends me its aura, which entices and emancipates my perceptions and thoughts."[1] The term "aura" implies an architecture that can speak for itself, for compelling places emanate an aura that an inhabitant intuitively recognizes without having to involve knowledge of its creator. The dialog between inhabitant and aura that Pallasmaa identifies should be recognized as one of the primary generators of significance in architecture. Architects can neither define nor control the inhabitant with any degree of determinism, but the aura of architecture is more within their control. What do we mean by "aura"? How do we recognize and create it in a manner that 'entices and emancipates' the inhabitant without requiring the architect's voice?

The Aura of Architecture

The *Oxford Dictionary* defines aura as "The distinctive atmosphere or quality that seems to surround and be generated by a person, thing, or place."[2] Recognition of an aura is not the product of cognitive effort, for its recognition precedes cognition. Peter Zumthor, one architect who has emphasized the importance of atmosphere in architecture, observes, "I enter a building, see a room, and—in the fraction of a second—have this feeling about it."[3] This is not to argue that the first recognition is a complete one, for the richness and depth of spatial atmosphere reveals itself slowly over time. But being pre-cognitive, at each stage the perception of aura is a subtle, intuitive and embodied awareness that does not translate effectively into linguistic description or cognitive construct.

Auras can have historical and cultural dimensions. Walter Benjamin argues that when a work of art is reproduced, it withers its aura by dislocating it from its contextual roots and shifting it into the exclusive domain of the viewer.[4] The question of reproduction[5] that Benjamin raises is not what I wish to focus on here, and while one can admit a historical and cultural dimension, for the purpose of this essay it is sufficient to recognize that the aura is a distinct and tangible presence that emanates from and is entwined with the work of architecture, possesses a holistic quality where the whole is more than the mere sum of its parts, is subtle and evades precise definition, and is known pre-cognitively through an embodied consciousness.

The aura of a place implicates the seemingly contradictory qualities of distance and communion. Benjamin discusses the quality of distance:

> The concept of aura which was proposed above with reference to historical objects may usefully be illustrated with reference to the aura of natural ones. We define the aura of the latter as the unique phenomenon of a distance, however close it may be. If, while resting on a summer afternoon, you follow with your eyes a mountain range on the horizon or a branch which casts its shadow over you, you experience the aura of those mountains, of that branch.[6]

This "unique phenomenon of a distance" indicates that the aura is a presence that is distinct from the observing self, and by this fact demonstrates that the observing self is not the only presence implicated in that moment. Benjamin uses natural phenomena, uncontaminated by human history, as examples that best illustrate how the aura demonstrates presences in the world that do not emanate from animate beings. But this quality of distance is not necessarily a primary or dominant characteristic. Benjamin also presents how the aura can connect through communion between presences:

> Looking at someone carries the implicit expectation that our look will be returned by the object of our gaze. Where this expectation is met ... there is an experience of the aura to the fullest extent ... Experience of the aura thus rests on the transposition of a response common in human relationships to the relationship between the inanimate or natural object and man. The person we look at, or who feels he is being looked at, looks at us in turn. To perceive the aura of an object we look at means to invest it with the ability to look at us in return.[7]

Peter Zumthor, writing about the warm affinity he feels with a town square he is sitting in, observes:

> What else moved me? My mood, my feelings, the sense of expectation that filled me while I was sitting there. Which brings that famous Platonic sentence to mind, "Beauty is in the eye of the beholder." Meaning it is all in me. But then I perform an experiment: I take away the square—and my feelings are not the same ... I could never have had those feelings without the atmosphere of the square. It's quite logical really. People interact with objects ... The real has its own magic.[8]

It does not necessarily follow that every aura will involve this sense of communion: one can have, for example, the experience of being captivated by the visual beauty of a house, while finding that beauty aloof and the place uninviting with respect to one's sense of domesticity, intimacy and warmth. Pallasmaa speaks about how architects' perception of space has been influenced by the perspectival characterization of space in the last few centuries. Perspective privileges a specific kind of vision: central focused vision, which implies a distance between spectator and object. In contrast, peripheral vision encloses us within space.[9] The bias implicated by perspectival perception has created a tendency in architects to focus on the precise delineations of form that focused vision picks up on, with comparatively less attention paid to the gradations of scale, light and texture on which peripheral vision depends. When such gradations are effectively scaled to achieve coherence with the enclosed human body, the inhabiting self is drawn into the aura and communion is established.

When this simultaneity of distance and communion is achieved, the aura of a place embraces transcendence. Through distance, the existence of a presence beyond the initially perceived boundary of the inhabiting self is demonstrated, and communion displaces that boundary outward to intertwine the self with this presence. The transcendence is of limits rather than entities: one is not moving from the self to a realm beyond. Through resonance with the aura, the self gets implicated in an expanded sense of being, realizing that its own intelligence and awareness is actually an integral part of a greater reality. The impulse is to harmonize with the aura rather than understand or conceptualize it.

When one enters into a place that projects an aura, one instantly and easily senses it: an ability that seems inherent to being human. But, just as recognizing good music and knowing how to perform it are worlds apart, knowing how to create a communing aura is an infinitely more challenging task. Given its subtlety, the architect will have to shift from the intellectual mode that underpins the modern notion of appreciation and learning, and develop a sensitivity that recognizes the life within what we are accustomed to consider as inanimate, liberating the dialog between aura and inhabitant that Pallasmaa, Benjamin and Zumthor refer to. This involves acquiring the gaze of a poet.

The Poet's Gaze: Recognizing Life beyond the Self

The poet Pablo Neruda devoted a great part of his oeuvre to odes that paid homage to everyday things around him. In *Ode to the Sea* he said:

> Here on the island
> the sea –
> and how much sea –
> can't contain itself,
> at every moment,
> says yes, then no,
> says no, no, no,
> says yes, in blue,
> in foam, at a gallop,
> says no, and no.
>
> It can't stay still,
> my name's sea, it repeats
> smashing on a rock
> unable to convince it,
> then,
> with seven green tongues
> of seven green hounds,
> of seven green tigers,
> of seven green seas,
> it goes all over,
> kissing and soaking the rock,
> beating its breast,
> repeating its name.[10]

To Neruda the sea is not a fact of nature out there. It is a living being imbued with personality, winning a recognition that compels the poet to give it voice. This animistic recognition of the world comes naturally to all of us when very young. In his extensive interviews of children, the Swiss developmental psychologist Jean Piaget found they perceive the sun, sky, flowers, stones, and other objects as alive: possessing emotion, character, action, sight and knowledge.[11] Initially believed to represent an immature and inadequate cognition of the world, later research has shown it is not so. Children, when asked to categorize, are easily able to differentiate between the animate and the inanimate. Challenged with simultaneously constructing self and context, they do so through bonding and compassion with what surrounds them; to the point where toys and other objects are sources of companionship and entertainment.

Morris Berman argues that pre-modern consciousness also viewed the world as enchanted, where all its elements are wondrous and alive. Humanity was a part of this network, and the cosmos was a place of belonging.[12] Berman terms this worldview as a "participating consciousness," involving a psychic wholeness, of merging with one's surroundings. Modernity, in contrast, sees knowledge springing most effectively from pure Cartesian thought, separating self and context, pushing thought from the body into a position of detached neutrality: a worldview that, along with its handmaiden laissez-faire capitalism, reduces the world to inert phenomena on a surface, with no ethical impediments to appropriation by humankind. This denial of a participating consciousness has led us to the overwhelming psychological and ecological crises we face today. Berman admits that attempting to turn the clock back to an earlier happy world of pre-modernity is both illusory and futile, and uses the ideas of philosophers such as Michael Polanyi and Gregory Bateson to argue for a more benign and holistic scientific model. Berman fails to account for any value that scientific detachment may have provided, and I shall return to this question later in the essay; but his call to acknowledge our participating consciousness, as a foundation for achieving existential wholeness with the world we inhabit, is an important one. This consciousness, natural to us when very young, gets eroded over time by the epistemological conventions of modernity that school us to distrust the embodied awareness it relies upon, claiming that all worthwhile knowledge is objective, explicit, and detached from the subjectivities of first person consciousness.

Poets, such as Neruda, are fortunate beings born with the innate capacity to resist these conventions,[13] and we need to discover how to empower a wider spectrum of humans with this ability. They retain the sensitivity of a "child-like" participating consciousness in empathetic communion with the world that surrounds them. If they write on things or places, they imbue them with personality and presence. If they write about emotions, such as love or anguish, those emotions characterize the compulsions of a force of life that is greater than the individual. They are artists who have achieved a level of mastery in their art that allows them to capture the exalted voice of the world in the aura of their art, and the bond between poet and reader derives from a common recognition of this voice.

The connection between mastery and a greater voice is empirically documented by Mihaly Csikszentmihalyi who studies moments of peak performance across many disciplines and fields, finding that at that moment people describe as being "in the zone," they lose awareness of their ego and their body, and feel they have merged with a greater reality that is "flowing" through them.[14] How can we reach this state of flow? To be in this spontaneous state of merger is to be beyond any perception of structure, difference, identity or hierarchy. As articulation of any concept is dependent on the existence of structure, this state of knowing is purely tacit: a state of embodied knowledge where, as Michael Polanyi has put it, "we know more than we can tell."[15] This is because the knowledge, while conforming to basic laws, cannot be reductively deduced from these laws. For example, riding a bicycle is an action that has to conform to the laws of physics, but knowing the laws of physics is of absolutely no use in acquiring the ability to ride a bicycle. The knowledge has to be acquired through bodily awareness, can never be adequately articulated, and because it resides in the body is not easily forgotten.

The paradigm of rationalism that permeates our models of learning tends to devalue tacit knowledge, seeing it as subjective and private; and since sharing knowledge is a prerequisite to its critique, only explicit knowledge is believed to meet a standard of rigor. Given that tacit knowledge is transmitted by personal contact, it is an experiential domain, and to examine it on intellectual terms is not only unjustifiable, but also likely to lead to premature condemnation. When a phenomenological rather than analytical standard of rigor is applied, a different picture emerges. An example popularly cited is that of a famous musician whose knowledge of how to perform music is purely tacit; and intellectual understanding an obstruction if applied at the moment of performance. But the knowledge is so tangible and communicable that it possesses commercial value: people are willing to pay substantial sums of money to hear the musician perform, either live or through recordings. It is not knowledge of how to perform music that is communicated. It is awareness of what music *is*; a voice that the musician articulates through music, and the captivation compelled by this voice establishes a common space that both musician and listener occupy. The transmission of tacit knowledge that occurs is enabled by an experiential rigor where substantive amounts of time, characterized by concentrated and immersive attention, are spent in the same space as the knowledge. Given this fact, we have more to learn from practice than from intellect.

Practice and the "Space Between"

Learning how to perform Indian classical music is predicated on *sadhana*, a term that would literally translate into English as "practice."[16] That would be an inadequate translation for *sadhana* also involves a level of discipline that commits the aspiring musician to long hours of daily practice. To distinguish it from rote learning, it is necessary to realize that *sadhana* is not just any practice; it must be an *ego-transcending* practice, which is best explained in the ninth verse of the *Isha Upanishad*,[17] "Into a blind darkness they enter who follow after ignorance. Into a greater darkness they enter who devote themselves to knowledge alone."[18] The meaning of the first line is apparent; the second seems at first glance to be counter-intuitive, but is actually a critique of how knowledge can have a negative impact on understanding. Firstly, if one has reached a sophisticated level of knowledge acquisition, it is very easy to delude oneself that a defensible position of expertise has been reached; or, alternatively, become desensitized to new learning. And secondly, knowledge is implanted into memory and memory is primarily related to the past: one cannot have a memory of "now." Therefore an attitude that gives undue centrality to knowledge will pre-empt its apprehension of the present, a sense of being rooted in the "here and now." Both of these barriers must be broken, for a prerequisite to connecting with a reality beyond oneself requires a continuous and sensitive openness to discovery as well as a present-centered awareness of where/when one is. *Sadhana's* goal is a mastery that is founded on surrender rather than command. It is aimed at the artist's transcendental destiny: a unity and harmony with a sacred reality. This connection is not made initially at overarching levels, and is one that depends on dimensions that are far more intimate and subtle.

These dimensions were articulated in a conversation that a group of architects (including the author) had with Indian classical vocalist Dinkar Kaikini on parallels between music and architecture.[19] A striking feature of this conversation was that if you were to ask any of the architects in the room whether they designed in a classical tradition, the odds are that they would have been offended by the question, retorting that they were creative beings empowered by a modernist freedom that refuses to submit to the outdated constrictions of classical style. Kaikini, on the other hand, embodied a contemporary creative artist situated firmly and comfortably within a classical tradition that he did not perceive as either restrictive or anachronistic. This was clarified when he explained that the emotion in music was not located in composition, lyric, melody or scale. These elements only started the process by defining a space within which one had to be. The space may possess character and boundaries, but there are fundamental choices to be made in how one will occupy it. Would you cling to the boundaries or explore its full range? Would you dance joyfully or shuffle pessimistically across it? Would you move slowly or quickly? These choices determine the emotional and expressive power that is unleashed, and given that every journey begins with a first step, the founding choices are to be made at the basic levels of single steps. When a sequence of immediate choices is woven into a harmonious structure that resonates at all levels, then an aura is created within which there is no division between singer, music, composition, scale, emotion, and the universe. Kaikini locates this union as primarily springing from two levels: *meend* (the glide from one note to the other that includes all the microtones between the notes) and *laya* (the interval between one note and the other). He uncovers a powerful paradox here: the revelations of grand perspectives cannot be relied on; *the infinite is to be first found within elements that are immediately adjacent, for it is at this level that its intimacy with the self becomes perceptible.* The challenge lies in acquiring the level of mastery that can unify the choices made at this level of simple adjacencies with greater hierarchies of scale. This is a far cry from the belief system of architects, which tends to align with the quotation attributed to the renowned Chicago architect Daniel Burnham, "Make no little plans; they have no magic to stir men's blood and probably themselves will not be realized. Make big plans; aim high in hope and work, remembering that a noble, logical diagram once recorded will never die ...."[20] This orientation places most power in overall concepts, with comparatively little attention paid to immediate adjacencies. To Kaikini a classical tradition is neither the constraint of a predetermined style nor a grandeur of concept, but a renewing reunion achieved through emotional and liberating choices involving dimensions that are most subtle, proximate and intimate.

Sadhana is a means of accessing this subtlety. At a conceptual level the musician may know the position of a note. But this knowledge obtained either by theoretical knowledge or a novice ear will only reveal an approximate position. Through *sadhana*, the musician gradually becomes aware of subtler and subtler aspects of the note's position, till eventually the note hits an exactitude of great power. In an interview, the vocalist Pushkar Lele speaks of this discovery when he changed teachers in order to break through a plateau he was trapped in after 15 years of training. He expected his new teacher Vijay Sardeshmukh to begin with revealing the higher level to which he aspired, but to his consternation Sardeshmukh forced him back to basics, asking him to sing a single note "sa" ("do" in Western scale) for months. Lele said, "When I started learning from him, he made me sing just 'sa' for six long months! It was utterly frustrating after having studied for 15 years. But one day, when I hit the 'sa' he wanted, he smiled and I realized that I had, till then, never hit the centre of a note before!"[21]

Lele's epiphany and Kaikini's observations reveal an orientation that is radically different from the conventions of an intellectual and individualistic tradition which, in wanting to know more about reality, adopts a strategy of movement and conquest, of learning more by commanding the "space beyond." *Sadhana*, in contrast, adopts a strategy of compassion and bonding, a discovery through intimacy and surrender. Just as personal relationships acquire greater depth through immersion in an extended and non-judgmental time of rapport, Kaikini and Lele embody an attitude that perceives music as a living field imbued with divine energy, yearning to know it better. They use increasing levels of discernment that can only be enabled by *sadhana* to delve deeper within this living reality, learning to recognize it with a far finer grain than was previously visible, seeking the "space *between*" rather than the "space beyond."

In this 'space between' is an energy whose power can be comprehended by visualizing the difference between two professionally trained musicians: one who is good and the other who is truly great. The good musician, like the great one, cannot be criticized on tunefulness or faithfulness to the composition. It is in subtle differences of microtones and timing where the virtuosity of the great musician breaks away to a powerful magical realm whose exactitude in the "space between" has the capacity to provoke rapture in the listener. Slight shifts in the position of a note away from the center of such exactitude may be of little significance dimensionally or in departure from tunefulness, but are of immense significance in relation to the soul-stirring resonance struck between listener and music: a resonance that provokes a participating consciousness in the listener bonding him/her with a music that is instantly recognized as a living field of emancipatory energy.

An architecture that speaks for itself is one that provokes a participating consciousness in the inhabitant through the exactitude with which its aura reveals the "space between." To achieve this, the architect must shift away from an over-reliance on intellectualism, and through the discernment that *sadhana* empowers two key capabilities. First is the ability to empathize with the living energy in the key dimensions of architecture (such as space, material, form, light, landscape and inhabitation), and channel this energy through one's embodied awareness and skill in order to reveal it in the final creation. And second is to strike the center of exactitude in the "space between" at all levels of the work: from the overarching concept to the smallest detail.

The need for exactitude at all levels requires a recasting of the role of detail in architectural design. The prevalent predisposition, seen in the structure of professional training as well as most critical texts on architecture, is a focus on conceptual intent, with detail typically abstracted to the level of technique or production. But if one's approach prioritizes detail, a different orientation can emerge. Detail is the scale at which the body first engages with space: it relates to the ranges of human scale, from the height of the body, to the reach of an arm, to the width of the palm or fingertip. It is the level where the intimate senses of touch and smell are most acute. As Kaikini pointed out, the self's connection with the infinite is to be found first in what is immediately adjacent. Detail not only provides this level, its intimacy facilitates realization of an embodied participating consciousness. To incorporate detail as a key element of the design process is to increase the likelihood of carrying this consciousness to broader concepts. In contrast, to privilege concept is to foreground abstraction and therefore resist the possibility of a participating consciousness.

When the center of exactitude is struck at all levels, from the spatial concept down to the smallest detail, architecture presents an aura of stillness because an unchanging spirit presents itself whichever way the body may move or the gaze may focus. Ron Hassner, in his study of conflict over sacred sites, points out that proposals for resolution by dividing the site between the conflicting parties invite rejection from all concerned because sacred sites are inherently indivisible.[22] This inherent indivisibility of the sacred is the reason why the transcendent is most powerful when it spans from the grandest to the smallest things, for it confirms the pervasiveness without which we could not consider the sacred as truly being so. This is at odds with the prevalent intellectual paradigm, as its epistemological method is based on reductionism that resists recognition of indivisibility. When indivisibility is expressed through an all-pervading exactitude at all scales, the resultant stillness creates an aura of sacred timelessness.[23] While it may not be what Mies van der Rohe meant, there is truth in the adage, "God is in the details."

Wonder, Wisdom, and Mastery

While it is a powerful methodology, it would be shortsighted to rely solely on *sadhana*; for that would deny the value of critical thought and scientific detachment. As Karl Popper has pointed out, this value is ethical, for without critical detachment the imperative of acknowledging individual freedom of thought that forms the foundation of liberal democracy would go unrecognized. We would remain within tribal or totalitarian regimes that are intolerant of departure from defined collectivist beliefs.[24] And at the other extreme, a total reliance on scientific detachment would result in the pathological denial of participating consciousness that Morris Berman identifies. Modernity's dominant focus on intellectualism has resulted in a weak epistemology of practice, seeing it as little more than applied theory pragmatically validated by experience. As Donald Schon has shown, this attitude would assume a model of "reflection *and* action," whereas effective professionals demonstrate a capacity for "reflection *in* action."[25] The value of practice and theory lies in their relationship, and is often most powerful when they contradict each other. Practice becomes the means for critiquing theory and theory the means for critiquing practice, and the conversational shift between the two is foundational to building a unity of grandeur and intimacy. We tend to pre-empt this potential by spatially segregating the two, believing that theory belongs to the reflective world of academia and practice to the action-oriented world of design firms. While one may sometimes find the two combined within individuals, we need more spaces that contain the combination. Our methodology will then rest on a conversational shuffle rather than a logical sequence, and building unity from this shuffle will call for an enabling attitude: one that is founded on wonder, wisdom and mastery.

To remain in the state of mind of the poet, channeling the energy of the world into one's creations, we need to be continually rooted in wonder, the capacity to be amazed by *anything*, the means by which we resist anaesthetization by the familiar. Wonder is crucial to maintaining the freshness of gaze that sustains discovery in "the space between." Wonder is the bridge that integrates us with wider horizons. Ingrained in us as children, we must resist the tendency to lose it as we grow up and get acculturated. A first step would be to avoid succumbing wholly to formal education's exhortations to learn more, and to not just receive information from the world but to also begin pushing back at it; questioning it, and even remaking it through metaphor. In doing so, we not only deny that we are merely passive vessels that must be filled with knowledge and skills, we assert ourselves and reach out to develop our relationship with the world. And like in our personal life, if we find we have more relationships than we can handle, we do not divide our relationships into categories and wholly drop some categories; we prioritize among similar relationships on the basis of the affinity we feel for them, and develop an inner circle of close friends. We do not relegate those whom we have not chosen to some subsidiary category of life; we accept them as being equal to our friends, it is just that they do not happen to be our friends. So to remain in wonder we must choose our friends carefully, and if the poet adopts language as a close friend, and the dancer befriends the human body, the architect must seek the company of the dimensions of architecture and wonder.

To be rooted in wonder is to be acutely aware of the scale of one's bodily sense of being compared to the context into which one is inserted. Children, given their diminutive size, have the humility of personal scale relative to context forced upon them, and context therefore remains a significant factor in their consciousness. Societies that remain rooted in ancient folk traditions also retain this awareness of scale, for their daily routines of work and living are based on bodily engagement with context. It is only in modern technological society that one begins to see a comparative separation from context, enabled by prioritizing a conceptual realm detached from material reality[26] and a faith that technology can master nature. To live in humility with respect to context implies that the only way of coming to terms with one's surroundings is through empathy, affection and respect: and this is crucial to remaining in a poetic state of wonder. Inculcation of this attitude must become a primary goal of education.

Wonder is the foundation of compassion, for to be in wonder is to refuse reduction of anything to inert form; acknowledging all existence as possessing intrinsic history, character and potential, and therefore worthy of respectful recognition. When we remain in wonder, we are able to move from knowledge to wisdom; for while knowledge can exist in isolation, wisdom can only constitute itself in terms of its appropriateness to the world. Knowledge lives primarily at the level of third person experience, whereas wisdom blurs the boundaries between the first, second and third person levels. Knowledge remains neutral, whereas wisdom seeks out ethics and balance. Knowledge stays confined to the animate, whereas wisdom encompasses the whole world. In Julio Ollala's articulate phrasing:

> Knowledge has become another possession and therefore it has also become the object of greed. Wisdom, on the contrary cannot be a possession. It cannot be traded, regulated or registered. It cannot be owned by any individual, because it lives in a territory that is not solely human, it is shared with the gods. Wisdom is not what we know about the world, it is what the world discloses for us. If knowledge can live in greed, wisdom can only live in gratitude. If knowledge belongs to thought, wisdom belongs to the soul. If knowledge creates silos and divisions, wisdom integrates. If knowledge is knowing about it, wisdom is being it .... Wisdom has a sense of timing and relevance that is mostly hidden to knowledge. Knowledge may deny meaning, wisdom is inseparable from it. Knowledge lives in the mental domain, wisdom also lives in soul and spirit.[27]

Knowledge that is tempered by wonder leads to wisdom, and wisdom that is tempered by *sadhana* leads to mastery. If wisdom is founded on relationships, mastery takes it further to intimacy. Relationships characterized by intimacy involve intense and open engagement over a long duration of time. This catalyzes a blurring of boundaries; while both parties are aware of each other as separate beings, common experiences have a shared quality where the division between the two perceptions can never be located with precision. This is the nature of the relationship between art and the artist. A master stone carver will have worked with stone so much—felt it, embraced it, sensed its resistance when hammered, smelt it, and so on—that eventually his or her experience with carving leads to a unity between the carver's body, stone, chisel and mallet. The energy in stone, carving tools and the world contributes as much power to the final creation as that springing from the creativity of the craftsman; and this energy is like a wind in the sails of the craftsman.[28]

Experts who achieve mastery see the world differently from novices, for their intimacy has granted them access to the "space between," and the texture they sense is of a much more refined grain than what is apparent to the novice. Novice players cannot come close to the number of patterns that chess grandmasters perceive in a single momentary glance at a chess game. Scans of the brains of dancers when they watch a dance performance show different results from the brains of non-dancers; and even among expert dancers, their brains react differently when they watch performances of a dance form they have mastered versus those of an unfamiliar one.[29]

Mastery is a difficult goal, requiring patience through arduous but long periods of stasis while waiting for revelation to occur. To sustain this we need to see light at the end of the tunnel, so while learning mastery we must also live in the presence of mastery, which requires that our choice of teachers must be wise. Architects who wish to pursue true mastery of architecture will have to shift from the current paradigm of believing that the sophistication of their intentions will carry their day. They will have to submit with humility to the living context of architecture, engage in conversation with it, commune with its energy through *sadhana*, and thereby give to the aura of architecture a voice that is not only intelligible to the inhabitant, but also emancipatory.

A sacred aura in architecture is only possible through mastery, for mastery enables the level of command of one's art that extends exactitude across all scales of the work to demonstrate the indivisibility of the sacred. There are very few architects whose mastery across a body of work has consistently achieved this spread of exactitude together with the gradations of scale and texture that provoke the spatial bonding of peripheral vision: Frank Lloyd Wright, Carlo Scarpa, Geoffrey Bawa, Peter Zumthor—to name a few. Where it has been achieved you find a striking characteristic: these architects are internationally acknowledged as masters, but unlike many similarly acknowledged masters they do not breed schools of followers and imitators. There are no shortcuts or "isms" that allow you to easily imitate these architects: achieving this ability requires that you invest in the rigor of mastery yourself.

Conclusion: The Pursuit of Beauty

If we are to empower wonder, wisdom and mastery with an energizing purpose, it is necessary to engage once more in the pursuit of beauty. For many centuries this pursuit, where beauty reflected divine purpose, was a central goal in architecture. Eventually this degenerated into a set of ossified compositional codes that were out of touch with changes in society and technology. Modernity justifiably rebelled against this straitjacket of canonical prescription, but the pendulum swung too far in claiming the false freedom of *context-free* desire. The architect was now afforded the indulgence of privileging his/her voice; beauty was no longer a dominant ideal, and it was sufficient to appear avant-garde, radical, reformatory, innovative, or even just interesting. There is no longer an overarching frame of reference that architects can agree on that validates any of these positions. Charles Taylor has written on how the lack of a wider "horizon of significance" has incapacitated idealism, for without it one cannot differentiate between choices we make: a choice involving normative value is reduced to the same level as one that does not rise above self-gratification. We initially received our horizon of significance through inherited tradition, but that was found wanting. We subsequently sought it in modernity through instrumental reason, but now that has also been found wanting. Taylor suggests a relatively unexplored source in spaces of engagement, for authenticity is like language: its potential is inherent within us, but will lie unknown and unrealized until we engage in conversation.[30]

This conversation will have to extend beyond fellow humans to the spaces we inhabit. Wonder and wisdom open us up to this engagement with the world, and mastery enables us to achieve union with it. The aura of architecture, as a product of mastery, reveals to the inhabitant a presence beyond himself or herself, a presence that can be recognized intuitively, whose resonance intertwines the inhabitant's sense of self with wider "horizons of significance." Architecture, like all the other arts, offers an exactitude that resists the entropic decay of life; offering to the inhabitant the potential to anchor his or her sense of being within a significant world. In the words of Gernot Böhme, "Because we ourselves are transient beings, we encounter beauty in the lighting-up of appearances which assure us of our existence. *Beauty is that which mediates to us the joy of being here.*"[31]

Endnotes

1   Pallasmaa, Juhani (2007). *The Eyes of the Skin: Architecture and the Senses.* Chichester, UK: John Wiley and Sons Ltd., p. 12.

2   *Oxford Dictionary*, http://www.oxforddictionaries.com/definition/english/aura (accessed November 2014).

3   Zumthor, Peter (2006). *Atmospheres: Architectural Environments—Surrounding Objects.* Basel, Boston and Berlin: Birkhäuser, p. 13.

4   Benjamin, Walter (1968). The Work of Art in the Age of Mechanical Reproduction. *Illuminations*, translated by Harry Zohn. New York, NY: Schocken, pp. 217–51.

5   The question of reproduction, and its impact on aura, is not one that is dominant in architecture given that every building is rooted to a specific site, each site has its unique features and context, and the aura of the building should resonate with the aura of its site. Given this constraint, architecture does not reproduce easily over multiple locations without dislocation from context—a dislocation that serves to erode its impact, making reproduction distinctively unappealing to any architect who is passionate about architecture.

6   Benjamin (1968). The Work of Art in the Age of Mechanical Reproduction, pp. 222–3.

7   Benjamin (1968)."On Some Motifs in Baudelaire. *Illuminations*, p. 188.

8   Zumthor (2006). *Atmospheres*, p. 17.

9   Pallasmaa, Juhani (2011). *Space, Place and Atmosphere: Peripheral Perception in Architectural Experience.* Inaugural Kenneth Frampton Endowed Lecture, Graduate School of Architecture Planning and Preservation, Columbia University, 19 October. The lecture can be viewed at https://www.youtube.com/watch?v=MFwrmIljdqo (accessed June 30, 2015).

10   Neruda, Pablo (2013). Ode to the Sea, in Ilan Stavans (ed.), *All the Odes: A Bilingual Edition.* New York, NY: Farrar Straus and Giroux, p. 594.

11   Piaget, Jean (1951). *The Child's Conception of the World*. London, UK: Routledge & Kegan Paul.

12   Berman, Morris (1981). *The Reenchantment of the World*. Ithaca, NY: Cornell University Press.

13   Pablo Picasso articulated this fact when he reputedly said, "It takes a long time to become young."

14   Csikszentmihalyi, Mihaly (2008). *Flow: The Psychology of Optimal Experience*. New York, NY: Harper Perennial Modern Classics.

15   Polanyi, Michael (2009). *The Tacit Dimension.* Chicago, IL: University of Chicago Press.

16   This is not to argue that Indian tradition is exclusive in this respect, similar concepts do exist in other musical traditions. I cite Indian classical tradition here purely because it is the one that is most familiar to me.

17   The *Upanishads* are foundational scriptural texts of Hinduism, particularly influential to the philosophy of *Vedanta* (End of the Vedas). While they cannot be precisely dated, the *Mukhya* (principal) *Upanishads* predate the Common Era.

18   Aurobindo, Sri (2003). *The Isha Upanishad: A Translation and Commentary*. Pondicherry: Sri Aurobindo Ashram Press, p. 8.

19   Unpublished conversation between a group of practicing architects and Dinkar Kaikini. The conversation was held in Bangalore, India, in August 2003.

20   While this statement is popularly attributed to Burnham, there is no record of his either saying or writing it. The quotation first appears in a Christmas card sent by Burnham's partner Willis Polk six months after Burnham's death. It appears to be assembled from a set of several speeches by Burnham, who probably never articulated this precise sequence of words. See Reardon, Patrick T. (1992). Burnham Quote: Well, It May Be. *Chicago Tribune*, Wednesday January 1, http://articles.chicagotribune.com/1992–01–01/news/9201010041_1_sentences-chicago-architects (accessed November 2014).

21   Ganesh, Deepa (2010). The Inner Spring. *The Hindu*, Friday August 6, http://www.thehindu.com/features/friday-review/music/the-inner-spring/article553469.ece (accessed November 2014).

22   Hassner, Ron E. (2009). *War on Sacred Grounds*. Ithaca, NY: Cornell University Press.

23   The connection between stillness and the sacred is emphasized by many spiritual traditions, ranging from the meditative practices of Eastern faiths to the Biblical injunction, "Be still, and know that I am God."

24   Popper, Karl (1945). *The Open Society and Its Enemies*. London, UK: Routledge.

25   Schon, Donald A. (1983). *The Reflective Practitioner: How Professionals Think in Action*. New York, NY: Basic Books.

26   Epitomized by the famous Cartesian dictum, "I think, therefore I am."

27   Ollala, Julio (2010). *From Knowledge to Wisdom: Essays on the Crisis in Contemporary Learning*. Boulder, CO: Newfield Network Inc., Kindle edition.

28   Yanagi, Soetsu (1989). *The Unknown Craftsman: A Japanese Insight into Beauty*. Tokyo: Kodansha International.

29   Horowitz, Alexandra (2013). *On Looking: Eleven Walks with Expert Eyes*. New York, NY: Scribner.

30   Taylor, Charles (2003). *The Ethics of Authenticity*. Cambridge, MA: Harvard University Press.

31   Böhme, Gernot (2010). On Beauty. *The Nordic Journal of Aesthetics* 21(39), p. 31.

Chapter 17
From Within:
On the Spiritual in Art and Architecture

Nader Ardalan

The great epoch of the Spiritual which is already beginning, or, in embryonic form, began already yesterday … provides and will provide the soil in which a kind of monumental work of art must come to fruition.[1]

Wassily Kandinsky

We reach for the light spiritually,
As the plant does physically.[2]

Frank Lloyd Wright

Introduction

Countless generations of architects and artists have been inspired by the aesthetic quest offered by the spiritual dimension of existence that transcends life's limitations. A long lineage of scholars attempting to define these elusive dimensions can be traced to this quest, which has variously been called Metaphysics, Mysticism, Sufism, Gnosis, Cabala, Zen, Yoga or more generally referred to as the Perennial Tradition. However, the Perennial Tradition, as an alternative to the empirical worldview, has remained misunderstood by the majority of the public. Yet, its profound influence has permeated to various degrees, all aspects of the great literature, art, architecture, music and dance of the world in every age.

This chapter is intended to position this alternative worldview as particularly related to architecture, and describe in summary the history and legitimacy of its root philosophic concepts. It will further discuss how in the beginning of the 20th century, the Abstract Expressionist Movement re-ignited the spiritual dimension in creative thought, and re-invigorated key metaphysical and aesthetic principles that radically changed artistic and architectural expression. The contemporary application of this design approach through a systematic framework will be explored and demonstrated through examination of selected case studies. The chapter will conclude with observations about the potential value of an encompassing Perennial Tradition to shift architecture from the dominant, contemporary machine-inspired functionalist aesthetic to a more holistic, sustainable, transcendent and spiritually inspired design approach.

The Spiritual Quest

What is the history and structure of this perennial spiritual quest in creative expression and how can it be described? Its Western roots can be traced from antiquity dating back to thinkers such as Hermes Trismegistus, Plato and Plotinus, to the leading figures of Middle Ages including Meister Eckhart, Dante, Robert Fludd, Jakob Boehme, to 18th- and 19th-century thinkers, such as, Emanuel Swedenborg, Goethe, William Blake, Ralph Waldo Emerson, and to the 20th century including, Theosophists, William James, Frithjof Schuon, Titus Burckhardt, Henri Corbin, Mircea Eliade, Huston Smith, Rudolf Otto, and Martin Heidegger.[3] Perhaps for an even longer period of history, in the East the lineage of such quests might include Lao-tzu,[4] Chuang-Tzu, and the Ikhawan al Safa, Ibn Arabi, Rumi, Suhrawardi, Hafez, Saidi, Liu Zhi, through to Tagore, Ighbal, Gibran, Coomaraswamy, Hassan Fathy and Seyyed Hossein Nasr.

The term "transcendent aesthetics" is used here to describe the simultaneous awareness of the hidden and the manifest aspects of external reality, as historically developed in the Perennial Tradition. However, it also requires a particular level of preparedness and inner awareness within both the artist and the beholder for the beheld to comprehend and appreciate its message. [This is important to the "resonance" between intent and experience.] The manifest is its phenomenal reality, while the hidden is its ontological link with its *a priori* non-existential reality. The artistic search to the deepest mysteries of the quest (also referred to as The Way), centers on the personal and direct state of confrontation with reality in its broadest aspects, and requires no intermediaries. The resulting comprehension is usually characterized by a sense of the universe as a single, living substance of which humans are an inseparable part.[5] Even if by this effort one is only able to catch but a brief and passing glimpse of an aspect of the non-articulated, the creative attempt is still inspiring and fulfilling. The creative challenge then is how to express most saliently the essence of this glimpse.

This "transcendent aesthetics" provides a particular "field" of consciousness or worldview where the "Creative Imagination" to take place.[6] The activation of the Creative Imagination may be of an audible nature that transcends the mere conventional tonal or linguistic frameworks of music, song, poetry or verse. In a similar manner, it may be of a visual nature in the form of light, color, art, architecture or movement in performance and dance. In both cases, the imagination is set into vibrations through abstract, transcendent symbols that have a propensity to pulsate the heart and thereby to touch the soul.[7] The soul serves here as the *modus operandi* within humans to spontaneously sense the ineffable and the sublime—to go beyond the mere phenomenal to higher levels of realizations about the realities of existence. This process has involved a symbolic and conscious death (*fana*) to the mere material way of perceiving existence and rebirth (*bagha*) to a heightened consciousness, where existence is perceived within a transcendent, ontological cause (Figure 17.2a). Art, therefore, offers an opportunity not only as a vehicle of aesthetic and experiential satisfaction, but also as a conduit between the microcosm of earthly existence and the macrocosm of everlasting spiritual existence. Such then is the nature and structure of this aesthetic quest.

> When you become the pencil in the hand of the infinite,
> When you are truly creative … design begins and never has an end.[8]
>
> Frank Lloyd Wright

To Unfold the Human Soul

In the field of the arts, most notably from about 1890 in Northern Europe and later in the 20th century in the United States, a group of artists moved away from representational art toward abstraction, preferring instead symbolic color and form as their means of expression in an attempt to reach a higher and deeper dimension of meaning, the most pervasive of which was that of the spiritual. It coincided with the late 19th-century reaction against what were thought to be limitations of the pervasive rationalist and materialist worldviews of their times.[9] They held that the role of the artist was to free modern painting and reinvigorate it with greater meaning. From that time to the early 1930s, an astonishingly high proportion of visual artists and some architects became involved and worked with these ideas and belief systems, particularly after the devastating effects of World War I. Nourishing such directions of thought were lessons learned from varied sources; Eastern mystics who had migrated to Europe; the discovery of African and "primitive art;" the theosophical and anthroposophical writings of Helena Blavatsky, Rudolf Steiner; and George Gurdjieff; and the influential impact of the book *On the Spiritual in Art* by Wassily Kandinsky, published in 1912.

Robert Rosenbaum's *Modern Painting and the Northern Romantic Tradition—Friedrich to Rothko*[10] lucidly presents this northern European tradition that profoundly departed from the more French tradition of "Art for art's sake." In particular, he analyzed the quest for the sublime in art, from Caspar David Friedrich to Vincent Van Gogh, to Kandinsky to Mark Rothko. How to express the spiritual experience outside organized religion became these artists' prime search.

Maurice Tuchman's essay in the *Spiritual in Art: Abstract Painting 1890–1985* observed that: "The five underlying impulses within the spiritual abstract nexus—cosmic imagery, vibrations, synesthesia, duality and sacred geometry—are in fact five structures that refer to the underlying modes of thought."[11] To these should perhaps be added two more key impulses evident in their works. The first is a silent sense of the unity of existence—a Oneness with the infinity of the universe—this was a pervading theme of the earlier Transcendental

Movement and, in particular the writings of Ralph Waldo Emerson and Walt Whitman, which continued to influence many of these artists. This theme is also the core of the *Wahdad-i-wujud* (unity of existence) thinking attributed to the 12th century, Andalusian mystic Ibn Arabi that had considerable and direct influence on later metaphysical contemplatives, including Emerson. The second is the appreciation of alchemy as a metaphor not only for the transmutation of external matter from its "dark heaviness to light," but also most importantly of the artist himself. The alchemical experience held for the artist the potential for a psychological catharsis that could both illuminate and purify the spirit.

> Light releases the energy trapped in matter.[12]
>
> Louis I. Kahn

Alfred Barr, director of the Museum of Modern Art in New York, charted this artistic movement in his book *Cubism & Abstract Art.*[13] He lauded, among others, the achievements and stature of Henri Matisse, Wassily Kandinsky, Piet Mondrian, Jean Arp, and DeChirico, to name a few. In the field of architecture and sculpture, this Western movement included such notable and foundational figures as Louis Sullivan, Frank Lloyd Wright,[14] Kazimir Malevich, Bruno Taut and Naum Gabo. Their creations reflect a desire to express spiritual, utopian or metaphysical ideals that cannot be expressed in traditional pictorial terms.

In the years leading up to and including World War II, the Abstract Movement was criticized from many quarters on rational and political grounds. However, after this cataclysmic war, a new wave of mostly American artists expressed a renewed urgency for asserting the universal truths of existence. Their spiritual sources tended not to be Theosophy, but beliefs and practices associated with Native Americans, Zen, Carl Gustav Jung's concepts of archetypal form, and universal world mythology as elucidated by Joseph Campbell. Abstract Expressionists artists, such as Barnett Newman, Jackson Pollock, Mark Rothko and Georgia O'Keefe sought an art concerned with silence and contemplation (Figure 17.1a).

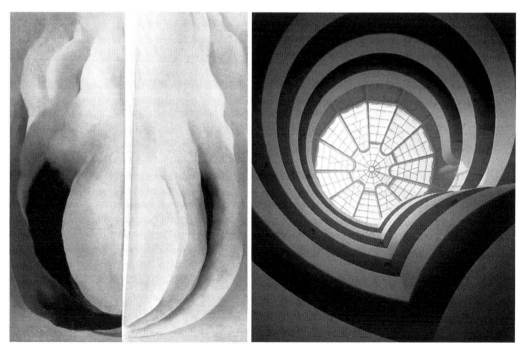

Figure 17.1   Abstract expressionism: a) Georgia O'Keefe, *Abstraction Blue*, 1927, b) Frank Lloyd
Wright, Guggenheim Museum, NY, 1950
Source: a) Courtesy Museum of Modern Art, b) Photograph courtesy of Nader Ardalan.

However, the great physical reconstruction of war-torn Europe and Japan overwhelmed any major impetus toward the transcendent in architecture. But, Frank Lloyd Wright and those of his school of thought (such as Bruce Goff and Paolo Soleri in his own unique way) practiced in this genre (Figure 17.1b). One of the later, leading metaphysically inspired architects, much influenced by Wright, was Louis I. Kahn[15] (Figures 17.1c and d), who left a few true disciples in America (perhaps architects such as Moshe Safdie, Daniel Libeskind and Antoine Predock) or in Europe (Carlo Scarpa, and Mario Botta), while inspiring some architects in the Middle East (the late Nader Khalili, Ali Saremi and this author in Iran), and in Indian the sub-continent, notably B.V. Doshi and Charles Correa. Independent of Kahn's influence, Hassan Fathy in Egypt generated a notable series of buildings based upon culturally relevant and transcendent considerations. More recently, E. Fay Jones, Steven Holl, and Christopher Alexander and artist James Turrell in North America; Luis Barragan in Mexico; Tadao Ando and Toyo Ito in Japan; Geoffrey Bawa in Sri Lanka; Keith Critchlow in UK; Anton Alberti in Holland; Peter Zumthor in Switzerland; Juhani Pallasmaa in Finland; Christian Norberg-Schulz in Norway and Alberto Campo Baeza in Spain, have explored dimensions of the phenomenology of the sublime in their architectural work. Due to this growing number of senior architects who have been basing their work on the intangible qualities of design, there is now a significant amount of scholarship being paid to this alternative, non-empirical and perennial approach to architecture.

Current Scholarship

During the past few years, a number of international academic and professional conferences have been held dedicated to the subject area of the relationship between nature, the built environment, culture and spirituality.[16] One of the most recent of such conferences was the multi-disciplinary symposium held at Harvard University in June 2014, entitled: *Urbanism, Spirituality and Well-being: Exploring the Past and Present/Envisioning the Future*.[17] Today, the urgency of this research subject has been greatly heightened by the apparent conjunction of three, potentially cataclysmic forces: the world economic crisis; global climate change; and the much-debated clash of civilizations. The need, therefore, for yet another cycle of artistic, architectural and cultural expressions of the unity and sanctity of existence is evident. The conceptual and general framework within which these diverse subjects might be holistically placed form a common ground for their wholesome integration, and, allow for a possible mitigating dialogue and constructive actions. With respect to this chapter, the context of geographic reference shall be the Middle East and its dynamic phenomenal and Islamic cultural situation. It will be shown how the financial crisis, global climate change, and clashing civilizations can be addressed within this cultural setting, and how these Perennial Tradition concepts can facilitate positive change.

In the book *The Sense of Unity*, published by the University of Chicago Press in 1973, I observed: "In the art and architecture of a traditional society the principles of the tradition inspire man's creative energies and integrate the whole of society into a totality. In such a society the distinction usually made today between sacred and profane is either transcended by a metaphysical knowledge that pierces through all veils of separation or it is removed through (enlightened rational) integration of all aspects of life into a unity outside of which nothing exists."[18] The above theme, as it may pertain to our contemporary times, will be explored in more detail. To begin with, it should be remembered that Islam sustains a unified character of society while elaborating upon its exoteric and esoteric dimension. The exoteric dimension concerns social behavior and is inculcated in the *Shariah*, but is not directly related to the creative process. Rather, it is the metaphysical aspects of the Way (*Tarigah*) in which the principles are found that govern traditional Islamic art, especially architecture. Therefore, this quest shall be pursued through a frame of reference that contrasts the relationship between classic Western philosophical thinking based upon Cartesian Logic, and traditional Metaphysics (*Erfan*) based upon contemplation and enlightened consciousness. It is important to note that recent scientific and academic research has shown that at the depth of key philosophic thinking there lies concealed a type of enlightened thought or heightened insight revealed by contemplative experiences.[19]

Expanding the Structure of Reality

Reason is modern man's most dangerous illusion.[20]

C.G. Jung

Your intuition is your most exacting sense;
It is your most reliable sense.[21]

Louis I. Kahn

Other recent signs in scholarly circles support this experiential knowledge approach, particularly in Martin Heidegger's influential philosophical conceptions of Phenomenology that views "existence" only possible within an ontological and hermeneutical structure.[22] By this he means that the very act of being ("existence") precedes all knowing—thus contradicting the famous dictum of Descartes: "*Cogito ergo sum*" (I think, therefore I am).[23] The noted French Iranologist, Henri Corbin, brilliantly compared the 20th-century philosophy of Heidegger to the 12th-century Persian mystical conceptions of Subhuddin Suhrawardi, who ranked everything in existence according to the intensity of light it possesses. The Ultimate Source, the Light of Lights, the Absolute is at the apex of a pyramidal hierarchy that descends through the World of Archetypes, which possess less degrees of light, and descends further through the World of Symbols, with even less light intensity, and finally reaches the World of Phenomenal Forms at the bottom of the pyramid that exists in total darkness. Suhrawardi holistically engaged in a "Trinal Knowledge" approach to ultimate knowledge combining philosophy (*Philos*-loving + *Sophos*-wise = lover of wisdom), mysticism and logic to pierce these veils that hide the pure light. The resultant fruit of his quest, he termed "The Red Intellect" (*Agl Surkh*)[24] (Figure 17.2b).

It is this heightened ontological consciousness, symbolized by the Red Intellect, and here termed "Luminous Thinking" that is proposed as the sublime planning tool, sufficient in scope and grasp to possibly generate a new holistic paradigm for our 21st-century challenges, especially in engaging the programming and design of the sustainable new habitats of the future, especially in the Middle East. In preparation for this Luminous Thinking approach, we need to first familiarize ourselves with some of the key principles of the traditional design-thinking of this culture. In particular, the significance of the meanings of such key terms as space, time, form/surface, and light/matter are critical, and are described below to better understand the fundamentals involved in this timeless approach.

There is nothing more timely today than that truth which is timeless, than the message that comes from tradition and is relevant now because it has been relevant at all times.[25]

Seyyed Hossein Nasr

Positive Space

Traditionally, space has been viewed as one of the most direct symbols of Being. It is primordial, all pervading and in the cosmology of Islam, the "locus" of the Universal Soul. This Hermetic concept forms a worldview in which the universe is composed of a microcosm and a macrocosm, each containing three great divisions: the body (*jism*), the soul (*nafs*) and the spirit (*ruh*).[26]

T'was a fair orchard, full of trees, fruit, vines and greenery.
A Sufi there sat with eyes closed, his head upon his knee,
Sunk deep in meditation mystical.
"Why," asked another, "Dost thou not behold
These signs of God the Merciful displayed
Around thee, which He bids us to contemplate?"
"The Signs," he answered, "I behold within.
Without is naught but symbols of the Signs."[27]

Jalalu'l-Din Rumi

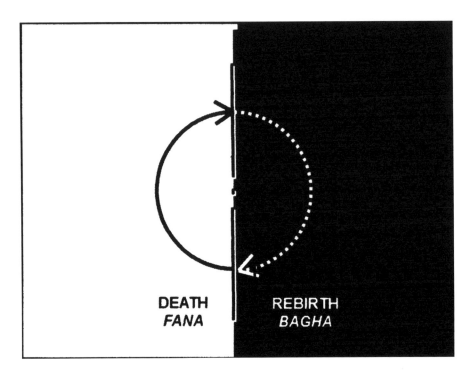

Figure 17.2a   Perennial Traditions: Death/Rebirth – *Fana/Bagh*
Source: Courtesy Nader Ardalan.

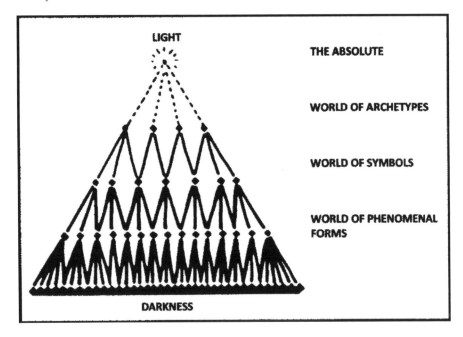

Figure 17.2b   Perennial Traditions: World of Shadows as conceived by Subhuddin Suhrawardi,
                12th-century drawing by N. Ardalan
Source: Courtesy of *Sufi* by L. Bakhtiar, Thames & Hudson.

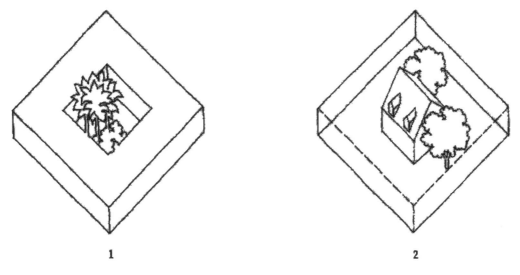

Figure 17.2c   Perennial Traditions: Positive Space in courtyard in 1 vs. Positive Shape in detached house in 2

Source: Photograph courtesy Nader Ardalan.

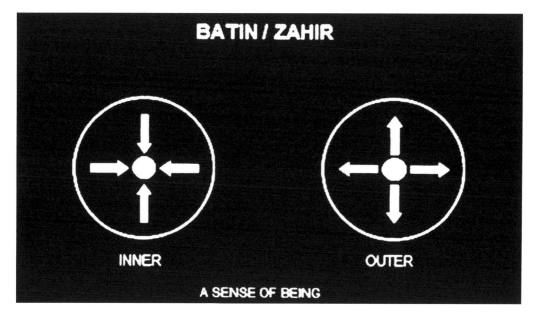

Figure 17.2d   Perennial Traditions: Diagram of Hidden/Manifest – *Zahir/Batin*

Source: Courtesy Nader Ardalan.

Rumi reminds us that in the traditional metaphysical worldview, particularly in Islamic cultures, reality has two structural dimensions, the "inner" (*batin*), understood by our enlightened thought and the "outer" (*zahir*) perceived by our sense receptors (Figure 17.2c). Architecturally, the Walled Paradise Garden (*bagh*) and the Courtyard (*hayat*) with their inward spatial orientation, have come to symbolize this duality in archetypal space making (Figure 17.2d). From this view the very unique conception of "Positive Space" comes into play where Spiritualized Space, not exterior shape or object, is the dominant focus of this planning and design approach. This is wondrously exhibited in the harmonic order of the bazaar of Isfahan[28] (Figure 17.3a)] which culminates in one of the world's most impressive Positive spaces, the *Maydan Nagsh i Jahan* of the 17th century, and leads to the Safavid courtyard mosque of the *Masjid I Shah* (Figure 17.3b).

> The essence of organic building is space;
> Space flowing outward, space flowing inward.[29]

Frank Lloyd Wright

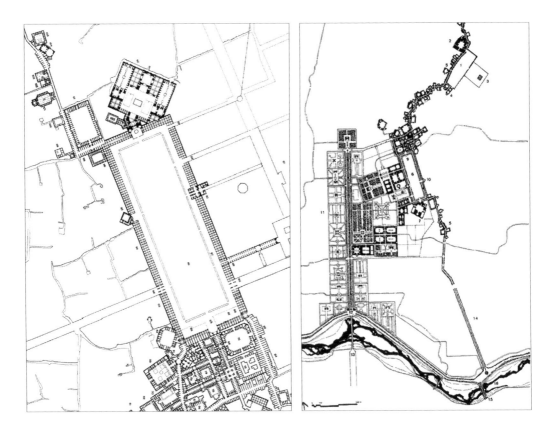

Figure 17.3   Examples of Positive Space: a) Isfahan, enlarged drawing of positive space of *Nagsh-i-Jahan* Square, 17th century, b) Growth of Isfahan Bazaar linear, positive space system, City Plan 10th to 19th centuries

Source: Courtesy Nader Ardalan.

Time

Unlike the classic Chinese conception of "Continuous Time" or the Greek conception of cyclical, "Circular time" or the orthodox Christian idea of "Linear Time" that begins with Genesis and moves progressively towards the Day of Judgment and the Apocalypse, the Sufi Islamic conception of "Spiral Time" commences with the Creation and through cyclical motion repeats the very act of creation, but in an ever ascending spiral, around an ontological axis, and seeking ever higher levels of transcendence, illumination and ultimate union with the Absolute. This brings us to one of the most remarkable realizations of this particular culture, termed *Khalq-e Jadid* or the "New Creation." The "New" means a cyclical, transcending, timeless yet innovative manifestation of archetypal ideas. It is this timeless world, which Louis Kahn referred to when he said: "Traditions are just mounds of golden dust, not circumstance, not the shapes which have resulted as an expression in time .... And if you can just put your fingers through this golden dust, you can have the powers of anticipation."[30]

> Were we wearied by the first creation?
> Yet, they are uncertain about a new creation.[31]
>
> Qu'ran L: 14

Form/Surface

The science of numbers stands above nature as a way of comprehending Unity. Numbers are the principle of beings and the root of all sciences. Geometry and number are the language by which form and surface define space. The Pythagorean system governs the traditional perception of the quantitative and qualitative understanding of mathematics. However, outer expression or form of a number does not exhaust its possibilities, there is a *batin* or inner essence that distinguishes the *zahir* or external personalities of phenomenal shapes, surfaces and patterns, which give symbolic meaning to their appropriate immanent (*tashbih*) and transcendent (*tanzih*) use. For instance, in the cosmology of the famous 10th-century Iraqi mathematical thinkers called the "The Brethren of Purity" (*Ikhwan al-Safa*), the number 1 represented the Creator; 2 represented the Intellect; 3 the Soul; 4 was Matter; 5 stood for Nature and 6 represented the Body.

> Naught there is but its treasures are with us and we send
> It not down but in a known measure.[32]
>
> Qu'ran XV.21

Light Matter

In Persian tradition the traditional craftsman, is called the *Jawanmard*,[33] the man of chivalry, who associates himself with the transformation of matter and temporal creation through the science of Alchemy, in order to transcend the "time-bound" materiality of the physical world. This Alchemical approach has a twofold aspect. On one hand, it deals with the transmutation of the soul of the artisan; on the other hand, it is the science concerned with the processes of adapting to nature, the environment and the transformation of heavy matter to pure light as both aesthetic metaphor and phenomenal product. The contemporary artist James Turrell, known for his light tunnels and light projections, also uses the alchemical process by creating shapes that seem to have mass and weight, but are created only with light. His creations have a transcendent and meditative quality of great power.

> All material in nature, the mountains and the streams and the air and we,
> Are made of light which has been spent, and this crumpled mass called material casts a shadow, and the shadow belongs to light.[34]
>
> Louis I. Kahn

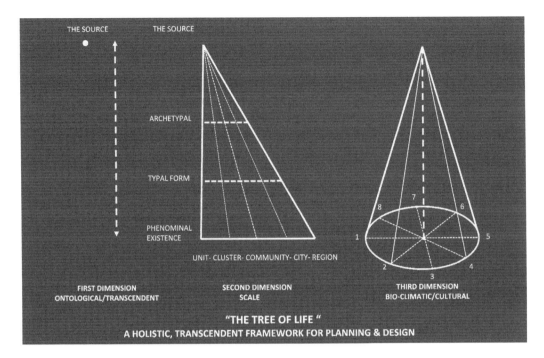

Figure 17.4   "Tree of Life": A Holistic Planning & Design Framework, 2010
Source: Courtesy Nader Ardalan.

A Proposed Holistic Design Framework

Based upon the preceding descriptions of transcendent design approaches, the following framework titled: "The Tree of Life Model" is proposed. This model can form a conceptual structure of design considerations that can qualitatively and quantitatively constitute a relevant and holistic model to organize sustainable design thinking for the Middle East region, with global implications. Furthermore, it may challenge architects to become *Jawanmards*, reinvigorating modern buildings and the built environment with deeper meanings and chivalrous acts of transcendent architecture (Figure 17.4).

It is important to acknowledge that cutting across all other issues facing the world today is climate change and it's practical, economic and elegant mitigation by designing environmentally and culturally sustainable built environments inspired by a transcendent vision is one of our greatest challenges. Regrettably, it has been demonstrated by the Fifth UN IPCC 2013 Assessment Report on Climate Change that current planning, design, building construction and real estate practices and models that are being used in the developed and developing countries, including the Middle East region, demonstrate serious shortcomings that are contributing to the jeopardizing of the planet. Global climate change, high fossil fuel and other resource consumption, urban sprawl, pollution and traffic congestion have resulted in a loss of the quality of urban life, social cohesion, and an indigenous sense of cultural identity.[35]

First Dimension—Ontological/Transcendent

Archetypes are the essential forms (suwar) of the Divine Names.
All things in phenomenal world come into existence depending upon the level of preparedness to meet the essence of their Archetype.[36]

Toshihiko Izutsu

Inspired by the spiritual and poetic traditions of Islam, the first dimension, a vertical axis representing the hierarchy of manifestation can first be considered. This vertical hierarchy transcends on an Ontological Axis from the measurable world of Phenomenal Existence (Nature/Man) through the World of Traditional Forms (the Typal) and beyond to the World of Archetypes, and on to the Divine Names that ultimately leads to the immeasurable, transcendent Universal Source, The Absolute, The Divine. In the words of Ibn Arabi: "All causality (the self-externalization of the Divine, in Arabic *Tajalli*) is in the Divine Names, in the incessant renewal of their epiphanies from instant to instant."[37] This axis brings the spiritual dimension of design and planning into our consciousness, which for far too long has been over shadowed by the post-Renaissance materialist determent philosophical worldview.

> The Divine was a hidden treasure that wished to be known,
> Therefore, he created the world.[38]

Hadith of the Prophet

Second Dimension—Scale

In Planning/Design terms of the second dimension, the Horizontal Axis commences at the scale of the Individual and the smallest building unit—the Dwelling—and moves outward to the social Cluster of dwelling units, to the Pedestrian Precinct and to the Urban Community, and finally encompasses the Regional Domain. Criteria for each of these scales have been thoroughly researched over the years, and one notable contribution was made by Iran at the first United Nations Conference on Human Settlements held in Vancouver, Canada in 1976, entitled the "Habitat Bill of Rights."[39] This research work also demonstrated that much of modern city development lacks this hierarchy of human-scaled, social groupings that can provide a sense of identity, connectedness and belongingness.

Third Dimension—The Bio-Climatic/Cultural Zones

Scientists and sociologists have determined that the world can be categorized into eight bio-climatic ecological zones, ranging from the Tundra to Tropical Forests, as determined by their temperature and geographic hydrological gradients in proximity to the sun. The Third Axis pivots around the Ontological Axis generating eight branches of the World Bio-Climatic Cultural Zones, each with their respective sub-zones.

To illustrate, I was commissioned to master plan the Pardisan Environmental Park Project for Tehran, which when realized, contains six of the eight world biomes. When these zones were layered by the characteristic, indigenous cultural types, a fine grain of bio-climatic cultural definition of the country was obtained. Within this framework, it would be possible to develop optimum criteria for excellence in passive design principles that could minimize energy demand in the various regions, and that are also culturally relevant. Compared to many existing "business as usual" developments now prevalent in Iran and the region that exhibit high energy demand, a more sustainable strategy, possibly based upon "One Planet Living"—10 Principles, could conceptually significantly reduce the current energy demands of Iran's towns and cities. The benefits would also be more economical and culturally more sustainable habitats, imbued with a meaningful identity of place.[40]

Tree of Life

The resultant conical form created by these three primary dimensions can be viewed as a "Tree of Life," representing multiplicity within the unity of the world, based upon a central, transcendent cause. This conceptual framework can form a model of design guidelines that can qualitatively and quantitatively direct a holistic sustainable design process. In context of the history of literature, art and poetic references in the Middle East, the Tree can also be metaphorically viewed as a Cypress (*Sarv*), which has symbolized longevity of life, self-fertilization, freedom and sustainability.

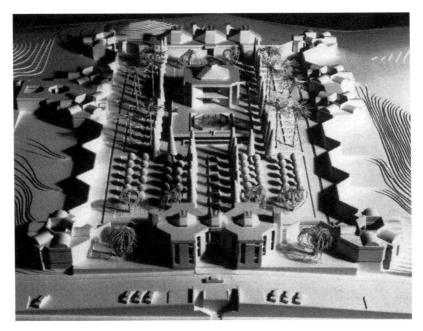

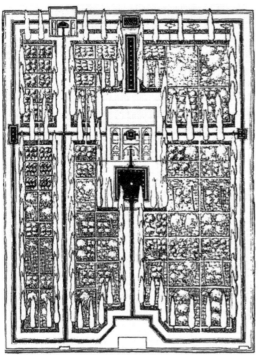

Figure 17.5   Imam Sadegh University (formerly Iran Center for Management Studies with Harvard
University), Tehran, designed by Nader Ardalan with AFFA, 1972: a) View of project model,
b) Example of typal form, the Bagh-i-Fin, Kashan, Iran, 17th century, c) Living courtyards
of Imam Sadegh University

Source: Courtesy of Nader Ardalan.

Applications of the Theory—Case Studies

Three case studies of actual project designs based upon the above holistic theories of sustainable design, commencing from the early 1970s and continuing to the present, can demonstrate the efficacy and benefits of the "Tree of Life" Framework of Design, based upon a "Luminous Thinking" approach. The three case study projects are: Imam Sadegh University (Iran Center for Management Studies), Tehran, Iran; Nuran, City of Illumination, Isfahan, Iran; and The Intelligent Tower, Doha, Qatar.

Case Study 1: Imam Sadegh University (Iran Center for Management Studies), Tehran

I designed this project in 1971 as a Design Partner of the Iranian firm, AFFA, and the functional curriculum of a graduate school of business was developed in cooperation with Harvard University Business School. The design was based on the innovative integration of the concept of a traditional Persian Paradise Garden, a traditional courtyard college (*Madrasah*) and the principles of "Positive Space Continuity" that were documented in my book, *The Sense of Unity*. The design survives today after nearly four decades in a most sustainable way, both physically and culturally, while serving the new functions of the Imam Sadegh University (Figure 17.5).

Case Study 2: Nuran, City of Illumination, Isfahan

The master plan and concept design of Nuran were planned in 1978 and, although never implemented, were recognized by Massachusetts Institute of Technology as one of the first low-carbon solar-energy-based cities in the world. This city of 100,000 people, located in the vicinity of Isfahan, was oriented so that its central town axis was on direct alignment with the great Blue Dome of Masjid-i-Imam in the city center of Isfahan. Solar ponds, photovoltaic roof panels, locally sourced cyclopean concrete structures (a primitive masonry construction technique using large irregular-shaped stones embedded in concrete); compact, high-density, courtyard housing, mixed-use design, and natural ventilation schemes characterized this pedestrian oriented garden city (Figure 17.6).

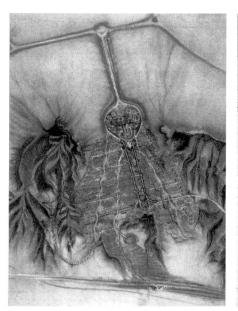 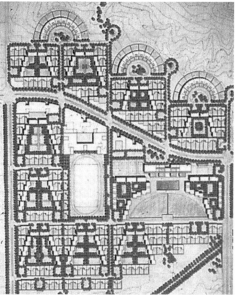

Figure 17.6   Nuran Solar City Master Plan, Isfahan by Nader Ardalan, Mandala International, 1978:
a) Illustrative master plan, b) Phase 1 Nuran concept courtyard housing design
Source: Courtesy of Nader Ardalan.

Figure 17.7   The Intelligent Tower, Doha, Qatar, Concept Design model: a) Lucite concept model,
               b) Sustainable building skin enclosure, c) Sustainable strategies: intelligent structure,
               energy system, roof top wind & solar & mixed mode HVAC System
Source: Courtesy Ardalan Associates & Klingstubbins with Arup.

Case Study 3: The Intelligent Tower, Doha, Qatar

The new typology of a sustainable high-rise architecture presents a significant design challenge. My 2007
entry into a world design competition was awarded first place, and the 70-story tower, located on the West
Bay Corniche of Doha, will provide an environmentally-adapted, socially-friendly and sustainable "Place for
Business." The tower minimizes energy demand by its high performance envelope of three layers of glass with
a sun protecting movable shade, and produces energy through wind, solar and energy efficient technologies,
while, also creating a dramatic, cultural symbol of an "Eternal Tree"—the Cypress (Figure 17.7).

Conclusion

During the course of urban history, human cultures have relied on their spiritual foundations to locate, plan
and design their cities and architecture. The organizing principles and precepts upon which ancient places
such as Karnak, Jerusalem, Mecca, Delphi, Lhasa, Kyoto, Beijing, Angkor Wat, Fez, Isfahan, Chartres,
and Machu Picchu have been built, produced intimate relationships and conversations with the cosmos,
divinity, and processes of nature and the universe, through profound and subtle levels of consciousness.
The vitality, fertility and longevity of these cities and built environments attest to the value given by social,
cultural, economic, ecological, and religious endeavors to spiritual sanctity. More concretely, the spiritual
dimension of a city arises from its capacity to induce and maintain a sense of existential and transcendental
meaningfulness, connectedness, reverence, authenticity, and experience in its dweller, both at the individual
and collective levels.

To truly understand this transcendent, sustainable design process (beyond merely satisfying resource needs and consumption), we need to begin with a culturally attuned cosmic, systemic awareness of the context and physiology of human existence on both a phenomenal and spiritual level. A holistic design model, such as "The Tree of Life," that has been proposed herein can form one basis for a luminous design process that is capable of beautifully reflecting this poetic vision with contemporary means, thereby transporting the beholder beyond mere material existence.

Throughout humans' presence on the earth, the relationship between spirituality, urbanity and the built architectural environment has, continues to have and will have profound effect on each other. How we draw from past and present experience to cultivate a new vision for architecture and city building is an imperative that scholars, planners, poets of architecture, landscape architecture, and artists must address through philosophical, theoretical and practical considerations and most importantly through inner contemplation. We ask from within themselves– what is the role of spirituality on the human and natural condition within the context of contemporary and the unfolding of future life?

What we need is the development of the inner spiritual man
The unique individual whose treasure is hidden
In the symbols of our mythological traditions and
In man's unconscious psyche

Carl. G. Jung[41]

There is no intuitive certainty until you burn:
If you desire that certainty, set down in the fire!

Jalalu'l-Din Rumi[42]

Endnotes

1   Kandinsky, Wassily (1912). *On the Spiritual in Art*. Munich: R. Piper & Co.
2   Hoppen, Donald (1998). *Seven Ages of Frank Lloyd Wright*. New York, NY: Dover Press.
3   Houman, Setareh (2014). *From the Philosophia Perennis to American Perennialism*. Chicago, IL: Kazi Publications.
4   Lao-Tzu: "The Tao that can be told is not the eternal Tao.
    The name that can be named is not the eternal name.
    The nameless is the beginning of heaven and earth.
    The named is the mother of the ten thousand things.
    Ever desireless, one can see the mystery.
    Ever desiring, one can see the manifestation."
5   See Lovelock, James (2000). *The Ages of Gaia, a Biography of Our Living Earth*. Oxford, UK and New York, NY: Oxford University Press.
6   See Izutsu, Toshihiko and Toyo (1981). *The Theory of Beauty in the Classical Aesthetics of Japan*. The Hague/Boston, MA/London, UK: Martinus Nijhoff Publishers.
7   Kandinsky, Wassily (1912). *On the Spiritual in Art*. Munich: R. Piper & Co.
8   See Hoppen, Donald (1998). *Seven Ages of Frank Lloyd Wright*.
9   Regier, Kathleen J. (1987). *The Spiritual Image in Modern Art*. Madras/London, UK: A Quest Book.
10 Rosenbaum, Robert, (1977) *Modern Painting and the Northern Romantic Tradition – Friedrich to Rothko*.
11 Los Angeles County Museum of Art (1986). *The Spiritual in Art-Abstract Painting 1890–1985*. New York, NY/London, UK/Paris: Abbeville Press.
12 See Hoppen (1998). *Seven Ages of Frank Lloyd Wright*.
13 Barr, Alfred, *Cubism & Abstract Art, 1986*.
14 See Hoppen (1998). *Seven Ages of Frank Lloyd Wright*. F.L. Wright's marriage to Olgivanna in 1928 introduced Wright to the teachings of the mystic Gurdjieff, who had a strong influence on her and subsequently on Wright and the Taliesin Fellowship. This complemented the pre-existing influences of Whitman, Thoreau and Lao-Tzu on Wright.

15 See Lobell, John (1979). *Between Silence and Light: Spirit in the Architecture of Louis I. Kahn.* Boulder, CO: Shambala. Louis Kahn: "The poet is one who starts from the seat of the unmeasurable and travels toward the measurable, but who keeps the force of the unmeasurable within him at all times."

16 These include: (1997). Making Sacred Places, Built Form and Culture Research Conference. Cincinnati, OH: University of Cincinnati; (1997). Pilgrimage and Complexity. New Delhi: Indira Gandhi National Centre for the Arts; (1999). Space, Place & Spirituality in the Built Environment. Muncie, IN: Ball State University; (2007). Constructing the Ineffable. Contemporary Sacred Architecture. New Haven, CT: Yale University, October; (2008). Research Symposium: Paradoxes of Appearances. Copenhagen, Denmark, 9–11 June; (2008). The Symposium on Architecture, Culture and Spirituality. Mt. Angel Abbey, Oregon; (2008–2009). Traces of the Spiritual. Art exhibit at the Haus der Kunst Museum Munich, Germany September 19–January 11; (2013). Urbanism, Spirituality & Well-Being. Cambridge, MA: Harvard University; and, (2014). The Architecture of Spirituality in a Multicultural Setting. Toronto: Trinity College, University of Toronto.

17 See http://www.acsforum.org/usw_symposium/ for video recordings of the entire proceedings, accessed June 2014.

18 Ardalan, Nader and Bakhtiar, Laleh (1973). *The Sense of Unity, the Sufi Tradition in Persian Architecture.* Chicago, IL and London, UK: Chicago University Press.

19 Beauregard, Mario and Denyse O'Leary (2008). *The Spiritual Brain, a Neuroscientist's Case for the Existence of the Soul.* New York, NY: HarperCollins Publishers.

20 Jung, C.G. (1959). *The Undiscovered Self.* New York, NY: Mentor Books.

21 Twombly, Robert (2003). *Louis Kahn: Essential Texts.* New York, NY: W.W. Norton & Company.

22 See Corbin, Henry (1976). "From Heidegger to Suhrawardi," Interview with Philip Nemo, recorded for *Radio France-Culture.*

23 Durant, Will and Ariel (1961). *The Story of Civilization: Par VII, the Age of Reason Begins.* New York, NY: Simon and Schuster.

24 Shihabuddin Yahya Suhrawardi, (1982). *The Mystical & Visionary Treatises of Shihabuddin Yahya Suhrawardi,* translated by M. Thackston Wheeler Jr. London, UK: The Octagon Press.

25 See Ardalan and Bakhtiar (1973). *The Sense of Unity.*

26 Ibid.

27 Nicholson, R.A. Rumi (1964). *Poet and Mystic.* London, UK: George Allen and Unwin.

28 See Ardalan and Bakhtiar (1973). *The Sense of Unity.*

29 (1994). *Frank Lloyd Wright, Architect.* New York, NY: The Museum of Modern Art.

30 (1970). *The Interaction of Tradition & Technology.* Report of the Proceedings of the First International Congress of Architects, Isfahan. Ministry of Housing & Urban Development, Government of Iran.

31 A. Yusuf Ali, *The Holy Qur'an.* Jeddah: Dar Al-Qiblah.

32 Ibid.

33 Ridgeon, Lloyd (2011). *Jawanmardi – A Sufi Code of Honour.* Edinburgh, UK: Edinburgh University Press; and Bakhtiar, Laleh (2013). *The Sufi Enneagram – The Secrets of the Symbol Unveiled.* Chicago, IL: Institute of Traditional Psychology.

34 See Twombly (2003). *Louis Kahn: Essential Texts.*

35 *Climate Change 2014.* IPCC Fifth Assessment Report, United Nations. London, UK: Cambridge University Press.

36 Izutsu, Toshihiko (1966). *The Key Philosophical Concepts in Sufism and Taoism—Ibn Arabi and Lao-Tzu, Chuang-Tzu.* Tokyo: Keio University Press.

37 Corbin, Henri (1969). *Creative Imagination in the Sufism of Ibn Arabi.* Princeton, NJ: Princeton University Press.

38 *Hadiths of the Prophet.* Sahih al-Bukhari.

39 (1976). *The Habitat Bill of Rights.* Ministry of Housing & Urban Development, Government of Iran, edited by Nader Ardalan, Jose Luis Sert, Moshe Safdie, George Candilis and B.V. Doshi.
    In 1974, The Ministry of Housing and Urban Development of Iran convened the Second International Congress of Architecture at Persepolis. At the conclusion of the Congress the delegates passed the following Resolution:
    "Through research studies, a code of human habitat should be developed with such procedures and strategies necessary to the achievement of principles essential to the creation of a wholesome, balanced and equitable habitat. This code should be so prepared that it may form a working tool suitable for use by all the decision makers involved in the shaping of the human habitat in time and place."

An international team of architects and professors from some of the leading schools of architecture worked on a volunteer basis over one year to prepare this document. It was entitled the "Habitat Bill of Rights" and presented to the first UN Habitat Conference. The *New York Times'* June 8, 1976 headline on the conference read: "Architects Have a Blueprint for Habitat" and featured the Iran contribution that emphasized "human scale and modest, vernacular architecture as opposed to the often abstract quality of much modern design, particularly as expressed in government-built housing." Recently it has been translated and republished in Farsi by IAARA and used as reference model for India by B.K. Doshi.

40 Department of the Environment, Government of Iran (1975). *Pardisan, Plan for an Environmental Park in Tehran.* The Mandala Collaborative/WHRT. The Pardisan Project was one of the 1975 winners of Progressive Architecture Magazine Award of Excellence.

41 *The World Within – C.G. Jung in His Own Words*, Bostuston Video Production, C.G Jung Institute of Los Angeles.

42 Nicholson, R.A. Rumi (1964). *Poet and Mystic.*

Index